J.S. Cummins is Emeritus Professor of Hispanic Studies, University of London. He is a member of the Council of the Hakluyt Society, a Fellow of the Royal Historical Society and a member of the Advisory Board, British Library.

A QUESTION OF RITES

A Question of Rites

Friar Domingo Navarrete and the
Jesuits in China

J. S. Cummins

Scolar Press

Published by
SCOLAR PRESS
Gower House
Croft Road
Aldershot
Hants GU11 3HR
England

Ashgate Publishing Company
Old Post Road
Brookfield
Vermont 05036
USA

British Library Cataloguing-in-Publication Data.
A catalogue record for this book is available from the British Library.

ISBN 0 85967 880 6

Typeset in 11pt Garamond 3 by Photoprint, Torquay
and printed in Great Britain at the University Press, Cambridge.

In memory of Joachim Ko and Juan Miu,
martyrs of the Rites Controversy,
et alibi aliorum plurimorum sanctorum martyrum

Contents

Acknowledgements

Edward Meryon Wilson, of Emmanuel College Cambridge, first drew my attention to Domingo Navarrete and suggested I should consult C. R. Boxer for guidance in research into his life and writings. And it is Boxer to whom I owe the greatest debt of all for his unflagging support and encouragement, and for access to his manuscripts and specialist library at all times. I have also been stimulated by Dr Joseph Needham's keen interest in Navarrete and I have been generously helped by him on many occasions. In addition, I remember warmly my long conversations with Dr Gregory Blue when he was a member of the Needham Research Institute in Cambridge.

Among Dominicans to whom I am also indebted are the late Dr Benno Biermann of the Walberberg priory (Cologne), and Fr Honorio Muñoz from whom I received constant assistance when I was working in the archives of Santo Domingo in Manila. I also received useful advice from a number of Jesuits, including Fr Henri Bernard-Maitre in Paris, and the archivists of the Jesuit Curia in Rome, always unfailing in their readiness to help. I acknowledge too the assistance of Charles d'Orban, specialist Chinese Librarian, the School of Oriental and African Studies, University of London.

Professor John Lynch of University College London kindly read the draft of Chapter 8 and made a number of suggestions for which I am thankful. In the section on Adam Schall, I am much obliged to Dr Irene Pih who shared research material with me during our discussions of the China mission. Information about John Locke's interest in Navarrete I owe to the kindness of Dr Esmond de Beer, editor of Locke's correspondence. I also thank both Daniel Farrell and John Pisani who read the book in draft and made many useful comments from which I have profited. I am indebted to Christopher Woodward who introduced me to the mysteries of the computer. I wish to express gratitude to Helen Hodge for her patience and expertise in the final stages of preparing the text; as also to John Smedley, of Scolar Press, who has done much to enable both this, and an earlier book, to be published.

Of course, none of these is responsible for the use I have made of their support and interest.

The Leverhulme Foundation granted me a Fellowship to assist my research during 1985–87, and publication was made possible by a grant from the Twenty-Seven Foundation in association with the Institute of Historical Research. I am grateful for this generous help.

J.S.C.
University of London, 1992

Preface

On the night of 15 February 1686 an old man lay dying in the island of Hispaniola, Spain's imperial slum in the Caribbean. He was a friar of the Order of Saint Dominic, Archbishop of Santo Domingo, and Patriarch of the Spanish Indies. His name was Domingo Navarrete.

The doctors, unable to diagnose his illness, could not deal with the physical cause of his obviously imminent death. This was hardly surprising, for on that island his were rare ailments: overwork and anxiety springing from an acute social and religious conscience. He was distressed by the fate of his diocese with its illiterate clergy and ramshackle churches; the poverty of many of the colonists; the plight of the few remaining natives; the degradation of the black slaves; but worst of all was a hopelessness brought on by an inefficient bureaucracy, locally and at home in Madrid. His own efforts seemed to have failed too. His attempt to lift elementary education standards had been thwarted, and eyebrows were raised when he, a Dominican, had turned for support to the local Jesuits, who in return praised him loudly.

Yet despite these parochial concerns, his thoughts, he confessed, kept turning halfway across the world to China where, years before, he had glimpsed Utopia and was left restless ever after.

To die in tropical Hispaniola dreaming of China perhaps requires some explanation, and those innocent of Catholic lore and legend may wonder why a Dominican bishop should cause comment by turning to Jesuit priests for help. For an explanation it is necessary to start at the beginning – the very beginning.

(a)   (b)

Friar and Jesuit in Chinese dress: (a) Dominican (b) Jesuit

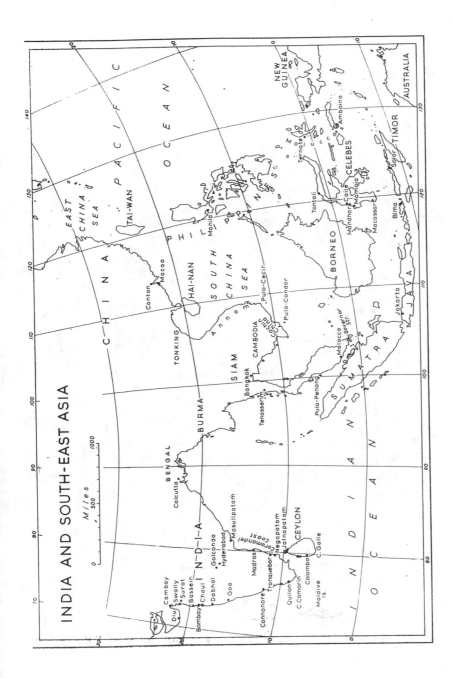

INDIA AND SOUTH-EAST ASIA

India and south-east Asia

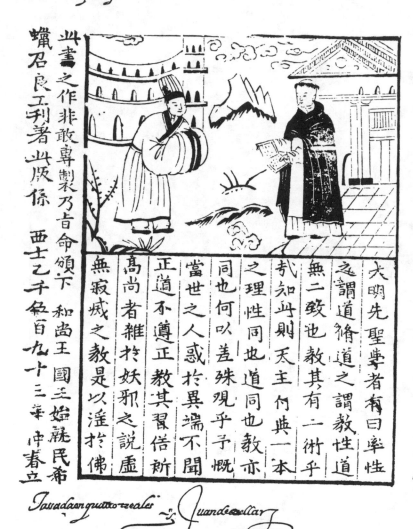

A Dominican friar catechizing a Chinese scholar

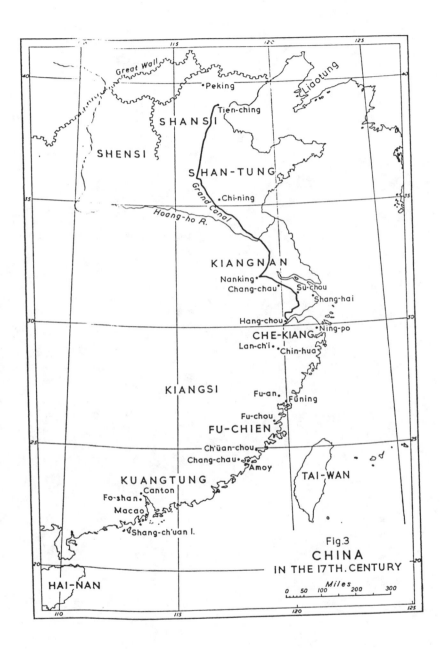

Great Wall
Peking
Liaotung
Tien-ching
SHANSI
SHENSI
SHAN-TUNG
Chi-ning
Grand Canal
Hoang-ho R.
KIANGNAN
Nanking
Chang-chau
Su-chou
Shang-hai
Hang-chou
Ning-po
CHE-KIANG
Lan-ch'i
Chin-hua
KIANGSI
Fu-an
Füning
Fu-chou
FU-CHIEN
Ch'üan-chou
Chang-chau
Amoy
TAI-WAN
KUANGTUNG
Canton
Fo-shan
Macao
Shang-ch'uan I.
Fig. 3
CHINA
IN THE 17TH. CENTURY
Miles
0 50 100 200 300
HAI-NAN

China in the seventeenth century

Prologue

In the first place, this is the story of a friar. It is also the friar's story, and as such it attempts to show things as he saw them and as he believed they were. It is therefore a personal, minority report, stressing one side of a many-sided experience. It is an alternative, dissenting version of the usual account of the Roman Catholic attempt to convert Ming and Ch'ing China. That attempt by the Jesuit 'mandarin-missionaries', using science and technology as strategic weapons to win acceptance for their Faith, was as celebrated as the story of Troy, when the story of Troy was still celebrated. Even in modern times it has engaged the attention not only of historians and biographers but of poets too (as in Browning's *The Ring and the Book* and Ezra Pound's *Cantos*).

The work of these Jesuit 'geometers' gave rise to the 'Chinese Rites Controversy', with which this book is concerned. That complex debate can be reduced to one point. Certain Chinese observances and rituals appeared to be of a doubtful nature: some missionaries thought that they were religious liturgies; others that they were merely civic and social customs, tinged perhaps with superstition, but separable from it. There was, then, room for a difference of opinion, and there was indeed a great difference of opinion, which eventually became a venomous quarrel, running through the greater part of the 17th century and the first half of the 18th.

The Jesuit Fathers entered China in 1583 disguised as Buddhists. Twelve years later they switched to the garb of the scholar-mandarins, and in 1601 penetrated Peking itself. The pioneer Jesuit, Matteo Ricci ('one of the most remarkable and brilliant men in history', in Joseph Needham's words), presented himself to the Chinese as a 'Wise Man from the West' rather than as a clergyman in any offensive sense of that term. Early reports were optimistic; first, the ruling class would be converted, and the rest would follow. This fair hope, always a step ahead, skipped along before the Fathers for decades, until finally it touched down where the rainbow ends. For China

1

proved intractable even to the Jesuits and, in the plain blunt words of C. R. Boxer, the 'Fathers had as much hope of converting the emperor as they had of converting the Man in the Moon'.

That spiritual and intellectual adventure is seen as one of the great might-have-beens of history, an epic turned into a tragedy by stupidity and malice. It figures as such in staid encyclopedias, poetic biographies, prosaic church histories and enthusiastic vestry pamphlets. Non-Catholics are in sympathy with the Jesuits here, seeing them as builders of a bridge between the East and the Renaissance West. In doing so they forget that the bridge was weakened, when the builders suppressed knowledge of the heliocentric system in deference to papal decree.

Catholics, also, though more understandably, welcome this Jesuit approach as being agreeably enlightened and they recall the not dissimilar policy of Gregory the Great towards the conversion of England – but in doing so they forget that Gregory's policy failed to uproot paganism among the Anglo-Saxons.

Chesterton puts the accepted view with characteristic verve: 'Saint Francis Xavier very nearly succeeded in setting up the Church in Asia, as a tower overtopping all the pagodas, but he failed because his followers were accused by their fellow-missionaries of representing the Twelve Apostles as Chinamen'. Lest this be thought unique, it is worth pointing out that much the same was said recently by an American Jesuit in a work that was awarded the Catholic Book of the Year prize. Another writer concludes that the Jesuits were attacked 'by calumnies and misrepresentation in a controversy marked by ignorance and blindness, until finally the "integralists" triumphed in their questionable crusade'. These opinions are not confined to Catholics, for the Jesuits who failed to win over the Chinese have converted the historians, so that there are surprising lamentations over the failure of the China mission from writers who would presumably regret it had the Jesuit-mandarins' English contemporaries succeeded in *their* mission to the Elizabethan world.

History, however, is not always 'the propaganda of the victors', for the Jesuits, who lost, were among the earliest practitioners of modern public relations techniques, and it is their account of events which has survived and found wide acceptance. Remarkably, the narrative of so contentious a matter is usually allotted to them as though they could be impartial witnesses to their own defeat. The relevant entries in the *New Catholic Encyclopedia*, in the *Dictionnaire d'histoire et géographie ecclésiastiques*, in *Catholicisme* and in the *Dizionario ecclesiastico* are all by Jesuits. Even Ludwig Pastor's magisterial *Lives of the Popes*, in 40 volumes, is not as impartial as is sometimes thought, for the grateful Pastor was guided through the quicksands by Jesuit collaborators (Fathers Brucker, Kneller and Kratz). And much of Pastor and his discreet co-workers has passed into lesser, more popular, church histories and biographies, so that it is as if the only well-known versions of Charles I and the Puritans were written by Cavaliers.

Where there are victims there must be villains; where there is failure, scapegoats, and in the China mission these roles are filled by the Dominican and Franciscan friars working there at the same time as the Jesuit Fathers. These mendicant friars are presented as diminutive moralists, as medievalists out of place in a Renaissance setting, narrow-minded bigots sabotaging the efforts of the scholarly and accommodating Fathers. By simplification, the situation is described as though a meeting of diplomats, engaged in delicate but hopeful parley, was broken up by a motley, ill-dressed crew of enthusiastic but misguided and tactless volunteers. The problem, says Pastor quite succinctly at one point, was that 'there survived in the friars something of the spirit of the conquistadors, that would not hear of discretion'. This assertion is much helped by ignorance of the great Dominican humanitarians and of the earlier work of the friars in America, many of whom, far from sharing 'the spirit of the conquistadors', never ceased to denounce that spirit, thereby earning themselves rough names and reputations from their fellow Spaniards.

But stupidity is always fascinating, so that if the popular version of the story were true, it would nevertheless still be worth investigation. One way to do that is to examine the situation from the friars' viewpoint; to reveal what they thought was happening and so explain why they acted as they did.

Yet it may fairly be asked why a Samaritan, knowing little of Jerusalem, should attempt this. The answer is that nothing similar has been presented in English, though the need for it was perceived years ago by Raymond Mortimer who, reviewing yet another popular biography of Jesuit Father Matteo Ricci, asked 'when is some friar going to give us a glimpse of the other side of the coin?' And the 19th-century writer Juan Valera complained that Spaniards take no interest in these matters: 'You'd never guess that St Francis Xavier and Domingo Navarrete were Spaniards, though the latter was the first to give us a detailed account of the Chinese literati'.

This book, then, is an attempt to satisfy that request and meet that complaint. I have tried to redress the balance and to show that both popular and academic evaluations of the situation are often based on stereotyping and misrepresentation.

Love (they say) conquers all things. But hate is not idle, and just as some personalities are fated to clash with others, so entire communities are unable to live with others. Throughout church history a hierarchy of hatreds descends in procession from official hatred of heresy and schism to particular hatreds of order for order, school for school, province for province, and theologian for theologian.

One such was that between the Jesuits and the Dominicans, and it was soon a byword. 'Let me see a Jesuit and a Dominican reconciled in doctrinal papistry', cried John Donne in a sermon, confident that his meaning would be taken by his congregation. Professor Meyer's verdict on the English mission is applicable elsewhere. 'The hatred of members of the same religion for one another was both the disgrace and the tragedy of English Catholicism; its forces were not united and it presented a broken front to the enemy'. The clash in Ch'ing China is therefore only a localized manifestation of a universal phenomenon, and as Professor Murdoch writes, 'between Jesuit and friar it was all but war to the knife, and no amount of Church historianizing will conceal that truth.'

That animosity is the theme of this book, which will try to show its effect on one man at a particular time and in a particular context. It is a very human story, for even Jesuits are made of men and so, *a fortiori*, must their opponents be. It was of these missionaries that Sir George Sansom declared, 'their combination of self-sacrificing zeal and sheer wickedness is astonishing!' Certainly the spectacle of Jesuits conniving at the hijacking of friar colleagues and arranging their protesting deportation from the China mission, is not what one expects to find in church history. For this is the unacceptable face of missionary endeavour.

Yet it should be no surprise. Lionel Fielden's autobiography (*Natural Bent*) discusses charity and good intentions, advertised aims and actual performance: 'The Quakers, the Near East Relief, the Save the Children Fund, the British Red Cross and the American Red Cross . . . you might have expected such organizations to show altruism and team spirit [but] instead they might have been a collection of prima donnas. Not one of them would disclose its plans, activities or funds to another; and, except for the Quakers, they kept up a quite disreputable struggle to requisition all the best houses and the best cars for themselves'.

Nor are others exempt from selfishness and passion: 'I have known even a scientist change his views because of personal animosity for a rival', confessed Sir Peter Medawar once, and James D. Watson in *The Double Helix* showed that 'In contrast to the popular conception, supported by newspapers and scientists' mothers, a goodly number of scientists are not only narrow-minded and dull, but also stupid' and, it seems, capable of coming to fisticuffs. Watson destroyed forever the image of the detached scholar, selflessly dedicated to the pursuit of scientific truth.

In his poem 'The Persian Version', Robert Graves presents the Greek victory at the battle of Marathon through Persian eyes. In the same way, I have here attempted to present 'A Friar's Version' of the missionaries' battle over the Confucian rites and terms. The friar giving evidence is the leading Dominican critic of the Jesuits' strategy, Friar Domingo Navarrete (1618–86), a Spaniard from Old Castile, who suddenly threw up his university lectureship at the age of 28 and volunteered for the Asian missions. That his view of the China Jesuits is hostile is only to be expected: a sore finger feels the slightest brush, and Domingo Navarrete was both a loyal Dominican and a sensitive Spaniard. Yet if his world seems crowded with scheming Jesuits, it was not a viewpoint peculiar to him. Many others, not only Dominicans, would have recognized it as regrettably normal, for as Bishop Burnet said of Innocent XI's aversion to the Jesuits, 'he is not singular in the hard thoughts he has of that order'. This book is intended to reflect that side of the picture, to explain the reactions of those who feared the Jesuits, and to sketch some of the consequences of that deep-rooted hostility.

Yet Navarrete is not merely negative or carping. There is another side to Friar Domingo, whose intelligent curiosity made him an ideal traveller. He ignored Gregory XIV's condemnation of missionary-sightseers, and his account of his journey around the world, with its wasps-to-whales approach, is vivid and personal. 'Reading it one feels as if one had stumbled on old Domingo himself in some tavern', writes Joseph Needham. And C. R. Boxer sees him as 'a 17th-century Herodotus who had the happy knack of inserting himself into all the remarkable happenings and interesting places of his time and surroundings, and had the observant eye, the open ear and the recording pencil of his great prototype'.

His *Tratados* (1676) was widely translated (English, French, German and Italian) and attracted the attention of Bossuet, Leibniz, Quesnay, and Voltaire. The English version (1704) was the result of warm recommendations from John Locke in whose *Human Understanding* he makes an appearance, called as a witness once more.

Navarrete is our contemporary in his concern for social justice and his defence of the downtrodden. In his determined praise of China and the Chinese he makes a rare Spanish contribution to the European vogue of chinoiserie and the sinomania of the following century. If his China is as idealized and utopian as that of any Jesuit, it is because his is a lover's tale: 'Sinologists are not inclined to smile upon Navarrete' (Needham again) 'yet his was a distinctly attractive character, and though he disagreed with the Jesuit "geometers", he fell completely in love with the Chinese themselves and their civilisation'.

Navarrete shows that just as much as any Jesuit Father he too wanted not only to convert the Chinese but to understand them and their culture. In this he was following the mendicant tradition of the pioneer American ethnographer Friar Bernardino de Sahagún, and of Friar Ramón Llull in the medieval Islamic world. Though his analysis had neither the depth nor sophistication of the Jesuits at their best, he had the innate urge to comprehend. But he was working alone, marginalized and excluded from the Jesuits' parleys, seminars and conferences. After all, it was not, they believed, in their interest to help or share confidences with a friar.

Navarrete's lifetime spanned a crucial period of Chinese history: it witnessed the fall of the Ming dynasty, the ascension of the Ch'ing (Manchu) line, and the 'Tartar Wars'. The years 1640 to 1652 in particular were a time of turmoil and civil war, and Navarrete, bringing a Spanish eye to bear on it all, comments on this agitated scene. His general conclusion is that, religion apart, they order things better in China.

The Spain to which he returned was also passing though a crisis. Distressed by what he found there he prescribed Confucian remedies towards national recovery, presenting Carlos II with a political prospectus and urging the example of an almost ideal world — an empire not of noble savages but of wise sages. Since this is part of his story I have included it here.

This is not, however, a formal biography. It is rather an evocation and an examination of Navarrete's career in Asia, of the effect of that experience on him, and of his role in the ecclesiastical drama being played out in Peking, Rome and Madrid. His final years as an archbishop in central America show him still obsessed by China, but co-operating with appreciative Jesuits while confessing at the same time that he 'would not die for them'.

II

As a group, the friars lacked the collective assertiveness which marked the Jesuits. But they had alternative strategies to offer. Where the Jesuit approach (through science) was curtailed — even damaged — by the papal condemnation of Galileo, the friars were able to continue with their less spectacular methods. This involved, for instance, some medical work, for they were the forerunners of the modern medical-missionaries, and in Japan they had caught the imagination of the populace with their hospitals and leprosaria. The China friars, in a lesser way, tried the same technique. Too much should not be made of this, but to ignore it is unjust.

But the friars differed from the Jesuits in their suspicion of too easy accommodation to such Chinese practices as ancestor veneration. They feared that it is in the nature of elastic to grow looser, and with their vast American experience behind them, they were less optimistic than the Jesuits. They were well aware that grafting one belief on another does not usually lead to a fusion but to the production of a bastard third (Haitian Voodoo, then unknown, would have made their point). They knew nothing of Jesuit Fr Parennin's parlour-tricks ('scientific blasphemy' in Needham's words), but it would have made another point: that standards can slip in science as well as theology, when a desired end comes to predominate. The friars also believed that shallow, glibly comfortable catechisms do not win whole-hearted converts: conversion requires some psychic payment; ideally, the payment should be felt and sometimes even hurt.

The difference between the two groups was referred to Rome, 'to the Feet of the Apostles', in the traditional way. The result was the 'Chinese Rites Controversy', of which Monsignor Baudrillaert has said: 'Never in the Catholic Church was there ever so remarkable a controversy — not even in the early centuries, the period of the great Councils', when quarrels over a diphthong could throw the civilized world into darkness. Of this same quarrel Father Bernard-Maitre has said: 'Without exaggeration, one can say that never did controversy within the Church ever preoccupy so many of the best minds for so long a time — three hundred and fifty years'. Before it ended, the 'Chinese affair' involved nine popes, two emperors, three kings, two papal legates, the Roman and Spanish Inquisitions, Propaganda Fide, the universities, and writers such as Bayle, Bossuet, Fénélon, Leibniz, Pascal and Voltaire.

The controversy involved more than mere theologians. Though it started, said Voltaire, as a monks' quarrel it ended as a philosophers' concern and, to quote Needham again, 'it is hardly to be ignored by historians of science, even though at first sight it has little to do with science'.

The allegations against the Jesuits were varied. They were accused of excessive and dangerous tolerance of Confucian and other ceremonies; of too discreetly concealing the crucifix from the Chinese (who found the story of

Christ's Passion repugnant) and of dabbling in astrology, even 'black magic', all for the greater glory of God. In short, the friars found much in the Jesuits' China Church which smacked of idolatry and they feared that the purity of Catholic doctrine was being contaminated – at the hands of its own evangelists.

Some Jesuits, Father Schall was one, admitted that the friars' approach was theologically *safer*; but would it work? Some friars admitted that the Jesuit approach might make it *easier* to convert the Chinese – but to what? They remembered the old saying that 'China is a sea that salts all the rivers flowing into it' and feared the religious syncretism (that amiable amalgamating of deities, and indifference to doctrinal niceties) for which Asia is famous – or notorious.

The Chinese Rites Controversy is closely linked to the history and fate of the old Jesuit order. Thirty years after Benedict XIV condemned the Jesuits' China policy, the controversy was cited as partial justification for their suppression by Clement XIV in 1773. Benedict perceived a link between the Rites Controversy and Jesuit moral theology: a link which enabled him to joke that the Jesuits fought as obstinately for 'Confucius Loyola' as, in their beginnings, they had fought for their own peculiar theological system. The discussion of the Jesuits here is limited to the old Society as it appeared to many. In some respects the modern Society of Jesus bears small resemblance to the awesome body it was before 1773.

III

This third attempt to Christianize China failed: the harvest was not ripe – it was destined never to be, for the crop was of unique stuff, and the field strewn by too many obstacles:

1. East and West failed to meet because their respective world pictures differed fundamentally and there was too great a cosmological divide. The Chinese mind, rooted in concepts from the Sino-Tibetan family of languages, found many Christian ideas, evolved from the Graeco-Roman-Judaic-Scholastic mental world, to be inconceivable, and the Chinese literati, by and large untroubled by metaphysical anxieties, showed an interest in the Jesuits' Renaissance technology, but laid aside with contumely their religion and Tridentine 'Ptolemaic' theology.

2. Ancestor veneration, an ancient practice which pre-dated Confucius, was like an ongoing memorial service, with deep collective psychological roots, a relentless coercive force summing up in itself all that was most sacred in family, clan and state. How small a thing was the salvation of a single soul, compared to the august continuity of that family tradition, 'which rises', said one missionary, 'like a mountain barrier between us and them'.

   Christopher Dawson sums it up: 'The Rites have the same importance for Confucianism that the Law possessed for Judaism; they are nothing less than the external manifestation of that eternal order that governs the universe'.

3. Polygamy (concubinage) was linked to ancestor veneration since it might ensure sufficient offspring for the sacred duty of venerating the dead, while imperial polygamy, as with Henry VIII of England, was basically utilitarian. The practice was also eugenic since those who could afford it would be the abler men in the community.

4. Syncretism: 'The two religions', said the Wan-li emperor, meaning Taoism and Buddhism, 'are the wings of the third', meaning Confucianism. Such tolerance baffled some Catholics, brought up in a sterner tradition and fresh from a Europe laid waste by the Thirty Years' War, or rejoicing over the Revocation of the Edict of Nantes.

5. Conversion, which brought no material benefits, could be an obstacle to career and promotion and, said Lord Macartney, 'a Chinese is more likely to be allured by an immediate benefit than a distant reversion'. He added, a practice such as 'Confession is repugnant to so suspicious a nature as theirs; and husbands must find a wife's imparting of her sins to a barbarian is particularly disgusting', particularly since many people's

harmless sexual pleasures would now be penalized by the missionaries.

6. As the squabbling missionaries themselves knew only too well, and were often reminded by the Chinese Dominican, Friar Lo, their own inter-order quarrels scandalized and discouraged potential neophytes.

IV

Yet the stakes were high, as the aim was not simply to substitute one ritual for another. It was, rather, to change the philosophy of a nation. The difficulties of this particular enterprise are fully discussed in Jacques Gernet's excellent *China and the Christian Impact* (1985). In a more general sense, John Donne, in a 'Voltairean' sermon, conveys vividly the extraordinary claims of Christianity as perceived by the 'uncatechised heathen'. On pain of eternal fire, the convert is required to believe in One God who is also a Trinity of Persons, the second of whom is God's virgin-born son, made Man yet still God, in order to be sacrificed for humankind's salvation.

In short, the Jesuit programme, outrageous in conception, was impossible in practice, since it called for a reversal of Chinese culture without a revolution. Nor is it sufficiently appreciated that, though the collar that the Jesuits had designed for the necks of the Chinese might seem smoother, in time it would have to be just as thick as any that the friars might bring. 'Above all', wrote Father Ricci, 'I want us to be in good standing with these people, because later we can do what we wish with them'.

Yet no matter how improbable the attempt, it is not easy to accept failure, especially of a dazzlingly adventurous strategy; thus the Jesuits, beguiled by their own effrontery in playing the power game, naturally laid the blame upon those in disagreement with them and, as they saw it, hampering them. But it was pointless to seek scapegoats. China, which had 'sinicized' Buddhism and Islam before accepting either, which was even then forcing its Manchu conquerors to become more Chinese, which in our own day 'sinicized' Marxism, was unlikely to yield to Christian missionaries – not even to legendary, land-leaping Jesuits, for all their clocks, maps and telescopes.

'The prime historical fallacy', remarked Lord Acton, 'is judging the past with the ideas of the present'. There is little danger of that here, since the Chinese Rites Controversy revolved around problems as contemporary as Vatican II. At the root of it all lay the question of *aggiornamento*: should the Church, having failed to convert the world, adapt itself to the ways of the world, in this instance, the world of Ming and Ch'ing China?

Zbigniew Brzezinski ('I have largely relied on Pastor's *Popes*') has 'modernized' this story, finding analogies between the Rites Controversy and the modern Sino-Russian doctrinal conflicts, equating Jesuit clocks and calendars with the sputniks of the 1950s; both represent the same 'soft-sell' approach to the Chinese. He makes the point that doctrinal conflicts, Catholic or Marxist, themselves generate further problems, jurisdictional, organizational or personal, which in turn intensify the very quarrel from which they sprang.

V

Among the aims of this book are the following:

1. To discuss the deep hostility between two great orders in the Church, and to outline the roots of their power struggle at home, before it was exported to the missions. As Brzezinski reminds us, 'power is always heavily involved in these disputes'.

2. To look at the Jesuits not as cultural bridge-builders, which has been done by so many others, but to consider them from the human angle as missionary-colleagues and men. As interpreters of East and West they were eminently successful; as strategists, daringly adventurous; and as priests undoubtedly devoted; but as co-workers they were sadly wanting. By the same token, I am also seeking to rescue the friars from the immense condescension of posterity.

3. To emphasize that the Jesuit approach was not static. Fr Ricci's tentative 'perhaps not superstitious' (of the Chinese rites) was expanded by later, less patient, Fathers. An interesting illustration of how Jesuit enthusiasm dealt with Ricci's early cautious approach is to be seen in the phenomenon of Jesuit 'Figurism', an 18th-century extension of the 'accommodation' policy which some modern Jesuits find an embarrassing aberration. Finally, Rome, the first European centre of Asian studies, condemned such developments and, alarmed by the venom and viciousness of the struggle, banned all writing on the problem. That ban, not always observed of course, ran from 1710 until 1940, when the situation in East Asia was seen to have changed.

4. To suggest some of the results of Jesuit policy and style on the converts, on the missionaries themselves, and on Navarrete, one of the best representatives of the friars. He came to know the Fathers during the nearly four years when he was interned with them in Canton in the persecution of the late 1660s. That formative period deeply affected his attitude, especially when he witnessed their own doubts and divisions, normally hidden from outsiders, from anyone who was 'not one of us'. Having briefly 'joined the Jesuits' in Canton he learned much; some thought too much.

5. This survey of the rites controversy ends with Navarrete's death in 1686, but, for any who may be interested, I have briefly outlined later developments, including Navarrete's own contribution to knowledge of China, the 'Middle Flowery Kingdom', and to the 18th-century vogue of Chinamania.

VI

Although the pinyin method of transliterating Chinese names has been in use since 1958 (street signs, etc.), and officially adopted since 1979, I have preferred the Wade-Giles system which has been used for most English language books on China. (Some amusing reflections on this subject are expressed in Herbert Sandford's 'Beijing or Peking?', a paper delivered at the Annual Meeting of the British Association for the Advancement of Science and Technology, August 1991.)

Chinese personal names are given in accordance with Chinese practice, where the family name precedes the given name, as in a directory. The given name is hyphenated. An exception to this convention is found when some Chinese living abroad follow the Western style, as in Lo-shu Fu. It is not always possible to tell nationality from a particular name; for example, Antonio Fernandes was a Chinese, and Bartolomeu da Costa a Japanese, Jesuit. This is also true of foreigners working in Spanish territories, thus Friar Tomás de Santa María was in fact the disreputable English Dominican Thomas Gage.

To avoid sprinkling the text with digits I have grouped reference notes in paragraphs as relevant. In this way I have tried where possible to make each reference note a bibliography in miniature for the passage to which it refers.

1 Hounds and Foxes

The Order of Jesuits is a great and effectual instrument for Spain, and the Dominicans, I take it, are much Spanish too.

— Francis Bacon

A great desire came over me to know something of the history of the Dominican Order.

— James Joyce

The Jesuits — so fascinating to study, so curious to touch.

— Lord Acton

The Dominicans, a more hellish order than the rest: witness the Inquisition, of which they are the managers.

— Thomas Astley

The history of Spain is in great part the history of her religious orders. Indeed the story of the two chief orders, front-line regiments in the army of the old Church Militant, is a chapter in the history of the Catholic Church at home in Europe, and in the foreign missions, her spiritual colonies overseas. Twice, when the survival of the Great Church was threatened, salvation came from Spain: first through the Dominicans, the Order of Preachers (or Blackfriars), who fought the thirteenth-century Cathar heresy; and secondly, through the Jesuits, the Society of Jesus (or Blackrobes), who saved half Europe from the Protestant Reformers' grasp. Without these two orders the history of the world could not have been the same.[1]

The Iberian Peninsula was the first of all the Muslim-conquered lands to

---

[1] 'Had our religion not been brought back to its original condition by Dominic and Francis, it would soon have been extinguished' (Machiavelli, *Livy*, 3, i). But Dominic is nearer to Ignatius Loyola than to Francis in the comparison drawn by Bennett (26).

fight its way back to Christianity and was never sullied by national heresy in either medieval or modern times. It seemed fitting therefore that Iberia should have given birth to these two orders, typical too that they should be the most self-consciously Roman and Catholic of the religious corporations. Their unmistakable character and personality are symbolised in a slight but significant way: Anglican groups have borrowed the name, dress and manners of the more malleable Benedictines and Franciscans, but no successful attempt has been made to do the same with the Jesuits or Dominicans. The Spanish saints, Dominic and Ignatius, are not easily assimilated, and could never fit into an Anglican frame.

The more regrettable, then, that from the start these two orders devoted themselves to a vendetta both unremitting and universal, and that, in the words of the Prophet Micah, 'they hunted every man his brother with a net'.

Early in the 13th century, when Albigensian heretics were threatening the basis of western society, a woman in Spain dreamt of giving birth to a hound, holding in its jaws a flaming torch with which to set the countryside ablaze. The pope in Rome, too, had a dream: he saw the Lateran Basilica collapsing, until a young Spaniard ran forward to support it. These prophecies were considered to be fulfilled in the person of Dominic de Guzmán, founder of the order of Friars Preacher. First of the four great Spaniards who profoundly influenced the universal Church, he was seen by an early biographer as an 'evening star rising out of Spain', forecasting the end of the world and preparing for the last judgement. For Dante, he was the Wrestler Saint, the Sacred Athlete, the Messenger of Christ, for, as Dom David Knowles puts it, 'The most apt word for St Dominic is virility: he was to the depths of his being virile'. Nevertheless Dominic is not a popular saint. A few enthusiastic contemporaries created and bequeathed the obligatory hagiographical legends; but he lacks charisma and his name has never been a battle-cry, despite his qualities as founder, organizer and missionary. (1)

In the struggle against the Albigensians he took hints from their ascetic way of life and dress, and so his Dominican friars wore a plain, white woollen tunic covered by the traditional black outdoor cloak of the Spanish clergy, hence the nickname 'Blackfriars'. They were mendicants, begging their daily bread and renouncing possessions by a vow of evangelical poverty. Dominic left it to another group of radical newcomers, the Franciscans, to convert through the heart; his new order was to convert through the mind. He aimed to confront error with all the resources of a trained intellect. He rejected illiterate volunteers, demanding of postulants a knowledge of grammar and elementary logic before acceptance. They then went through a course of advanced studies in theology, philosophy and history. The Dominican rule so emphasized this intellectual training that to join the order was the equivalent of enrolling in a university. Nothing was allowed to interfere with these studies. Manual labour, a traditional part of a monk's way of life, was abandoned because it would take time and energy away from the friar, whose work was intellectual. To this end, dispensations from the rule were permitted: friars were allowed to stay up at night to study, fasts could be broken, and choir attendance excused. The daily chanting of the the the conventual liturgy, the divine office, was to be speeded up and performed briefly and briskly (*breviter et succincte*). Even their way of celebrating mass was somewhat abbreviated to that same end, to get back to their books – to study was to pray. (2)

The Dominicans formed the first order in the Church with an academic mission, the first preaching order of perpetual students. It must also be said that no religious order in the modern sense existed till then. They produced works of theology, philosophy and apologetics in an effort to meet the demands of the time. The Dominicans aimed 'to pass the fruits of contemplation to others' and to satisfy the intellectual demands of the most intellectual century of the Middle Ages.[2] They were not afraid of change, as a Church which exists in time must necessarily change with the times, and continuity must include innovation, declared a Dominican inquisitor in 1241. Yet pluralism is not a theological condition with which Dominicans are equipped to deal. Their charisma is for truth, their motto is 'Veritas', and (Knowles again) 'Their peculiar glory has been to preach the traditional gospel, to maintain a massive fabric of truth against the attacks of every kind of agnosticism, illuminism, eclecticism and opportunism'. This disdain for whatever they saw as opportunism partly explains the Dominicans' attitude to the problems encountered later in the China mission and which are discussed below. (3)

These professional mendicants, a protest movement against the growing commercialism of the age, were men who, witnessing the rise of capitalism, chose to negotiate the sacred merchandise of the gospel (*divina mercadería*) without touching filthy lucre. But the Dominican friar, a canon in profession, a monk in austerity, an apostle in preaching, was seen by Dominic himself as a hound – a watchdog driving back into the safety of the fold any sheep wandering away to destruction.

The Dominican order was one of the most perfect of the medieval conventual corporations, and its commonsensical, flexible rule was so sophisticated a creation that in seven centuries it has never needed reform. The order was centralized but democratic. Superiors were elected by those they were to govern and, unlike the monastic abbots, were not aloof and distant lords, had no privileges, were granted no external signs of respect, and lived and dressed as did their subjects. High office for the Dominican was an onerous burden, not an honour: *onus non honus*.

The Dominican revolution (it was nothing less) in the world of monastic institutions ended the old system in which the only religious had been

---

[2] *Contemplata aliis tradere*: the order's other motto, was first used in Aquinas's *Summa* (2. 2: 188: 4–6) where he defends the concept of the order.

monks, living apart from the world, committed to a particular monastery, not primarily concerned with evangelizing. The new, more assertive friars contrasted sharply with this tradition as they tramped across Europe, preaching, teaching and confessing. They saw themselves as men of action, ready to dispute in the market-place or to teach from pulpit and rostrum. They were 'fitted for all the perils of these modern times'. They lived in new buildings, taught in new universities, worshipped in new churches, debated new ideas, found new approaches to old problems, proclaimed new standards in theology, philosophy, poetry, prose; and, in every branch of knowledge, felt themselves well-equipped as modern men. They appealed especially to the more dynamic elements in society, to the young, to the merchant class, the universities, but it was their espousal of poverty that endeared them to the populace at large.

So well did the friars acquit themselves that soon after their foundation Gregory IX chose them to staff the Inquisition. It is ironical that an intellectual order, founded to correct error by reasoned persuasion, should have been chosen to suppress dissent by force. This, says Chesterton, is why Dominic is seen as cruelly devising thumbscrews, while St Francis is accepted as a humanitarian deploring mousetraps. Perhaps he was thinking of Thomas Astley, one of Navarrete's English editors, who warned readers that Friar Domingo belonged to 'a more hellish Order than the rest: Witness, the Inquisition, or Hell in Miniature, of which they are the Managers; and their Founder Dominic should have been called *Demoniac*, for he was a Limb of the Devil'.

Subsequent popes, to whom Dominicans made a special vow of obedience, placed similar confidence in them, employing them as agents, diplomats, and collectors of the papal revenues. Their spiritual reputation brought further temporal privileges: for instance, they were confessors to the kings of France, Aragon and Portugal. In England (where the royal confessional was their monopoly for centuries) during the reigns of Edward I, II, and III they occupied the sort of position later to be filled elsewhere by Jesuits in the castles and palaces of the Counter-Reformation. But in Spain, above all, the Blackfriars were the royal confessors from 1218 until 1700. (4)

They did not escape criticism. Their novel conception of the religious vocation disconcerted some, and many officials in the Roman chancery saw Dominic as a dangerous innovator. Their success aroused jealousy: parish priests feared them as supplanters, bishops suspected they were papal spies, conservatives saw them as heralds of new and dubious trends in theology. They witnessed the birth of Oxford University and fostered its growth, but they were not always welcomed in the academic world, where many regarded them as unfair competitors who ingratiated themselves with the upper classes, used devious methods, and were unscrupulous rivals. In part, this resentment arose because they attracted the keenest students, who were drawn by their fresh way of thinking.

The friars did not limit themselves to the schools. They also worked among the lowly and uneducated; and here too their story is one of spectacular success. Nothing better summarizes the Blackfriars' versatility than a comparison between their introduction of the rosary, a simple chaplet of beads, and the mighty *Summa theologiae* of their St Thomas Aquinas. The rosary, poor relation to the elegant bourgeois *Book of Hours*, cost little to acquire, was easily carried about, and helped the illiterate to meditate through a rudimentary form of 'composition of place'. As opposed to the simple rosary, the *Summa* has been the intellectual bedrock of Catholic theology ever since its appearance: 'Reason, as borne on the wings of Thomas, can scarcely rise higher', said Leo XIII.

Aquinas produced another great work, the *Contra gentiles*, which was a missionary handbook written at the request of his brethren, who did not confine their activities to Europe. Indeed, both the age of discovery and the counter-reformation began when these mendicant friars began their work and wanderings in the 13th century. Dominic himself had longed to be a missionary, and in keeping with that spirit, his 'Hounds' spread worldwide. This diaspora began in 1217 when there were only sixteen friars. They spread rapidly, widely and effectively, and for the next three centuries the burden of missionary work fell on the two mendicant orders of Dominicans and Franciscans. (5)

About 1300 the Blackfriars formed the 'Society of pilgrims living in foreign parts for Christ's sake' (*Societas fratrum peregrinantium propter Christum*); soon there was even a friar archbishop of Peking, and a few years after the discovery of the New World, mendicant friars laid the foundations of the American Church. Such was their reputation as missionaries and pioneers that when the first Spaniards reached the Philippines in the 16th century and found the remains of what looked like Christian images, they accepted them as evidence that friars had somehow anticipated them.

When a new order is founded, it is truly the child of its begetter and as such is dearly loved and nourished. There is a kind of pathos in the stories: the splendid birth of the idea, its embodiment against all odds, the excitement of the early years, but then, as the organization grows and matures, it changes and becomes stiffer and hide-bound, and loses much of the early vitality. The Dominicans were no exception and, by the end of the 15th century, the friars' Golden Age seemed over. The scholastic learning of this later period became a mere shadow and counterfeit of the thought of the pioneers. Radicalism and adventurous thought surrendered to conservatism; the revolutionaries became reactionaries, and dialectics an end in itself. Latter-day 'schoolmen' confined themselves to defining, classifying and categorizing, losing themselves in a maze of conceptual arabesques and conceits. Many of these Aristotelians of the Stricter Observance looked upon the learning that they had inherited as sacrosanct and unchangeable. They dared not alter classical positions even when the need arose, as Aquinas himself would have done, for he had often stressed that he was only putting forward hypotheses, the rejection of which would not compromise his metaphysics. These Dominican word-warriors, 'Masters of the Sacred Page', saw themselves as guardians of an inviolable orthodoxy.

It would however be a vulgar error to generalize this 'Bronze Age' into a description of all the later scholastics without distinction. A recent survey warns against such readiness to reject scholasticism out of hand. It is 'not to be dismissed unheard as if it were disingenuous official propaganda by ideological hacks'; we are reminded that 'almost all branches of linguistics, logic and philosophy were developed by the scholastics'. Their 'quaint illustrations' should not be misunderstood, yet 'it is still often said that all scholastic philosophical debate turned upon the question of how many angels could stand on a pinhead'. The German Jesuit Georg Schurhammer best summarizes the attitude of modern defenders of scholasticism: 'the scholastic method with its sharp, clear concepts, its long logical training, and its daily disputations was precisely what the humanists with their confused ideas about philosophy and theology needed, and what the battle with the heresies of the time required'. (6)

Nevertheless, it cannot be denied that there was a period of sterility against which there were two reactions: one from the humanists, who rejected the methods of the schoolmen, and the other from those friar-scholastics who themselves sought self-reformation. Above all, it was the Spanish Dominicans who worked for the restoration of scholasticism, and in time they came to dominate the whole European revival of Thomistic philosophy and theology. They rejected pseudo-dialectics, and they applied the latest knowledge to the service of theology: in particular, bringing the new philology to bear on textual criticism of the Bible.

The Dominican Francisco de Vitoria (1483–1546) brought about this renaissance in Salamanca, the leading Spanish university. A reforming liberal who made a point of writing elegant Latin, his modern biographer finds that 'even in our day his views [on international law] seem ahead of the times'. Both at home and abroad he was consulted on current affairs, not least of which were the nature and rights of the American Indians, and Henry VIII's plans to divorce his Spanish queen. The greatest teacher in the imperial Spain of Charles V, Vitoria 'earned more praise when disagreeing with Aquinas than he ever did when agreeing'.[3] It was typical of him that he challenged his students 'not to accept Aquinas's words blindly, without scrutiny', and reminded them of Aquinas's dictum that 'in philosophy, the appeal to authority is the weakest of all arguments'. In Spain, then, the old generation of 'schoolmen' was replaced by another, intent on creating new approaches,

---

[3] 'Maioremque, meo judicio, laudem dissentiendo, quam consentiendo assequebatur' (Cano, De locis, XII, Intro.). Cf. Wittgenstein: 'Aquinas's questions, not his answers, give the measure of his philosophical gifts' (Kenny, Aquinas (London, 1980), 81).

and as a result his pupils used to divide the history of theology into two periods: 'before and after Vitoria'.

Vitoria's most brilliant, if tempestuous, pupil was his fellow-friar Melchor Cano (1509–60), audaciously ranked by some as next to Aquinas himself. Cano is the classic author on theological proof, whose revolutionary work, based on the methods of Aristotle and of Cicero's *Topics*, earned him a reputation as the founder of modern fundamental theology, which investigates the primary elements of Christian revelation. Cano asserted the right to criticize anyone, including Aristotle and Aquinas. His fulminations against decadent unthinking scholasticism and schoolmen show that there is no need to turn to Erasmus or Vives for such objections. His *De locis Theologicis* (1563) contains fierce denunciations of 'those so-called theologians whose writings sound more like the ramblings of little old crones. At this moment (I am writing this in tears), when our theologians should be armed from top to toe and mounted like knights to do battle with the German heretics, they equip themselves with sticks and children's hobby horses. These sophists think they know theology, but are only following its shadow. Oh, how much longer must we endure their idle disputations over Maximum and Minimum, Infinite and Finite – topics on which I'd be ashamed to waste my time'.

A humanist in his style and rejection of sophistry, Cano searched profane history and secular literature for anything to reinforce the Church's doctrines. Pagan antiquities ('the jewels of the Egyptians') were to be exploited for Christian culture: 'Those who ignore the lessons of history are neither theologians nor even educated men'. He himself systematically collated biblical texts in the light of archaeology, philology (Greek, Hebrew, Latin) and ancillary studies.

For Ernst Curtius, Cano's 'real revolution in theological method has the same classical significance as has Aquinas's *Summa* for philosophy'. Lord Acton praised his hard-headed view of pious fables, for Cano spurned even the miracles associated with his own patron, St Dominic: 'in the lives of our saints it is wrong for the truth to be contaminated with the false and fabulous'. Gibbon praised 'Cano's honest complaint that the biographies of Laertius and Suetonius showed a stricter regard for historic truth than can be found in the lives of the saints and martyrs from Catholic writers'. Samuel Purchas added that Cano was right to reject these 'Lies of the Saints, Misse-stories and Leaden Legends'. (7)

One of the finest Spanish Christian humanists, Cano passed on these gifts to his own pupils – men such as Friars Luis de León and Domingo de Soto. León, an Augustinian theologian, philologist, mystic, exegete, student of the classics and Hebrew, was a lyric poet of beauty and force who provided a model for future generations. It was of him that the Spanish academician Dámaso Alonso wrote, magnificently, 'When they ask if there was a Renaissance in Spain, we can answer that there was indeed, for this, that, or some other reason. Or we can simply say: "Yes, there was, because there was Friar Luis de León!" ' (8)

The first Jesuits learnt their theology at the feet of friars such as these. Fr General Ledóchowski thought it was 'a Divine Providence that our Holy Father Ignatius, and his first companions were taught at Paris and Salamanca by professors of the scholastic system as it had been restored in accordance with the mind of St Thomas'. Ignatius Loyola himself even urged Francis Xavier to attend only the Dominicans' lectures in Paris and to avoid those of the regius professors. (9)

II

The Jesuit order was the creation of Ignatius Loyola who, like Dominic de Guzmán, came from northern Spain. Austere, detached, an *hidalgo*, Loyola was a natural leader, gifted with that talent for detail which marks the successful organizer. Dominic, 'God's Athlete', was now to be followed — supplanted, said some — by Ignatius, 'God's Bureaucrat'. All this came about when, convalescing from a wound, Loyola demanded his favourite novels of chivalry to while away the time; nothing could be found except romantically written saints' lives. Inspired by this hagiography, Ignatius became a born-again Christian, changed his way of life, and in due time created the Society of Jesus, rather as though a multinational corporation was born of absorbed readings of *Alice in Wonderland*, followed by the accidental but electrifying discovery of Samuel Smiles's *Lives of the Great Engineers*. (10)

Despite diligent propagation of such devotions as 'St Ignatius Water', the Saint himself, like Dominic, never became popular. Goethe revered St Philip Neri, Shaw enthused over St Joan, and English sentimentalists love Francis of Assisi, but there were no ready approaches to Loyola, perhaps, as Giovanni Papini remarks, 'because in a sense he is the most absolutely Catholic of the saints'. Nevertheless Ignatius, 'his beautiful Spanish eyes always a little filled with tears', was not without tenderness. His companions remarked on the 'motherly strain' in him, and until the end of the 18th century he was the patron of expectant mothers. Moreover, according to one Jesuit visionary, he was the recipient of such rare spiritual favours as 'the grace of an exchange of hearts with Christ'. (11)

Since Vatican II it is unfashionable to see Ignatius as a soldier-saint raising a new regiment of eucharistic warriors, so Captain Ignatius Loyola has been demobilized. Yet that is how he and his men appeared to friends, foes and each other. The military terminology to which they were addicted is not of course unique to them, for it dates back to St Paul and the early Church Fathers. But he broke with tradition by styling his group not an order, but a 'company' — a word, says Fr Herbert Thurston, 'patient of a military interpretation'. *Compañía* in contemporary Spanish meant a soldier-band of 'companions' under a *caudillo*. Ignatius composed a *Summa Instituti* in which he makes references to 'military service for God' in the ranks of what Julius III called 'this soldier band of Jesus Christ'. The military metaphor is also enshrined in the Bull with which Paul III established the Society.[4] Ignatius himself assured the pope that his Company, the Light Cavalry, the shock troops of the Church Militant, were ever ready for the thick of battle at any time or place, to support the heavy regiments, the older orders, who by their nature were less mobile.

---

[4] The *Imago primi saeculi*, the extraordinary Festschrift which the Jesuits presented to themselves on the Society's first centenary (1640), is full of military imagery.

This disciplined approach also accounts for the 'blind obedience' demanded of the Jesuit by his superior. Democratic rule, such as that favoured by the Dominicans, was distrusted because it might weaken the order's united impact: there would be 'as many opinions as members'. The Jesuit Society was probably the most centralized and disciplined non-military body that has ever existed. The general was elected for life and lived in a Roman headquarters, at the centre of a communications network (not unlike the mercantile organizations) through which he appointed all subordinates to their posts. Certainly the friars never achieved an equivalent internal discipline, as some lamented when they saw the novel efficiency and successes of the Society.

The rule of the Society was a development of tradition. Even the Jesuits' celebrated 'blind obedience' goes back as far as the early Desert Fathers. Ignatius's 'I will believe that the white object I see [before me] is black if that should be the decision of the hierarchical Church' is more emphatic than original.[5] The traditional element may also be found in parts of the Jesuit *Constitutions* which sometimes show a marked, almost literal, dependence upon the earlier Dominican rule, though they surpass it in centralization and efficiency.[6]

Some of Ignatius's innovations were suspect in certain quarters. The Society's name seemed arrogant: 'Who are these men', asked the too readily indignant Sixtus V, 'whom we cannot name without bowing our heads?' Sensitive souls, noting that the Jesuits did not wear a distinctive religious habit, interpreted this as contempt for those who did. And where Dominic had abbreviated the communal liturgy, Ignatius abolished it; Jesuits did not assemble daily in choir for community prayer, though they emphasized the daily practice of private mental prayer and meditation. They did not perform special corporal austerities, being content to observe the same fasts and abstinences as layfolk. They did not 'take the discipline' (that is, indulge in the monastic ritual of self-flagellation), did not wear the hairshirt, go about barefoot, with head uncovered. Such practices, though good in themselves, were not suited to Fathers occupied day and night in the care of others. Instead the Jesuits practised mortification of the will. They also decided not to undertake the spiritual care of nuns, or to allow women to be associated with their Society. Franciscans might have their 'Poor Clares' and the Dominicans their Sisters, but there were to be no Jesuitesses.[7] This cautious

---

[5] He was reacting to Erasmus's remark of 1527: 'White can never become black, even if the pope should say so'.

[6] Recalling the friars' early help to Ignatius, the Dominican historian Mortier adds, meaningfully, 'Of course, in ageing, memory is the first thing to fail!'

[7] With one exception: Princess Juana, the emperor Charles V's daughter, was a female Jesuit. (By contrast, St Dominic began his apostolate by founding a nunnery and seems to have had a particular care for women, and a special skill in their spiritual direction. This was one of the many lessons he learned from observing the Albigensians.)

attitude continued into modern times and General Ledóchowski declared in 1923 that '[Our] Institute is more rigorous than others in what pertains to dealings with women; others may have the care of Sisters but we may not. In this matter, therefore, in which by our very Institute we differ from others, we should attend to and follow our own laws'. (12)

In order to avoid personal ambition, and so that the individual might work only for the Society and not his own advancement, Jesuits were forbidden to accept bishoprics, posts in the Inquisition, or similar dignities. This was intended to make the organization flexible, mobile and adaptable. Its elite members took not only the usual vows of poverty, chastity and obedience, but an additional fourth vow of personal loyalty to the pope, committing themselves to go wherever and whenever he might command. Macaulay waxed romantic on the topic. 'If a Jesuit was wanted at Lima, he was on the Atlantic in the next fleet. If he was wanted at Baghdad, he was toiling through the desert with the next caravan . . . They glided from one Protestant country to another under innumerable disguises, as gay Cavaliers, as simple rustics, as Puritan preachers, as Mandarins'.

For the Jesuit, everything was done for 'the greater glory of God' (the phrase is repeated or implied 376 times in the Society's *Constitutions*). This too gave offence, for it seemed to suggest that the older orders had done no more than work merely for the 'glory of God'. Furthermore, the Jesuit's well-meant references to his *mínima compañía* were resented as a slur upon the Franciscan 'Friars Minor'. Even Jesuit terminology was new, with talk of *residences*, not convents, of *rectors*, not priors.

Not even the marginalia of the spiritual life were neglected by the 'holy legislator' who laid down instructions on how to ring the door bell properly, forbade sleeping with the windows open, prescribed the correct amount of salt on food, and ordered his Jesuits, when in conversation with people of authority, not to stare them in the face, but rather to keep their eyes slightly lowered. Wrinkling the forehead, and still more the nose, was to be avoided, since an even forehead and a bonny face indicates a good heart and interior tranquillity. There was also a practical reminder that morning was appropriate for discussing spiritual affairs with layfolk; after dinner was a better time for seeking favours. Nothing was too detailed for Ignatius and there were barrack-like inspections of rooms to check that beds were properly made up, had no fluff under them, and that any books were neatly laid out on the table.

More basic was his insistence upon the use of 'human means' to attain spiritual ends.[8] Jesuits were to pray for God's help as fervently as though their own efforts were useless, but at the same time to resort to practical means as though everything depended upon them alone. Like the friars

---

[8] In 1925 Jesuit General Ledóchowski urged missionaries to acquire the practical skills of Boy Scouts: '*illas res practicas quas exploratores* [Scouts] *discere solent*' (*Acta Cong.*, 96).

earlier, they too used the new humanism, adopting and adapting the sciences (mathematics, astronomy) and the arts (literature, painting, drama, opera, even the ballet), for 'the greater glory of God'. (Sometimes to startling effect: fourteen conscience-stricken courtiers ran from the première of Fr Bidermann's *Cenodoxus* (1602), to a nearby Jesuit house, begging admission to the Society.) Moreover the Fathers introduced the most effective education system the world had seen until then, though Macaulay thought they had merely 'discovered the precise point to which intellectual culture can be carried without risk of intellectual emancipation'. (13)

Exceptional men were needed to carry out such tasks and indeed no other religious community produced men so variously distinguished. To achieve this, superiors carefully sifted candidates for admission, seeking men of virtue, intelligence and stability. Since the pioneer Jesuits shared the contemporary view that physical appearance was an outward sign of the inner man, and that deformities signified shortcomings, they looked for a pleasing appearance, and a good voice and figure in postulants. There are records of applicants turned away for blackened teeth or a facial scar, though such defects could be overlooked if there was some compensation. Nobility of lineage was a considerable advantage. Novices who overcame these hurdles were put through a rigorous course of discipline and study, for the Jesuits aimed to equal the best of their opponents in everything; theirs was an army in which every private soldier was given a general's training. (14)

The Fathers' strengths were legion and their faults, they knew, were few. But the self-styled *mínima compañía* suffered from a fatal flaw which, though permissible, even praiseworthy, in a secular corporation, could only be a collective disease in the heart of a spiritual community. For the Jesuits were proud. 'You will', said Diderot, 'find every possible kind of Jesuit – yes, even unbelievers – but you will never find a humble one'.[9] That spirit contributed to the dissolution of the order under Clement XIV in 1773. The last official historian of the Old Society, Fr Giulio Cesare Cordara, witnessed the suppression of what was 'dearer to me than my eyes'. Indeed, on hearing the sentence pronounced he fainted, but recovered sufficiently to analyse possible causes. He rejected the vulgarities alleged against the Society (regicide, sedition, poisonings), but was left with the inescapable fact. Finally he diagnosed two possible causes, one natural (human hatred and malice), the other supernatural (God's Will). 'And why did God allow it? If you consider a little you will see that not only has He allowed it – He willed, even arranged it. In short, it was not human intrigue that brought it about'. Fr Cordara concludes by finding in his beloved Society a peculiar blemish, one

---

[9] This was an early problem and the Society's first General Congregation (1558) had to take action against it. For Jesuit disquisitions on the problem see Fr Ludwig Koch, *Jesuiten-Lexikon* (Paderborn, 1934) s.v. Stolz; Fr H. Becher, *Die Jesuiten. Gestalt und Geschichte des Ordens* (München, 1951), 80.

that had moved the Almighty to allow its punishment, and that blemish was the Jesuits' sin: 'the subtle vice of pride, from which God shrank . . . and so subtle is it that the Jesuits even prided themselves on their virtues, especially on their record of chastity, which distinguished them from the common herd of religious'.

Cordara believed that one day the Society would be revived, but not until 'our pride has vanished'. This opinion was apparently shared by his English confrère Fr Charles Plowden, who lived to see the re-establishment of the English novitiate (1806) and wrote: 'I trust the novices will never share the fault of contemning other ecclesiastical bodies which, I fear, existed in too great a degree in the Old Society'. Another contemporary, this time an outsider, who shared Cordara's view was Alphonsus Liguori, founder of the Redemptorists. St Alphonsus warned his own fledglings to take care, 'pride could destroy us, as it did the Jesuits'.

On the other hand, the Jesuits had reason to be proud. They had an immense sense of purpose; the reassurance of brotherhood; a gratifying awareness that they were unique, and were the most extraordinary organization that the world had seen, using the most modern techniques in the service of the timeless. Moreover, in everything they were successful. They were producing saints and politicians, preachers and scientists, martyrs and scholars. They were the confessors of the mighty and consolers of the lowly; the educators of the day, and in eternity, advocates pleading for frail humanity before the bar of Justice; ever seeking worldly power, the better to serve unworldliness. There was, it seemed, no task for which they were not prepared and willing, except that of co-operating with their elder brothers.

The Jesuits quickly spread abroad, and where they managed to combine their teaching skill with missionary activity the results were startling. Within a few years of their establishment (1540) they were in Abyssinia, Brazil, Japan, and the Congo. In time there were Jesuits at the courts of the Great Mogul, Ivan the Terrible, and James II of England. Jesuits converted Queen Christina of Sweden (though a French cynic maintained she only adopted Catholicism because it was a convenient religion for travelling). In Paraguay Jesuits established a benevolent dictatorship, in North America they were admitted to blood-brotherhood by the Iroquois; in the East they appeared as bonzes, brahmins or mandarins, and associated with gurus, samurai, and yogis. It was part of their policy of being 'all things to all men for the greater glory of God'. They were said to be versatile enough to educate a French nobleman, an Indian chief, a Chinese mandarin's son, and a Polish squire, all with the same tact and charm. Nor was that all. They provided men as resourceful as they were varied: theologians for the Council of Trent, papal nuncios for Poland, Egypt and Tudor Ireland; martyrs and privy-counsellors in England; and in Styria, guerillas who disrupted Calvinist services by tweaking the prayer-books from the worshippers' hands and deftly substituting missals. They adopted a policy of working through the elite, often with success, as in Bavaria and Poland, and they continued this dangerous policy elsewhere from Louis XIV to President Nixon.[10] They took care that all this was well publicized at home, where it made compulsive reading. (15)

The Jesuits soon enjoyed more prestige and influence than the other orders. This aroused antagonism, especially in Spain, where they found themselves disputing the leadership with the Dominicans, hitherto the most powerful of the religious corporations. These two, the Jacob and Esau of the Church, were such rivals from the start that, said Benedict XIV, they seemed almost to have forgotten that they had any common cause. (16)

Many reasons account for this. The orders were competing for vocations, popularity, prestige, and property.[11] There were also psychological reasons. A man joining an order as an obedient celibate renounced part of his personality and many of his rights, committing himself totally and irrevocably to his new family, new emotional home and new intellectual centre. Once entered, he clung to the order which guaranteed livelihood and welfare until old age, and after death a place in heaven, at least to every Jesuit who died in good standing. A religious became as zealous for his Institute's honour as he would for his mother's (especially in 'Golden Age' Spain, where honour was a national obsession and a social tyranny).[12] A religious corporation, like any other living organism, is primarily concerned with its own survival and the order's welfare became the prime concern of its members. Church history then became a drama in which the leading role was played by 'my' order. (17)

Analysis of the questionnaires completed by prospective Jesuits in the 16th century shows instances of a romantic infatuation with the Society, some postulants describing the discovery of their vocations in terms similar to those used by frustrated lovers: 'inflamed with desire they burst into tears; their love for the Society had taken away their appetite'. Juan de Mariana, the Jesuit historian, even while deploring recently-developed faults in the Society, admits that when he joined he had found it to be 'Paradise on earth'. St Robert Bellarmine's enthusiastic Jesuit biographer speaks of his 'devotion

---

[10] Nixon's Jesuit adviser, Father McLaughlin, 'the Administration's "hired collar" . . . appeared ready to bless whatever cause was placed before him' (P. Hebblethwaite, *The Runaway Church* (London, 1975), 191–2).

[11] Dominicans grumbled that the Jesuits distracted the rich so as to grab their possessions, 'as we do jokingly with children when we point to the sky, and, while they are staring into space, snatch the apple from their hands'. There was even a proverb, 'Guard your wife from the friars, but watch your wallet with the Jesuits'.

[12] Powerful unconscious elements underlay these loyalties. Fr Brancati, for example, once sprang to defend his Society from Dominican accusations, saying he would strike a blow for his 'Father and Mother, *hoc est*, the Society of Jesus and its Glorious Founder'. For group hostilities and fantasies: M. Kets and D. Miller, *The Neurotic Organization* (London, 1985).

to the Society which might without exaggeration be described as passionate'. (18)

A comparison might be made drawn with the Cistercians who, having begun as modern reformers, unwittingly hit on the route to economic success, and in time developed an arrogant and even military temper. In the 17th century, however, the Strict Observance branch of the order came to prevail and it 'exerted a morbid fascination which was probably akin to that of the Foreign Legion earlier this century'. (19)

The founders of the orders, ecclesiastical lords, received the fealty of the novices entering their communities to profess poverty, chastity and allegiance, in exchange for temporal and spiritual security. The specific teachings of each particular order were constantly stressed, those of others often denigrated; the older communities were despised by newfangled ones which claimed to supersede them; new institutes in turn were regarded by the more venerable religious families as upstart imitations. Erasmus reckoned there were 'as many factions as religious communities'. Alonso de Valdés went further: he blamed the opening moves leading to the Reformation on Luther's Augustinian jealousy of the Dominican Tetzel and his indulgences. The notion is far-fetched but need not be rejected outright: it is not improbable and these quarrels were often public knowledge. Sometimes there were street brawls over bizarre questions (as, for example, Augustinians and Trinitarians in 16th-century Salamanca, disputing whether or not Adam was physically weakened by losing a rib). In Spain however such passions were relished by a nation of enthusiastic amateur theologians who supported their favourite team with the zeal and violence of modern sports fans.[13] This team spirit spread to those missions where evangelists were in disagreement and in China in the 1650s a friar saw Jesuit converts putting up posters proclaiming that 'there's no room for both black and white birds in this nest!'.

The world-wide rivalry between Dominican and Jesuit was conducted with venom and vigour for over two centuries, until the suppression of the Society. 'A Jesuit is never happier nor more in his element than when deriding a Dominican'. The witness, Cardinal Domenico Passionei, was biased, but he was corroborated by a respectable contemporary, the Jesuit historian Giulio Cesare Cordara who declared that his brethren 'sought especially to excel the Dominicans and considered it a feather in their cap that they had broken the power of that order; that they, and they alone, had managed to dim its glory'. Cordara added, sententiously, 'such emulation would have been legitimate, even praiseworthy, had it been directed towards

---

[13] Thomas Gage's father sent him (1612) to join the Jesuits; angered that he joined the Dominicans instead, he declared he would rather see him a scullion in any Jesuit college than General of the entire Dominican order.

a mutual zeal and incitement to study, but it was not so, for the Fathers gloried only in being the Dominicans' chief enemies'.

What was said of the Jansenists — that they appeared always to be fighting — often appears true of the Jesuits too. What is certainly true is that they developed a hypersensitivity to all criticism and never let their quarrels become lapsed legacies. As Jonathan Swift noted in his sermon *On Brotherly Love*: 'Christ's last legacy was peace and love; but then he prophesied that he came to send a sword upon the earth: the early Christians accepted the legacy, but their successors have been largely fulfilling his prophecy'. Yet some Jesuits welcomed such strife, applying to themselves a line from Livy, that the more aggressive they were the more God seemed to favour them. [14] Despite, or because of, this reassuring reflection they justified themselves furiously to everyone, everywhere, everlastingly. In self-defence they were tireless, if tedious; in counterattack, robust and resourceful. And they were consoled to know that they would outlive every one of their critics, even Pope Clement XIV. Yet there seemed a curious vulgarity about this constant straining to prove they were always right; a vulgarity which sat oddly with their otherwise sophisticated procedures. [15] (20)

This zeal was still marked in modern times. In 1923 when the French Jesuits founded their journal the *Archives de Philosophie*, some of the more combative Fathers wanted it to be devoted to answering Dominican periodicals, which 'continually attack us and undermine our reputation and authority in many ways.' In 1931 the Fr-General, distressed by the 'adversaries who encompass us on every side', demanded information on 'their machinations thus to track down more readily the source of such persecution and make our defence more easy'. A little later, 'anonymous attacks are intensifying in practically all parts of the world by means of handbills, tracts, pamphlets and newspaper articles'. To combat these he instructed his regional superiors to collect hostile comments and news of 'plots against the Society'. These were to be forwarded to the Roman headquarters because 'it is important for us here to have complete information on file . . . to know *who* said *what* . . . out of love of the Society be diligent in reporting plots to me'. Local superiors were to gather evidence on affidavit from those who had received 'unsolicited books, especially if they

---

[14] '*Nescio quo fato magis bellantes quam pacati propitios habemus deos*' (*Imago*, 144). Few contemporaries would recognize them as Robert Southwell's 'meek Society' (Meyer, 195). Fr Guido Sommavilla's *La Compagnia di Gesù (Milan, 1985)* divides the Society's many controversies into two series (73–92, 127–42).

[15] The French Dominican Bruckberger noted 'the Jesuits have an odd vocabulary: they talk of "winning souls, winning Paradise"; with them it is always win, win, win; it intrigues me.' (*La Nef* (1974), 146–54). But over-concern with winning can end in cheating, as Frank Sheed once pointed out.

are influential men; the wrappers in which the books were mailed should be sent [to HQ]. The less evidence there is of financial profit in the circulation of these publications, the clearer it becomes that our enemies are motivated by a conspiracy of hate against the Society . . . For this purpose we can make use of those clipping agencies whose business it is to clip from newspapers for the payment of a small fee the information their clients request'.[16] Sometimes, he added, recourse to law might be necessary.[17] (21)

Conflict between the two Spanish orders was inevitable. The Dominicans had always been popularly regarded as the custodians of truth and orthodoxy, were proud to be the 'Hounds of the Lord' (a play upon their name, *Domini-canes*), ever quick to bark at, and ready to bite, intruders into the 'Household of the Faith'. Furthermore, they regarded themselves as superior to the Jesuits both socially and intellectually, for their masters-general ranked as Grandees of Spain, and their order was considered suitable for gentlemen at a time when to join the Jesuits 'was equivalent to putting one's entire family in the public stocks, for ever'. (This referred to those early Jesuits of Jewish blood admitted to the Society by Ignatius, who was engagingly sympathetic to Jews.) The friars had no intention of losing their high reputation to this band of upstarts whom they regarded with suspicion. They were especially incensed by the Society's claim (once their own) to be peculiarly fitted to solve modern problems and to be seeking realistic solutions to contemporary questions. They had no liking for the view of themselves as exhausted athletes, handing over the baton to supercilious Jesuits, those Benjamins who were claiming to be better able to carry it forward.

Dominicans were further irritated by those Fathers who saw significance in the alleged coincidence that St Ignatius, the new Moses, had been 'converted' in the year of Luther's break with Rome; or by those extremists in the Society who regarded themselves as a fulfilment of the blessed Joachim de Fiore's 12th-century prophecy of future military squadrons called forth to oppose heresy. To such boasts the friars retorted that they had been fighting Luther for 30 years before the Jesuits appeared. For the friars did not appreciate that in one sense the struggle in Europe was really between Luther and Loyola, and that, compared with these two, Charles V and Francis I were like boys fighting over a broken toy. Envy, the Spanish vice, seized the friars when they saw Jesuit churches packed; and their indignation was inflamed by a well-meaning but clumsy papal nuncio who chose the Jesuits to help him in a plan to reform the other religious orders in Spain. At once there was an

---

[16] 'The central dynamic [of institutions] is paved with the fantasies or "world-view" of their top executives . . . the fantasies that come to characterise one's "internal theatre" which composes one's view of the world' (Kets and Miller, *op. cit.*, ix).
[17] This had already been done when Fr Bernard Vaughan sued *The Rock* newspaper for saying that under the English Constitution Jesuits were outlaws who could not, therefore, be libelled. Fr Vaughan got £300 damages (*The Jesuit Libel Case* (London: Catholic Truth Society, 1902)).

outcry from the friars and in Andalusia alone hundreds of them gathered to discuss retaliation for the insult.

By the end of the 16th century this rivalry had developed fully, and competition had turned into antagonism and vendetta. The Companions of Jesus had moved from defence to attack, and the Brothers of St Dominic could not retreat. The result was an ecclesiastical civil war. It was taken into the pulpit and headstrong preachers indulged in some ferocious oratory. In 1651, Cromwell's chaplain, Thomas Gage, published an account of one such 'sermon-duel' between a Jesuit and a Dominican fought out before the king in Valladolid. Gage was repeating a cliché when he declared that no hatred was comparable to that between the Dominicans and the Society; but he had the right to repeat it, for he had studied in each of the orders before deserting both.

The Jesuits had established colleges which provided them with a steady stream of recruits, and led the friars to accuse them frequently of stealing vocations. One Dominican master-general, Ridolfi, used to recall how as a boy he had studied in a Jesuit college where one Father, nicknamed 'The Fisherman',[18] was particularly skilled in drawing aristocratic or intelligent youths into the Society by telling them that the old religious orders, like the Old Law, were now out of date and trammelled with legalistic observances, while the new Society of Jesus, like the New Law, dispensed with such superficial trimmings. Pronouncements of this nature inevitably reached the wrong ears.

On its home ground, one of the most violent of the Society's critics was the Dominican Melchor Cano, of whom mention has been made. Cano, who did so much for Spanish culture and theology in the Renaissance, had a vehement and vindictive character. His fear and suspicion of the Jesuits led him to mistrust their novelties. He found room in his great theological work *De locis* to sneer at those new orders who seemed to think they had dropped from heaven just because the pope had approved them.

Of all the Society's many enemies throughout its history only Pascal and Palafox come anywhere near Cano for hostility. He suspected Jesuit orthodoxy, showing how revolutionary and disturbing they and their new forms of piety could be, how near to heresy they seemed to some. In his wilder moments Cano alarmed his colleagues by calling the Jesuits 'precursors of anti-Christ', describing them as worse than the German heretics, as 'flatterers with forked tongues', and 'mealy-mouthed wretches

---

[18] In 1942 the Jesuit general referred to 'the spiritual fisherman's art, of which our first Fathers spoke, not without pleasantry'; adding, 'in this quest for vocations you must proceed as prudently as businessmen. First of all, they make a thorough survey of a region to discover its richest source of wealth; then they omit no suitable means to accomplish their purpose . . . The Society has always made use of "fishing" for which it set down in writing careful and prudent directions' (Ledóchowski, 140, 155). Navarrete's experience of this 'fishing' in Manila (by Fr Colín) is at NC 423.

who, when they catch a man, transform him into a hen; and if they were to catch a hen would turn it into a chicken'.[19] Curiously prophetic, Friar Cano foresaw the suppression of the Society. 'If the members of the Society continue as they have begun, the time may come when kings will want to resist them, but be unable to do so'. His fears were groundless, however, for when the time came, two centuries later, the Catholic kings found it possible to get their way: the Jesuit lions of the 16th century had become unicorns in the 18th.

Cano's anxieties can only be understood in context, for the Church was then beset by the Reformation, and by new spiritualist movements, by popular mystics, seers and visionaries, any of whom might well prove heterodox.

---

[19] The English Jesuit George Tyrrell writing to the general in 1904–5 felt that while young men were battling with the world, the novice Jesuit was fenced away from the conditions of moral growth and vigour. 'If there is any manhood left in him it is in spite of and not because of your methods' (G. Tyrrell, *Autobiography*, II (London, 1912), 486). Fr Bernard Basset comments 'no English critic of the Society wrote a more penetrating attack' (435).

III

The hostility between the two orders broke out in the early years of the Society's existence and was fought out in three distinct but inter-related battle fronts. These concerned free will, probabilism, and the Immaculate Conception.

In each of these the Jesuits diverged from the Dominican teaching to a greater or lesser extent, and since the friars reverenced their master theologian Thomas Aquinas as an oracle, any divergence from his teaching ('Thomism') was automatically denounced. The Jesuits, however, while accepting Thomism in its fundamentals, saw no reason why it should not be developed, even modified, by their own 'in-house' theologians. They believed that a new age had come bringing new requirements, methods and approaches. In 1558 Diego Laynez, the second Jesuit General, declared that what was needed was a new theology, 'better accommodated to the needs of these times'. In other words, it seemed, something different from the sacrosanct teachings of Aquinas.

Having created new theories, the Society needed university chairs from which to proclaim them. This led into the struggle for the monopoly of Catholic education, and so what had started as theological differences began to take on economic, political and sociological overtones. Power politics and emotional theology were intertwined, and each side took its stand under the banner of 'My order, right or wrong!'.[20] Each side emerged from these forays into speculative theology to fight for its own particular theorizing as though that consisted of facts self-evident to all but the malicious and perverse.

Since some understanding of these complex problems is essential for an understanding of the China mission the following brief outline is offered. The account of the first, the doctrine of free will, is necessarily an over-simplification, maybe grossly so, but it is hoped that it may help to make the matter sufficiently intelligible for the telling of Navarrete's story.[21]

Free will

It's not the crucifix but the Jesuits' *scientia media* that should be kept hidden from the Chinese (NC 238, 464).

This concerned the reconciling of divine grace with man's free will.[22]

---

[20] A century later this spirit was still alive, and in a chilling page of his *Memoirs*, Saint-Simon (a hostile witness) describes Fr Le Tellier, single-mindedly working 'for the Jesuit school, prepared to put state and church in an uproar and to start a persecution.'

[21] For Molinism in the China mission: Gernet, *Impact*, 286; Gaubil, 335; in Japan: Mortier, VI: 269.

[22] Grace is a supernatural gift of God, freely bestowed for our sanctification and salvation, since our own natural powers are not sufficient. Augustine explains 'grace is not rendered for any merit on our part, but gratis, hence the name grace.'

A problem, baffling as the mystery of the Trinity, and described by Bayle as 'a sea with neither shore nor bottom', it dated back to the quarrel between Augustine and Pelagius (a British lay theologian of unacceptably optimistic views, who flourished in Rome in 400 AD). It should be noted that the question was not whether free will is compatible with predestination (i.e. with God's foreknowledge of man's actions), for both are Catholic doctrines. The problem was rather how to formulate a definition that would safeguard one doctrine as against the other. What was at issue, then, was a fresh attempt to define, not the nature of God's grace, but the mechanics and workings of grace, and its relation to man's liberty of choice. (22)

This, the no-man's land of theology, was best avoided or at least skirted. Instead the challenge was taken up by a Spanish Jesuit, Luis de Molina, who published a highly subtle work which laid the foundations of the Society's own brand of divinity.[23] This theological bombshell, ironically named *Concordia* ('The Harmonization of Man's Free Will with Divine Foreknowledge'), came out of Lisbon in 1588, together with the Spanish Armada, and it would be difficult to decide which of the two ultimately made the greater commotion, even in England, for the *Concordia* proved to be the most fateful and provocative work the Society ever published.[24]

Molina's *Concordia* completely alienated the Dominicans who considered that their own moderns — Friars Vitoria, Soto, Cano — had already satisfied the needs of the times by revitalizing 'scholastic' theology, bringing it from the 13th into the 16th century, and they saw no need for new masters in Israel. But there were other levels of significance behind it all. The Jesuits — impudent siblings, unwilling to remain in second place — needed to assert themselves by casting off the tutelage of their elders, ageing Thomists, and to be seen publicly to have come of age.

Fr Molina's *Concordia* did not reject Aquinas, though it departed from him by emphasizing man's ability 'to work his passage to heaven'. The novelty was relative, but any novelty, given the delicate situation, crystallized the diffused indignation. In the end the *Concordia* led to the greatest outpouring of metaphysical and theological energy in the history of modern Catholic thought, or what a Dominican, Alvaro Huerga, has called the greatest theological struggle of all time.

Molina's chief novelty lay in his attempt to reconcile man's free will with God's knowledge of the future: humans have a free choice and God has foreknowledge of those choices, but we do not sin *because* of that foreknowledge. Molina solved this dilemma by announcing that the

---

[23] A poet, even a Jesuit poet, is not necessarily the best authority in historical theology, but Hopkins was right: 'Molina is the man who made our theology' (Letter to R. W. Dixon, 1 December 1881).

[24] It went through five editions in six years and marked a turning point in the history of speculative theology.

Almighty has a special 'middle knowledge' (*scientia media*), whereby he knows the future possible actions of men as being possible. Not surprisingly, *scientia media* eventually became a catchphrase meaning 'an easy way around a knotty problem'.

On her conversion to Catholicism, the Oxford philosopher Elizabeth Anscombe was relieved to learn she did not have to believe 'that stuff, according to which God knew how someone would have spent his life if [that someone] had not died a child'. But 'that stuff' was no joke, for in its day it could be a burning matter. Ostensibly a question of divinity, much more was involved, for the Dominicans now feared to lose control of theological policy. Whereas previously the Jesuits only had to contend with the attacks of individual friars, suddenly the entire Dominican order mobilized for 'St Thomas and the Truth' and thenceforth the Society smarted under the concerted criticism of the Blackfriars. Some Jesuits, Juan de Mariana for one, thought they ought to avoid trouble with the Dominicans 'who are our Masters and Teachers'. But Fr Mariana was no typical Jesuit, and the majority were ready to fight, since to lose that battle would suggest theological, i.e. professional, incapacity. They therefore had no choice but to defend their man, and by 1598 definitive battle lines had been drawn. (23)

One Jesuit general, reflecting on it all later, thought the affair had nearly finished off the young Society, which in those early days was indeed often fighting for survival. But if the Jesuits were fighting for their existence, the Dominicans were fighting for Aquinas, their 'Angelic Doctor'. They rushed to his defence, even though the Jesuits protested that they were following him as closely as the friars, and were merely restating his theology of grace so as to prevent it appearing to favour the Protestant Reformers. This implied that Aquinas had had to wait three centuries for a Jesuit explicator, that the Dominicans had been teaching his doctrine for 300 years without properly understanding it.

There could now be no reconciliation: each side denounced the other to the Inquisition, and held public meetings to defend its cause. Molina's Jesuit supporters branded the Dominicans as semi-Calvinists ('pessimists'). They in turn retorted with cries of semi-Pelagians ('optimists'). Doctors and students in every university took sides and in the Dominicans' schools the mere mention of Molina's name sufficed to rouse the students to violent foot-stamping in obedient detestation of his doctrine. Spaniards, from poet to peasant, accustomed to crowding into the *autos da fé* and *autos sacramentales* (eucharistic dramas), were soon eagerly debating grace and free will in the theatre, the plaza, or convent parlours.[25] Within a few months the Spanish Jesuit provincial superior reported to Rome: 'there's bloody war in Castile

---

[25] Free will, being about choices, is at the heart of all drama, and a number of plays from the Spanish Golden Age repertoire deal with the workings of divine grace in sinful humanity. In modern literature Burgess's *Clockwork Orange* may be cited.

where our young men, in their youthful fervour, have risen in defence of Molina and, as they put it, for the honour of our Society'.

Fr Leonard Lessius, writing from Belgium in 1588 to his fellow-Jesuit Cardinal Robert Bellarmine in Rome, doubted 'whether Catholics were ever as zealous in opposing heretics as are the Louvain and Douai theologians against us, and unless the Holy See intervenes it's all over with us here. Throughout the whole country we are defamed as heretics even by rustics and mechanicals'. Soon Bellarmine was appealing to Clement VIII to 'deliver the Church from these scandalous quarrels, restore peace between the two orders, and deprive the heretic of his amusement at our expense'.

This head-on clash disturbed Philip II who, after the Armada disaster, needed unity and harmony at home. But the controversy did not die down: it spread out into the empire from Chile to the Philippines, and even into China, where Jesuit missionaries were soon requesting copies of the history of 'the great debate', and Friar Domingo Navarrete, getting the Jesuits twice with one stone, thought it was not the crucifix but Molina's *scientia media* theories that ought to be kept back from the Chinese. (24)

The pope ordered that the question be setttled in Rome. The result was the celebrated and energetic 'Working Party on Aids' (*Congregatio de auxiliis*) which began its sittings in 1602. By the end of that first year, 68 of its total of 181 sessions had been held. The Romans, always less reverent than the Spanish, derived much entertainment from these proceedings and squibs and pasquinades circulated throughout the city as folk enquired of each other 'What's new from the [Jesuit-Dominican] front today?'

The debates were held in the presence of Clement VIII who, more than once, had to admonish the contestants severely, and, acting as a sort of pontifical referee, denounced and penalized foul play. The Dominicans' chief spokesman, Friar Tomás de Lemos, proved a redoubtable opponent.[26] In the 84 sittings at which he spoke, he took on, and exhausted, six different theologians successively, without apparent strain. The Fathers attempted the well-known stratagem of having him 'kicked upstairs' to a bishopric (*promoveatur ut amoveatur*). But Lemos refused the honour.

The Jesuits' leading advocate was Gregorio de Valencia. A keen debater, he earned himself a niche in Pascal's notorious *Fifth Provincial Letter* half a century later. Towards the end of one prodigious series of bouts between these two, Lemos got a chance to finish off his opponent when Valencia, in backing up one of his statements, quoted a passage from Augustine's *City of God* (xix, 13). But Friar Lemos's fabulous memory detected a misreading of the text, for Fr Valencia had accidentally substituted one word in the original with another of his own, which happened to be more suited to his argument.

---

[26] Lemos was later involved in Galileo's trial (Santillana, 30, 140).

At once the friar pounced, accusing the Jesuit of falsifying evidence. He grabbed the volume from Valencia's hands and read out the passage correctly to the outraged pontiff. This incident was later cruelly embellished by the Jesuits' adversaries. (25)

Amusing it may have been to some, but a decision either way would have been harmful, for on the one hand the Dominicans — Inquisitors, and traditionally the leading theologians of Catholicism — could not appear in the wrong; but then neither could the Jesuits, by now regarded as the chief opponents of the Protestant heresy in northern Europe. What, it was asked, would be the impression abroad if either were to be condemned?

Clement's successor, Paul V, though distressed by the controversy, was said to be terrified of having to decide. He was supposed to have a bull of anathema prepared against the Society, but instead tried to solve his problem by dismissing the Working Party on Aids *sine die*, ordering both sides to abstain from further discussion, or even reference.

Though there was no decision either way, the Spanish Jesuits interpreted this outcome as a victory and (says Fr Brodrick, II, 66) they seem rather to have lost their heads. They granted three days' holiday to their students whose boisterous celebrations included bullfights, masques, firework displays, triumphal arches and posters bearing the pronouncement, 'Molina Wins!'[27] There were other, more ecclesiastical, entertainments such as processions (with musicians and drummers borrowed from the army), masses, solemn offices, and *Te Deums*, in thanksgiving for their triumph. Rome was often amused by the Spaniards, and even Paul V could not help laughing good-naturedly when he heard an account of these rejoicings. For the sake of propriety, however, he and the Jesuit general issued a rebuke to the merry-makers.

The Aids debate between the two orders, who ought (in Donne's phrase) to have been 'sister teats of God's grace', had widespread repercussions, and it may even be argued that the terrible Jesuit-Jansenist controversy was sparked off by reaction to the 1609 Antwerp reprinting of Molina's *Concordia*. But what matters most for our purpose here is that this further poisoning of relations between the two orders deepened their mutual mistrust in the Chinese Rites Controversy which was to follow. (26)

No pope has ever dared to decree on the matter, so that in the end the Aids and Grace controversy was shelved, not settled. The most that could be hoped for was a truce, not peace. All writing about the matter was forbidden, but as usual the ruling was sometimes ignored, and though the play was officially over, the players continued squabbling in the wings.

---

[27] The Jesuits often used fireworks in their celebrations, particularly on St Ignatius's feast-day, so that some Dominicans nicknamed him 'the canonized skyrocket'.

Probabilism

> We friars do not, as alleged, frighten the Chinese by making God's law a heavy burden, full of precepts binding on pain of mortal sin (NC 492).

Another clash between the two orders directly affected the missions and played a part in Navarrete's story, since the Jesuits' China strategy rested on a theory evolved by them.

This was probabilism, or the system of 'probable opinions', neatly defined as 'The doctrine that in matters of conscience where authorities differ, the opinion favouring greater liberty may be followed, provided it is solidly probable'. In other words, between two reasonable though differing options as to a course of action, one *may* follow the less secure option if it is backed by a recognized authority.[28] Probabilism, then, did not give rules for saints, it gave guidance for sinners.

Similar arguments for moral freedom to follow the less secure (but usually more agreeable) option are found in the writings of the Dominican St Antoninus of Florence (1389–1459), and the hypothesis was revived by another Dominican, Bartolomé de Medina in 1577. Yet probabilism, though neither the invention nor the monopoly of the Jesuits, became the cachet of the Society.[29]

Jesuit advocacy of probabilism gave them a broader work-base than that of their opponents. It allowed them to be conscientiously less scrupulous. It made Catholicism less oppressive, possibly less neurotic. But it could also make the Jesuits disturbing to the nervous who were not reassured to find them asking daring questions which pushed back the boundaries of conscience. And the naturally devout were distressed when probabilism evolved to admit looser concepts such as the 'probably probable'.

The Council of Trent, by emphasizing the importance of confession, led to a greater interest in casuistry. Consequently, helpful handbooks began to appear, and confessors welcomed the guidance of the specialists. And though 'casuistry', that is, case analysis, has a dubious ring to the man in the street, it is only an admission that circumstances alter cases. It is not an absurdity, as Pascal would have it, but an attempt at adaptation to the complexity of the believer's everyday life. Casuistry, now possessed of the new weapon of probabilism, appealed to the maxim *lex dubia non obligat*; aimed at humanizing inhuman precepts; favoured liberty of action against mere legalism; and offered the sinner the benefit of the doubt. Nevertheless, there was an inherent danger that, in Harnack's words, it might 'transform the vile into the venial', and become merely a set of rules for evading the rules. (27)

---

[28] Casuists say 'may', not 'must'.

[29] Classical precedents include Cicero's *De officiis* which discusses possible conflicts between expediency and duty: whether friendship should prevail over claims of law and religion; and whether the vendor of a badly built house should advertise 'an undesirable residence for sale'.

The Jesuits became the champions of probabilism, but for many onlookers they carried it too far. The Dominicans, in particular, felt that the 'reasonable probabilism' of their own St Antoninus and Friar Medina was being taken to extremes: casuistry was becoming 'the new casuistry' and was seen as essentially pharisaic. Rigorists rejected this 'doctrine of the lukewarm', and regarded probabilist confessors as bad lawyers defending bad cases. Repelled by this apparent search for wider moral frontiers, they believed that where doubt existed the generous soul would keep to the strict sense of the law, without 'haggling with God'. Christ had said 'Give up what you have, and follow me', but Dominicans saw the Jesuit probabilists twisting this into 'Give up the least you can get away with, and follow me at a comfortable distance'. They seemed to be creating a moral code for spiritual malingerers, reducing to a minimum what had to be rendered both to God and to Caesar. Pierre Bayle thought something similar: 'These advocates in the court of conscience discover more distinctions and subtleties than do lawyers in civil cases. They are turning the confessional into a moral laboratory'. Other unsympathetic observers, such as Macaulay, saw the Jesuit here at his ingenious worst and as 'having at his command an immense dispensary of anodynes for wounded consciences, and doctrines consolatory to transgressors of every class'. (28)

The Dominicans practised safe morality and, with their 'hatred of opportunism', were repelled by these new theories. So it was to them that Alexander VII turned when, wearied by the endless debates (and what Bossuet privately called the *ordures des casuistes*) he attempted to return to the simplicity of the Gospels. He ordered the friars to draw up a definitive work to settle the matter. They, however, went further than the pope intended, for the entire Dominican order now solemnly renounced probabilism, their Chapter General publicly called attention to the dangers inherent in it, and recommended scrupulous adherence to Aquinas and tradition.

Hostility to Jesuit probabilism spread, and the year of Alexander VII's decision (1656) also saw the publication of Pascal's *Provincial Letters* which dealt the French Fathers their most damaging blow before their expulsion in 1764. 'All Europe', it was said, 'read and admired, laughed and wept'. Probabilism lay at the heart of the Pascal–Jesuit debate as with terrible irony and artful selection from Jesuit writings, he made mock of the Fathers, picking on the work of one particular casuist, Fr Antonio Escobar (1588–1669), whose name became a byword for elasticity of conscience.[30] Pascal referred to another, Fr Bauny, with the words 'Behold him who takes away

---

[30] Escobar, the 'quintessential probabilist', figures in a La Fontaine ballad, and has given disobliging nouns, a verb and an adjective to French. But he was a saintly man, concerned for the poor and underprivileged and François Bertaut (*Travels*, 1669), who met him in Valladolid in his last year, found 'a good fellow, looking a decade younger than his age'. Since, incredibly, he had never heard of Pascal's *Letters*, Bertaut promised him a copy which, one hopes, never reached him.

the sins of the world', and quotes yet another who 'has made many opinions probable which before were not so: it is no longer a sin to follow them, whereas it was before'.

On the other hand, these casuists were spiritual consultants writing on their special subjects for general practitioners. For instance, Fr Sánchez in his classic *De Matrimonio* was at times writing almost as a gynaecologist; and some confessors' manuals dissect humanity in a manner worthy of the modern psychological novel. Yet to unsympathetic outsiders this very conjunction of religious precept with 'delicate' physical matters appeared grotesque and smacked of a morbid, perverted ingenuity. To others the casuists appeared as moral acrobats and they were subjected to merciless satire, especially in France where Jansenism, a harsh neo-Augustinianism, was spreading.[31]

The Society seemed to bow before the storm. The Fr-General compromised, offering obedience to the pope's wishes. Quietly, however, he prevented any Jesuit from making a public withdrawal from their old position: in 1673, for instance, a Jesuit who tried to write against probabilism was 'silenced'. This made it seem that the Society was playing a double game. The pope therefore secured the election as Jesuit general of a militant who could be trusted to oppose probabilism. (He was lucky to be elected: he only got 48 out of 86 possible votes, and that at the third scrutiny.) The new man, Fr Tirso González, promised 'to save the Society from the pit into which it was falling', and devoted the rest of his embattled life to the cause. Nevertheless, the controversy continued and a whole line of Dominican theologians took part in the debate which came to a climax in the middle of the 18th century. (29)

The Jesuits' missionary methodology in China was partly based on probabilism, and, since the friars never fully admitted the legality of that base, they had *ipso facto* to reject whatever was founded upon it. This explains much of what follows below of Navarrete's career in Asia.[32]

The Jesuits emerge from all this as humane advocates of greater liberty, and their attempts to decide whether moral standards were absolute or modifiable may be seen as an assertion of personal independence.[33] The difference between them and their opponents was a revival of the old quarrel between the benevolent Pelagius and the rigorous St Augustine at the start of the 5th century. The Jesuits saw their opponents as legalists out of touch with everyday problems. Yet, as so often, the Fathers were wrong for the right reasons. Probabilism was more humane and compassionate than

---

[31] Augustine took the worst of Paul, and Calvin the worst of Augustine (Harry Williams); and in Jesuit eyes, the Jansenists were near-Calvinists. Hence the mutual antipathy.

[32] Probabilism as a disturbing element in the missions: Boxer, AFP, XXXIII(1963), 86.

[33] This humanizing of theology is not unique to Molina; it owes much to such Dominicans as Cano and Soto (J. S. da Silva Dias, *Correntes de sentimento religioso em Portugal*, I [Coimbra, 1960]: 453); and Schneemann, 112–136.

Augustine's gloomy theology, but their determination to get their own way over those mistrustful of it, created still more enemies. And some of their claims did not help their cause. In 1640 they celebrated their first centenary by publishing the *Imago primi saeculi*, a volume of 952 pages of triumphal arches, giving scandal to many with its statement (readily misunderstood) that 'Thanks to the Society of Jesus, sins are now atoned more speedily than formerly they were committed'. Some saw the Jesuits as pedlars of pliable moral theology 'who abbreviated the Commandments by lengthening the Creed; not daring to abolish hell, they suppressed sin'.[34]

Fortunately for the Church, a way out of the dilemma was found by the adoption of 'equiprobabilism', the moral system of St Alphonsus, who was called in as a peacemaker. This middle way between extremes of laxity and rigorism has been welcomed as a brilliant service to the Church.[35]

The Immaculate Conception

Some [Jesuit] books in Chinese present the Immaculate Conception of Mary in such a way that the converts think it's an Article of Faith, though it's not. So delicate a matter shouldn't be mentioned to converts (NC 264).[36]

This third controversy between the two orders centred on a problem less theologically significant, but of immense sociological import; a controversy which had noisy repercussions throughout the Iberian world. It was a quarrel which the Jesuits welcomed, because it worked to their advantage. It damaged the Dominicans and led to a decline in their popularity with the faithful.

The debate concerned the Immaculate Conception of the Virgin, the belief that Mary Unblemished was unique in being born free of Adam's original sin.[37] The matter was only settled in 1854 when Pius IX solemnly defined the pious theory as an article of faith. Stigmatized as 'only rhetoric crystallized into dogma', now it had to be believed, and the Dominican 'Maculists' were finally defeated, after centuries of resistance. (30)

---

[34] An unfair exaggeration. Fear of hell still flourished, thanks partly to the Jesuit pulpit-thumpers thronging the pages of Piero Camporesi's *La Casa dell'Eternità* (Milan, 1987), and encountered in James Joyce: there are all sorts of Jesuits, said Diderot.

[35] Laxism, a perversion of probabilism, weakened the strict sense of morality but, according to Fr Miquel Batllori, Jesuit laxism only obtained for the period before Innocent XI (1676–89), that is, during Navarrete's lifetime.

[36] Navarrete also complains of exotic national devotions in the Jesuit mission (handcuffs at confession, padlocks around the neck, symbolizing 'Slaves of Christ' etc.); 'this puts the decorations before the foundations of the house': NC 208, 214, 239, 265, 286, 432.

[37] It has nothing to do with a virgin birth but refers to Mary's own conception by her mother St Ann. Destined to be Christ's mother, Mary had to be free of the stain of Adam's sin, which caused a mutation in the rest of humankind, henceforth born with the genetically-transmitted guilt of that 'original sin'.

In earlier times the Dominicans were committed to the Thomistic position, for their own Aquinas had opposed the Immaculate Conception theory, believing that so unique a privilege would detract from Christ's role as Saviour of all humanity. It would mean that for Mary the Redemption had been unnecessary. The Jesuit St Robert Bellarmine tried to come to Aquinas's aid by declaring that the 'Angelic Doctor' did not have all the evidence when he was writing in the 13th century; and that if he could see how the Church celebrated the Feast in the 16th, he 'would *probably* have inclined' to the popular opinion.

Some Blackfriars went to great lengths in defending their viewpoint, and once at least they went too far. In Bern in 1507, a group of them, determined to redeem the reputation of their order, arranged bogus apparitions of 'souls from purgatory' who declared to the dumbfounded populace that the Virgin had been conceived in sin. The affair caused a great stir, and an even greater one when the fraud was discovered and four Dominicans were burnt at the stake. (31)

The Jesuits fervently encouraged popular belief in the 'Inmaculada' which, in 1593, became part of official Jesuit teaching. The friars suspected this determination, and Philip III's Dominican confessor thought that 'the Fathers hope to ruin our order through this'. Unfortunately for the friars, devotion to 'La Inmaculada' was abnormally popular in Spain with both high and low alike. The devotion was a national phenomenon, with deep psychological roots. The Spaniard wanted 'La Inmaculada' almost as a supernatural lover, but at the same time seemed to want to lift her out of the feminine arena. It was, said Richard Ford, 'the crowning and protecting mystery of Spain, and so peculiar and national, occurs so frequently in church, chapel, and gallery, and occupies so many pens, pencils and chisels, that some explanation is absolutely necessary'. (32)

Whatever the explanation, no other country has produced so many passionate advocates of the doctrine, even down to modern times. In 1904, the 50th anniversary of the declaration of the dogma was celebrated with rejoicing throughout Spain, and a Jesuit writing then recalled how through the ages Mary Immaculate had inspired Spanish theologians, missionaries, writers, artists and heroes: 'She led Columbus to the discovery of the New World, where the first island after El Salvador was named Concepción in her honour; she it was whom Magellan had painted on the banners of the ship, named after her, in which he sailed to the Philippines'. (33)

The Immaculate Conception became a matter of national and political concern in 1616 when Philip III managed to have a special committee established to press for the formal definition of the doctrine. This junta, which met periodically until 1770, survived until the the first Liberal government in 1820.

The populace at large took an almost morbid interest in the subject. For them the the matter was settled, and there was no need for promotion-committees and juntas. Enthusiasts regarded the denying Dominicans as 'enemies of the Virgin'; some compared the Blackfriars to the Turks; others feared that a statue of our Lady in a Dominican church was as much a prisoner 'as is the Holy Sepulchre in the hands of the Muslims'. Others expressed the opinion that St Thomas Aquinas 'drank more than water on the day when he declared Mary was conceived in sin'. So the friars found themselves in a curiously anomalous position: they, terrible symbols of the Inquisition to heterodox and heretic alike, were regarded as deviants on their home ground. Once, a group of them, travelling with some Jesuits, fell into the hands of bandits who promptly released the Fathers, but robbed the Dominicans on the grounds that they were 'enemies of the Virgin'. A French visitor noted that for all their connections with the Holy Inquisition and their spiritual kinship to the royal confessor, Spanish Dominicans were often abused by tradesmen who refused to sell goods to them. The Blackfriars vainly tried to defend themselves, showing their devotion to the Virgin by multiplying public processions and recitations of the rosary in her honour. All to no avail, however, and in the early part of the 17th century the friars found themselves in disgrace throughout the land. (34)

The 'Marian War' reached its peak in Andalusia in 1613 when a misguided Dominican preaching in Seville expressed his doubts and caused an uproar. The archbishop denounced the friars for doubting what the apostle James himself had taught to Spaniards. High words were followed by hard blows as Marianists and Maculists fell upon each other, first in the pews and then in the plazas. Their quarrels resembled nothing so much as those in the early Church when the faithful fought over the nature of the light of the transfiguration on Mount Tabor, or were so obsessed by Arianism that, complained St Gregory Nyssa, 'if you ask for change of a shilling, they start ranting about the Begotten and Unbegotten; if you ask the price of a loaf they reply, "The Father is greater than the Son"; ask if your bath is ready and your man solemnly informs you that the Son was made from nothing'.

As the Marian war continued juntas were established, death-vows taken, pictures painted, medals struck, statues erected, persecutions set on foot, and forgery and violence resorted to, all in honour of the Virgin *sin pecado concebida*. In those days the common everyday Spanish greeting was 'Hail Mary, full of grace' (a Spanish 'Great is the Diana of Ephesus'), and woe betide anyone who failed to answer properly, 'Conceived without sin'. (35)

Nervous Dominicans slinking through the streets were accosted by impudent urchins with the query, 'With or without sin?' Other, brasher, friars bribed youngsters with sweets to taunt 'concepcionistas' by yelling at them, '*With* original sin, so there!' Once they ruined a Marianist procession by chanting 'with, with, with *pecado original*' from the safety of a tower overlooking the marchers whom they pelted with tiles. The Church deplored such conduct but was powerless to stop it, and though in 1616 Paul V issued a decree calling for a truce, all was in vain.

This debate, too, raged throughout the empire.[38] The Spanish India Office became involved when Borghese, the Cardinal-protector of the Dominican order, heard that Jesuits were despatching anti-friar pop-songs ('*coplas*') to the colonies as a form of propaganda. At the same time the Inquisition received reports of Dominican sonnets attacking the Immaculate Conception. From Madrid to Formosa missionaries squabbled, preached and staged plays for and against. The English renegade friar Thomas Gage, while still a Dominican missionary in Guatemala City, had loyally defended Aquinas's Maculist view in a public debate at which 'Jesuits stamped with their feet; clapped with their hands, railed with their tongues and condemned with their mouths' what they regarded as the sort of heresy only to be expected of an Englishman and a friar. In China, Jesuits were denounced by Navarrete and others for preaching a pious opinion as a doctrinal certainty, thereby confusing the heathen with inessentials. Some later Jesuits, however, went farther than that, claiming that the Immaculate Conception was prophesied in the Confucian classics.

The accumulated quarrels involving the two orders harmed their reputation even in the sympathetic Spanish milieu. Though the Jesuits advocated the people's viewpoint in the 'Marian War', it did not win them popular support. Their confidential correspondence from the period shows how much this alarmed them; they complained that some of their firmest admirers were beginning to doubt them in the face of so many accusations hurled from pulpit and rostrum. In his apologia of 1605, Pedro de Ribadeneyra begged his readers to take a more benevolent view of the Society. Keeping to the old Ignatian metaphor, he reminded the friars that in battle 'the cavalry do not despise the infantry, nor the musketeers the pikemen, and regiments in the army of the Church militant should do the same.' Since the Jesuits were neither monks nor friars they should not be judged as such, but for what they were, and by their own standards. And Ribadeneyra discreetly complained of those religious [the friars], who were so contented with their own vocations that they were unable to see good in any other. (36)

Navarrete was personally involved in this third debate. Earlier, his relative Friar Baltasar Navarrete had served on Philip III's committee investigating the Mystery. Friar Domingo as a firm 'Maculista' faced potential problems, especially at the end of his life when officialdom began to demand oaths of support for the 'Inmaculada' thesis. One bishop of Segovia resigned his diocese rather than take the oath and, a week before Friar Domingo's death, Charles II of Spain issued a decree forbidding Dominicans to preach at official

---

[38] Elsewhere Bishop Smith reported to Rome (1626) that the Jesuit Immaculate Conception Sodality was dividing the English laity, since the Fathers obliged members to confess only to Jesuits. Some devotees died without the sacraments rather than disobey (Philip Hughes, *Rome and the Counter-Reformation* (London, 1942), 339).

celebrations unless they first pronounced a eulogy of 'La Inmaculada'. As we shall see, Navarrete's own obituary complained of his following the Dominican party-line ('espíritu de escuela') to the end. (37)

From popes to saints, all alike intervened at one time or other to make peace between these two rivals, but what little success they had was short-lived, though Santa Teresa foretold that in the end the two would join together to fight the antichrist himself. The generals of both orders strove equally to repair the widening breach. Periodic exhortations to harmony were issued, admonishing local superiors and urging tranquillity at all costs. As early as 1549 the Dominican master-general launched an appeal for friendship with the new Society. In 1590 another called a peace conference in Alcalá; in 1646 and 1661 appeals for fraternal love were again issued and in 1656 every Dominican in the order was instructed to say a mass for the Fathers of the Society.

Jesuit superiors on their side made similar ecumenical efforts and in 1679 Father-General Oliva wrote specially to congratulate his subjects, the Bollandist hagiographers, because they had managed to publish an item on Aquinas in their monumental *Lives of the Saints*, which was so written that it could not possibly offend the Dominicans.[39] The Inquisition was more accustomed to threatening than to appealing, and in 1674 it forbade both orders to abuse each other in sermons or writing, 'under penalty of major excommunication, banishment from the province and confinement in a religious house elsewhere'. From time to time optimists declared the war was over, and in March 1635 the poet Francisco de Quevedo (the Spanish Jonathan Swift) reported a recent friendship-pact between the two. He considered the event worth a sonnet. (38)

The sonnet was in vain, for the peace did not last. The anti-Jesuit coalition would not be placated, nor would the Fathers themselves yield, and in 1696 their General Congregation urged the defence of the Society against the friars. So whether the Church was in a state of persecution or progress, Fr Ribadeneyra's 'regiments in her army' found the time, and created the opportunity, to bicker among themselves. Sometimes innocent bystanders, such as Galileo, were used by one side to strike at the reputation of the other. As long as the old Society existed the rivalry never died, so that the 18th-century Spanish government seeking the suppression of the Jesuits knew what it was doing when it enlisted the Dominican general of the day as one of its agents.

---

[39] As a fraternal gesture, he visited the death-bed of the Dominican Master-General Marinis, and in a lugubrious scene the two, reduced to tears, were unable to speak 'for fifteen minutes'.

IV

Events in Europe set the stage for further dramatic productions overseas, for both friar and Jesuit took resentment as well as mass-kits when they went out to the missions. It seemed that wherever they met, from Brazil to Japan, a clash was inevitable. The American historian Bailey W. Diffie has said 'the history of the Church in Latin America was a constant quarrel between the religious orders'. The same could be said of other areas. In England, the Jesuits, jealous because friars had managed to re-establish their old province, dubbed them 'Archbishop Laud's trencher-flies and blue-bottles'. In Canada, where inter-order rivalry was nearly co-extensive with the history of New France, the two groups never managed 'to set their Horses together'. Echoes of the disputes about free will and grace reached the gates of Nagasaki, where the dispute went on even as the executioner was about to transform rival missionaries into quarrelling martyrs.

In 1712 the London *Spectator* published a letter, allegedly from the Chinese emperor K'ang-hsi to Pope Alexander VIII, exhorting His Holiness 'to keep in peace two good Religious Families of Missionaries, the black robed Sons of Ignatius, and the black and white robed Sons of Dominicus'. Though a spoof, it was near reality. *The Current Intelligence* of 4 June 1666 had already reported from Rome, as a front-page news item: 'The differences betwixt the Dominicans and the Jesuits, are now grown to that height that they spare not the pulpits but use them as so many advantages to vilifie each other'. This animosity found particularly extravagant expression in the Philippines, where alarming accusations were made against the Jesuits by those passionate friars of whom one governor wrote that he would rather face up to the rebels in the Spanish Netherlands than tangle with them.

Preaching became so ferociously satirical that the pulpit was described as a 'lectureship in revenge'. In 1636 the Lenten sermons in Manila caused alternate merriment and scandal, as one friar called the Jesuits the 'pickpockets of the Church', while another declared that neither Calvin nor Luther had done as much harm as this, the Society not of Jesus but of the Devil. Another friar urged his congregation to attend a forthcoming Jesuit sermon on the 'The Good Thief': it was 'a topic specially befitting that order'. Yet, even in Manila, there were moments of harmony and Fr Murillo Velarde, in 1749, recounted how in 1702 the two orders came together to celebrate each other's good qualities, 'a novelty, the like of which was never seen before'. He further commented that only the lower classes believed there was any real hostility between the orders, their differences being merely a matter of style, not substance. (39)

A break-through for the Jesuits came towards the end of the 16th century when they obtained a papal mandate making the newly-opened China mission a Jesuit monopoly and forbidding friars from trying to reach there. But this attempt at peace through ecclesiastical demarcation also failed, for the Hounds penetrated the Foxes' covert. The result was a fourth and profounder struggle between Jesuit and friar in the 'Chinese Rites Controversy'.

That controversy, as we have seen, had been rehearsed long before it was enacted.

2 The Jesuit mandarins

Ricci, Pantoja, Aleni, these were the giants of the mission.
— Navarrete, Controversias, 356

Whether in pretence or in truth, Christ is being proclaimed.
— Philippians 1:18

We are only blamed by those whose praise would be a reproach to us.
— Father Louis Le Comte

Sleeping China awaited the Christian kiss.
— F. W. Drake

Christianity is always adapting itself into something which can be believed.
— T. S. Eliot

China, 'The Middle Flowery Kingdom', sat apart in solitary grandeur, self-sufficient, proud and unaware that during the 16th century she was under holy siege as Jesuit (Francis Xavier) and friar (Juan de Zumárraga) gazed longingly towards the empire, the one from India, the other from Mexico. Throughout the century sporadic exploratory expeditions were made, and finally a friar and a Jesuit managed to enter the empire at almost the same time: Fr Melchor Nunes Barreto in 1555–56 and friar Gaspar da Cruz in 1556. From that point onwards more and more religious sought to follow. But the Jesuits in particular had set their hearts upon China and Japan, partly as a result of Xavier's despatches from the moving frontier in Asia. At first there seemed no hope of establishing the Society there, but then in 1576 Gregory XIII, by the Bull *Super Specula*, raised the Portuguese concession-port of Macao into an official diocese to include 'forever' all China and Japan.[1] At once there seemed enormous possibilities. Macao, the gateway

---

[1] Macao lies on the west side of the Pearl River estuary on the south China coast; nearby Hong Kong lies east of the estuary.

into the Ming empire, might become the Jesuits' Trojan horse. Then, through China, all the neighbouring countries might be converted in their turn.

The Jesuits were in a special position, as China was their monopoly, granted by papal decree and later guaranteed by Gregory XIII's bull *Ex pastorali officio* of 1585. They were granted this favour because Gregory believed they were the pioneers in China: 'The begetters, teachers, and as it were the parents of the Christian religion in that land'. In fact, theirs was the third attempt to evangelize China, for Christianity had been introduced there in the 7th century, and again by the Franciscans in the 13th.[2] So the Jesuits were re-opening an old mission but, unaware that friars had worked there earlier, they presented theirs as *the* mission to the Middle Kingdom, and there is no doubt that it was an event without parallel in the history of East–West contacts. (1)

The most outstanding member of this Jesuit forlorn hope (in both senses of the phrase) was the Italian Matteo Ricci, who arrived in China in 1583. He saw at once that special care would be needed. The Chinese were xenophobic, especially at that time when Ming dynasty policy aimed to keep aliens out of the country. They despised foreigners in general as ignorant barbarians. The different European nations seemed to them merely different tribes and they would have been dumbfounded had they known that for the Jesuits their 'Middle Flowery Kingdom' was just one more 'vice-province' of the Society's international organization, within which Japan rated as a full 'province'. Further, the Chinese preferred subtlety and conservatism to change, and they lived in accordance with a rigid code of etiquette in which appearances counted for much, and refinement of behaviour was demanded at all times. 'A European', warned a later Jesuit, 'is naturally lively, passionate, and eager; but when such a one arrives in China he must become a quite different man. He must form a resolution to conduct himself, for his whole lifetime, with calmness, complaisance, patience and seriousness'. It required a special effort from vehement Latins, but they soon learnt that even when preaching they must forego gesturing or excitability, which was received with contempt and the laughing question: 'Who is he trying to pick a fight with?'[3] Even an Englishman from the sedate 18th century was impressed by the Chinese: 'How can I scold my servant for breaking a glass when I see one of these hear the crash of a whole porcelain service without any visible emotion?' (2)

The Jesuits began with a false start. They dressed first as Buddhist bonzes,

---

[2] Even after the close of the medieval mission, Rome continued appointing prelates to Peking until 1426. The fourth attempt to convert China was that of the Protestants in the 19th century.

[3] In 1636 Father Aleni was noted as preaching 'with thundering voice and with great emotion' (Zürcher, 437).

but realizing that these were not widely respected, in 1595 they changed into the silk robes of the literati, or scholar-officials, from whose ranks were recruited the mandarins who administered the empire. Adopting Chinese manners, they let their beards grow (but drew the line at Ming fingernails), hired servants, gave expensive presents to the influential, and had themselves carried about by porters in sedan-chairs. By 1595 Ricci was reporting that his life style was completely Chinese. This way of life was costly so that later, in order to support themselves in the manner to which they had grown accustomed, and to keep their mission independent, they were obliged to become traders. As missionaries they were prepared to do everything permissible to bring the gospel to the unconverted; ready to become literati to the Chinese, or indeed anything to anybody. (3)

The Jesuits realized the immensity of the work involved in persuading an ancient and highly developed civilization to change its way of life by adopting Christianity. Their task was all the harder because the Chinese seemed so choked with intellectual pride — greatest of obstacles to the Faith — that the possibility of earning their respect was remote, and much more so was any hope of converting them. The pioneer, Ricci, saw that he must gain the interest of this sophisticated people and for that he played on their curiosity and love of knowledge.[4] In his mission he was assisted by a natural charm which helped him to make friends, and the Chinese saw 'a person of virtue, with a curly beard, blue eyes, a voice like a great bell, intelligent, witty and of manifold ability; he could read off anything he had once glanced at'. His memory techniques helped him master Chinese, which eventually he wrote unaided, though he sought correction before publication. He was not an astronomer, but had studied mathematics in Rome under Christopher Clavius, and cosmography in Portugal under Pedro Nunes. During the five-year-long journey from Europe to China he had devoted his leisure to the study of the natural sciences, and he had brought with him a number of maps and scientific instruments which he decided to use as bait: they were to be the engines of his attempted spiritual conquest. Gradually, polite visits to educated officials developed into discussions; amused and tolerant regard changed into interested questioning when it was discovered that there was after all something to be learnt from the barbarian newcomer. (4)

Ricci grasped every opportunity. He observed, pointed out, and corrected errors in Chinese mathematical texts. Above all, he captured interest with a world map revealing Europe and America to the Chinese for the first time.

---

[4] In 1552 St Francis Xavier had alerted Ignatius to the possibility of exploiting this national characteristic. The Japanese, for example, were curious about natural phenomena, asking where rain, snow, comets, thunder and lightning came from. 'You cannot imagine how much explanations of such things dispose them in our favour' (*Monumenta Xaveriana*, I (Madrid, 1899), 738).

Ricci himself claimed that his earliest work in China, a treatise on friendship, 'won more credit for me and for Europe than anything else we have done', for the Chinese were as interested in moral philosophy as in science. Maybe he recalled that it was Cicero not St Monica who converted Augustine.

This, however, was only the beginning. From his arrival in the empire in 1583 to his entry into Peking in 1601, Ricci kept his eye fixed upon the imperial 'Dragon Throne', realizing that in such a hierarchical society the best hope for Christianity lay in getting the emperor's favour. 'We should begin at the top, and mathematics are useful in the whole of the East, for how else could we approach these proud kings?' So in China, as elsewhere, the Jesuits gave priority to the conversion of the ruling class. It was a policy laid down in their Constitutions and carried out in practice. Eventually this trickle-down theory would pay dividends as converted rulers led their peoples into the Church. (5)

None but courtiers and high officials had any contact with the emperor, the 'Son of Heaven', who dwelt in godlike splendour, isolated in the Forbidden City within Peking, which was controlled by the imperial eunuchs. For 18 years Ricci worked conscientiously, and waited quietly, until, after managing to establish himself near the capital, he sent to the palace a number of gifts calculated to excite the emperor's interest: books, paintings of Christian subjects, a clavichord, maps and above all, a striking clock. As he had hoped, the clock intrigued the emperor, and when it wound down, Ricci was summoned to carry out 'repairs'.[5] Thus he succeeded in what had seemed impossible and maybe for the first time since Friar John of Montecorvino (1289-1328), a European entered the palace.

Although he never saw the emperor himself, Ricci continued his efforts, striving to make himself indispensable, holding open that door, as he put it, which he had prised ajar with such patience. He had given his colleagues an example of the Ignatian use of 'human means' for divine ends and, since the wisdom of his imaginative policy was apparent, the Society now began to send to China some of its most talented members: mathematicians, such as Fr Adam Schall von Bell (who produced the official state calendar which served China until the 20th century), architects, court painters, topographers, surveyors (whose work was not superseded until the 19th century), mechanics such as Fr Magalhães, who made a clockwork puppet which could walk for 15 minutes, and Fr Verbiest, who invented a rudimentary form of steam engine. Since these technical experts were ready to turn their hands to anything, Fr Schall cast cannon for the imperial armies, and in time Jesuits

---

[5] The stormy mission produced no canonized saints, though Ricci became the clockmakers' patron, and a possible inspiration for 'Speedy Gonsales' in Godwin's scientific romance *The Man in the Moone* (1638), (Needham, *Science*, III: 440).

became part of the state bureaucracy, and for 200 years were the interpreters between East and West.[6]

If Ricci had only had to insinuate himself into the emperor's favour all would have been achieved, but there were stumbling blocks. There were, for example two serious technical problems demanding solutions. The first, the so-called 'Term' question, concerned the need to find the correct Chinese word for the Deity. There were two possible words, *T'ien* and *Shang-ti*, and it was essential to decide which coincided most with the Christian conception of God as he than whom no higher can be conceived; he who alone exists of himself, is infinite in all perfections and who rewards and punishes for all eternity. This question was both vital and urgent, since the translation of prayers and of the liturgy was practically impossible until a decision was reached. Furthermore, if, as some feared, the Chinese had no word for God, then it followed that they must be a nation of atheists. Ricci could find no satisfactory expression, but he began to use the term *T'ien chu*, meaning 'Master of Heaven', because it seemed to him that the Chinese adored Heaven as the supreme numen, and so by referring to God as the 'Master of Heaven', the Christians were showing that their God was greater than Heaven. This solution did not satisfy all his colleagues, some of whom feared that the Chinese word might have connotations unknown to them, which would detract from or contaminate the Christian idea of God. In fact the Chinese had no concept or word for a creation *ex nihilo* in the Christian sense, but this was not yet known to the missionaries. This semantic problem troubled the Fathers for years, and was serious enough to drive one of them to suicide.[7] (6)

The second problem had more widespread consequences, for it concerned the rites performed by the Chinese in honour of their ancestors. These ceremonies — which it was impious to neglect — were practised by the entire nation from bandit to emperor and involved offering meat, fruit, silk or perfumes, and burning joss-sticks and paper money in front of the corpse, grave, or commemorative tablet (*p'aiwei*). These rites dated back to the beginning of recorded history and were the foundation of the social system of the empire. Any interference with them was bound to cause violent reactions. Parallel with these were other ceremonies, performed by the scholar class as part of the state cult (a form of hero worship) of Confucius. These twice-monthly minor ceremonies consisted of prostrations (*kotow*), and the offering of incense before a statue of the Sage. At the spring and autumn

---

[6] Others tried the same ploy elsewhere: Elizabeth I (1599) seeking an ally against Spain, presented the Grand Turk with a clock surmounted by singing birds. For automata as royal gifts, and philosophical, theological and political symbols: O. Mayr, in *Smithsonian*, XI (1980), 4–52.

[7] This old problem had disturbed newly arrived Buddhists in ancient China. Should they adopt existing (i.e. Taoist) terms, risking distortion of their message? For term problems in modern science: Needham, *Science*, II: 409; V(3): 255.

equinoxes the rites were more solemn: dead animals, food and wine were offered up, and the participants usually fasted and abstained from sex before the ceremony. The missionaries had to decide whether these practices were religious; whether or not they were sacrifices or mere commemorations; whether they could be permitted to converts. To these were added other problems: if the ceremonies were judged illicit, how far could Christians co-operate in them indirectly? Could a Christian kill animals for the sacrifice? Could a convert official assist the emperor when performing the rites? Such problems were similar to those encountered by the early Church in the Roman empire.[8]

There were other popular practices based on primitive animism, or derived from Taoist and Buddhist mythology, which were banned by all the missionaries, since they were defined clearly as superstitious; however, the rites in honour of ancestors and of Confucius were more difficult to interpret. For years Ricci studied these rites which, he was encouraged to note, were not accompanied by prayers to the dead or to Confucius. He had been assured that they were meant only to inculcate obedience to parents and to authority in general, and as a result he concluded that they were merely social acts. Ricci was not always sure of his ground, but putting the spirit of the much disputed probabilism to one of its most dramatic and indeed most fateful uses, he declared that the ancestor rites were 'certainly not idolatrous and perhaps not even superstitious'. That 'perhaps' is to be noted, because in time his followers, the 'Riccistas', went farther than did Ricci himself, and his cautious 'perhaps' became first 'probably', then 'a very great probability', and finally an exuberant 'certainly'. Ludwig Pastor, for example, managed to get away with 'certainly not superstitious'. (7).

Within a few years these questions were being debated not only by missionaries in China but by philosophers in Europe. The result was a controversy that raged for decades, helped to change the history of ideas, and in time became a fresh if exotic incentive to ancient quarrels about grace and Christ as Mediator. (8)

Ricci advanced yet another theory which, though at first glance a masterstroke, was later turned against him both by the Chinese and by those missionaries opposed to his methods. He appealed to texts in Chinese classical literature to prove that the religion of China had once been monotheistic. He concentrated on showing the Chinese the similarities between their own ancient religious beliefs and Christianity.[9]

---

[8] Similar problems *mutatis mutandis*, agitated priests in the English mission: P. J. Holmes, *Elizabethan Casuistry* (London, 1981) 8, 48, 49, 63, 77.

[9] This thinking was not limited to the Catholics: 'We find an almost persistent effort among Manchu dynasty scholars to explain away Christianity simply as an old Chinese religion somehow transplanted into Europe' (C. S. Ch'ien, *Philobiblon*, I (1946), 15).

To his sympathisers, Ricci seemed to be assuring the Chinese, as Paul had done the Athenians, that he had come to preach their 'unknown, unrecognized God'. Like Paul, he too found grains of truth in, and quoted adroitly from, their own classics. He did not accuse them of being in the wrong, he assured them they were only different. There were advantages in this approach. Chinese pride was not upset by any seeming arrogance on his part; converts need not fear that their revered ancestors had been damned. Confucianism was a prelude to the gospel, a *praeparatio evangelica*, and its adherents were simply at an arrested stage of their unconscious journey to Christ; indeed, some missionaries thought that they were already halfway there and needed only the light of revealed religion to put them in possession of the whole truth. They were 'Anonymous', i.e. unwitting, honorary, Christians, a people who, without knowing Christ, had nevertheless reached a Christian position.

Ricci's approach was seductive but dangerous. Seductive because by stressing analogies he could show that all this was not something new, foreign, and therefore 'barbarian', but rather common to both civilizations; identical in essentials if not in accidents with the creed of their ancestors. Christianity then became a 'new' link with the venerated past. But dangerous because it could lead to syncretism, a vague amalgam of Chinese and Christian beliefs.[10]

More daringly, Ricci wrote a catechism in which he made no mention of six of the seven Catholic sacraments, and he ignored the six 'Commandments of the Church', which meant that his converts were not bound to fast or to abstain from meat on the prescribed days, nor did they have to observe the obligation to attend Sunday mass on pain of mortal sin. This catechism, a brief synopsis of Christian teaching based on natural reason, was suited to the situation and was what the pioneer friars had done earlier in the New World. (9)

Preaching to the Athenians, the apostle Paul was given a polite hearing until he mentioned the resurrection of the dead. At that point he lost his listeners' respect, for they were repelled by the idea of a 'standing-up of corpses'. Equally, the Chinese were scandalized by the concept of the crucifixion. They expressed their love of self-control by presenting Confucius or the Buddha with a serene smile. Beside these, the agony of a gibbeted God was shocking. He must have been a criminal to be so put to death? His worshippers must be sadists? Faced with this reaction Ricci and the early Jesuits were cautious about displaying the crucifix too openly. Nor did they

---

[10] Ricci's attitude accords with some modern thinking: in 1975 an English Benedictine described Tibetan Buddhist services as the Catholic divine office in an unfamiliar rite. On the dangers here ('no one ever entered someone else's intuition and came away unmarked'): G. Moorhouse, *Against all Reason* (London, 1969), 225–6.

discuss Christ's passion until they were sure of the seriousness of their enquirers. 'It is true', admitted Fr Francisco Furtado to his general in 1636, 'that we keep the crucifix withdrawn and not in public, but we do not hide the mystery of the passion from those worthy of being catechized. Indeed *if there is time* [my italics] the whole of the Lord's passion is explained to those who are to be baptized'.

What seems most likely is that the Jesuits distinguished between cross and crucifix, and were cautious about indiscreet public displays of the latter. But many were uneasy about this policy, which was to cause the Fathers much anxiety in the years ahead, especially after 1654 when the moral theologian Pedro de Tapia urged that the doctrine of the passion be not postponed until after baptism. (10)

In short, Ricci, carrying out the Jesuit policy of being all things to all men for the greater glory of God, was taking a calculated risk. His efforts to accommodate Catholicism to Confucianism led him to preach a natural religion which seemed to many almost akin to Deism. The outcome was that, in trying to soothe Chinese susceptibilities, in lessening the 'scandal of the cross', the Riccistas led the Society into one of the gravest controversies it had to face and one which, in the end, contributed to its suppression.

China, therefore, presented enormous problems, but the sort of problems the young Society welcomed, for the Middle Kingdom and its people seemed the answer to a Jesuit's prayer. Silk was about to meet silk. First, it was a vast empire governed by a refined intellectual aristocracy who would only be converted by superiors, and no Jesuit doubted that the order most fitted to this task was his own, which, 'though the merest newcomer to the Culture of the Church, has been chosen by divine dispensation and made into the first after St Thomas the Apostle, to cultivate the remote Orient'. Additionally, they had their monopoly of the mission. That papal donation was as resented by the friars as it was treasured by the Fathers. Any friar who tried to enter the empire got a less than cool welcome, as the Franciscan Martín Ignacio de Loyola discovered when he arrived there in 1585. Although a relative of their founder, Ignatius Loyola, the Jesuits did not hesitate to have him deported. According to his story they laid false information against him, alleging that he was a Spanish spy preparing the way for an invasion.[11] Another Franciscan, Antonio Caballero de Santa María, was manhandled, tied up, and carried off by a Jesuit's servants, with the Father's connivance — for which he apologized in later years.[12] (11)

---

[11] The closeness of his relationship to the saint depends on the historian: for the friars and Jansenists he was the saint's nephew but modern Jesuit research shows he was only the 'cousin of the son of the son of the brother of St Ignatius' (D'Elia, *Fonti Ricciane*, II: 637).

[12] Sometimes Jesuits exiled each other: Fr Schall connived at the expulsions of Fathers Furtado and Martini (Dunne, 332).

Individual friars managed to enter China (one sold himself into slavery to do so) but only succeeded in establishing themselves there on their eighth attempt. Nevertheless they persisted, partly out of suspicion of what the Jesuits were doing, partly in response to the particular challenge presented by the mission. They were stimulated by their earlier success with the Chinese they had encountered in the Philippines and Mexico, and ironically, also by the Jesuits' efficient propaganda in favour of their own Asian missions. In 1615, for example, Fr Nicholas Trigault had arrived in Rome garbed exotically as a Chinese scholar, making a stir with optimistic talk of China as a source of hope and promise for the Church. Others, too, saw opportunities in Asia, and the fabulously rich Duchess of Aveiro, the 'Mother of the Missions', swore an oath to build as many churches in the missions as Elizabeth of England had destroyed. (12)

Jesuit hopes and plans did not please everyone. Their vision of vast oriental conversions, counterbalancing the losses suffered by the Church in northern Europe, drew comment from Samuel Purchas. Though grateful for the Fathers' contribution to geographical knowledge, he derided their 'Pranckes in Asia' where he saw them as busily 'seeking to repaire, with their untempered Mortar, the ruines of their Falling Babylon [at home] and there laying a new foundation of their after-hopes, [finding it] easier to conquer naked Americans and effeminate Indians, then in keeping what they had in Europe'. Pascal too was shocked by the Fathers' 'strange zeal and novel charity' which led them to 'suppress the scandal of the cross, preaching only the Saviour in his glory, not as suffering'. (13)

So the mendicant friars were delighted when in 1600 Clement VIII, breaking the Jesuit monopoly, permitted them to enter China under certain conditions. Further papal decrees in 1608 and 1633 allowed any religious to enter China. As was to be expected, the Jesuits resisted these attempts to rescind their old privilege, and almost till the end of the 17th century struggled manfully to keep the friars away and the mission to themselves. In 1638 the Jesuit Patriarch Affonso Mendes, resorting to Leviticus, reminded the cardinals of Propaganda Fide that 'a vineyard should not be sowed with diverse seeds; nor a garment woven of Linnen and Wooll; wherein is implied, that the severall institutions and different manners of living in religious orders, ought not be be entruded upon young and tender Churches. For many times, emulation growing among them, and many wanting prudence, and others abounding in an indiscreet zeale, they do many things, which tend rather to ruine than edification'. What he was expressing as a fear soon became reality, and his words a prophecy fulfilled.

To the Jesuits, the coming of the friars was 'an unwanted hairshirt', even though they themselves could not produce enough men to staff the mission. Occasionally they had to abandon territory because of staff shortage, and throughout the next century they were continually appealing for more recruits. But their many qualities did not include a readiness to co-operate with fellow religious.[13]

As for the friars, it should not be lightly assumed that they were unlearned or untalented. Many held university lectureships before volunteering for the missions; many more had experience of missionary work in America or the Philippines. For them, problems of terminology, rites and 'unknown gods' were no novelty: they had already met them in America, and a glance at the standard bibliographies would show the energy and devotion with which they applied themselves to the study of native languages and dialects. It was a friar (Martín de Rada) whom a generous Jesuit (Bernard-Maitre) has christened 'the father of modern Sinology', and it was Rada, not a Jesuit as is always said, who identified China with Marco Polo's 'Cathay'. Another friar, Bernardino de Sahagún, is regarded as the pioneer of American ethnography. It was not a friar, but a 17th-century Jesuit, who said that to understand the situation in China not much theology was needed, only a knowledge of the language, a remark echoed by General Ledóchowski: 'Nothing except Christ crucified, and Chinese', were needed for that mission-field.

By that standard the friars were more than well-equipped. Experience in America had taught them (and had it not, the decrees of the Spanish India Office were there to instruct their ignorance) not to interfere with harmless native customs or practices. A modern Jesuit recently denounced the folly of those friars who entered China intending to ram down the Faith with Toledo steel, yet in fact it was a Jesuit (Alonso Sánchez), and not a friar, who concocted a wild plan to invade China to do precisely that. The friars knew well (Aquinas had told them so) that there was more hope of converting men by reason than by main force, and they even had such guidebooks as Friar Luis de Granada's *Símbolo de la fe* and his *Breve tratado* which stressed the point.[14] (14)

Yet despite this, many Spanish friars had their full share of the national conservatism and dislike of novelty.[15] From home they brought old fears of fifth columns within the Church, since many never lost their doubts about the sincerity of the 'new Christians', former Muslims and Jews, who had been converted in Spain.

---

[13] NC 15, 408, 420, 437, 446, 537–41 and Fr Damboriena (133n) lists 23 occasions when his brethren obstructed friars from entering the mission. Yet, General Ledóchowski claimed that 'the Society has never hesitated to share with others the field of action assigned to it, when it considered it too extensive for the number of its own labourers' (*Writings*, 703).

[14] Granada's *Sinners' Guide* (1556), translated into English and Japanese in 1599, warned against conservatism: 'Prudent men do not weigh the newness or antiquity of things in order to approve or condemn them. There are things long-standing but evil; others new yet good; age cannot justify wickedness, nor novelty condemn the good; we must look at the merits of things, not their years.'

[15] The poets who introduced new Italian metres into Spanish 16th-century poetry caused scandal and, not entirely jokingly, were branded as literary heretics comparable to such innovators as Luther.

The Chinese Rites Controversy may be said to have started in America, for the collective experience of that mission, so helpful to later friars in China, had at the same time made them cautious. Friar Motolinía, the Franciscan chronicler of the spiritual conquest of Mexico, had noted that the Aztecs, who had a hundred gods, had no objection to adding another, that of their Christian conquerors: Christ might become merely a new deity in the American pantheon. In Mexico and Peru missionaries were still having to suppress native religious underground resistance movements, and to prevent Indians from hiding their old idols behind the crucifix which they appeared to be venerating so satisfactorily. In the Philippines, too, friars met similar problems in that many apparently sincere converts were suddenly detected observing their old rites in cheerful conjunction with their newfound creed. Many, it seemed, had 'not been so much baptized as sprinkled'.

After the encouraging papal permission of 1633 the friars began to make more organized efforts to reach the mainland. Following the Manchu conquest of 1644, when coastguard surveillance diminished, it became easier for them to sail directly to the maritime province of Fukien, either from their bases on Formosa or from the Philippines, without having to negotiate the unfriendly Portuguese concession-port of Macao.

Fukien now became the Dominicans' base in China and one of the two main locations of Sino-Western contacts, the other, of course, being the Jesuit establishment in Peking.[16]

In 1635, to the Jesuits' dismay, two celebrated friars, a Dominican, Juan Bautista Morales, and a Franciscan, Antonio Caballero de Santa María, arrived on the Chinese mainland. Undaunted by the open hostility of the Fathers, they continued the Chinese language studies already started in the Philippines, where the Dominicans were officially responsible for the spiritual welfare of the huge community of Chinese traders, mainly Fukienese. They also set about the study of the religious thought of China, going over the same ground as the Jesuits and meeting all the same problems. Their suspicions were aroused by their language teacher, who defined the word *ch'i* as a sacrifice ('like the mass') and as the ceremonial way to honour one's ancestors. Accordingly, the two friars arranged to attend one such ceremony in the house of a catechist, a member of the Miu family.

What they saw horrified them. In a richly decorated hall, with tablets bearing the names of ancestors inscribed in gold letters, was a table bearing food, flowers, candles and incense tapers. 'The divine office', directed by a Master of Ceremonies, included ritual prostrations, the sharing out of the 'sacrificial' foods of goat's flesh and pork, and libations of wine. The

---

[16] Adjacent to Canton province in south China, Fukien lies opposite Formosa (Taiwan) and north of the Philippines. Its people had some experience of foreigners since China's sailors have traditionally been Fukienese (and Cantonese), and they also had dealings with the Dutch, etc. See Idema, 460.

presiding official solemnly intoned the exhortations of Confucius, and gold and silver paper money was burnt to pay for the expenses of the dead in the after-life. The friars concluded that this was no mere civic ceremony, but a religious act, in which 'nothing more was needed to make it into a sacrifice'.[17] This experience, together with their readings, led them into conflict with the Riccistas. The rites which Ricci found 'certainly not idolatrous, and perhaps not even superstitious', seemed to them certainly superstitious and perhaps even idolatrous, and where the First Commandment was concerned they were prepared to be unpopular rigorists and to keep on the safe side. 'We say the gate is strait, but then so too did Christ', observed Navarrete who saw no place there for probabilism, or 'perhapses'. In this they were in good company, for the Christian God boasted of being jealous, was averse to syndicates, and had demanded the stoning to death of any who, unfaithful to him, whored after other gods.[18] (15)

The friars now forbade their converts to perform the rites, and with such conviction that at first they refused to credit reports that Jesuits were permitting them. Other, later, reports seemed equally unbelievable. Friars who had seen the Fathers' Church in Peking reported that it contained two altars: one dedicated to Christ, the other to the emperor of China. It was to this latter that Chinese visitors seemed to be paying reverence. To many friars, therefore, it seemed that they, like Ezekiel, were witnessing abominations in the Temple. They had already heard that the Jesuits were concealing the crucifix, for as early as 1631 word of it had reached Rome and had elicited an admonition from Propaganda. The friars were even more distressed when the Fathers, 'not content with hiding the crucifix themselves, told us to do the same'. What a modern Jesuit (Pastor Gutiérrez) considers 'excessive timidity' was called plain cowardice by contemporary friars. In reaction, and anxious to show that they, at least, were ready to 'preach Christ crucified without shame', the friars tended in the beginning to make the cross the pivot of their teaching. (16)

Beside the two principal problems to be settled, the Term and Rites questions, there were a host of lesser ones, for the friars disagreed in many respects with the Fathers' conception of the mission. It would have been wiser of the Jesuits to come forward at the start to explain any apparent laxity on their part, especially since the friars' attitude was the more scrupulous on most levels. The mendicant friars held that Christian missionaries should live poorly, observing their vows of poverty, begging their way through the country, instead of 'sallying forth in sedan-chairs on the shoulders of porters,

---

[17] The rites could be awe-inspiring, as is shown in Needham, *Science*, II: 32; see also Ebrey's translation and assessment of Chu Hsi's liturgical text, *Family Rituals*.

[18] Juan de Paz, a widely-consulted Dominican moral theologian, specializing in East Asian problems, rejected probabilism where the First Commandment was concerned. So too Jesuit St Robert Bellarmine (Le Bachelet, *Auctarium Bellarminianum* (Paris, 1913), 641). Cf. Bernard-Maitre, 'Becker-Brucker', 424.

surrounded by servants, and rustling silk whenever they stirred'. Moreover they disagreed with the Jesuit policy of conversion from the top, holding that the poor were the more naturally inclined to Christianity. (17)

They were most intransigent on the question of the rites. Where the Jesuits tended to compromise, the friars, reacting against them, tended to caution. Before long they denounced the religion taught in China by the Jesuits as contaminated with idolatry. If earlier they saw themselves as so many Ezekiels, they soon saw themselves like Joshua, come to lead the people into the Promised Land. Their arrival in China was an act of God: 'just as the friars had been called in the 13th century to save Europe, so now these same sons of the Church were being called to re-lay the false foundations upon which the House of God was being built in China'. (18)

Other discoveries complicated the affair, for the friars found that not every Jesuit in China was convinced of the legality of Ricci's method. During Ricci's lifetime there had been an apparent unity among the Fathers, and not until he was dead did an open rift appear. Soon after there was a full range of opinion within the ranks: those for whom the rites were *perhaps* superstitious, those who saw them as *certainly not* superstitious, and those who, seeing them as *certainly* superstitious, opposed all temporizing and in varying degree shared the views of the friars. Fr Jean Valat was regarded with suspicion by his fellows but, to the mendicant friars he was an ally and a source of consolation, for he forbade the ceremonies to his converts as though he were a Dominican.[19] Another Jesuit, Ignacio Lobo, witnessing the Confucian rites for the first time, excelled the friars in a demonstration of outraged orthodoxy, for he almost fainted: 'my flesh crept, my hair stood on end, my face went white, for the blood rushed to my heart'.[20] Some of these dissident Jesuits held high office and were influential in the Society. Luís da Gama, a narrow-minded Portuguese martinet who made the friars seem lax, was the official Fr-Visitor for China and Japan, and he caused considerable discontent among his Jesuit colleagues before he was overruled by Rome.

Not all the opposition was on theological grounds either. The Jesuit João Rodriguez, nicknamed 'The Interpreter', who had been in Asia since the age of 16, was an adversary of the Riccista line of thought, and his prestige as a linguist lent weight to his opinions. On the whole, however, and this must be stressed, the majority of Jesuits favoured the Riccista compromise, and the minority who wavered from the party-line never seriously influenced mission policy.

The most serious defection was that of Fr Niccolò Longobardi, precisely

---

[19] 'About Valat, keep what I've said to yourself; he's been good to us and we don't want to get him into trouble with his brethren', wrote one friar to another in 1672 (SinFran, III: 402).
[20] Dismissed from the Society, he became a secular priest in Macao where friends teased him for genuflecting to the emperor's portrait in the Peking church during his Jesuit career (NC 84, 518).

because Ricci had chosen him as his successor. This situation was disturbing for the Society which prided itself on the ability to swing the whole ecclesiastical corps into concerted action with no undisciplined stragglers.[21] Accordingly, conferences (no fewer than 74 up until 1665) were convened to discuss the disagreements, and the outcome was that all evidence of disaffection was to be suppressed, and the writings of the anti-Ricci faction burnt.[22] Unfortunately for the Fathers, a copy of a treatise by Fr Longobardi was leaked to the friars, was published by Navarrete in his *Tratados* and came to play a significant part in the subsequent controversy in Europe. (19)

There was not much likelihood of an easy settlement of the differences between the missionaries, and any such hope was tempered by the traditional rivalry. For example, Jesuit unwillingness to co-operate with other missionaries was such a byword that a mendicant handbook for the guidance of friar-couriers conducting volunteers to the missions warned of the futility of approaching the Fathers for help or advice *en route*. But an ironical passage pointed out that this unhelpful attitude could sometimes be useful. Occasionally a friar bound for the missions would lose heart and jump ship, but in places where the Jesuits were in control, the friars' leader had no need to worry, for the watchful Fathers could be relied upon to see the delinquent was firmly back on board when the vessel got under way. Such gossip kept animosity alive. So too did the Jesuits' contemptuous attitude towards the friars, whom they reckoned out of place in China, where they could only deter, rather than impress, the literati. The Jesuits were embarrassed by the friars' presence, and they made no effort to keep their opinions to themselves. The Jesuit Patriarch Mendes grumbled that 'these idiot friars are gradually ruining the mission with their imprudence and rashness'.[23] And the Jesuits in Japan contemptuously equated the word 'friar' with 'botcher', and described anything badly done as being 'friar-like'. (20)

On occasion Jesuits forbade their converts to shelter friars, to make their confessions to them, or even to recite the rosary (a particularly Dominican devotion), and they refused absolution to Christians who joined the rosary sodality.[24] The friars put a different estimate on their talents and usefulness, and protested indignantly at the arrogance of those who 'set themselves up to

---

[21] Perhaps an idealized view: 'The Society could be described as a group of individuals working against each other for the greater glory of God' (A. L. Martin, 'The Jesuit Mystique', *Sixteenth Century Journal*, 4 (1973), 33).

[22] More than 50 controversial Jesuit memoranda are recorded up to the time of the mendicants' arrival in the 1630s but all disappeared *ad extinguendas opinionum dissensiones* (Bernard Maitre, 'Dossier', 75).

[23] 'Idiot', as in English, can mean 'illiterate, uneducated', or better, 'simpleton by nature but sage by grace'. St Francis declared that anyone unable to bear the description would never make a good friar.

[24] For the Jesuit rosary-ban in 16th century Salamanca, see Barcelona Univ. ms. 968, no. 33, ff. 305–8.

correct Dominicans as though they were dealing with erring school-children.' (21)

Voltaire was later to say that the Jesuits' worst enemies were not the mandarins, but their fellow missionaries. He might properly have added that, had the Jesuits been able to bring themselves to show the mendicants some of the tact, diplomacy and understanding that they lavished upon the Chinese literati, much of the hostility might have dissolved, the attempt to convert the empire might have been more successful, and history have a different story to tell. At least the Chinese would not have been so disedified and bewildered. As it was, they often wondered if both groups were Europeans. There was a very real danger that, as had happened earlier in Japan, the converts would see themselves as being Jesuit-Catholics or friar-Catholics, or would split, as in Pondicherry, where two groups of converts worshipped in separate buildings. There were, of course, occasional demonstrations of mutual charity, but they were neither frequent nor lasting, and though the Fathers 'sometimes put on Palm Sunday faces to welcome newly-come friars, nevertheless, Good Friday always follows on behind'.[25] (22)

The divisions caused pain. Friar Varo had nightmares in which he saw ox-drawn carts loaded with the many memoranda submitted to Rome on the problem of the rites. Not only the priests but their converts could suffer mental martyrdom. One such, Juan Miu, sent a touching plea to Fr Giulio Aleni after he and his friend Joachim Ko, having moved from Jesuit-controlled territory into the Dominican zone, found to their distress and confusion that practices previously allowed were now forbidden them under dire threats: 'Neither Joachim nor I can eat or sleep for thinking of these troubles . . . [the friars] say "no", because mortal sin is involved. Now, you're supposed to lead us to Heaven but you are harming us and yourself in teaching the contrary. I'm blinded by tears as I write this and I can't see. Show me the way to go. Answer me soon and reassure me'. These two, seeking God among the wrangling divines, are a reminder of Gernet's words that to its enemies Catholicism often appeared to be a doctrine devised to torment humanity.[26] (23)

---

[25] Dom David Knowles writes of the English mission: 'At first the [other] missionary priests and the Jesuits worked together in amity and with abundant fruit. Then, through a series of deplorable mistakes and mischances, divisions began to appear and ultimately caused great and permanent harm to the cause for which each party was working and suffering' (*Religious*, III: 444).

[26] For other similar cases: NC 306.

II

The friars' position may be summarized thus: their viewpoint was shaped by experience. They did not underrate the difficulties before them, but they reached the East by the Spanish route, across America and the Philippines, and everywhere saw evidence of the success of their methods. They were therefore less psychologically resigned to compromise. In addition, what they encountered in Jesuit China drove them to strong reaction. Every bit as learned as the Fathers in theology and philosophy, and no less zealous or perspicacious, many of them also had more experience of pastoral work on their way out to China than had the sea-borne Jesuits.

There were still other causes of tension. Nationalism, for instance, was an old problem. In 1625 Francesco Ingoli, the first secretary of Propaganda Fide, had suggested that different nationals should live apart, in separate mission residences. Twenty years later Propaganda had to intervene to restore peace between the Italian and Portuguese Carmelites in India; on the Orinoco the Capuchins were obliged to segregate Catalans and Aragonese friars. From time to time Rome issued general appeals to missionaries to pluck out the root of the trouble from their hearts, but it was far from easy. In the China mission this problem, like many others, was still more complex, and the possibilities of dissension greater, for there it so happened that the Jesuits as an organization worked under the patronage of the Portuguese, while the friars were under Spanish auspices and each side was committed to its patron. This was happening precisely at a time when Spain and Portugal were at war. After 1640 tempers ran even higher, for in that year the Portuguese rebelled against Spanish domination, breaking the bonds of what they called the 'Babylonian Captivity'. There was at this time still another traditional rivalry between the Jesuits and friars, for the Fathers had the reputation of working in favour of the Portuguese house of Braganza and against Castile, whereas the Dominicans in Portugal were pro-Spanish. The old institutional rivalry was thus inextricably mixed with the national rivalry of Spain and Portugal, and the animosity between the two Iberian religious orders was linked to the struggle between the two Iberian crowns for supremacy both at home and abroad. The Portuguese in East Asia were anxious to keep their monopoly of the lucrative China-Japan silk trade; the Spanish in Manila were just as anxious to share in it. Similarly, the Jesuits wanted to retain their mission monopoly of China and Japan, and the Manila-based friars were equally anxious to share in the work and the spiritual rewards of the China–Japan missionfield. (24)

The Portuguese were the first to arrive in East Asia, establishing themselves in Goa, and then at Macao, the only European settlement allowed on the China coast. From there they tried to enter the empire. And though the Portuguese Church, with very few vocations, could hardly spare any clergy for overseas work, the authorities tried to prevent other countries from sending out missionaries.[27] As a reward for shouldering the responsibility of extending Catholic missions in East Asia, the Portuguese got privileges from the papacy. As a preliminary, they secured a series of papal bulls granting them ecclesiastical patronage rights (the *padroado*) over the area from the Cape of Good Hope to Japan. This meant that no bishop could be appointed, nor episcopal see created therein, without the permission of the king of Portugal, whose consent was also required before a single missionary could go into the East Indies. Foreigners only obtained this if they renounced their nationality and became Portuguese subjects. With great farsightedness, and even greater optimism, the Portuguese obtained an annulment in advance of any bulls of a contrary nature that future popes might utter. In return for these privileges they helped the mission with favours and money.

The Jesuits, realizing that they could only enter China via Portuguese Macao, submitted to the conditions imposed by the *padroado*, allying themselves, as an organization, to the cause of Portugal.[28] Once, at least, in Japan, to the scandal of some Spanish seamen, they gave bizarre proof of their loyalty by refusing to pray for Philip II of Spain during the 'Memento for the living' in the mass; this because he was regarded as an usurper after he annexed Portugal in 1580. Individual non-Iberian Fathers had to repress personal feelings *ad maiorem Dei gloriam* and in accordance with their rule, which urged the Jesuit to make his homeland a foreign country to himself, and every country his fatherland, so as to be at home everywhere. From the beginning this had been the policy of what it was hoped would be the 'Universal Company of Jesus'. With a view to creating a union of hearts, Ignatius had put a Frenchman in charge of the Roman College, a Spaniard in the Paris College, and a Fleming in Perugia. The early Generals Acquaviva and Vitelleschi had stressed that nationalism and regionalism were to be 'drowned to death in the sweet sea of our holy Society' and 'the horrifying word foreigner' was banned from the Jesuit vocabulary. This was to seek perfection, yet the Society, emphasizing as it did a special loyalty to the papacy, succeeded in leading most Jesuits to an ultramontane view, and to a form of supra-nationalism which in 16th- and 17th-century Europe was no mean achievement. (25)

---

[27] This shortage was not a calamity for everyone: 'Of all the nations of Europe, Portugal was in the least favourable position for contact with the Eastern Christians. The Spaniards, French or Italians would probably have acted in a different way' (Cardinal Tisserant, *Eastern Christianity in India from the earliest times* (Calcutta, 1957), 68) and cf. 'The Portuguese temperament naturally despises all these orientals' (Fr Sousa, SJ., *Oriente conquistado*, Pt. II (Lisbon, 1710), 550).

[28] Some resented this: Valignano, area manager for East Asia, wanted to entrust China to Italians, in part to get revenge for the bureaucratic 'humiliations' imposed on foreigners by the Portugese *padroado* system.

The China mission, however, imposed a double burden upon a man's ideals, for there he often had to be loyal to different, sometimes differing, nations: his own, and whichever of the two Iberian powers was patronizing the order to which he belonged. Portuguese Jesuits, loyal to their country on the double count of birth and membership of the protected Society, frequently fell short of the Ignatian ideal. One Portuguese Father, requesting more missionaries, stipulated that they not be foreigners, particularly not French priests, who only wanted 'to pluck the golden apples from the tree of Asia, watered with our blood and nurtured by our labours'. Some Portuguese were capable of welcoming a friar, provided he were from home, rather than a brother Jesuit from Spain. Portuguese friars too sometimes preferred Jesuits from home to fellow friars from abroad. 'It is no good having foreigners in these parts', wrote one Capuchin in Asia, with more force than accuracy, 'up to now they have not made a single convert . . . this harvest was sown and reaped by us Portuguese, and we alone are fitted for it'.[29] (26)

Whereas the Portuguese had gone East following Vasco da Gama, the Spanish pushed West after Columbus, and from America crossed the Pacific to the Philippines, their gateway to China. They had as allies the Spanish friars, who were able to devote themselves at one and the same time to the welfare of Church and fatherland, unlike the many foreigners among the more cosmopolitan Jesuits, who had had to make a deliberate act of faith in Portugal. Many friars mixed with their nationalism a belief in Spain's mission to save the world. Nowhere else on the face of the earth, the 16th-century writer Pedro de Medina asserted, was the Faith confessed and practised as in Spain. The zeal of this people, whose rulers were dubbed by a Catalan pope 'the Catholic Monarchs', was in part a legacy of the centuries spent struggling for national and religious unity against the Muslim invaders. The final victory of 1492 was accompanied by that yearning for racial and spiritual purity which fostered an Inquisition proudly described as unique in Christendom. Out of this grew the Spanish view of themselves as a new Chosen Race, and the self-confidence that could denounce even popes and that Roman Curia whose conduct had brought about the Reformation, thereby imposing yet another burden upon 'our Blessed Lady Spain'. The outspoken Cano declared that all talk of reforming Rome was useless: 'no one who knows that city can hope to cure it'. One pontiff, driven to complain of Spanish pride, and thinking of the converted Jews and Moors there, taunted 'God alone knows what race they are descended from'. No jibe could have hurt more in a country where 'clean blood' was a necessity of life. (27)

Some Spaniards seemed to consider themselves the only true Catholics. A Dominican treatise, after comparing the Spanish empire to the Church itself on the grounds that both were 'one, holy, Catholic and apostolic', went on to conclude that the Spanish were preordained to rule the world politically as

---

[29] Portuguese friars never attempted to work inside China.

the Church ruled it spiritually. The chronicler López de Gómara declared that, Incarnation and Redemption apart, the greatest event since the Creation had been the Spanish discovery of America. For many of his fellow countrymen it was self-evident that the new lands had been given to Spain by God, as a reward for saving Europe from Islam. Only Spain, the 'garden of Christ', was free of all heresy and kept its colonies equally pure: 'Oh, Holy See of Peter', cried Bishop Palafox, 'how much you owe to Spain! Thanks to her you are venerated from Japan to Chile!' (28)

When they came to China, therefore, the Spanish Friars-Preacher had a threefold purpose: they came to convert; they came as *Domini Canes* to preserve orthodox Catholicism, and to rebuild what they saw as the shaky house erected by the Jesuits; and they came as representatives of the 'Catholic Monarch' and the new Chosen People. In these circumstances it would have been miraculous if trouble had not followed their arrival. Yet some writers play down the division between the different religious orders with all its consequent disparate loyalties, and look elsewhere for the cause of the controversy, dehumanizing the situation as much as possible by representing it as a clash between two civilizations, East and West. This explanation is novel, and saves face; unfortunately, it is not true. The missionaries themselves knew where to look for the source of their troubles. One Portuguese Father dismissed a piece of gossip by asking: 'Is it likely that a Jesuit would pour out his secrets to a Dominican, or a Portuguese confide in a Castilian?' There, in miniature, lay the tragedy of the Asian missions. A French Jesuit remarked that when a Spanish Dominican met a Portuguese Jesuit trouble was inevitable. He himself may well have been persecuted by both parties, for the seething pot was freshly stirred towards the end of the 17th century when French Fathers reached China. Faced with this new threat, Jesuit, Iberian and friar were united, not by charity, but in jealousy of the unwelcome newcomers. The sending of the latter was a prudent move by the administrators of the Society in Rome, for by that time the power and resources of Portugal were in decline and the French were about to replace them.

The Portuguese, however, were still capable of resistance, and the French Jesuits, like the Spanish friars of the earlier period, were obliged to enter China by a back door, since the front was firmly closed in their faces by their Lusitanian brothers. German Jesuits were no more welcome than the French. The Iberians objected that these would have done better to stay in their own 'German Indies', fighting the heresy flourishing on their doorstep, leaving the work of spreading the Gospel in China to those who had put their houses in order before venturing abroad to proselytize.

Of all the missionaries, the least nationalistic were the Italians, who were outside the common rivalries, had no colonial axe to grind and were not empire-builders. In addition, they were by nature generally more tolerant and broadminded than the Iberians. The Portuguese Jesuit António Vieira was ashamed to note that the Italians 'understand so much better than us things which so little concern them'.[30] In the late 18th century ambassador Lord Macartney found the Italian Fathers in Peking were 'more learned and liberal than the Portuguese who still retain a considerable share of ancient bigotry and rancour'. The Italians often had to act as peacemakers but despite this the wrangling continued, and it fell to the Chinese Dominican Friar Lo to warn his European fellow priests that the fate of the Church in China would be the same as that in Japan if their quarrels did not end. (29)

---

[30] Heterodox Italians of the period showed a similar breadth of vision. 'Out of Italy emerged the greatest leaders of tolerant Protestantism in Europe' (H. Kamen, *Rise of Toleration* (London, 1967), 81), and 'An impassioned plea for religious toleration was the most far-reaching Italian contribution to the Reformation' (P. McNair, *History*, 60 (1975), 361).

III

This was the backcloth to Ricci's heroic and dramatic attempt at cultural subversion through technological transfer: the end was to change the soul of Confucian China; the means, Renaissance science. He confessed this in 1595 declaring he hoped to 'destroy China's ancient Law and to replace it with the Christian Dispensation'. This was only an extension of Jesuit practice in Europe, and many saw it as a harmless pious deception. The strategy, the sociologist's 'dual-identity ruse' still survives, and any disquiet over an element of deceit in this double posture can be soothed by recalling a sacred precedent, for Jesus himself came out of Nazareth disguised as a carpenter. (30)

Ricci died in 1610 in an aura of optimism; he was leaving his successors 'an open door', and knew that 'for centuries to come we'll be remembered in this kingdom and, furthermore, it'll be a good memory'.[31] He could not know that in that same year Galileo would publish his planetary discoveries. The rainbow was already beginning to fade.[32] (31)

---

[31] Cf. Fr Manoel de Nobrega in 1552: 'We [Jesuits in Brazil] are working to lay the foundations of [religious] houses which will last as long as the world endures' (Boxer, *Race*, 87), and Verbiest: 'Is the name of Scipio Africanus or Drusus Germanicus greater than that of a missionary in a Chinese province?' (*Corr.*, 236).

[32] At Ricci's death there were 12 Jesuits, including Macanese catechists; the converts numbered some 5 000. Even his death was useful to the mission since two of his companions were officially allowed to remain in Peking to care for his tomb and to perform the necessary sacrificial rites (Zürcher, 418, 423).

3 Jesuits' strategy: friars' scandal

The Rites Controversy was the heart of the matter; at first sight it had nothing to do with science or chemistry, but it can hardly be ignored by historians of science.

— Joseph Needham

La querelle des Rites est absurde: mais la question des Rites était légitime.

— Pierre Grison

The conversion of all East Asia depends on that of China alone.

— Fr Antoine Thomas

Of the four Catholic mission centres in Asia (Goa, Malacca, Macao and Manila) the first three were under the Portuguese. Only the last was in the Spanish zone of influence, and it alone was not dominated by the Jesuits in the ecclesiastical sphere.

In China the division was cleanly cut: the Portuguese with their cosmopolitan Jesuit allies, based in Macao, held China as a monopoly until 1633. The Spanish, poised on their Manila springboard and using their own nationals, the friars, tried to enter China by any means they could. The Portuguese suspiciously watched these efforts, fearful that Spain, backed by American silver, would be a formidable commercial competitor. The friars could not get into China through Macao, because the Portuguese would not let pass what they saw as a Spanish advance guard; nor would the Jesuits agree to their entry because, for the time being at any rate, they supported their Portuguese patrons, and they had heavy investments in the silk trade. They also wanted to keep China as their own special preserve. The Jesuits explained away their disobedience of the papal decrees abolishing their former monopoly, by pleading that they were forced to obey the Portuguese *padroado*. But whatever the excuses, the friars saw only the disobedience, and became the more distrustful of the Jesuits' activities. This mistrust grew when the Jesuits found reasons for ignoring the decrees of successive popes before the end of the controversy. (1)

The controversy began, as a domestic difference. The Fathers were divided among themselves about the preaching strategy to be used in China. Given time they would have suppressed these in-house differences. That was their way. But unfortunately for them, the atmosphere changed once the friars had seen Jesuit China. What began as a difference of opinion within a highly disciplined religious family then became a bitter quarrel, and became more wide-ranging as the seventeenth century progressed. Appeals and denunciations by both sides were made to Rome, each hoping for a favourable decision. It was the most damaging controversy to shake the Catholic world in modern times, for it scandalized both China and Europe, whereas that other great debate, over Jansenism, was largely limited to Europe. In an age of ever growing literacy the 'China Affair' had widespread effects, for the battle was mainly conducted on paper, and the contestants were distressingly addicted to print. The literature of the debate is enormous; already by 1680 a Jesuit bibliography had been compiled to fill an obvious need. Twenty years later the book-war was at its height. Much of the material is written in a lively style for, though the authors resorted freely to insults and personalities, they had no difficulty in securing official approbations for their work. It was in many ways a robust age.

On the credit side the dispute is cited as evidence that the Church preserved unity of doctrine even at the cost of losing the Chinese empire. Moreover, it showed that the papacy was not dominated by the Jesuits, as their enemies alleged; it also showed that the papacy was not unhesitatingly obeyed by them either, as they boasted. The controversy brought China before the eyes of Europe and led to the 'sinomania' of the 18th century. Apart from this, the quarrel was disastrous for those involved: it dealt a deathblow to the mission by dividing the missionaries, exasperating the authorities, and bewildering the converts. In Europe it scandalized the faithful, armed the Jansenists and delighted the Deists. It also contributed to the suppression of the Jesuit order.

II

None of this could have been foreseen in 1643 when the Dominican Friar Juan Bautista Morales arrived in Rome from Asia to report on the situation. Having failed to get satisfaction from the China Jesuits, he returned to his Manila headquarters and attempted to convene a meeting of the religious orders to discuss the problems of the new mission. The local Jesuits refused to take part so, later, when the friars were accused of denouncing what they did not understand, they reminded the Jesuits of this initial refusal to help or explain. (2)

Everything conspired against a settlement. In Manila, a Jesuit, Bartolomé Roboredo, took it upon himself to answer the friars' doubts by publishing a defence of his China colleagues. He considered this an opportune moment because all Manila was gossiping about the novelties and mysteries of the new Church in China. Why the impetuous Roboredo felt himself equipped to intervene must remain a puzzle, for he had not been in China except for a few months in the Portuguese coastal settlement of Macao. His apologia, published on 26 December, 1638, caused a sensation because he conceded the friars' main point that the rites were superstitious; he talked of Chinese 'idols', 'altars' and 'sacrifices' but justified attendance at Confucian ceremonies by saying that a cross was put upon the altar, to which the convert could discreetly direct his or her devotions.

In a revealing slip he told the friars not to blame their troubles on the Fathers: 'The reason the friars' churches are pulled down and they are whipped, imprisoned or exiled, has nothing to do with Jesuit opposition, nor to the mandarins favouring our Fathers. It is simply due to their not permitting the pagans and converts their acts of idolatry and their political rites. There's no reason to complain of anything else, it's their own fault'.

The effect of this disastrous intervention, at such a critical time, cannot be overestimated, especially since Roboredo claimed that he was basing himself upon material submitted to the Father-General by the Jesuit area manager for Japan and China. To make matters worse, the unhappy Roboredo's admissions reached a wider audience than the Manila friars, for before long the Jesuits' arch-enemies, the Jansenists, were repeating them in Europe. (3)

The local Dominican provincial, Clemente Gan, made a moving plea to the Jesuit superior: 'Do not be surprised if we find it difficult to accept that Catholic converts can attend, even act as ministers, at sacrificial ceremonies which Fr Roboredo admits are idolatrous. We beg your Reverence to investigate the matter — if it be decided that it is legitimate to do all this, then we will suspend our judgement to the contrary and follow your practice, such is our desire for peace and the avoidance of scandal'.[1] (4)

---

[1] Other attempts were made to persuade the Jesuits to explain their method; all failed (NC 318).

Nothing came of this appeal. There was no joint discussion, nor did the Fathers immediately disown Roboredo. The Father superior offered no help, and about Roboredo he was grimly ambiguous: 'He will be called upon to give an account of what he wrote'. For the friars it seemed that the religious fate of Asia was at stake, and they saw no alternative but to appeal to Rome. The modern Jesuit historian Fr Bernard-Maitre, discussing 'this delicate affair', admits that 'one has to recognize that the Manila friars behaved very correctly; after having vainly tried to get answers to their doubts from the local Jesuits, they took the matter to their [Roman] superiors'.

They chose Morales as their agent. He left immediately and reached Rome in February 1643, to be warmly welcomed by the Secretary of Propaganda Fide, Francesco Ingoli, whose dislike of the Jesuits was notorious. Friar Morales' equally morbid fear of them led him to see their influence everywhere, and he even suspected the papal nuncio in Madrid because he had a Jesuit relative. (5)

The pope, then coming to the end of a long reign, was in constant ill health, and the Portuguese astrologer who had promised him another decade was soon to be proved wrong. Urban, now an irritable old man, tormented by remorse for his earlier nepotism, slept so badly that he had the birds in the Vatican gardens killed, to stop their untimely chirruping. Ever protective towards him, the Cardinal-nephew, Francesco Barberini, kept away all bad news, but he agreed to the interview with Morales.

The meeting was dramatic. The friar threw himself at the pope's feet and, not normally the man for half-measures, managed to restrain himself, telling the pope that he had not come to accuse anyone but only to seek guidance concerning certain propositions to do with the mission. The old man had an inkling of what was afoot, and without waiting for more, drew himself up and, weak as he was, struck the arm of his chair twice, crying out, 'Heresy! Heresy! To the Inquisition!'[2] He promptly ordered a commission of enquiry to be set up. (6)

Leaving the commission to its deliberations, Morales went to Spain in search of volunteers for East Asia. He had already recruited some Italians, among them a Florentine relation of Matteo Ricci, Vittorio Riccio, who, according to colourful legend, had changed his surname in repudiation of the methods of his celebrated relative.[3]

In Spain Morales was even more successful, and was soon reporting to Rome that he had gathered 'the cream of the Spanish province' to his cause.

---

[2] He had reacted similarly over the Galileo affair: 'Urban banged his fist on the table and ordered the *ad hoc* Commission to produce a case against that man on the double-quick' (Santillana, 195, 217). Rome was aware of the rites affair and Propaganda Fide had already debated the matter in 1641.

[3] Riccio is the only missionary to figure in contemporary Chinese fiction (Idema, 476–78; J. M. González, *Diplomático*); he also wanted to open a mission in Australia (Kelly, *Austrialia*, 388–91).

This was a triumph for him, since the well-known austerity of life in the Dominicans' Philippine province discouraged volunteers, and there were no postulants in the islands themselves, where the Spanish lay population consisted mainly of soldiers, merchants and civil servants. (7)

Outstanding among the volunteers was Domingo Fernández Navarrete del Rosario, who was to play a significant part in the Rites Controversy, and who 30 years later was also to return to Rome seeking a policy decision. It was his *Tratados de la China* (1676) which first revealed the divisions and quarrels to the general public, and helped to shift the centre of the action, turning it from a local into a universal quarrel.

Domingo was born in 1618, eight years after Matteo Ricci's death, in Castrojeriz, a small town in Burgos province which lies on the pilgrim route to Santiago de Compostela.[4] Any intelligent boy, seeing the endless trail of foreign pilgrims thronging the steep narrow streets of his home town, would have felt curiosity about the wider world, and longed to see things for himself. Certainly, everything in Friar Domingo's subsequent career suggests that happened to him.

There was a Franciscan friary in Castrojeriz and it would have been natural for a pious boy with a vocation to join the local order. Instead he chose deliberately to go elsewhere, to Peñafiel in Valladolid province, to join the Dominicans. One can only speculate as to the motives behind this deliberate choice. He may have found their intellectualism more appealing, or there may have been a family connection. He is said to have been related to the Dominican Friar Alonso de Navarrete, martyred in Japan in 1617, and to the Valladolid theologian Friar Baltasar Navarrete. But his joining the Dominicans was fitting as, apart from his love of nature, he had little of the gentler Franciscan quality. Be that as it may, nothing is known of Domingo's life before his career as a missionary. There are few intimate glimpses of him in his writings, and no personal letters survive. He was an ideal religious in that he shows no interest in family or home, and on his return from his quarter-century of travel it was not to his boyhood home that he went, but to his old mother-house, the priory of Peñafiel.[5] (8)

There he professed as a friar in 1635, completed his studies in Valladolid, where he was ordained in 1639, and almost immediately was elected a Fellow of San Gregorio College.[6] A 'seed-bed of scholars', San Gregorio would now be called a think-tank, and was frequently called upon to advise on current affairs. It had a name resonant in Spanish history, for it produced most of the great Golden Age Dominicans, Cano, Carranza, Granada, Vitoria, and,

---

[4] It consisted of 654 households, a friary of 20 Franciscans and a nunnery of 30 Franciscan Poor Clares (*Censo de Castilla: 1591: Vecindarios* (Madrid, 1984), 100, 163).

[5] 'Missionaries must be "homeless" for the sake of a metaphysical-moral vision held to be universally true' (Eliade, IX: 567).

[6] He was also connected with San Esteban College in Salamanca (NC 86).

above all, Bishop Bartolomé de Las Casas, the 'Protector of the American Indians'. Las Casas's old cell was a primitive archive of the Americas, for he had bequeathed his vast collection of papers to the College, directing that the younger friars (men such as Navarrete, in his time) put them in order, so that if God punished Spain for her sins in America there should at least be evidence to show why.

Friar Domingo made swift progress, first as a lecturer in humanities and, despite his youth, a College Councillor. But, suddenly, hearing of Morales' recruiting campaign, he decided to volunteer for the Philippines. He was then 28, so his was a late vocation, yet he gives no explanation for it beyond a few hackneyed phrases: 'On hearing of the austerity of life there, I decided to leave parents, friends, homeland, and to go'. (On the other hand, Thomas Gage alleged that *his* recruiting master had been Bacchus, for he had been recruited with copious drafts of sherry.) In Navarrete's case it is more likely that his tremendous latent drive was seeking a new field of action. A sense of duty, urge for experience, indifference to comfort, and that Spanish energy as rare as it is excessive, all combined in Navarrete, who could not be satisfied with an academic life. In this, however, he was following a long tradition, for as the Jesuit chronicler Murillo Velarde was later to remark, 'There are Masters of Theology and famous preachers working in those little native villages'. (9)

These same qualities made him the ablest of the Dominicans in 17th-century China, where he became superior of his order. The moment he reached China he fell in love with it, finding lessons there for the edification of Europe, becoming the only important Spanish contributor to the sinomania of the Enlightenment. His *Tratados* reveals a typical Castilian, grave to the point of over-earnestness, with a slightly malicious but clumsy sense of humour. To his theology, he brought a lawyer's sharp pedantic mind, and he could be stubborn over matters of small importance. To the end he remained oddly innocent, never losing his naivety, for all his travels and experiences.

But his mind was never a closed one: he was saved by his curiosity. That quality, which kept him spry until the end, distinguishes him from many of his fellows, who concentrated on the apostolic side of their vocations, and noticed little in the countries they worked in. No such complaint could be levelled against Friar Domingo. Indeed one Jesuit critic later accused him of being too interested in worldly affairs and of not being sufficiently apostolic: 'If he has not converted many Chinese, he has eaten a lot of fruit'. This complaint, about Navarrete's many botanical notes, was Spanish rather than Jesuitical. An sharp observer, Domingo comments on everything from tailors' needles to the Great Wall, from manuring methods to women's shoes, from ginseng to flash-lock gates. Some of his comparisons between Europe and China are critical of Catholicism, and of social conditions in Spain. His insistence that, religion apart, Spain was inferior to China, made unpalatable reading for some, and later got him and his works hauled before the Inquisition.

The sixth and most entertaining chapter of his *Tratados* recounts his adventures from 1646 until his return home in 1673. Although he wrote with a purpose he was anxious not to bore the general reader, and so included incidents reminiscent of a picaresque novel. Curiosity is revealed in his opening pages, for on the second day of their journey south to the embarkation port, he and his group reached Salamanca, then in the middle of one of its frequent student riots. A student was killed and Friar Domingo insisted on seeing the body. Recalling the incident thirty years later, he drew a parallel between Spain and China, and generalizing wildly declared that in all its two thousand years of history and three million students, no such behaviour was ever known in China. In similar vein, reporting atrocities committed by Spanish soldiery he reflected that the Chinese were in all ways better disciplined than the Spanish, the most uncivilized people in the world. 'Barbarians are never where one expects them'. (10)

On 12 June 1646, Morales' party of 27 Dominicans set sail for Mexico, the first stopover on their journey. The Atlantic voyage, six to eight weeks long, was trying. Boredom was a problem: loneliness was not. Quarters were cramped, water rationed, food poor, and nerves kept on edge by such unaccustomed noises as the cracking of the canvas, the wheezing and groaning of the timbers, and by fear of storms and pirates.[7] On board ship the Friar-Commissary, manager and courier of the fledgling missionaries, had his hands full: idleness and the many inconveniences could lead to melancholy, restlessness and short tempers, which could end in violence. Sometimes a ship might be devastated by an outbreak of *rabies theologorum*. One Augustinian overhearing a Franciscan claim that his was the older order, retorted, 'to the scandal of all and honour of none', that St Francis was a bastard. High words were followed by blows, and the Commissary without hesitation clapped the offenders in irons, trusting that his 'show of teeth' would undo the bad example given to sailors and passengers alike. In the interests of discipline, therefore, the prudent Commissary kept his friars as occupied as possible. Weather permitting, the day began with mass, followed by spiritual conferences, sermons, or study. A great part of the time was spent reciting the liturgy until, at sunset, after the Angelus, 'a sailor went out at the hatch and having rang a little bell in the saddest and most doleful voice that ever I heard, cried out, "Death is certain, the hour uncertain, the Judge severe. Woe unto thee who art slothful; do now what thou couldst wish thou hadst done when thou diest." And all the crew repenting for their sins went to rest without the least noise'.

One experienced Commissary wrote a guidebook in which he stressed that

---

[7] The fears were justified: 376 Jesuits left for China in the 17th century; only 127 arrived (*Synopsis Hist. SJ*, 295; Chappoulie, I: 59).

some friars, 'babes with beards', had to be stripped of romantic illusions, and to be faced with the reality of their new lives. The voyage was the right time to begin preparing them for their future. (11)

For this Morales was well-equipped, for he had a fund of anecdotes and lore with which to hold the attention of his bearded babes. It was rare to meet anyone who had been inside the fabulous Chinese empire, about which strange stories had been told from the first, so that Marco Polo had earned himself the nickname of *Il milione* and Spanish travellers had given the language a catch-phrase, *cuento chino*, meaning anything unbelievable. (12)

Before leaving Spain, Morales had been relieved to receive a decree from Rome intended to clarify mission policy and condemning Catholic toleration of the Confucian ceremonies. On 31 May 1645, while still in Seville, he had written a long and revealing letter about his experiences in the Asian missions. He recounted how Fr Giulio Aleni was questioned by the writer Huang Chen about the eternal fate of those ancestors who had practised polygamy. Morales accused Aleni of side-stepping difficult problems to please the Chinese.[8] He alleged that Jesuits permitted their converts to make 'sacrifices' in pagan temples, providing they held a cross in their hands to which they were 'directing their intentions', rather than to the image apparently being venerated. In Morales' opinion, the Fathers in trying to avoid one sin were authorizing two: one exterior sin of idolatry, and another interior one of hypocrisy, fiction and lying. He also included the story of how Fr Lobo's superior had ordered him to keep the cross in his church always covered, 'for the heathen detest it'.

Morales had, of course, been scandalized by stories of a Fr Cypriano, who in the 1630s and 1640s, had travelled widely in the east, leaving a trail of bizarre complaints in numerous archives. In 1638 he had delivered a three-hour-long sermon in Macao in which he demanded transport to Japan to reactivate the mission and to convert the emperor. Failing help from the faithful, he threatened to go there anyway, airborne on his own cloak. The proposals of this pioneer airman alarmed the merchants who found trade with Japan difficult enough already and saw little profit in exporting martyrs there. Obviously deranged, Cypriano nevertheless had a following who thought him a saint, especially since he claimed to have died earlier and been resurrected. He stopped people from cutting bits off his habit as pious souvenirs, by himself handing out remnants of clothing as relics, while his Chinese barber, with characteristic resourcefulness, sold his hair clippings to devotees.[9]

---

[8] D. Lancashire in *Church History*, XXXVIII(1969), 231–2, shows that Aleni failed to satisfy his questioner.

[9] Morales does not mention a Franciscan ('the miracle-monger') who in 1614 attempted to walk on water in the hope of making converts; fortunately he was rescued (Farrington, II: 264; Boxer, *Christian Century*, 236).

Next, Morales related his own experiences at Jesuit hands and how they had tried to get him driven out of China. This section of the letter becomes a catalogue of their hostile manoeuvres against would-be friar collaborators. Before concluding, Morales reveals that some Jesuits dissented from the majority view, and tells an improbable story about a Fr Rodrigo de Figueiredo ('Jesuit in dress, though not in opinions') who sent three young Chinese for seminary training in Manila, but wanted them educated by friars, not by his own fellow Jesuits.

Morales' letter, which concludes with the story of his reception two years previously by Urban VIII, is signed, certified as true, and dated Seville, 31 May 1645. Obviously written by Morales as he waited for transport back to the mission, the revealing letter shows the anecdotes this veteran retailed in Rome, and to his impressionable young volunteers. This is the atmosphere in which Navarrete and his companions were trained; these are the stories which survived from one generation to another, spread abroad, reached non-Catholic ears, found permanence in print, and were brought forward later in the 18th-century campaign for the suppression of the Society. The stories are not necessarily untrue, but were told, and accepted, without qualification or attempt at understanding. For example, the Aleni story does not reveal the Jesuit's deep concern over the embarrassing problem, to which he had given much hard thought. The possibility that Fr Cypriano might quite simply have been mad is not considered. And in the account of Jesuits who had apostatized in Japan under torture, there is no sign of compassion for a fellow missionary's personal tragedy.

Yet the Fathers themselves were largely to blame. The fatal pride, the over-estimation of their ability to survive all criticism, the refusal to explain themselves, and their resort to higher authority as a solution to their troubles, alienated those who could and would have been their allies. In the end such stories helped to create the popular picture of Jesuit craftiness, moral opportunism and double-dealing.[10]

Morales' experiences were not the cause of his prejudice; they confirmed it, for he had inherited from an earlier generation of friars suspicions that Jesuit Asia was a world in which probabilism, even moral laxism, ran wild and unrestricted, in the interests of clerical power politics. A mission with one or two oddities might be tolerable, but one with so many grave violations of doctrine, practice and propriety, where the very missionaries seemed, in Paul's phrase, to be adulterating the word of the Lord; where the cross was hidden, and where universal liturgical rites and rules were altered to suit local tastes, while friars were kidnapped and deported in order to preserve a dubious monopoly — all this was, quite simply, frightening.

---

[10] Morales would have been horrified to find his letter included in one of the many anthologies of anti-Jesuit writings published in the later 18th-century to prepare the public for the coming suppression: Anon., *El Retrato de los Jesuitas* (Madrid, 1768), 220–48.

In the nature of things, what had started badly must end worse: the possibility that heterodoxy and schism were being planted in a virgin field contributed to the friars' anguish and frustration, making impartial judgement unlikely. And there were many others who felt the same as Morales.

Navarrete admired Morales, and now, on board ship, he and the young friars with him must have been influenced by his lessons and experiences. Long before he reached China, Domingo saw and heard much to confirm those opinions with which he had been brought up. His Dominican training, and the climate in which he had lived, biased him. Valladolid, where he had studied and taught, was one of the principal battlegrounds between the two orders, whether in the mundane rivalry for vocations, or in the more subtle disputes over the mechanics of divine grace. Further, the friars of Valladolid had a distinguished missionary record, and Domingo had already heard of their trials in China and the Philippines, had seen and venerated the relics of the Japanese martyrs, had listened to the letters of former community members, now on the missions, being read aloud during meals in the conventual refectory. In Valladolid his namesake, the theologian Baltasar Navarrete, had earlier taught a spiritualized sinomania, urging his students to look to the east where the cooling ardour of Catholic Europe was being offset. (13)

Nevertheless, the entire voyage was not spent in prayers, lessons, or gossip, and the friars were allowed time for reading history as a relaxation. They were given plenty of fruit with which 'they entertain themselves like children'. The secular passengers whiled away the tedious journey by putting on plays. Earlier, Thomas Gage had seen one of Lope de Vega's comedies done 'as well as in the best theatres of Madrid'. Cockfights, shark-baiting and other sports beguiled the days, and on St John's Eve Navarrete was amused by a ship-board 'bull-fight' in which the horse consisted of two apprentices tied together with a saddle between them, and the bull was only two-legged.

Finally, on 13 August 1646, after a voyage of two months, the party reached Mexico, and stopped at Puebla de los Angeles, where 20 years earlier puritanical Tom Gage had been scandalized to see fellow friars teaching the Indians to dance and to play the castanets. Navarrete's stay there was to be of momentous significance for him, since it coincided with the opening rounds of the notorious 'Palafox affair'.

The religious orders, as self-governing bodies, claimed exemption from episcopal scrutiny, but the local bishop, Juan de Palafox, in common with many prelates, resented this independence within his diocese. He had already been denounced to Rome by the Franciscans, whose privileges he regarded as an encroachment on his authority. That particular trouble was soon settled. But the Jesuits, with whom he next clashed, inevitably proved tougher. The quarrel rumbled on for some time, becoming serious in March 1647, a few months after Navarrete's arrival, when the Jesuits refused to show the bishop their permits to preach and confess in his diocese. Resentment quickly warmed and was followed by excommunications and interdicts.[11] Tension mounted and the city seethed with rumours. The climax came on 31 July, feast-day of St Ignatius, when Jesuit students rode in a procession that became notorious even in Europe, for they poked fun at the bishop (who had a wen) and as they rode through the streets they chanted 'Deliver us, oh Lord, from Palafox'. (14)

The dispute became the most bitter and scandalous yet in the rich history of the New World Church. Anti-Jesuit groups inevitably found it an abundant source of ammunition. A century later echoes of the quarrel were still to be heard when Palafox was used as a symbol by both the Jesuits and their enemies. Defending the bishop's memory became equivalent to attacking the Society, and a proposal to beatify him was exploited by the Fathers' enemies, who seized the opportunity to deliver an indirect blow at the Society. The Jesuits naturally contested this project, so that few *beati* can have had so many zealous Devil's Advocates; Palafox's shade had a halo alternately thrust at it or plucked away, according to the allegiance of the faction predominating for the moment. In the end the bishop did not reach beatification and is still a mere 'Venerable'.[12] But cynics derived some harmless amusement from the sight of free-thinkers besieging the Holy See for a canonization.

'The affair' had a marked effect on Friar Domingo, who saw in it evidence that the Jesuits put the Society's reputation before the spiritual welfare of the colony, that if necessary they were prepared to resort to violence to gain their ends, and were willing to discredit their opponents to save the labour of refuting them.

Bishop Palafox and Friar Domingo had much in common. Both were interested in educational problems and Domingo later persuaded Manila University to adopt the statutes drawn up by the bishop for Mexico. Both had firm ideas about just treatment for the Indians. Both were deeply disturbed by the decline of Spain, and coincided in their analysis of its causes. Palafox was also fascinated by China, and felt some responsibility for the missions there in his capacity as one of the nearest bishops to the empire, a claim which would have been noisily contested had it been more widely

---

[11] An interdict (*cessatio a divinis*), ecclesiastical strike, inevitably caused distress, even terror, among the more pious.

[12] After the Jesuits' suppression their enemies lost interest in the cause, and individual secular priests have less hope of canonization than religious, whose order, from collective self-interest, can press a case for generations, sometimes too zealously. Benedict XIV, for example, suffered much from Jesuit determination to have Aloysius Gonzaga canonized (*Corr.* ed. Heeckeren, I: 386). Palafox's cause is not officially closed but is now too delicate to reactivate; in 1950 a Jesuit declared that his beatification would be 'the glorification of Jansenism' (Poulain, 233). The volcano is only dormant: R. Olaechea, SJ, *Montalbán*, V (1976), 1053–1130; Arteaga, 592–616; Luis Martín [SJ general], *Memorias*, I (Rome, 1988), 488.

advertised. He kept himself informed of events in China by means of half-yearly reports, and so was able to show the friars a treatise written by Fr Diego Morales, Jesuit Rector in Manila. Though he had never been to China, Fr Morales, like Roboredo earlier, justified the policy of his brethren there, and in fact defended what the pope had just condemned. The friars carefully studied this report to see what objections to expect when they showed their new decree to the Jesuits. (15)

When Palafox saw the decree, he pointed out what their innocence of bureaucratic ways had not seen: since it had not been approved by the India Office in Madrid, it could be rejected on a technicality. On the friars' behalf he now addressed a long report to Philip IV of Spain, calling upon his Catholic Majesty to intervene in a struggle which was daily growing worse; it was the king's duty to know of the controversy, for the Faith was his royal heritage and many of the missionaries were his subjects. Further, if the truth were not taught properly it would be a stain upon the monarchy, for the heretics of Europe could accuse the Church of spreading error and Spain of permitting it. Such arguments were calculated to impress a Spanish king. (16)

III

The friars' hopes of sailing to the Philippines in the spring of 1647 were thwarted, for there was no Pacific galleon that year. Obliged to remain in Mexico, they did their best to spend the time usefully. Friar Domingo found the New World fascinating, and he enthused over the beauty of the scenery. Ordered ahead to Acapulco to buy supplies for the journey, he rented a house in which they awaited the arrival of transport.[13] In the meantime he studied Palafox's anthology of literature on the rites controversy, and there, in Mexico, he met his first Chinese.[14]

In the following spring, 1648, they boarded the *Buen Jesús* bound for Manila; not, however, without some drama, for in a fire which devastated Acapulco Navarrete lost the 300 hens he had bought for the group's Pacific crossing. On the other hand the voyage itself was relatively uneventful, except when two white-faced sailors ran up on deck to tell how, searching for drinking water, they had bent into a open barrel of gunpowder with a lighted candle which, fortunately for all, went out at that moment.

If the journey was quiet, their landing was not, for as soon as they arrived there was trouble from the Manila Jesuits on two scores. Ever since he had set out, Friar Morales had been darkly forecasting that the Jesuits would refuse to recognize his new decree. Along the route he had despatched pessimistic letters back to Rome, saying that since the Jesuits always found a loophole to get out of everything that did not suit them, they would be sure to do so again; the disobedience of these 'disturbers of the Church' was inevitable; one could only hope that the Holy Father would know how to deal with their resistance. The Jesuits ran on wheels when their interest called, but had lead in their heels when there was nothing in it for them. In one letter Morales made clear his feelings about the Society, praying that God would give patience and strength to the Dominican order which alone seemed to be left to sustain the perpetual struggle with the Jesuits: 'While these blessed Fathers exist there cannot be peace in the Church, and if I had the power they would already be finished'. (17)

Once in Manila, he published the decree condemning the Chinese rites. In Rome, they knew something about the Jesuits' skill in finding *escapatorias*, so the document had been carefully addressed to them, specifically and by their name: 'to each and everyone of the missionaries of whatsoever order, including even the Society of Jesus'. That phrase (*etiam Societatis Jesu*) was invented by the Roman curia in an attempt to prevent the Fathers from finding ways around decrees not to their liking, and though some dismiss the

---

[13] For the special problems encountered in Acapulco: BR, XIV:102. That he was entrusted with this task suggests he was already regarded as a 'senior' man in the group.

[14] About 300 Asians (Chinese, Japanese, Filipinos) were smuggled into Mexico annually (Israel, 75).

phrase as an empty cliché, it is noteworthy that no other order requires its usage. (18)

Yet, given their conviction that the 'idiot friars' were denouncing what they did not understand, the Jesuits could only see in the decree the ruin of their mission. They were therefore relieved to find a way of postponing the papal ruling, thereby giving Morales the melancholy satisfaction of being right in his forecast. The resistance he had foreseen found its justification in an apparently innocent phrase at the end of the text: 'until the Apostolic See ordains otherwise'.[15] The Jesuits seized on this rider, holding it to mean that the decree was not definitive and could be revoked if further and better evidence were submitted in favour of the rites. Declaring that the friars had misled the Holy See, they promptly arranged to despatch yet another spokesman, Fr Martino Martini, to put their case to Rome once more.

In vain the Dominicans explained how the clause came to be there: by the time the working party had finished its task and prepared the document, Urban VIII was dead and Innocent X had succeeded him. The new pope was asked to sign, but, characteristically, he dithered, demurred, and fretted that it was 'perhaps a bit too strong'.[16] The attendant cardinals urged him to pass it as it stood; the affair, they said, had already dragged on too long. Finally he yielded, ordering only the insertion of the clause on which the Jesuits now fixed their hopes.

What the pope had in mind cannot be surmised, but he must have been in general agreement with the terms of the decree and this is borne out by his confirming it in 1652, as also by the curia's sending copies of it to the generals of the three orders involved. There is further evidence that the curia had no doubts about the validity of the decree, for they ordered that the China Jesuits be monitored to see if they were obeying it. (19)

Rome was not often hurried. Its slowness, deliberate, even professional, usually worked in its favour. Here, however, was a rare instance of impatience which had given the Jesuits their loophole, and they now declared they would continue their old mission strategy until their representative (Fr Martini) returned from Rome. For them, the controversy was far from decided.

Resentment was not confined to the Jesuits' side. The newly arrived friars were incensed to learn (through a letter from Palafox) of the loss of Formosa to the Dutch. This was a severe blow to the Manila-based friars, who used

---

[15] The phrase was not uncommon, i.e. Gregory XIII, recognizing Elizabeth I as rightful sovereign of England, thoughtfully added 'until the Holy See decides otherwise'.

[16] Innocent 'stands out as a negative quantity. Depressed, nervous, well-intentioned, he was not a bad man. His fame rests on nothing he did, but on the fact that Velázquez painted him. He played bowls, set his hand to papal bulls and went through the religious duties of the Holy Father but his life was swamped by an ambitious sister-in-law', who was said to govern the Church (Wedgwood, 411). 'In the City she acted a man in woman's apparel, and in the Church a woman wearing the breeches', said Gregorio Leti.

the island (only a day's passage from the Chinese mainland province of Fukien) as a spring-board, and to bypass the obstacles placed in their way by the Jesuit-Portuguese coalition in Macao. Naturally the Jesuits regarded Formosa as a threat to their China monopoly, and the friars were consequently convinced that they had manoeuvred the loss of the island. Gossip had it that when the Dutch had moved against the island in 1641, Governor Corcuera's Jesuit confessor had persuaded him to abandon the place, on the grounds that it was of no strategic importance. True or not, many believed the story. So the loss of Formosa was seen as a double blow to the friars: it deprived them of their backdoor into China, and it was a national humiliation for Spain, brought about, they believed, by the machinations of the cosmopolitan Society of Jesus which, as usual, preferred the Portuguese *padroado* to the Spanish *patronato*.

In order to be useful, the newcomers needed to learn the local dialects, and Friar Domingo concentrated on Tagalog, the language of the Manila district, claiming he made swift progress: 'If grammar and other arts were followed with such application in Europe, as we out there learn languages, men would soon be learned. At the end of five months we all heard confessions and preached, and at the year's end did both with ease, and conversed with the Indians about their everyday affairs'. The Philippine Dominicans were also known for their Chinese language studies, and Friar Domingo now started to minister to some of the many thousands of Chinese living in the islands.[17] But if he had hoped to be sent to China he was now disappointed, for on completion of their training the friars were allocated to their stations, and in the postings, which were purely arbitrary, Navarrete was ordered to continue working in Manila among the native Filipinos. For the moment there was nothing to suggest that he was later to play so decisive a role in the China affair.

Morales and three others were ordered to cross over to the China mainland from where they sent news at once exciting and infuriating.[18] The good news was that a Dominican, Friar Francisco de Capillas, had been martyred. The friars were encouraged by this, the first martyrdom in the mission, for 'the blood of martyrs, being the seed of the Church' would stimulate conversions. Friar Vittorio Riccio hastily wrote off to Rome pleading for volunteers from among the many Dominicans in Italy, adding a laboured pun that he must have heard from some Spaniard, 'God wants chapels (*capillas*) in China, for the first martyr there was a Chapel (*Capillas*)'. (20)

---

[17] The American Dominicans, for instance, were denounced for devoting too much time to linguistic studies rather than to theology, and for burying learned men among ignorant villagers (Brading, 308–9).

[18] The Fukien–Philippines voyage was made in February or November; the reverse journey in May or September. For the Manila–Canton crossing: Visschers, 16–32.

The bad news concerned the Jesuits, and it came in despatches that made unusual reading. One of the first Jesuits encountered by Morales and his group on the mainland was a Pietro Canevari, to whom they offered help because he had recently been robbed of everything and was unable to continue his work. At first all seemed well. But when they showed him the Roman decree denouncing the rites, he turned hostile, accusing them of misleading the pope. He now opposed them in everything, forbidding his converts to have any dealings with them, and putting up posters announcing that he alone was entitled to be there as Catholic priest. He denounced the friars to the local judge, claiming they had falsely accused him of living with a woman. The judge refused to believe the story, whereupon the Jesuit counter-charged that the friars themselves had dealings with women. This too was thrown out of court. But he was undaunted. His next move came on 8 September (it was Our Lady's Birthday). As the friars were singing high mass they were picketed by Canevari's negro servant, who interrupted them, reciting a claim that the only legitimate parish priest there was his master, the Jesuit, that the friars had no right to hold services, that hitherto it had been unheard of that missionaries should interfere with the work of those already established. The friars' report of this incident concluded by admitting that 'the Jesuit Fathers are mighty in all the world and it is certain that they can have us banished from this kingdom if they wish, and our staying here depends entirely on their goodwill'. (21)

In fairness, Canevari thought the friars were trying to displace the Fathers throughout China; and, as a loyal Jesuit, he regarded the mendicants' decree from Rome as 'a slap in the face of our Society'. Further, he was apparently mentally disturbed.[19] Again, the converts were fond of tale-bearing and often created bad blood between the missionaries. But whatever the mitigating circumstances, the friars only saw their suspicions confirmed. A year later they reported that the local Chinese, out of fear of the Jesuits' influence in Peking, were afraid to let the friars settle even in places where there was no priest at all. Other despatches told how the Fathers treated friars as though they were members of a different religion. In Manila these reports caused anger but not surprise, for they were neither new nor unexpected.

Friar Domingo concentrated on his work among the Filipinos, and the task was congenial, for he shared the common Dominican view that the natives were to be protected by the missionaries. This zeal for their welfare is a pleasing aspect of his character, which was strong rather than gentle. His

---

[19] Sin Fran II: 380. 'Insanity among Religious was the fashionable [sic] disease' (BR, I: 78, XLIV: 85, LV: 115). Loneliness afflicted men used to community life, and fear of accidents, illness, death without the sacraments, all caused anxiety. Others, amid the exotic temptations of Asia, had to sweat for their chastity (BR, XXVIII: 244, 294–5). Language-learning too was a heavy challenge for some (coded account of Fr Trigault's suicide in ARSI, JapSin 161, II, fols. 116–7); for Fr Murillo's suicide: Gregorio Arnáiz in AOPM, Docs. *sin clas.*, and Ocio, I: 477.

passion for justice had been aroused by his early readings of Las Casas; in Mexico he heard much in favour of the Indians from Palafox, and in the Philippines he found a firmly established tradition to follow, for there the friars had another Las Casas to imitate, Bishop Domingo de Salazar. The early Dominicans in the Islands went to great lengths to protect the natives, once even keeping secret the whereabouts of a mine known to them, rather than be the indirect cause of more native exploitation. Friar Domingo could always find an excuse for the natives, who in religious matters were the innocent victims of their own ignorance. They were easier to convert than the Chinese, any one of whom gave a missionary more trouble than two Indians. Patience was the basic requirement for dealing with the latter, and one friar, questioned by the pope, explained the difficulties of converting them by giving an example: while his holiness had been addressing a short homily to him during an audience, the friar had managed to look most attentive, although in fact he confessed that he had been concentrating only on counting the 33 buttons on the pope's cassock, 'without paying the slightest attention to a word your holiness has said to me. And that, Holy Father, is what the Indian is like'. (22)

On the other hand they were intelligent, and when their interest was aroused they asked acute questions and had a disconcerting way of interrupting sermons to demand more precise information on some point. Their piety was exemplary: 'I often remarked how the fervour of old Castile has passed to the Filipino men and women'. Praise of the natives had a natural concomitant: criticism of their Spanish overlords. 'On occasions I set myself up as an advocate for the Indians of the Philippines as others have done for those of America. There is no other fault to be found in those poor creatures, except that which was found in the Holy Innocents, whose only crime was to have been born'.

In particular Navarrete denounced the heavy taxes imposed upon the natives, to escape which many fled: not a ship left Manila without refugees on board, and Filipinos were to be met with all over Indonesia. Yet the colonists constantly bewailed the decline of the native population, although the remedy was obvious. Navarrete's interest in this problem was also spiritual. When he saw Filipinos driven to seek asylum among the heretic Dutch, he denounced their Catholic masters whose harshness was responsible for a great loss of souls, and he scornfully rejected the boasts of those layfolk who claimed they had gone to the Indies to cooperate in the salvation of the natives. For these unwelcome strictures he was himself denounced. Unrepentant, he used the occasion to repeat his charges. (23)

He spent nine years in the Philippines, both in Manila and in up-country stations. In addition he served as a humanities lecturer in the Dominican University of Santo Tomás in Manila. But the climate, especially the humidity, was exhausting: 'a man can hardly keep on his feet, for the body is perpetually feeble, drooping, spiritless, without will or energy'. And the friars' severe regime, which allowed no dispensation, soon undermined the strength of those who were naturally restless. He also suffered from the common complaint of anaemia and the dysentery which killed many. A steady decline in his health set in, and since the doctors seemed helpless it was decided to post him back to Europe. (24)

Some forty years later the Dominicans decreed that incurably sick friars must not be released from their obligations to the mission: they must remain and suffer patiently as a form of apostolate and as an example to others. Those seeking a dispensation to leave the Islands on health grounds never came to any good: far too often they ended up with secular folk in Mexico: out of the frying-pan into the spiritual fire. Had the China Jesuits known of that circular, they must have wished that Navarrete had suffered that agreeable if unedifying fate and had left them undisturbed in the Middle Kingdom. But that was not to be. (25)

In preparation for his departure he gathered up his notes, by then plentiful, ranging from the habits of crocodiles to the mischievousness of a poltergeist. He claimed he was the first to bring fresh lichee ('a fruit for which to thank the Creator') into Manila, having found the plant in the Bataan mountains. He noted the abundance of wines and spirits in the Islands ('and no lack of those to drink them either'), and made pertinent remarks on the fortifications. Later, in India, he met a German engineer working for the Portuguese, and urged him to leave for Manila where he promised he would be well paid. Twenty years later still, when the coinage problem in Manila was still nagging him, he recommended that copper coins, such as those used in America, would be a solution. (26)

The governor offered him a place in a ship going to Mexico; but the return journey across the Pacific was known to be more severe than the outward voyage, and Navarrete, health worse and morale low, refused the offer. Never afraid to be afraid, he admitted that fear prevented him from embarking. Instead he opted to join a ship bound for India, hoping to reach Europe that way. He set off on 14 February 1657, taking books, papers, 'sixty pieces-of-eight, four tunics and two habits. I left my cloak with a friend, but afterwards missed it'.

The journey was not easy. According to him, the first lap, the 40 days' journey to Macassar, took nine months, owing to the appalling weather. This is so improbable that it must be a mistake, but certainly their food and water ran out; a treacherous wind carried away the mainsail; the tiller broke; nerves were on edge; the captain fought with the crew over the best route and, in accordance with Spanish standing orders, turned to Navarrete, as a priest, for advice.

Eventually they reached Tontoli where they bought maize. In the Philippines sago was despised, and the natives who had to live on it were pitied, but now hunger made it a 'great daintiness'. Navarrete was reduced to begging, even from those who had nothing to give, once from a kindly negro cook who told him the fish were counted but offered him a drink of the cooking water.

Hunger, though it drove him to pilfer food, and to fantasize that he could eat mice or soap-cakes, did not interfere with the work of taking notes on Indonesian temperatures, dress and manners. Self-respecting 17th-century traveller that he was, he saw the statutory hermaphrodite and a boy with 24 fingers and toes. Everywhere there were Filipinos to care for. In Borneo alone there were over 4 000 refugees. Destitute as he was, he begged enough to ransom two slaves, but the first turned out badly and the second died immediately. Yet his only regret was that he could not do more: 'I'd give the habit off my back to free an Indian'.

They reached Macassar in October 1657 where life was more comfortable, for the local prince took a liking to them, promoting Navarrete to temporary membership of his council, consulting him frequently, sometimes inopportunely, when an ambassador arrived from Djakarta. There was no way of continuing the journey until May 1658, when a ship arrived from Goa, carrying Jesuits to China. Navarrete, who had now become convinced that he could never reach Europe, decided to join them and, if possible, to go to China, 'there to end my life with my brethren'. On 13 May they set sail for Macao. The journey was quiet, except once when they were chased by enemy ships and Friar Domingo had prayed 'not that the sun might stop, as it did for Gideon, but that it might set more quickly'. On arrival in Macao, he went straight to the Dominican priory, arriving in time to join his Portuguese brethren in the chanting of the night office of Our Lady's Saturday. (27)

This meeting with the Jesuits in Macassar, mentioned so casually, was one of several momentous coincidences in his life, for among the party was none other than Fr Martino Martini, returning from Rome with yet another decree relating to the Rites Controversy.[20]

As we have seen, Martini had been sent there as a result of the Fathers' reaction to the decree of 1645 brought east by Navarrete's group. On arrival in Rome in September 1655, Martini had submitted a memorandum to Propaganda Fide, but the pope had referred it to the Inquisition. Fr Martini's report to Rome differed from that of the friars. He carefully distinguished between the rites as practised by the elite and by the commoners. He limited himself to asking if the ceremonies as understood by the educated (civic acts devoid of superstition), might be permitted to Christians. After five months' consideration the Holy Office answered his queries by declaring, not surprisingly, that the ceremonies, as described by him (*prout exposita*), were licit. And they issued a decree to that effect.

The situation now was that within the space of 11 years Rome had issued

---

[20] In the party was the still more famous Fr Verbiest, together with Frs Intorcetta and Gabiani.

two apparently contradictory decrees on the same subject, for the decree given to Martini permitted what was prohibited in the decree given to Morales. In reality, the contradiction lay not in the answers but in the questions submitted, for each party had described the situation as he saw it. The Holy Office's replies were also declared to be conditional upon the truth of the descriptions submitted (*si vera sint exposita*).

Yet it is difficult to see why Rome failed to comment on the obvious disparity in the two reports submitted, or to call for more information before giving a ruling. The problem was not to decide if Christians might take part in civic acts; not even the sternest Dominican rigorist disputed that. The problem was to decide if the rites were, in fact, civic or religious. If the Holy Office felt unable to answer this question it would have been wiser to say so, but amid the press of work of more local concern, and therefore apparently more important, this distracted combination of civil servants and theologians may well have felt the need to protect itself by stolidly doing no more than give straight-faced answers to apparently straight questions.[21]

This latest decree threw the China mission into turmoil, since both sides now had a ruling to back their opposing viewpoints. The Jesuits added to the confusion by announcing that they had a decree justifying their policy, and by characteristically refusing to show it to anyone. Consequently, for some time many friars did not know what was allowed and what was forbidden. The Jesuits defended their stance: they were content to *have* the favourable decree; they did not intend to *show* it since they did 'not wish to behave like victors in a contest'. A noble resolution which, however, was not kept, for 'in time their caution abated, and their shield was converted into a sword and this indiscretion renewed the war'. The 1656 decree was the only one throughout the controversy that seemed to favour the Society's China policy. Temporarily it put them in a strong position, but it was a deceptive strength. Alexander VII signed Martini's decree on Thursday 23 March 1656. On the Monday of that same week Pascal had dated his 'terrible' *Fifth Provincial Letter*. The battle was moving to undreamed-of fields, or, in the words of Fr Brou: 'c'est la grande guerre'. (28)

---

[21] The decree coincided with Propaganda's famous Magna Charta for all missions, which, following Augustine, Aquinas and decrees of the Spanish India Office, ruled that 'harmless local customs be left untouched', etc. The best version is in Metzler, III/2, 702; see Cummins, 'Two methods', 87, and NC 427.

IV

Martini and Navarrete did not travel together to Macao in the same ship. Friar Domingo sailed on 13 June, the Jesuit four days later. It was just as well, for Martini was a fiery man with a straightforward conviction that all would be well in China if the friars were deported. (29)

It became a Spanish friar to be circumspect in Portuguese territory, so in Macao Domingo trod delicately, taking to himself a Chinese proverb: 'In your neighbour's melon-patch do not stoop to tie your lace, nor loiter in his apple-orchard to arrange your hat'. Nevertheless, through the local ecclesiastical governor, he made one more attempt to get Martini to show his decree. But the Jesuit replied firmly that he had nothing to reveal or publish. There the matter stayed though it did not rest, because Domingo somehow managed to get hold of a leaked copy and that same day sent it across to Manila where the Dominicans (like the Jesuits when they first saw Morales's decree in 1648) refused to admit its validity, declaring that Martini's whole position took for granted what was not yet proved, namely, that the rites were merely social acts.

At this stage, Navarrete had no personal experience of the mission and there is reason to believe that his initial reaction to the new decree was to accept it as Rome's final decision, to which he was ready to bow: *causa finita est*. The copy despatched to Manila may have been sent in the belief that all was now settled and that it was possible to work with the Jesuits, and this may have influenced his decision to go to China and 'end my days there'. Later, as he points out, his studies of Chinese religious thought, and more detailed analysis of Martini's submissions, persuaded him that he had been mistaken. He never again wavered in his belief that Martini had misled the Holy See.

In the meantime, however, he contented himself with hearing confessions, and preaching with such success that 'even Jesuits came to hear my sermons'. At the same time he was making plans to enter China, and here he had his first experience of the Jesuits' apartheid policy. The only way to find out about conditions in the interior was by asking the Jesuits, who alone in Macao knew anything definite about the whereabouts of the missionaries. When approached, the Fathers were affable, even giving him a map, which however turned out to be no use, since it only depicted the provinces from 'Macao to Tartary, as though a man wishing to go from Madrid to Germany were told "go first to Catalonia, then make your way to Flanders" and so on'.

At this point he received a visit from a Jesuit on business from Canton, who promised to take him back with him when he returned to his parish. Domingo, ever gullible, waited some days for a call from the Father, then went to enquire for him, only to be told that he had already left. The forgetful cicerone (not named by Navarrete) was Andrea Lubelli, who later (in a private letter) claimed there had been a misunderstanding: Domingo had not asked for help, on the contrary he had said that he had his own Chinese guide. In this particular conflict of evidence Navarrete is probably right, for Lubelli's behaviour accorded with the Fathers' policy. For a Jesuit to have conducted a friar into China would have been unthinkable, especially at that time when, already worried by the numbers of friars managing to enter the empire, the Fathers were further alarmed by rumours that a friar bishop was about to be appointed by Rome – so that, as one Franciscan put it, smuggling oneself into Japan ('the Closed Country') was easier than crossing the few miles from Portuguese Macao to Jesuit Canton.[22] (30)

However, Lubelli had not seen the last of Domingo Navarrete. Had he guessed the trouble this particular friar was to cause he would have felt justified in taking far sterner measures to keep him out of the empire, for the greater glory of God. As for Navarrete, before long he was able to dismiss such incidents drily, declaring that nothing would surprise him. He made the most of the anecdote, of course, and of how it was a heathen Chinese who finally guided him into the interior when a fellow priest had refused to help. It was the sort of comparison he liked to draw. (31)

Jesuit apartheid increased mendicant suspicions. The Fathers might represent themselves as excellently equipped and trained troops invading China from their Trojan Horse of Macao. But to the friars they looked like a handful of impetuous scouts moving into isolated positions in the midst of unknown territory, cutting off their own supply-lines, and so busy waving away reinforcements from other regiments that they failed to notice that they were, in fact, walking into minefields.

---

[22] Flat contradictions of evidence were frequent, even though 'certified true on the word of a priest'.

4   In the Garden of the World

Great China is the fairest flowering kingdom, a fertile bosky garden, a place of delight situate in the middle of the world. Oh, in truth, 'tis all a beautiful pleasaunce and full of solace.

> — Navarrete

The greatest, fairest, and most fertile portion of the earth; such that it wants nothing to make it a real Land of Promise.

> — Fr Louis Le Comte

Friar and guide set off from Macao in October 1658, travelling part of the way by river and walking the rest. The two-day journey was severe, for winter had already set in, but without delaying in Canton ('another Babylon'), they pushed on towards the city of Fu-an where they had been told there were some friars. In Macao Navarrete had been warned that the journey was likely to be dangerous; further, he knew from an unhappy experience of Morales that travellers were sometimes beaten up and robbed; the execution of Friar Capillas was recent enough to inspire other fears. Later he used to boast that he was the first priest to enter China openly as a missionary. Those friars who in the past had managed to get in had gone in secret (partly to hide from the Jesuits) while the Fathers themselves went under some form of patronage, usually as imperial mathematicians or bureaucrats. (1)

Towards the middle of the month, as he approached the city of Chang-chau, the weather grew colder. The strain of the journey began to tell and once, when he called at a house to beg for food, he fainted on the threshold. But instead of being abandoned, he was wrapped in a blanket, fed, given the owner's bed so that 'no more could have been done for me in any town in Spain'. His precautions against being robbed failed him, but the culprits who stole his 50 pesos and mass-kit were not heathen Chinese but negro Catholics from Portuguese Macao.[1]

A century earlier, the Portuguese Galeote Pereira had noted: 'This nation is not only civil at meat, but also in conversation, and in courtesy they exceed all others. Likewise in all their dealings, they have no reason to envy us'. Navarrete enthused, 'I've said before, and if I have to, I'll do so again, this nation outdoes all others in the world in all particulars'. It was high praise from a 17th-century Spaniard. (2)

In China there seemed no difference in manners between courtier and commoners, and his mind, well drilled in patristic study, remembered how commentators on Isaiah and Amos had explained the elegance of the one and roughness of the other by showing that one was only a peasant. That explanation would not be valid in China, where 'the whole empire is a court, and all its inhabitants courtiers'. Navarrete was approaching dangerous ground: it was only a trifle but the Bible could not be wrong even about a trifle. Yet before the century was out the Chinese were to break many of the old yardsticks. (3)

The Chinese passed another test when, to his alarm, he had to walk through an immense crowd of soldiers. Yet there was no need to fear, 'I would rather go through two Tartar armies than one of ours'. To a patriotic Spanish Jesuit who later objected to this remark, he replied, 'I wrote it for our confusion, and whenever I've the opportunity I'll preach it from the pulpit. Every day in Europe we witness barbarities never seen in those people, who are dismissed among us as savages'.[2]

Continuing his journey through countryside, across which the soldiers had passed, he was astonished to find that they had not interfered in any way with farms or villages: there were no signs of pillaging; the crops and fruit were untouched. It would make a striking novelty for anyone fresh from the Europe recently devastated by the shunting armies of the Thirty Years' War. Again, on the last night of the journey he slept in 'an old castle' where some 50 soldiers were billeted. He was politely welcomed, and their captain insisted on giving up his quarters to him. This was an opportunity to observe the soldiers more closely: 'it is incredible what civility I met with there. I was amazed at this usage from infidels'. Five days' more walking and they reached Fu-chou, where there was a missionary. But they did not meet, for the Jesuit hid from the friar, 'so that I neither saw him, nor went to his

---

[1] Black Catholics came from varied places: Schall had a Bengali servant (Pih, 337); others jumped ship: e.g. from a Dutch fleet in Fu-chou in the 1620s (Zürcher, 434).
[2] Not everyone was so fortunate: see Maas I:73; and Fr Gayoso, on the Hang-chou road in 1682, found the inns closed, the owners having fled from the soldiery (*Maggs's Catalogue* 455 (1924), 21). This is more realistic than Navarrete's idealization, and he, it should be remembered, was in the middle of a war-zone at this time.

church, such are the humours of men. But I was saddened because I longed to confess and say mass'.[3]

Although many people recognized him as a missionary, none showed resentment. In the streets of Chang-chau he started to run when he heard people say, 'Look, there's a friar from Manila' because, 'considering how the soldiers there treat the Chinese, I reckoned I'd be lucky to escape with a beating'. Yet he went unharmed.[4]

Fellow-lodgers at the inns watched him rising early to recite his daily office before setting off, yet no comment was made, though they had fingered his rosary beads and a crucifix hanging round his neck, for at this time he was still wearing his Dominican habit. He risked another generalization. 'Here you never see anyone jeer at another person, no matter how one may dress or walk. Among us, neither gentleman nor sage, maid nor priest is spared'.

By the end of the journey his enthusiasm was boundless. Like many others he had fallen in love with China, so that when he stops singing the praises of the Middle Flowery Kingdom it is not because he fears to tire his readers, but because he has tired himself. The beauty of the country captivated him, Why had no one yet suggested that China might be the site of the Garden of Eden? Everything pointed to it. Chinese politeness, however, had disadvantages, and once led them to deceive him about the length of a journey, so that in one day alone he 'went up and down seven hellish mountains', although at the end of it there was the discovery of well-cooked Chinese rice, 'in all my life I never ate anything daintier'.

On 2 November 1658, late, in heavy rain, he reached Fu-an after almost 40 days' walk. The gates were already closed, so there was nothing for it but to spend the night lying on straw, sheltering under the walls. Next morning, however, all was forgotten when he found the Dominican church and the three friars there: 'the sight of them made me forget the long journey'. They too were delighted by his unexpected arrival, for there were now over a dozen Dominicans in the empire.

Friar Domingo adopted the Chinese name Min Ming-wo, so as to be more easily identified by converts, and he continued his study of Chinese. It was essential to be fluent enough to do without interpreters, for like the earlier

---

[3] Friar Escalona reported how Fr Antonio Rubino refused to hear his confession when they met and quarrelled in Cochinchina, 'I kept quiet, said my mass, and avoided trouble, as though I were among enemies, for their way of behaving amounts to war against us friars' (SinFran II: 310).

[4] Yet Friar Angel Cocchi (Fu-an, 1630s) was threatened by a mandarin because he was one of 'those wicked Spaniards in the Philippines' (Aduarte, *Historia*, II, 367); and, 'A "Luzon padre" became a byword in Hokkien for a domineering man who is always correcting others, but won't take correction himself' (van der Loon, 138).

friars in America he had a horror of intermediaries in religious teaching.[5] The friars were serious language students, and Jesuit allegations that they knew no Chinese were in part understandable strategic exaggerations, and in part the result of misunderstandings, because the friars concentrated on the dialect of Fukien, the location of their base.[6] This dialect would not be easily understood in Peking, where the court Jesuits could allege mendicant 'ignorance'. Navarrete, however, claimed to know both Mandarin and Fukienese. Fortunately the written language could be read and understood from one end of the land to another, so that concentration on one particular dialect did not prevent missionaries from studying the all-important classical texts.[7] At the same time some Jesuits wanted it both ways, and readily admitted that the friars knew Chinese, when they wished to accuse them of dangerous talk. According to the Franciscan Antonio Caballero de Santa María, Fr Schall in one breath denounced the friars for not knowing the language and in the next reproached them for alarming the Chinese with talk of bringing soldiers to impose the Faith and Spanish rule. In fact, of the first 21 Dominicans who entered China after 1631, only two failed to master the language.[8] (4)

Normally the Jesuits prepared their men for the mission by putting them to study in Macao for three years. The Dominicans were able to begin their studies in the Philippines or Formosa, and they devised an intensive course for newcomers. The divine office and community masses were said before dawn, and then all available time before dinner was devoted to private study or conversation practice, and anyone who accidentally spoke Latin or Spanish was punished. In the afternoon, following vespers, there were classes until supper time. Navarrete found the language difficult, but the Chinese love of reading was a constant spur and model, especially the sight of a mandarin studying as he was carried along in his chair, or of 'a cowherd sitting on the back of one of his beasts, with a book propped between its horns'. He was fascinated by 'that terrible language', which Bishop Domingo de Salazar thought the devil had invented to steal time and their creative genius from the Chinese. (5)

---

[5] For an amusing account of an Anglican parson in India preaching on the prodigal son to Hindu troops through a Muslim interpreter: G. M. Fraser, *Flashman in the Great Game* (London, 1975), 120.

[6] The best survey of early Dominican language studies is Piet van der Loon's 'The Manila Incunabula', *Asia Major*, 12–13(1966–67), 1–42, 95–186.

[7] Once during the Sino–Japanese war, Cantonese-speaking pilots landing in north China were killed by locals who thought they were speaking Japanese. However, written characters are understood throughout China, just as numbers, music and electronics-signs are understood equally by Scots, Spaniards or Swedes.

[8] Modern Jesuit admission that friars were adept at Chinese in 1679: review of SinFran VII/ VIII in AHSJ., XLIX(1980), 535.

Navarrete developed a deeper appreciation of Chinese than of his own Spanish, if we can judge from some of his comments, but he did not go as far as those missionaries who forgot how to write their own language. Enthusiasm and perseverance helped him. After the midnight office he often sat studying till dawn. Working with Manuel Chin, a young convert and later a friar, he progressed rapidly. By the following Lent he was able to preach a sermon, something that two months earlier would have seemed impossible. Yet his success with Chinese might have been forecast from his earlier achievement in Manila, where in five months he had mastered a Filipino dialect which normally required a year's study. Before long the work had such a grip on him that he could not put down his book, and so abstracted did he become that some nights he forgot to take off his spectacles when going to bed, and went around the following morning searching for them until he realized he was still wearing them from the previous night.

Intense study quickly absorbed two years, but he did not begrudge them, for exactitude was essential: how else could the mysteries of the Faith, transubstantiation for example, be explained? Nor were accuracy and precision enough, elegance was necessary in preaching the Gospel to a people as cultured as this: 'a meal needs no spice when offered to a hungry man, but it does when offered to one whose appetite is indifferent'.

Navarrete, who warns future missionaries of the difficulty of Chinese, was surprised to hear the Portuguese Fr Magalhães declare it was easier than any European language. Remembering Jesuit claims to greater scholarship in Chinese studies because the Society had been there longer, he pointed out that time itself is not enough to learn that language; the secret lay in perseverance and curiosity. (6)

Though absorbing, this study was not allowed to monopolize his energy, for over everything there hovered the question of the rites. Initially, and as an interim working measure, he decided to obey the terms of Fr Martini's decree of 1656. Gradually, however, study convinced him that the Jesuits' policy could not be justified. Undoubtedly he approached the problem with a bias, and despite his denials, he obviously regarded the China Fathers as different from the rest of the Society, and as fixed in opinions which they would never relinquish. Far too many a Jesuit, he thought, wanted to be his own pope; they would rather lose their lives than change their minds.

As Friar Domingo engrossed himself in these problems it became obvious to him that the fundamental difference between the Jesuits and friars lay in the interpretation of the ancient Chinese classics. Ricci and his followers based themselves on those venerable texts, appealing to the past to support their novelties: they were simultaneously 'Veteratores and Noveleers'. The friars, on the other hand, based their approach not upon the ancient texts themselves, but on the interpretations and exegeses of the later neo-Confucian commentators, the greatest of whom was Chu Hsi (1130–1200), a near contemporary of Aquinas. (7)

An analogy might be drawn between those who go directly to the Bible for their understanding of their religion, and those who rely upon the Church Fathers and tradition. The friars believed that theirs, the latter course, was the only proper one, because many of the ancient texts were so corrupt or obscure that the Chinese themselves could not fully understand them. Furthermore, Navarrete claimed, to ignore the definitions of the later neo-Confucians could only alienate the very people they wanted to win over. To draw a comparison, he asked what would Catholics say of a handful of Chinese who after only a few years in Europe claimed the ability to explain the Scriptures in a sense contrary to Aquinas and the Fathers? Ricci's successor, Fr Longobardi, had also been critical of those (he meant Ricci) who regarded the classical texts as inspired, canonical works. But Friar Domingo, not as tactful as Longobardi, emphasized that the beliefs of the ancients did not matter, they had come to save the present generation, and must come to terms with its evaluations of Confucianism. To Friar Domingo, it was futile for Europeans to speculate about Confucius's own beliefs, and he repeatedly declared that the opinion of a single Chinese was worth more than that of thirty missionaries.[9]

This divergent approach had far-reaching consequences. It meant that the two schools of missionaries could never meet in agreement, for they were not at opposite ends of a plane, but rather on two different planes, with no point of contact. Moreover each was right in his analysis: Ricci in his reading of the classics, and Navarrete in his understanding of the later commentators. For the Jesuits, the solution to many of their problems lay in a benign interpretation of any references to a 'Supreme Lord' in the Chinese classics. Their attitude was similar to St Augustine's approach to the Platonists: with some slight changes they could become Christians. The friars, on the other hand, concluded that the neo-Confucians, who followed Chu Hsi, were either atheists or materialists with no belief in an after-life, while the uneducated masses were idolaters.[10] The matter was confused by the fact that the neo-Confucians, instead of creating new terms for their definitions, had adopted the old expressions which they rationalized and to which they had given fresh meanings. Consequently the educated literati and the ignorant masses could use the same words and yet understand them differently: the former giving them a rationalistic, materialistic meaning, the latter understanding them in their old religious, superstitious sense. It was *double*

---

[9] He could have reflected that the Jesuits, who had not shirked from putting the Dominicans right about the meaning of their own Aquinas's teaching, were unlikely to flinch from the self-imposed task of telling the Confucians what Confucius had been trying to say.

[10] 'Chu Hsi said a hundred times, "The immortality of the soul is a Buddhist error". The Confucianism of Confucius is not essentially opposed to Christianity, but any conciliation with Chu Hsi is impossible. The antithesis is Jesus or Chu Hsi, Christian or literatus' (Fr L. Wieger, *The Religion of China* (London, 1909), 1925). Hence the neo-Confucians' question, 'Does the sharpness then remain even after the knife-blade is destroyed?'

entendre, a new nominalism, it was *Alice in Wonderland* language ('words mean what I want them to mean') in metaphysics. So one set of missionaries could talk of 'offerings' on 'tables' in 'halls', while the other set could describe those same ceremonies as *sacrifices* on *altars* in *temples*. Such differing comprehensions also meant that Ricci's use of old terms to express novel Christian concepts was understood in one way by the literati, and in another by the uneducated.[11]

The 18th-century ambassador, Lord Macartney, was to describe this religious scene in homely terms for the benefit of his fellow Englishmen. 'The educated, higher ranks are what in England we call free thinkers. The rest are disciples of Confucius, of whom there are two sects. The one considers Confucius as a superior man of wisdom and virtue; these venerate his name, sing his praises and drink bumpers to his memory, as the Whigs of Ireland do, honouring the glorious King William [III: the Orangeman's "King Billy"]. But among the other Confucians [the plebs], this grateful recollection has degenerated into a corrupt superstition, the toast has changed into a libation: the original tribute to deceased merit is now become a mixture of sanctified ceremony and convivial abuse. Even here the perversion did not stop. Sacrifices were added, and sheep and oxen immolated to the Manes of Confucius. Every person who presents the offerings acts as hierophant. This sect of enthusiasts is like our Quakers, for China too has its religious subdivision, its Methodists, Moravians, and Muggletonians as in England'. Navarrete would have recognized the scenario. (8)

Both sides appealed to the Chinese to interpret disputed points, and for information about the exact nature of their beliefs. Ironically, however, this deepened their division, for since each group was comparatively limited in its contact with the people, the replies confirmed their assumptions. Thus the Jesuits were assured by the educated courtly elite with whom they associated that Confucianism was simply a code of ethics, neither religious nor superstitious, whatever it might have been originally. And the friars, working in the southern provinces mainly among the unsophisticated poor (Macartney's 'Methodists and Muggletonians'), found an amalgam of religions and of superstitious idolaters and sects. The respective beliefs of these social classes were scrupulously reported to Rome by the two missionary groups, so the Holy See could receive a Jesuit declaration that the Chinese were agnostics, and on the same day receive another from friars affirming that they were a nation of superstitious idolaters. All this, of

---

[11] For neo-Confucian rationalizations of Confucian terms: Needham, *Science*, II: 490 (table 21); v(3): 255. Modern term problems: (i) in computerese 'Euclid' and 'Pascal' do not mean what they suggest; (ii) for objections to the expression 'the Lord's Table' which 'to Catholics is offensive. Tables are for meals, God's sacrifice is offered on an altar' (see letter, London *Times*, 2 February 1978); (iii) the success of the modern Japanese technological revolution depended partly on solving terminology problems.

course, signed *in verbo sacerdotis* as each side paraded native witnesses to back its assertions.

The veteran Longobardi had warned that it was misguided to appeal to converts' opinions, because they did not appreciate the weight attached to their replies to apparently trivial questions; and because they tended naturally to favour Ricci's approach, since it would be safer for them if Christianity were proclaimed, as he had suggested, to be a link with the ancients. Converts need not then fear accusations of having joined a new foreign sect. This tendency to favour Ricci's interpretation explains why the Jesuits could always field more witnesses than could the mendicants. (9)

Navarrete found the religious situation a tangle of beliefs and half beliefs. One thing alone was sure: the Chinese divided into two groups, the literati, and the rest; the atheists, and the idolaters. He abhorred the former, whose indifference to metaphysics baffled him; they seemed blinded by pride of mind. (He found them portrayed in ch. 13 of the Book of Wisdom.) Worse than atheists, they appeared to be cynical hypocrites pretending to believe in the popular religion because it kept the masses in their place. As Augustine said of the ancients, they sinned more grievously because for political and social ends they venerated 'feignedly and only in outward show, gods in whom they no longer believed'. In Navarrete's China, as in Gibbon's Rome, religion was considered by the people true, by the philosophers false, and by the magistrates useful. (10)

As for the ceremonies, Navarrete distinguished between those that were purely civic, those in veneration of the emperor (with which he had no quarrel) and those that in his opinion were religious, the Confucian rites and the ancestor-veneration ceremonies. He was also deeply concerned by the problem of the correct Chinese word for the concept of God, and to this he gave a good deal of time, writing a treatise (*De nominibus Dei*), opposing the use of the terms *Shang-ti* and *T'ien*, which he considered inadequate.

Throughout the controversy the friars were unmoved by Jesuit justification of their conduct by appeal to the theory of probabilism, which the friars regarded as dubious, and, only slightly *avant la lettre*, jesuitical.[12] The Dominicans would have agreed with Pascal: 'I'm not content with the merely probable, I seek the sure'. (11)

Confirmation of Navarrete's doubts came from the notorious disunity among the Fathers themselves, which was highly infectious: 'Seeing their disagreements, our own doubts increased'. The Fathers sought unanimity and secrecy, but Fr Lubelli, forgetting the secrecy, revealed to Friar Salvador de Santo Tomás (1681) that on arrival in Macao every Jesuit was handed a policy statement setting out the party line, to which he had to adhere;

---

[12] Some Fathers admitted to skating on theologically thin ice, and Fr Schall once admitted the friars' position was safer, though his colleagues suspected this was an example of his notorious sarcasm (Intorcetta, *De cultu*, 304).

Lubelli boasted he had never deviated once in eight years. But this was the rare ideal, for there was no point on which all the Jesuits agreed, although they constantly urged the friars to fall in line with their broadminded approach. Disingenuously, Navarrete inquired which particular Father was to be followed: it was difficult to accompany those marching in opposite directions.[13] He realized that some of the Jesuits who were contemporary with him had moved and were still moving away from the earlier cautious, more tentative approach of Ricci. (12)

He quoted Jesuit estimates of Confucius. 'Here, as in all else, there are two opinions amongst the China Fathers': Frs Couplet and Rougemont considered Confucius as a teacher of the Natural Law; Intorcetta thought him a prophet; Brancati and Morales thought it sinful to criticize him; Ricci found no wrong in him; Gravina believed he was in hell; for Valat and Motel he was a 'great knave'. Which view was official opinion? Which Father should a submissive friar follow? They were divided on other points too, for Fr Visitor Gama and Fr Lubelli thought it wrong to use mathematics as a means of establishing the China mission.

This disunity enabled Friar Domingo to quote Jesuit against Jesuit, a tactic which years later saved him when they denounced him and his offending book to the Spanish Inquisition. He was able to show that every single one of the friars' opinions had been held by one or other of the veteran Jesuits. To complaints that there had been peace in the mission before the coming of the friars, he answered impolitely: 'Read your own Fr Longobardi and you'll soon come off your high horse, for we friars argue along the same lines as he did'.

It should be noted that Navarrete wrote his two accounts of China in 1676, when disillusion had sharpened his insight and recent events seemed to prove him right. He had just witnessed persecution in the mission and the future of Christianity there was then doubtful. This he believed had discredited the Jesuit technique. In China, the Faith, far from being firmly rooted, was only 'stuck on with spittle'. Some friars found symbolism in that the first person they met in Canton, back in 1579, was a lapsed Jesuit convert, once christened 'Simón' but now an 'apostate'. For the friars forgot that every convert is someone's apostate. (13)

Compared to the more advanced Jesuits, Navarrete was narrow in his views. He believed in accommodation as far as was reasonable and legitimate, but the definition of what is reasonable and legitimate tends to differ, particularly among theologians. Navarrete was never slow to denounce those who appeared to be introducing religious novelties, which

---

[13] He was like Pascal's provincial, who asked the doctor of theology whether he 'admitted *proximate* power in the sense of the Molinists [Jesuits]? Whereupon he, quite unmoved, asked: "Which of the Molinists are you referring to? Because far from holding the same views they are quite divided amongst themselves".'

his narrowly ecclesiastical mind feared. A difficulty he found in the Jesuit approach was that on the one hand they praised the intelligence of the Chinese, considering them (as did he himself) superior to any people they had ever met. On the other hand the Fathers advocated ritual and other changes, on the grounds that these were necessary to make the Faith more comprehensible or agreeable to the Chinese. Now, no one denied the need to adapt traditional methods when dealing with people of limited intelligence. The friars' experience in America had proved that, but the Chinese needed no such spiritual molly-coddling or pampering. Let the missionaries beware, then, of becoming 'spiritual confectioners, recklessly adding sugar to taste', for some day the diet, if it were to be health-giving, would have to be taken plain, whole and unsweetened. Did the Jesuits really believe that those who for years had been fed on milk and pap would one day be willing to eat their bread with the crust on? (14)

In this he was right. The Jesuits were hypnotized by their own brilliance, and their natural enthusiasm for Ricci's imaginative policy was hardening into dogmatism. They failed to see that some day the rules of universal Catholicism would have to be imposed, with the danger of consequent confusion and schismatic splits into 'new' and 'old' factions, as had happened with the Chinese Muslims. (15)

There were other dangers. One was especially serious: religious syncretism. The friars' American experience made them aware of it, but others, more optimistic, were not haunted by fear of yet another pagan– Christian syncretism, and Samuel Purchas, for example, appraising the work of the Jesuits in China, thought that if the Chinese became Christians it did not matter what brand they were to be; any form of Christianity would be better than none: 'Better a mixed truth, than total errour, and a maymed Christ, than none at all'.

Spanish friars could hardly be expected to share this easy-going view, or to tolerate a contaminated form of the Faith. Moreover, there was a peculiar danger in China where Catholicism, proud of its clearly defined character and personality, might be absorbed by the three teachings of the Middle Kingdom (Confucianism, Taoism, Buddhism), for the endemic oriental drift towards amalgamation meant that religions were not mutually exclusive. A Chinese might belong to any or all of them simultaneously and without embarrassment. In general, the Chinese were willing to see the three cults, the *San chiao*, move over to make room for a fourth. Navarrete had personal experience of this tendency in the well-meant but alarming plan of a distinguished Jesuit convert in Peking ('one of the pillars of the mission') for uniting Catholicism to Confucianism, Taoism and Buddhism, thus evolving a new state cult. This convert was later defended by Fr Verbiest who denied any knowledge of the affair, but there is no doubt Navarrete's allegation was correct. (16)

This distressing, baffling Asian tolerance of all religions, an amiable politeness towards possibilities, showed the need for Catholicism to retain a firm character if it was to survive, especially there, where of necessity converts often received no more than a brief catechizing, and easily lapsed or evolved their own private, sometimes weird, versions of the Faith. Friar Caballero came upon a group of a thousand Christians who, after eight years without a priest, had developed a religion of their own, a jumble of Christian and pagan beliefs which involved the veneration of images of Christ and the old idols together.[14] The friars insisted that toleration of traditional practices could be dangerous where links with the pagan past were not yet broken, for they might still retain some of their ancient significance. How, they asked, could an emasculated form of Catholicism, such as the Jesuits were teaching, survive in a country that was gradually absorbing its Jews, and Muslims? On a number of occasions Navarrete pointed to these latter as proof that his was the right attitude. They had been four hundred years in China and, knowing the nature of Confucianism, refused to celebrate the rites, held the literati for atheists, and declared apostate any Muslim who joined them. For all that, Friar Domingo observed, the Muslims had never suffered persecution for their religious loyalty. The Fathers, in turn, investigated the Chinese Jews to see if they too offered incense to the imperial tablets (they did) and if they used the terms *T'ien* and *Shang-ti* to designate the Divinity (they did).[15] (17)

When the quarrel with the Jesuits was put aside, however, Navarrete showed that his approach, though narrow, was not negative. He, more than the generality of friars, appreciated the feelings of the Chinese, and brought both psychological insight and understanding to his work; for he was far from those who thought that a healthy fear of hellfire was a main ingredient for conversion. Constantly seeking a middle way through the divergent views of the missionaries, and without resorting to probabilism, Friar Domingo stretched his theology as far as possible in favour of 'these new plants which could easily be flattened by any slight wind'. He prescribed practical rules for his fellow friars, urged gentleness and warned against over-confidence. Reason and an appeal to the 'Natural Law' were to be the basis of their arguments: questioners were to be answered on their own grounds, out of their own texts, and on their own terms. Here he was simply following Aquinas's *Contra gentiles* (I, ii).

---

[14] In Japan Captain Saris (1613) found converts venerating a Venus and Cupid: 'thinking it to be our Ladie and her Sonne' (Purchas, 1: 367). Even in Catholic Portugal (c. 1550) an astounded Archbishop met a peasant procession chanting 'Blessed be the Holy Trinity and his sister the Virgin Mary' (Lady Herbert of Lea, *Life of Bartholomew of the Martyrs* (London, 1880), 242).

[15] Some Jesuits hoped that the Chinese Jews' ancient Torah scrolls might contain references to Christ the Messiah which, in the West, had been expunged by malevolent rabbis. Their discovery now might finally convert the European Jews. So the Fathers tried to get copies of them, but the Chinese Jews refused: 'to sell the Torah would be to sell the Lord' (Dehergne-Leslie, xv–xvi, 21).

His middle-of-the-road approach is seen in his proposed solution to the minor problem of missionary dress. The friars are usually alleged to have refused to change their religious robes for Chinese dress.[16] In fact they had no problem. The early friars, working among the Mongols around 1300, got permission to wear secular clothes. And in 16th-century Mexico, the Franciscans for local reasons changed their brown habits to blue, while their English nickname, 'Greyfriars', speaks for itself. But the friars, disagreeing with the Jesuits' practice of wearing the silken robes of the literati, were shocked to see Fr Martino Martini travelling in state 'like a Knight of the Golden Fleece and Mandarin of the First Degree, dressed in silk with a golden dragon embroidered on his breast, surrounded by banners, lances and harquebusiers, more like a marquis than a religious bound by the vow of evangelical poverty'.[17] This was too much for the mendicants who, though they agreed that Chinese dress must be worn, thought it should be made of cotton, or some other inferior material more becoming to missionaries. Navarrete suggested that for everyday dress Chinese robes of poorer quality than silk might be worn, but that each church or residence should have one simple black silk robe for official purposes. (For holy poverty's sake, this was also the policy of the Jesuit Cabral in Japan.) (18)

The friar-missionaries, who rejected the Jesuit dual-identity strategy, make no appeal to outsiders, and are harshly judged, whereas the Jesuit geometers' humanistic learning is a link between themselves and modern writers. They were mathematicians, astronomers, engineers, painters or linguists, united in the selfless task of spreading learning; sophisticated pioneers blazing a trail along which East and West might meet; dedicated, if accidental, cultural diplomats. They were, of course, also missionaries, but their flexibility suggests a willingness to put aside oppressive dogma and doctrine when convenient. 'The Jesuits', said d'Alembert, 'though odious, were a complaisant set, provided one did not declare oneself openly their enemy'. The friars, on the other hand, are represented as the wild Cossacks of the Church Militant, innocent of any learning except the narrowest divinity, blinkered bigots frustrating the Jesuits' sophisticated and subtle efforts. A simple equation is laid down: mendicant versus Jesuit equals ignorance versus enlightenment; intolerance versus flexibility; medieval versus modern. Yet it could be argued that even if the friars' only knowledge was of theology, that was precisely what they most needed. To deny that is like

---

[16] Fr Verbiest 'used to say, it was a shame for a Jesuit to be clothed in the silken livery of the world and not that of Christ' (Le Comte, 46). Navarrete agreed but, not reluctant to wear Chinese robes, even wore them on his return home, peacocking around Lisbon in a camp gesture suggesting a show-off streak.

[17] Similarly scandalized cries were heard in England at this time where Fr Jasper Heywood's 'port and carriage was more baronlike than priestlike. Was he not wont to ride up and down the country in his coach? Had he not both servants and priest attendants that did hang on his sleeve in great numbers?' (Fr Basset, 100).

complaining of engineers who only know engineering: it is not a drawback to being a specialist engineer. (19)

These, like most generalizations, are not without some truth, but qualification is needed before either can be accepted. In the beginning, both sides made tactical errors, and both are denounced for these original sins as though they were also guilty of final impenitence. In the early days both sides seemed to have decided on spectacular methods of conversion: a missionary had to be either a mathematician or a martyr. The ever-practical Jesuits held that a live evangelist was preferable to a dead one, and though Fr Semedo admitted the 'zeal and heat of those who want to convert the world all of a sudden' was commendable, he also thought they were best left in their pulpits back home. The friars, on the other hand, having decided on their course sometimes carried their conclusions to logical but inadvisable ends, and often ran risks in reacting against compromise. Fr Schall complained that the Franciscans had gone to China not to preach the Law of God but to break the law of the land. Fr Magalhães denounced them to Rome for appearing more eager to earn themselves private palms of martyrdom than to get on with the prosaic business of converting the heathen. They seem, wrote Fr Furtado in 1640, to be inciting the Chinese to martyr them. The friars, always straightforward, were impatient with Jesuit disguises, and could have argued that martyrdom might be preferable to conversion through 'black miracles' such as Fr Parennin's.[18] (20)

The friars later admitted their initial mistakes, but claimed that they had quickly learnt that 'this is not the time for naivety and seraphic ardour, but for prudence'. The claim was true. Under the influence of such superiors as Navarrete the mendicants changed considerably, without departing from their principles. They took fewer risks, abandoned their early practice of preaching in the streets, and confined their proselytizing to the churches where they could more freely discuss and argue with their listeners. Before Sunday mass they divided their congregations into two groups, the better to recite a dialogue rosary. Before the service itself there was a catechism lesson followed by questions on the creed, and in this work they were helped by trained catechists. The Chinese were skilful in argument and used to take quotations from the missionaries' writings and turn them against the preacher. Their questions were always acute and went to the heart of a problem; some, said Navarrete, 'left me swooning with surprise', and Friar Coronado warned: 'in China the man who hasn't his feet firmly in the stirrups will quickly find himself flat on his back'. Friar Varo begged the doctors of Salamanca University to come to exercise their learning in the Middle Kingdom. It was the same in Japan, where Zen priests asked questions

---

[18] Provoked martyrdoms are not recognized by the Church; Thomas More (*Dialogue of Comfort*) thought a courted martyrdom was suicide.

which not even Aquinas and Scotus could have answered satisfactorily.[19] In addition, the Chinese had Muslim allies who would join in, arguing with the missionaries while the Chinese stood by, carefully noting reactions. In short, the Asians, unlike the American Indians, 'were not wax waiting for the imprint of the seal'. Nor were they easily satisfied: the Chinese often 'reply to the reply'. (21)

Again and again, friars appealing to Spain for volunteers warned that care be used in selecting the right men for the mission. They must not be 'plucked casually from the heap, but scooped carefully from the cream', for, as the Franciscan Caballero informed the Jesuit general (who hardly needed a friar to tell him), 'the Chinese, though only husbandmen, are no fools'. (22)

The ideal missionary, stipulated the friars, must be fit, energetic, pious, sound in theology, and linguistically gifted. In character he must be calm, urbane, modest, and long-suffering; the Chinese are converted through the eyes not the ears, by example not argument. Above all, volunteers must be realists, and all introspective, romantic dreamers, would-be saints and mystics, 'going about with head on one side, are best left in their friaries'. Friar Ibáñez thought there was no place in China for Mary, lost in meditation at Christ's feet; what was needed there was Martha's energy. (23)

The Jesuits maintained that God operated through secondary channels, so 'human means' and natural resources were to be systematically worked for His greater glory. The early friars had insisted that God's grace alone was sufficient. But here again they changed, and later they adopted human means as aids to evangelization, sometimes outstripping, even shocking the Jesuits, as when they opened a fencing school in Japan. They had already adopted secular means, and devised audiovisual aids, in America and the Philippines, in order to win and hold converts. The friars there taught mechanical skills, building methods, agricultural techniques, tailoring, bookbinding, music, and painting. They occasionally produced mathematicians, such as Friar Martín de Rada (a pioneer Copernican), and Friars Ignacio Muñoz and Juan Cobo who taught astronomy and included a treatise on cosmography in his *Shih-lu* ('Veritable record') of 1593, written in classical Chinese, mostly in dialogue form.[20] (24)

In early 17th-century China the Jesuits were able to present themselves as scientists because Ricci and his colleagues had arrived at a moment doubly lucky for themselves. First, the triumph of neo-Confucianism had allowed Ricci to interpret the rites as merely civic ceremonies; if he had arrived before

---

[19] Franciscan San Pascal noted (1674) how literati loved to argue over the notion of the creation, immortality, and sin. But the friars believed they had an advantage: 'the Chinese do not know the device of the syllogism and can be floored with an effective *consequence*, or conclusion' (SinFran, VII (i): 141–2). And see Fr Gaubil on Chinese incapacity for logic (*Corr.*, 339).

[20] An analysis of the ideal missionary concludes that it is no accident that some sciences (comparative linguistics, anthropology) have roots in missionary activity (Eliade, IX, 568).

1530 he would have had to condemn them as idol-worship. Second, he arrived when Chinese science was in decline, and there was no one to tell him of China's former mathematical glories, or that science there had often been in advance of medieval Europe. The three inventions reckoned to be among the keys to the transformation of Europe came from China: printing, gunpowder and the compass. The Jesuit newcomers could have said (as did Raphael in More's *Utopia*): 'Before we arrived, they didn't even know the name of a single European philosopher. Yet despite that, they had already discovered for themselves much the same principles, in music, arithmetic and geometry, as our own early authorities'. (25)

There was a curious irony in the situation. Those Jesuits who proclaimed they were bringing home to China native but forgotten religious beliefs, together with western science, were, unknown to themselves, doing the opposite: bringing native, but forgotten, science, and a new religious belief, Tridentine Catholicism. The Fathers emphasized that their science was 'western' since their religion was also western in Chinese eyes, and they aimed to commend Christianity by the prestige of the science accompanying it. Some Chinese suspected this: the K'ang-hsi emperor himself declared that since all mathematics derive from the 'Book of Changes', the so-called western methods were obviously Chinese in origin, and in 1669 he decreed that it be called 'new' science. The Chinese were willing to adopt 'new', but not 'European' science. That is, they were willing to adopt what was new to both worlds, but not something predominantly linked to Christian Europe: they would accept the philosophy, not the theology.[21] (26)

Jesuit science was the handmaiden of Tridentine Catholicism. 'Did you ever seen a scientist genuflecting to the world (unless he be a Jesuit, but then he is not a pure scientist, he is an apologist in disguise)?' As if answering Jacques Maritain's question, we find Fr Dominique Parennin (1665–1741) performing scientific 'miracles' for the greater glory of God. He informed his Paris headquarters that 'one must gain the esteem of Chinese scholars through a knowledge of natural things, for nothing better disposes them to attend to our preaching of Christian truths'. He went on to relate how he had impressed some literati by freezing a bowl of water standing beside a hot brazier, because he had surreptitiously slipped saltpetre into it. Next day, after another such 'miracle', an onlooker declared he would now believe anything Parennin said, but feared being deceived. 'I couldn't deceive anyone', replied the Father, 'On the contrary I would happily undeceive you from your religious errors'. And later, 'you must promise me you'll now listen with greater docility when I speak to you of a far more elevated subject, which will bring you happiness for all eternity'.

Quoting this, Joseph Needham comments, 'Parennin was an outstanding

---

[21] Navarrete too resented the use of 'European' since it attributed the 'superstitions' of the Jesuits' Chinese calendar to Europe (NC 133).

linguist, estimable man and devoted priest, yet his using physico-chemical knowledge to perform tricks with the object of inducing belief in the religious dogma which he represented, and without explaining the meaning of his demonstrations to his listeners, was something we may find hard to forgive today. Missionaries of all religions everywhere have sought to accredit themselves by signs and wonders, but seen in the light of the ethic of the scientific world community of today there was something almost sacrilegious in Parennin's attitude. Thaumaturgy was in bad taste when what was called for was the transmission of true chemical knowledge and understanding'.[22] (27)

Clearly, the temptation to take shortcuts was strong, and suggests a link between the Jesuits' elastic theology and their science. We have an earlier instance (1654) of 'superior knowledge' used for divine ends when Fr Schall drafted a fictitious oracle, allegedly based on astronomical observations, in order to influence the young Shun-chih emperor.

On the other hand some Fathers were under a nervous strain. 'They don't give me time to breathe', Ricci had said, and in 1668 Fr Magalhães, was 'so busy that night and day I've a hammer or file in my hands, all in order to make friends for the mission'. Sometimes working conditions were harsh, the task unremitting and the vocation of divine drudge too much for some. In 1754, after painting night and day for weeks in crowded, malodorous workshops in Jehol, Fr Attiret wrote to Peking: 'Will this farce never end? I find it hard to persuade myself that all this is for the greater glory of God'.[23] Fr Gaubil, in 1726, lists his scientific achievements, but it was all done under obedience and à contrecoeur: 'I'd give it all up willingly to be able to baptize, confess and instruct pagans'.[24] (28)

There was a strain, too, in having to appear ever-omniscient and some yearned for the luxury of admitting ignorance. Fr Verbiest, puzzled by a curiously shaped comet, nevertheless had to come up with a quick answer to a questioner. He explained to a colleague in 1668: 'If one were talking to Tycho Brahe or Ptolemy it would be possible to say modestly "I don't know"

---

[22] Such manoeuvres were not confined to China: the 19th-century orientalist Francis Whyte Ellis reported the finding in Pondicherry of a collection of Sanskrit mss. 'These were shown to be compositions of Jesuit missionaries, who had embodied under the title of 'Vedas' [Brahman sacred books] their [own] religious doctrines in classical Sanskrit verse, with a view to palming them off on the natives as being the work of the inspired authors of their scriptures' (*Asiatic Researches*, XIV(1822), 1–59; and *Dict. Nat. Biog.*, VI(1938), 694).

[23] Under the Ch'ing the Fathers were 'reduced to artisans in imperial service, but always felt the pull of the idea of becoming the king's confessor' (Zürcher, 421).

[24] Evangelizing through 'human means' could be hazardous: Fr Bouvet's imprisonment was allegedly because he declined to enamel a dildo for the Manchu heir-apparent, Yin-Jeng (Guy, 'AMDG', 68; cf LEC. III(1843), 145). Enamelling was popular and K'ang-hsi had a passion for it (Sullivan, 54).

without losing the least credit; but to a fat-bellied Mandarin one has to give a reason on the spot without batting an eyelid, and under pain of losing face and reputation'.[25] (29)

Verbiest does not mention here Copernicus or Galileo, which reminds us that the missionary scientists were hampered in their tactic. In Europe science was making such strides that the Jesuits' situation soon became ambiguous. 'The Society', writes Santillana, 'the most powerful organization within the Church, self-charged with controlling the flow of new ideas' was finding the current dangerously strong, for the Jesuit could be ordered to 'sacrifice his scientific conscience to the political convenience of his superiors'. Urania's feet were bound as tightly as those of any Chinese lady of fashion.

Galileo had published his *Siderius Nuntius* in 1610, the year of Ricci's death. News of his work had reached China relatively quickly (1615), and at first the Jesuits propagated his theories. But after the Roman condemnation of 1633 they had to stop doing so. The result was that Jesuit science then became essentially medieval, for though they spread the knowledge of Galileo's telescopes, they could not mention the heliocentric theory. Thus they retarded rather than advanced Chinese astronomy, cheating the Middle Kingdom of the most startling discovery that man had so far made.[26]

Silence was no solution, for when the Chinese eventually discovered the suppression of Galileo's discoveries, they doubted the Fathers' other doctrines. The never-changing Faith had been tied to ever-changing science. And since acceptance of Copernicanism could raise doubts about all Ricci's teachings, Schall misrepresented Copernicus's work to give the impression that in principle there was no disagreement between him and Ptolemy. (30)

The Jesuits' chosen intellectual weapons had back-fired and their stratagem proved vulnerable. Parennin shows how they hoped to catch the Chinese with the bait of science, but just as the 17th-century Englishmen of the Royal Society gratefully received Jesuit contributions to geographical knowledge, yet repudiated their religion, so too the literati of China learnt to distinguish 'new' science from 'western' religion. 'Their knowledge', wrote Lu Lung-chi in 1675, after visiting Buglio and Verbiest and seeing their clocks and spheres, 'their knowledge is generally credible, except for the stories about Adam and Eve and the birth of Jesus'. Another researcher reported that 'Jesus was born during the Han dynasty and his religion still

---

[25] The best study of the Jesuit scientific contribution concludes that their work was favourable and impressive, yet 'on the whole their coming was by no means an unmixed blessing for Chinese science' (Needham, *Science*, III: 437, 447).

[26] 'It is really with the condemnation of Galileo that the paths of East and West diverge, not to meet until the 19th century' (P. Pelliot, *T'oung Pao*, XXXVIII(1948), 328–9). For the telescope in Ch'ing fiction, see Idema, 466 ff.

has followers who have composed over 100 books, the contents of which discuss Heaven and Fate in a way confusing to the intelligence'.[27]

Meanwhile, the Fathers, handicapped in the speculative sciences, were more secure in their engineering, architecture and other technical fields where advances in knowledge were unlikely to lead to a clash with orthodoxy. Here they could, and did, make a name for themselves. So strong was the memory of the missionary technicians that when French Lazarist priests went to Peking in the 19th century, local Christians asked if they were clockmaker Fathers, or perhaps, painter Fathers.

If the Jesuits were not free to compete fully with disinterested secular scientists, the mendicants were not able compete fully with the Fathers. Instead they devoted themselves to the use of 'human means' in a manner that has successfully survived into contemporary missionary practice. Already in 1650 Friar Bonaventura Ibáñez urged that the best approach to the Chinese was as medical men. As a warning, he pointed to Japan where the Jesuits had opened a hospital, but closed it when work there conflicted with their policy of concentrating on the upper classes, who criticized such activities. The friars, however, who aimed at what the Jesuits called 'the poor, lepers and people of little worth, poxy rabble', later found their policy justified. Medical work, of course, included rescuing foundlings who, promptly baptized, were counted as convert statistics. (31)

Friar Ibáñez wrote to his Manila headquarters explaining that friar-physicians and surgeons would gain ready admission to Chinese homes, could earn their keep, and attend sick colleagues. Friar Caballero, more insistent, begged his superiors to send a friar-physician 'even if you have to drag him from the altar!' Later, these medical missionaries enjoyed some success, not only in China, but in places as diverse as Siam and Persia. It would be wrong to over-emphasize their limited skills, but it would be unjust to ignore their inventiveness. The friars too realized the need for official favour, and they sought it, but as a group they never acquired the Jesuits' versatility in the use of 'human means'. Rightly or wrongly, they remained more at home with crucifixes than clocks. (32)

Where the friars (especially the Franciscans) were narrow-minded was in observance of their vow of evangelical poverty. This meant that unlike their rivals they could not present mandarins and bureaucrats with the expected gifts and bribes. This hampered their work. If they had been able to regard money as a mere instrument, and imitated the more realistic Jesuits by trading, they might have had greater success. As it was, they relied mainly

---

[27] Of the scriptures, he added: 'Their topic is Heaven and Hell, but the style is atrocious. Our Sacred Dynasty makes use of their calendar but bans their heretical doctrine. We should continue this policy for all eternity'. Even in the 19th-century, some were still muddled: 'It appears that the Jesus-religion preached by Ricci was Catholicism, whereas the Jesus-religion preached afterwards by Verbiest was Christianity' (in A. Waley, *The Opium War Through Chinese Eyes* (London, 1958), 97).

on contributions from Manila which often came late, if at all. Consequently, they were sometimes reduced to a state far beyond the demands of holy poverty. Friar San Pascal warned newcomers that life in China was hard, for there were 'no full porridge pots'. One Franciscan spent the six weeks of Lent living on turnips, except once when a visitor gave him a fish. Another two friars in Canton were so hungry that they had to eat grass from the city moat, and this at a time when they saw those 'ecclesiastical knights of the Golden Fleece', the Jesuits, angering one of their own Fr Visitors who complained that 'if anything be lacking in their diet (I don't mean necessities, but delicacies) one can do nothing with them'.[28] (33)

Holy poverty sometimes prevented the friars from leaving home, and then they relied on Chinese curiosity to bring callers. In a single day Friar Domingo received 23 separate groups of eight or nine people. Pious medals and pictures sent over from Manila easily aroused interest, and the friars took to handing them out freely. Friar Piñuela once had to erect crash-barriers around the altar in his church to keep back the crush of people who, disconcertingly, wanted to handle the sacred vessels. Baptisms of women were especially popular and attracted large crowds, for the bonzes had spread stories about the indecency of the ceremony. One friar had an alarming experience at a baptism: so many spectators assembled that an entire wall of his chapel was knocked down. This curiosity sometimes led to conversions. But Friar Pascal, after answering one man's questions for a whole day, was disappointed, for in the end he refused baptism, although later it was consoling to hear that by repeating the friar's arguments he accidentally converted one of his friends. (34)

Disappointments were frequent. Friar Piñuela describes how he was visited by two mandarins who prostrated themselves before the altar, and after polite questions declared the 'law of God' to be good, but showed no desire for baptism. Too often visitors sat listening intently, even politely agreeing with what the friars said, in the end only to pat their stomachs, smilingly: 'this is all that matters'. San Pascal once sat from noon till nightfall talking to a mandarin and his suite of a hundred attendants. But finally the mandarin left, saying, 'Master, what you say is right, but we Chinese love only cash and women'.

Such polite indifference was discouraging, for opposition was what the evangelist thrived on. 'Here there are many martyrdoms, yet no blood is spilled', wrote a Franciscan, 'not to be martyred is itself a martyrdom' — describing the frustrated desire to save the uninterested. To one enthusiast, enquiring eagerly from Manila for news of the latest miracles, the friars replied drily that they had only two to report, both remarkable: the first,

---

[28] One friar denounced the Fathers who 'speak of the dried radish leaves which they consume for their nourishment, but make no mention of the delectable chicken that follows' (Boxer, *Christian Century*, 479; *Maggs's Catalogue* 515, 34).

that any Chinese were ever converted; the second, that any missionary had the heart to go on loving China and working there. As Fr José de Acosta had explained, miracles had been needed in apostolic times when illiterates had to convert the learned; the situation is now reversed and miracles are superfluous. (35)

The missionaries' different living standards, and the effect that had on their success further deepened their divisions, and led to continual wrangles about the number and social standing of their respective converts. Nothing in all the literature of the controversy is as demeaning as this soul-tallying. Fr Brancati jibed that the Dominicans had converted only a handful of wretched peasants who were so poor that, having nothing to offer their ancestors, they were not discouraged by the friars' prohibitions of the rites. Certainly the mendicants did not equal the Jesuits' numerical success. Friar Vittorio Riccio lamented in 1657 that in two years he had only converted 98 people. A Franciscan on the other hand saw no cause for despondency. He resorted to a simile to make his point: some grapes grow in the open and require care and attention, though the yield is low; others are grown in hothouses with comparatively little effort, but when the time for the wine-pressing comes the difference in the quality of the two types is apparent. Every friar knew that those inferior hothouse plants were the Jesuits' converts.

The friars indeed sometimes took on work in particularly tough territory, sometimes even in places that the Jesuits had given up as hopeless. The latter, after 12 years' fruitless work in Shantung, abandoned the area, and the friars remained alone there in the 1650s. They worked for 15 years almost in despair, then suddenly the tide turned and by 1670 they had 4 000 converts. Within a few more years they reported that for Christian fervour it was the best province in all China. The Dominicans catechized in Fukien province, which both Jesuits and mendicants agreed was a specially unrewarding area: 'the conversions in these parts go something like the tides', wrote the Jesuit Gouveia in 1653. Moreover, before 1655 the Dominican missions lay in the middle of the war zone in which the Manchu conquerors of China were fighting supporters of the fallen Ming dynasty.

The nature of the people of Fukien province was an obstacle to easy evangelizing, for they were, as the K'ang-hsi emperor said, lovers of daring deeds, and there the very scholars carried shields and swords. A contemporary Dutchman described them as 'given to riot and lasciviousness, of a savage and cruel nature, and still retaining something of their ancient barbarism', but a Dominican found them materialistic, obstinate in clinging to their rites, yet capable of becoming fervent Catholics.[29] (36)

---

[29] For some peculiarities of the Fukien mission see Zürcher, 439–41 where the view is taken that there was less interest in science than in religion, with 'extreme emphasis on the person of Jesus'.

But there was yet another explanation for the difficulties of working in Fukien. Friar Riccio wrote sadly to his Roman province 'the people here are hostile to the Faith because many of them have been over to the Philippines and seen the bad example of the Spaniards there, and that's the truth of it'. Navarrete had personal experience of this. Once when preaching there, a listener called out, 'why give us your sermons? We know how to behave. Go back to Manila where you're needed more'. Friar Juan García in a similar situation was 'covered with shame, went as cold as snow, and took myself off, too depressed to continue'. Gregorio Lo, the Chinese Dominican, always kept a tight rein on any converts he had to take to Manila on business, and made sure that they never went out alone in the city. Others learned to practise this holy apartheid and in Japan the Fathers said separate masses for the converts, to protect them from the unedifying sight of Portuguese cradle-Catholics at their devotions. Navarrete thought it could only be God's mercy that the Chinese were ignorant of conditions in Europe, for 'if they knew about that, they'd spit in our faces'. In 1685 this problem drove an English preacher to warn, 'If we ever expect to convert India, the Justice and Integrity of our Merchants and Factors must prepare the way, for they will never think the Christian Religion better than their own, unless they are well assured by men's Practices, that it enjoyns more Honesty than theirs. They will no more believe the Gospel whose professors Cheat and Lye than they will go to Heaven with a Spaniard'.[30] (37)

At the same time, the Chinese were all too easily shocked and even some pious pictures of the Madonna gave offence, because for the Chinese a woman's foot was the centre of her sexual appeal, so that not even the most explicit pornographic drawings dared to depict a naked foot.[31]

Again, some Chinese, already shocked by the crucifixion and resurrection, were disturbed by the incarnation. A prospective convert in Lan ch'i changed his mind on hearing friars use the familiar 'thou' in their prayers. Others were scandalized to see Catholics in Church genuflecting to the divine presence on only one knee: to do that before a mandarin would earn a whipping. Others were amazed to hear that, despite the gospel precepts, there were poor people in Europe, and they showed scepticism before the resourceful explanation that God allowed those few to remain so that the rich might exercise their charity.

For Friar Domingo the natural goodness of the Chinese, their fine scruples

---

[30] Referring to the notorious anecdote of an Amerindian refusing baptism lest it lead to eternity with Spaniards (Thos. Manningham, *Sermon* (London, 1686), 15).

[31] Only true of bare *bound* feet; unbound feet were not considered obscene. Representations of the asexual deity Kuan-Yin, a Chinese version of St Uncumber, were the only exception to this convention (van Gulik, 218, 222). By extension a woman's shoe became taboo, and in the 1630s Jesuits created an uproar in Canton when caught sending to Europe a map of China and, worse still, a sample of female footwear.

and high standards made them a living example of Augustine's saying, 'Behold the pagans are become the teachers of the Faithful'. (38)

The devotion of the Chinese to parents and ancestors also presented problems. Christ's saying that he had come to 'set son against father' distressed converts who, unable to bear the prospect of an eternity separated from their ancestors, eagerly inquired if Confucius himself was saved. Here the missionary felt trapped. If Confucius was saved, Christianity seemed superfluous; but to deny his salvation would alienate them. The Jesuits were divided on this issue, though the majority believed he was saved. Whatever their individual opinions, however, they followed a common policy, and when asked to pronounce on the fate of the Sage they nimbly replied with a syllogism of which, they said, the major proposition was certain, though the minor was conditional:

1.   All those who know and love God above all else, and die in that knowledge and love, are saved.
2.   If Confucius had done so, then he was saved.

Beyond that they refused to particularize and threw back the question, urging the literati to consult their own books.

A frequent Jesuit accusation against the mendicants was that, quite gratuitously, they preached the damnation of Confucius and of all unbaptized ancestors. But in fact, they were not so reckless, although there were difficult moments, as the following anecdote shows. A missionary (called 'Ai Ju-lüeh') was quizzed by a Chinese who later recorded what happened.

> According to the Christians' ten prohibitions if a man takes a concubine because he has no son, then he has broken a great commandment and will go to hell. Now, if this is true, then the past emperors who had concubines cannot avoid hell.[32] So I put this to the missionary: 'King Wen had many concubines, what do you say to that?' He sighed deeply for a long time, but made no reply.
>
> I enquired again the second day. Again, deep sighs but no answer.
>
> On the third day I said, 'The matter must be thoroughly discussed and clarified, for only in that way can you bring people to understand and rally to you, and no longer harbour any doubts.' Ai once again thought long and deeply, then he said with great hesitation, 'At first I didn't want to tell you about this, but now I will.' Then he sighed again for quite a while and gravely announced, 'I shall speak frankly to *you*, old brother, though in the presence of others I certainly wouldn't have said anything. I very much fear that King Wen too has gone to hell.' Then, reconsidering, he said: 'I am speaking of the principle, not the man himself, for it could be that, having subsequently repented sincerely, King Wen was not damned after all'. What mean and shifty phrases with which to defame and slander the sages. (39)

---

[32] In all Chinese imperial history, there was apparently only one monogamous emperor (F. W. Mote, *Cambridge History of China*, 7(i) (Cambridge, 1988), 350).

Now, contrary to what might be expected, the embarrassed missionary, Ai Ju-lüeh, here cornered into harshness rather than compromise, was no friar, but Fr Giulio Aleni who was praised by friar and Father alike as 'intelligent, circumspect and courteous in both word and deed; everything he does is preceded by mature reflection'. A modern Jesuit finds him 'well acquainted with Chinese psychology, one of the greatest of the early Jesuits, he had an extraordinary mastery of Chinese culture and never failed to observe in minute detail the ritual of cultivated society which endeared him to the hearts of those who met him. He was known as the Western Confucius' and Navarrete thought him 'one of the giants of the mission'.

But the 'Western Confucius' seems to have been unaware that the Dominican theologians Vitoria and El Tostado had declared that polygamy among non-believers was not a sin.[33] Nothing shows more clearly how some Jesuits could suffer as much as friars when faced with persistent questioners, and that, like the friars, they too, sometimes limited their concessions. In other words, it suggests that the general picture of the all-accommodating and permissive Jesuit is as simplistic and overdrawn as is the picture of the harsh, uncompromising friar. (40)

On this particular topic Navarrete trod as delicately as Agag, and Friar Varo noted approvingly that he never broached the subject himself, and when questioned always side-stepped skilfully. However, his private analysis was as severe as Fr Alieni's, for he was antagonized by Confucius's refusal to discuss the possibility of an after-life, and he decided that the Sage was an atheist who recognized only a material First Cause. (41)

This distinction made, Navarrete's sinomania was limitless. His Chinese readings continued to astonish him; he found sayings of philosophers, moralists, emperors, fit to be compared with anything from the Apostles, Church Fathers, Saints Francis or Dominic. The Chinese were an example not merely to the laity but even to religious. Their piety in performing their pagan rites was a reproach to priests who were slovenly in offering the holy sacrifice of the mass. Even the detested Buddhists were better then Christians, and many years later, at the end of his life, in poverty and near despair, he would remember their temples 'spotless, sumptuous, and packed with worshippers', and their monks whom the 'very Desert Fathers could not have equalled in austerity.' The converts too were models. Not only did they hear three or four masses daily, but they did so devoutly, kneeling throughout. Seeing them, Navarrete repeated his conclusion that 'these new Christians are better than the old!' Such was their natural goodness that it was unnecessary to preach some of the Commandments to them: they were already observing them.

---

[33] Augustine (*De doc. christiana*, 3:18) thought it more commendable to use the fertility of many women for an unselfish end, than to use the flesh of one woman for lust. This referred to the Old Testament but seems to fit the Chinese situation.

For Friar Domingo these were the 'Athenians of the East'.[34] He was impressed by their cultural life: by the examination system, which, he naively believed, ensured a meritocracy. He praised its precautions against cheating or bribery, making it worthy to be introduced into all the universities of Spain. Chinese students had no vacations, only eight annual 'play days' and were obvious models for the rioting students he had seen in Salamanca a dozen years before.

Sinomania enabled him to accept the peaceful nature of the Chinese which others dismissed as cowardice. He admitted they were less warlike than the Japanese ('the Spaniards of Asia'), but saw their lack of martial ambition and preference for learning as a God-given virtue. Even Ricci saw them as cowardly effeminates, their very anger was womanish, and for them it was no dishonour to run away. An earlier Spanish visitor, Friar Martín de Rada, put them down as 'the wretchedest warriors in the world', and for the Jesuit Baltasar Gracián 'Cowardice dwells in China'. It is certainly true that after the Manchu conquest many Chinese literati reacted against their new masters' military prowess by rejecting martial arts and physical exercise as vulgar, suitable only for barbarians or professionals. They themselves adopted delicate ways, became hypochondriacal and sensitive, took to books and flowers, became poets or monks. Later, this was to appeal to the Europeans of the Enlightenment, who, indulging simultaneously their *rêve chinois* and pacifism, found here yet another Chinese virtue to admire.

Jonathan Spence's *Death of Woman Wang* shows provincial life in Shantung at the time when Navarrete travelled through the area. Spence's picture is one of hardship, heavy taxes, levies, crop failures, floods, plagues, feuds, bandits, corrupt officials, arrogant soldiers, all giving the lie to Domingo's cosmetic version. But determined to show China as a model for Europe, and as a living text for his social sermons, he ignored this inconvenient evidence.

---

[34] It was not Athens to everyone: 'Here I am, alone and unhappy in the darkness of this Egypt of China', began a gloomy letter from Friar Riccio, and the Jesuit Gouveia at the same time reported 'Not a hand's breadth of land in all China is at peace'; Friar Coronado found the 'iniquities of this kingdom are incredible: the fidelity, piety, and respect common to all the nations of the earth, are unknown here'.

II

The Dominicans had had a mission station in the small town of Fu-an, in Fukien province, since 1632.[35] Friar Navarrete arrived there in 1658 to join three friars: Juan García, Francisco Varo, and the Chinese Gregorio Lo, whose ordination in Manila he had witnessed two years earlier. García had been in the Philippines since 1632 and in China since 1636, so that his long experience was helpful to Navarrete, who was also fortunate in being with Varo, a notable language scholar. All three profited by the presence of Lo. (42)

García had gossip about the Jesuit Martini who had brought the new decree from Rome. In particular he related an incident when Martini had travelled through the area as an official gunpowder-mandarin. Local converts asked their priest, Friar Francisco Diez, to wait upon the Jesuit-mandarin and to be seen talking with him, so showing that Diez and his converts belonged to the same religion as the powerful courtier Jesuits in Peking; in that way they would suffer less harassment from local petty officials. Diez agreed and set off to seek an audience, but the Jesuit-mandarin, seeing the friar clad in cheap cotton, sweating and dishevelled after the journey on foot, did not dare acknowledge him, lest he himself should lose face with the magnates who were his fellow travellers. This affront excited universal hostility among the friars, and later it found its place in the anti-Jesuit propaganda soon to be so popular in Europe. (43)

Navarrete found the story credible, for 'once we were resting in the heat of the day in a Bonze's temple where we were treated with every courtesy by those heathen, when a party of people passed by. Travelling with them was a certain person [i.e. a Jesuit] who seeing us said with a gesture of contempt, "Oh, these friars!" We were ashamed but answered with silence'. So Martini, gorgeous in silk dragon robes, and brandishing his unwelcome decree, remained a subject for warm discussion among the friars for long afterwards. (44)

In 1661 the Dominicans decided to break the deadlock created by the two contradictory papal rulings and so, early that year, they called a conference at their new church at Lan ch'i in Chê-kiang province.[36] Navarrete could not attend, but sent a memorandum stating his opinion of the two decrees. The more educated converts were consulted and, gratifyingly, confirmed the friars' belief that the concessions granted to Martini in Rome were based on misleading information. The new decree was therefore declared 'invalid'. The

---

[35] Fu-an (Fogan, to Spaniards) in Fukien province, then a town of 3 000 inhabitants, six days' journey north of Fu-chou. The friars' residence there was named after the Holy Rosary. On Fukien see Zürcher, 427–456 *passim*.

[36] St John the Evangelist Church, built by friars Juan Bautista Morales and Domingo Coronado in 1656 with help from a convert literatus, Lin Tcho.

meeting then drafted 22 questions for submission to Rome in the hope of clarification. Navarrete was one of the signatories of this document (dated April–May 1661) which was forwarded to headquarters in Manila, from where it was taken to Rome by Friar Juan Polanco. The Holy Office did not answer until 1669, when it straightfacedly declared that both the apparently contradictory decrees of 1645 and 1656 were valid and each missionary was to observe them according to his own conscience. Rome was still refusing to commit itself, and this temporizing inevitably led to further dissension. (45)

In the meantime, however, there was work to be done in Fu-an. It was frustrating for Navarrete when, in the summer of 1661, he fell sick with fever after having been caught in a rainstorm when making a sick-call. He was forced to remain inactive until November, when he was posted to Chin-hua (Chê-kiang province) replacing Friar Polanco who had left for Rome with the Lan ch'i conference minutes. The 11 days' journey to Chin-hua provided Friar Domingo with more examples of Chinese civility. In the provincial custom-house, for instance, the officials gave him tea, and, much to his relief, made no attempt to examine his baggage which contained altar wine and 50 pieces of eight, half the entire resources of the 11 Dominicans scattered throughout the empire.

In Chin-hua ('City of the Golden Flower') he performed some baptisms at the newly-built church, but was less successful than in Fu-an where earlier he had baptised over 250 converts in two years. This is hardly surprising, since the Dominicans had some success in Fu-an county where by 1746 about 20 to 30 per cent of the population were Catholic. This was possibly because the locals had contact with outsiders from the Philippines, Japan, Malacca, and Sumatra, and so adapted more easily to foreigners and their ideas.

Soon after his arrival he overheard a conversation between two Chinese, one of whom was a Catholic. This convert was asked by his companion why God had consented to be born in barbaric Europe, leaving the Chinese in ignorance for so long. Navarrete had ached to join in the dispute but had to content himself with giving the questioner a book to study, and later, to his delight, the man was baptized. Convinced now that he should devote himself to explaining Christian doctrine in Chinese, he went to a nearby village where there were educated converts who could help him. He was careful to submit all his work to the criticism of natives, and also to choose Christians converted by Jesuits as well as by friars, in the hope of achieving the best approach.[37] (46)

In Chin-hua again, he found so many daily enquirers that the friars were never off duty and had at all times to be ready with patient answers, never showing weariness or falling short of Chinese standards of courtesy.

---

[37] All the missionaries needed native help before publishing (Vaeth, 243). Modern Jesuits (1925) found it difficult to learn the language after the age of 30: 'all our priests speak the language, some very well, but those able to write a short newspaper article are rare' (*Acta Cong.*, 22).

Navarrete wanted to help future missionaries prepare themselves, even before they left Europe, for the peculiar difficulties of the China mission. Newcomers must realise that the Chinese would regard them much as they themselves regarded the Amerindians. Unable to resist a dig at earlier writers, he urged the appointment of foreign ambassadors to China, pointing out that one benefit could be more accurate reports.[38]

So he began the translation of a book of moral precepts, known to him as the *Ming-hsin pao-chien*. 'The first book I read in that country, and which I took a great fancy to because of its plainness and brevity, is the book called the Precious Mirror of the Soul'. He saw it as a kind of Chinese *Imitation of Christ*. He regretted he could never match the elegance of the original, and had to content himself with expressing the sense of the Chinese as nearly as possible. He finally translated enough to make up the fourth section of his *Tratados*, which consists of moral exhortations and apophthegms attributed to Confucius and other sages.

Once more he was struck by the many sayings which could have come from the saints. The whole book, he found, was full of Christian doctrine; even the printer's preface admonished the reader that life was like crossing a frozen river, and that at any moment the thaw might come. Indeed, some of the precepts in the *Precious Mirror* were too exacting. Navarrete comments of one that it is a Counsel of Perfection, 'This heathen spins too fine a thread! His advice is well enough for the saintly but the rest of us must settle for less'. Other sayings set standards which, though not beyond attainment, were still too lofty even for good Catholics: 'I wish those who regularly go to confession and communion would observe this last precept. But no, the author of this excellent moral teaching has more faithful disciples in his own heathendom than he would ever find in Europe. Shame on us!' The *Ming-hsin pao-chien* denounced games and play-going as frivolities, and Navarrete heartily agreed, though he noted the theatre in China was less dangerous than in Europe where it provoked licentiousness. The Chinese, very properly, never allowed a woman to appear on the stage. But then their general attitude to women was laudable, though they tended to be too severe 'as though God had created Eve not from Adam's rib, but from his foot'. There were 'entire books, and not small ones either', dedicated to the subject of marriage, detailing the grounds for divorce, which included loquaciousness in a wife: 'If this were so in Europe, there's many a marriage would be dissolved'. The difference lay in that the Chinese women seemed exemplary, and there was no need to imitate Democritus who married a small woman, saying 'when I choose evil I choose only a little of it'. Chinese women were hard workers, modest dressers, used no cosmetics, were rarely seen in public and, in general, behaved like nuns. The custom of foot-bandaging, which

---

[38] Shortly after (1701), Rome set up a diplomatic school, just as Cardinal de Tournon's legation to China was in the making.

helped to keep them at home, was loudly praised by Navarrete, who would have liked the practice to spread.

The busy rhythm of work and study went on as the friars catechized their neophytes and in turn were themselves edified. Then, in 1664, they suffered a serious blow when Friar Juan Bautista Morales died on 17 September. He had been sick for four months and his colleagues brought him down from Chê-kiang to Fukien, where it was warmer. They advised his return to Manila, but love of China kept him there. For Navarrete it was a personal loss, because during the 18 years since they had left Spain together he had come to admire and respect Morales, and hoped he had caught something of his zeal. Narrow but sincere in his views, Morales was implacable in his distrust of the Jesuits and even as he lay dying he urged Friar Varo to write a treatise showing the rites were superstitious.

Navarrete succeeded him as superior of the China Dominicans and soon afterwards the provincial chapter in Manila appointed him to the church of St John in Lan ch'i. But it was an appointment he never took up, for suddenly persecution broke upon the mission.

5 Progress and persecution

One can't confine oneself to writing only edifying stories if the truth is prejudiced thereby.

— Fr Adam Schall

One morning in 1661, Navarrete, entering the sacristy of the Fu-an church, was surprised to find the ivory crucifix lying face downwards on the floor, although the nail was still in the wall and the cord of the cross was unbroken.[1] He knelt down, kissed the cross, and reverently replaced it. He was told that it had happened before and usually foretold trouble. Later it came to be seen as an omen of the persecution of 1664. Navarrete does not mention the incident because, always sceptical of 'omens', he was impatient with the 'foolish fancies of miracle-mongers, for God has need of no man's lie'.[2] He agreed with the Jesuit José de Acosta that the only miracle needed was that a missionary's manner of life should be in harmony with his preaching. So the anecdote comes from one of his Jesuit critics, who not unnaturally wished that in his writings he had confined himself to recounting this and other edifying passages, instead of continually sniping at them. (1)

The 'omen' came in the golden days of the mission. In Peking the Jesuits seemed firmly entrenched. Suitable men had been found to enter the door pushed open by the dying Ricci, including the German Fr Adam Schall von Bell, and later the Belgian Ferdinand Verbiest, men of extraordinary ability, in every way worthy of Ricci, and successful in continuing his work.

---

[1] I have supplemented Navarrete's version of the persecution with the more realistic account by the Franciscan Antonio Caballero de Santa María in SinFran, II: 502–606.

[2] Belief in 'omens' was widespread, and Keith Thomas notes 'Archbishop Laud was badly shaken when he found his portrait on the study wall had fallen to the floor' (*Religion and the Decline of Magic* (Harmondsworth, 1988), 105).

In 1630 Schall took on the work of preparing the Chinese state calendar in accordance with the latest European mathematical calculations. The calendar was all-important within the empire, for it was also an almanac with astrological functions and used, said Fr Semedo, to select 'fortunate, or unfortunate days, to do or leave undone such things as to take a voyage, to go out of doors, to make marriage, to bury the dead, to build, and other similar affairs; whence the Chinese in all their business, do so observe these rubrics, that merely not to go against these rules, they hasten, defer, or let alone whatsoever they have to do'. Fr Verbiest believed that 'in all the countries of the world there is no other book which is so solemnly promulgated every year as the Chinese calendar'. (2)

So Fr Adam Schall as reviser of the imperial calendar-almanac was a person of power and influence. But his position was never a happy one, for he met serious opposition. First, there was resentment among the officials supplanted by him, and this ultimately led to the persecution of 1664; second, some of his own Jesuit colleagues worried about the propriety of what he was doing. Of these the most hostile was a Portuguese, Gabriel de Magalhães, who, nonetheless, on one occasion, saved in a crisis through Schall's influence, cried in relief, 'Oh blessed Calendar, by which we live!' (3)

Needless to say, Schall's new post was also criticized by the friars, and in Europe enemies of the Society professed themselves scandalized that Jesuits were resorting to 'black magic *ad maiorem Dei gloriam*'. Appeals and counter-appeals to Rome brought a pronouncement that Schall might retain the post, provided he had nothing to do with the superstitions attached to the calendar. This distinction was too nice to be practical. Navarrete had a good deal to say on the matter, and getting two Jesuits with one stone, related that Fr Fabre had once told him how he himself had been present when Adam Schall received a mandarin's request to signify a propitious day for a certain business deal 'which the Father did with such ease that Fr Fabre wondered at it, though he himself is easy-going enough'.[3] Many were dissatisfied with Schall's explanation that he only put into the calendar what was scientifically true, and that the superstitious accretions were nothing to do with him. Other critics felt that even though he saw the distinction there was a danger of scandal, since the calendar circulated throughout the empire under his name, 'the work is public: the explanation secret'. Schall, then, had to soothe troubled colleagues, and calm the impatience of others who thought that with his new influence he ought to have converted the entire court. Unfortunately Schall was not good at either soothing or calming. He was playing a slow game which demanded skill and patience and in a moving

---

[3] Schall had a sense of humour, and when a mandarin asked if he would be lucky in marriage, Adam answered yes, provided he avoided old women, who would 'bring rain on the feast'. To a scandalized Portuguese, Adam explained that 'silly questions get silly answers'.

passage of his *Historica Relatio* he defended himself. On the face of it there seemed to be every reason to hope for success, but, unfortunately for the Fathers, trouble was imminent. (4)

The early 17th century found the ruling Ming dynasty near collapse. There was a general deterioration in government, civil war was close, invaders advanced from the north, and the authorities remained indecisive. In the 1640s, when Manchu invaders were bold enough to make raids against Peking itself, the emperor drafted Schall to the work of casting cannon. By then, however, it was too late, and not even Jesuit cannon, engraved with saints' names, could help.[4] Provincial uprisings added to the prevailing chaos; the capital fell to rebels, and in 1644 the last Ming emperor (Schall's 'greatest ruler in the whole world'), committed suicide, or as the chronicler put it, 'the emperor of the Great Ming ascended to heaven on a dragon'. (5)

A general still loyal to the old dynasty now called upon the Manchu trespassers to help him subdue the rebel uprising within the empire, hoping that when this was done the Manchus would withdraw. But they who went to help remained to rule, for, said Navarrete, 'lions were called in to frighten off dogs'. The Jesuits had prepared for the unknown by backing both sides: they divided into two groups, one remaining with the Ming in case they survived; the other preparing to welcome the invading Manchus if they were successful. Schall refused to leave the city when it was overrun by rebels, and he saved the Jesuit residence by combining courage (which enabled him single-handedly to rout a group of inquisitive intruders) with a simple faith (which resorted to throwing pious emblems on to the roof).[5] In all, Schall had to endure a month-long reign of terror, but he stayed at his post, armed only with a Japanese sword and 'a beard long enough to supply the entire attacking force'. In the end the rebels, impressed by such bravery, left him alone.

Finally, when the new Manchu rulers were established in the capital, Schall presented a memorial explaining who he was, and after investigation, was allowed to remain. Not only did he keep his post as state astronomer, but in time he won the affection of the Manchu boy who ascended the Dragon Throne as the first of a new line.

The remnants of the Ming imperial family fled south with their supporters, including a Polish Jesuit, Michael Boym. One of the claimants to the dead emperor's throne was a Catholic (as was his wife, the symbolically christened Helena and a promisingly named son, Constantine), who

---

[4] Cannon founded later by Fr Verbiest were more successful and a grateful emperor declared they had turned the tide in crucial battles.

[5] 'The Jesuits, with all their brilliance, were a strange mixture, for side by side with their science went a vivid faith in devils and exorcisms. Though some superstitions wilted in their presence, philosophers might opine they brought as many with them' (Needham, *Science*, III: 457).

despatched Fr Boym to Rome for help. But no help came. Navarrete heard a story that Boym's mission failed because of the machinations of the Jesuit Martini then in Rome who, having written off the Ming, declared that the new rulers were there to stay and alone deserved support.

Navarrete disapproved of the Manchu 'usurpers', and criticized the Jesuits for working under them, thereby abandoning the old imperial family. To him it seemed that since the Ming pretender was a Catholic the powers of Europe should have taken action to restore his line to the throne. As always, the Jesuits were realistic; they had gone to China to save souls not dynasties, and did not care who ruled, if they could continue their work, preferably with imperial favour. When therefore the Manchu ruler accepted them they gave him their whole-hearted support.[6]

Schall had served his courtier's apprenticeship in the last decades of the Ming, when, says Zürcher, access to the Inner Court meant associating with the group that dominated both throne and harem and terrorized the bureaucracy, namely, the imperial eunuchs. Yet even with them the Jesuits had their successes, baptizing some of these elite, but hated, members of the royal household.

In that dangerous and slippery world Schall's experience now stood him in good stead and, as time went by, the new emperor, the young Shun-chih, seemed to grow more dependent on the priest, showing him such unprecedented favours that from 1651–60 the Jesuit seemed almost the *de facto* regent of China, and at one point he moved into private quarters in the east end of the palace. In 1652 he reported that the emperor had publicly praised him on a number of occasions and had excused him the ceremonial kowtow; that the empress, in a recent illness, had refused to call in Buddhist bonzes to offer prayers, but instead had sent Fr Schall generous alms and asked him to intercede on her behalf with his God. Others told similar stories, and optimistic reports to Rome left the empire by every post.

Where Jesuits were mistaken, simple friars had no hope of being right, and they too misread the signs. Friar Morales welcomed the Manchu invasion, and, reporting the death of the Ming emperor, the existence of three separate claimants to the throne, and the state of chaos throughout the empire, reminded Propaganda Fide that 'when the river is in turmoil, Christ's fishers find opportunities'. It was too early for anyone to know it, but the fishermen had overestimated the catch.

For the moment the future looked promising, and Navarrete thought this was 'the August of the harvest'. In fact Christianity had already had its chance, when, under the last of the Ming, a liberal reaction against Confucianism had been strong, a reaction which might well have been made to work in favour of the missionaries. Under the new Manchu dynasty

---

[6] Such realism irritated their critics. 'While Spain was the greatest power the Jesuits were all Spaniards, but, since the declension of the house of Austria, they're all French', said Bayle.

imperial prestige restored orthodox Confucian conservatism, making the spread of Christianity more difficult.

Navarrete never had much faith in the vaunted dependence of the young Shun-chih emperor upon Fr Schall. He dismissed it (on Jesuit evidence, he claimed), as merely the result of a young man's interest in an old man's curious lore. (Whatever the truth of that, the second Manchu emperor, the great K'ang-hsi, distrusted the Europeans. He warned his successors that the clever Westerners turned everything to their profit. He went on to say that while he reigned there would be nothing to fear; but future rulers were to keep a close watch over the foreign barbarians.)

But whether Navarrete was right or not, under the Shun-chih emperor the Jesuits enjoyed power and prestige and had few anxieties, other than that they were only a handful, and that friars, in increasing numbers, were trespassing in their Manchu vineyard.

II

However, some Jesuits in Peking wanted to get rid of other Jesuits. and there grew up among them an anti-Schall faction which worked for the removal from the mission of the brilliant but abrasive Father. Schall's chief opponent was Fr Magalhães, an engineer and mechanical genius, born of the same family as the navigator Magellan. In 1644 when he and an Italian, Fr Luigi Buglio, were evangelizing in Sichuan province, they fell into the hands of a sadistic freebooter, Chang Hsien-chung, the self-styled 'King of the West'. Forced against their will to serve him as astronomers, they suffered threats, torture and near-execution for the next three years. When after this gruelling experience they managed to get back to the safety of Peking, they were suspected of having willingly collaborated with a rebel. Magalhães and Buglio were condemned to two years' imprisonment. Schall claimed he was powerless to help his two colleagues without risking his own position. 'And why,' he asked with characteristic tactlessness, 'should I risk my own head for a pair who had evidently lost theirs? They lay down in the mud, why should I get dirty pulling them out?'

After their release from prison, the anti-Schall campaign began. Magalhães, too ready to pick up slanderous chit-chat, soon found allies for his cause among tale-bearing servants and gossiping converts. In letters of alarming content and regularity, he began to confide his suspicions to Rome. The Jesuits were later to publish a popular series of *Lettres édifiantes et curieuses* retailing pious stories and optimistic statistics from the missions, but their private, unpublished letters are often more curious than edifying. Certainly, Magalhaes's reports were more hostile to Schall, and more scurrilous, than those of any friar. (6)

Schall was in a unique position. During the 1650s he was on the friendliest terms with the young emperor, to whom he had access at any hour. Similarly the youngster would call on him informally, sitting cross-legged, or stretched out across the bed, talking for hours. The two clearly felt affection for each other, and the youth respected the priest who had so much to teach him. Schall was appointed the first European director of the astronomy bureau,[7] given titles of honour, had his imperial salary doubled, and inevitably came to resemble a courtier, even a state minister, living in style, giving and attending elaborate receptions, wearing one of his twenty silk robes. (7)

Schall now made a mistake. He adopted his servant's son as his own 'grandson'. The servant, P'an Chin-hsiao, who seems to have had Schall completely in his power, then automatically became Schall's 'son'.[8] The

---

[7] No European was ever president of the bureau.

[8] There was a story that during the Ming-Manchu war, Schall had summoned Portuguese help for the Ming from Macao. But his servant treacherously held on to the letter and, after

adoption was encouraged by the emperor, concerned that the Jesuit had no children to venerate him after death. 'There are three things,' Mencius had said, 'which are unfilial, and the worst of them is to have no posterity'. On that score, Schall was now provided for. But the emperor's pious manoeuvre was misinterpreted by the Jesuit's critics. Pained requests for denials and clarifications, in this and other puzzling matters (the superstitions linked to the calendar, the casting of cannon) came in from Manila and Macao; denials and attempted clarifications (accompanied by fresh accusations) went back to Macao and Manila, but above all to Rome. In the Jesuit Curia, where the reports were filed as 'the disorders in Peking', the authorities must sometimes have felt the need for the ecclesiastical equivalent of a stiff whisky. (8)

Unfortunately, Adam Schall had a way of alienating others. Some years earlier he had engineered, or connived at, the ejection from Peking of two Franciscans, and he did not hesitate now to do the same with two of his fellow Fathers, Martini and Furtado. Moreover, he knew how to inspire fear. Jesuit Visitors (area inspectors) officially investigating the mission, might mutter in private that Schall's residence was a 'hell house' (as did Fr Simon da Cunha) but in public showed him an indulgence bordering on complicity (as did the same Fr Simon da Cunha). Magalhães himself noted nervously that on one occasion he was forced to write his report on Schall away from the residence because 'there the very walls and floors have ears', and the place abounded in spies. (9)

Magalhães ('I am a mere goose among these swans') had opened his attack in 1648, giving vent to his feelings in rather shrill prose ('furious passion and passionate fury'; 'weeping tears of blood') about 'one of our own Brothers, a son of our common mother the Society of Jesus, a European, a priest, a religious of the four vows, and a preacher of the Faith of God, the good Fr Adam — a man without charity, justice, or humanity: *Filii matris meae pugnaverunt contra me* [my mother's sons were angry with me]'. He denounced Schall for violating the Jesuit rule; for pandering to Chinese superstitions by choosing lucky days and burial-places; complained he had been refused entry into his house ('the better to hide his misdeeds'); lamented that Schall was spending community funds on his servant, and on extravagant personal ventures; that when depressed he made his house-boy sing 'lewd' songs to cheer him up. Magalhães quoted Fr Manoel Dias's request to Schall to dismiss the servant, P'an Chin-hsiao, 'who', said Dias, 'twice dared to say to Your Reverence [Schall] that you didn't love him any more, because you now have your eye on someone else, on whom you lavished affection'. (10)

By the following year (1649) Magalhães and Furtado began to imply that

---

the Manchu victory, used it to blackmail Schall and thenceforth 'lorded it over his lord' (NC 26). Fr Buglio reported to the general that the servant ruled Adam even 'in matters concerning our Society' (ARSI, JapSin 162, fol. 58r).

this was a matter for the Inquisition. Backed up by Frs Longobardi, Buglio and Ferrari, they urged that Schall be dismissed from the Society. If he proved obstinate they would dissemble until such time as they had enough friends in Peking to permit them to punish him without endangering the mission: 'The five Fathers who sign below, judge in the Lord that this is necessary for the greater service of God, the credit of the Society, and the welfare of souls'. (11)

This would not have worried Schall, if there was any truth in their claim that he had once said to a student anxious to join the Jesuits, 'You're all dying to get into the Society, well just let me out and I'll be satisfied'. Two days later, Fr Longobardi on his own account wrote a confidential (*soli*) letter to the provincial reporting the 'disorders of this residence' and warning that any reply should be sent in such a way that it would not fall into the hands of 'our friend here'.[9] (12)

1649 was a busy year, but so was 1650. The range of complaints widened. Now, it seems, only the well-dressed could get an audience with Fr Schall, the poor were sent away. Again, Schall had acquired 'dirty' pictures from members of a Dutch embassy which he showed to his houseboy and guests, and he had developed immodest tastes 'not only for women, but also for boys'. After that it was no surprise to read that the Jesuit residence was known in the city not as the house of God, but as a pothouse, a tavern for gossips. Magalhães's evidence suggests that the little Peking Catholic community was alternately shocked and fascinated by Schall's antics. But there was something near schism in the congregation: some parishioners refused to attend Schall's mass; others demanded his recall; one group, including old folk who had known Ricci, admonished him, possibly feeling resentment at his attachment to the Manchus. (13)

Later, in 1659, there was a rumour that Adam Schall was to be appointed provincial superior of the north China mission, and this sparked off more hurried denunciations. Life did not seem to have changed much, as, reported Magalhães, Peking was ringing with talk of Fr Adam's doings. Far from taking the advice to dismiss his servant and adopted grandson, he had had them promoted to mandarin rank. And he had taken up games of chance over cups of wine with 'prostitutes'.[10] Moreover, his intrigues at court had led to the downfall, torture and even the death of some officials. Magalhães,

---

[9] A Jesuit's letter to a superior, if marked '*soli*' on the envelope, is 'for the addressee's eyes only', thus allowing a subordinate to go directly to the top. The system was not infallible: Schall opened confidential mail entrusted to him, and once broke into Furtado's room, while he was out saying mass, to remove a letter of complaint about his servant (Pih, 82). (The system continues: in the first quarter of 1969 the general received 5 480 letters, 72 of which were '*soli*': ISJ, I (1969), 240.)

[10] '*Micare digitis*', the Finger Game (*Morra*) in which the loser has to drink a cup of wine. Popular in China as Chi-moee: 'A bacchanalian game played during the last course of a meal, accompanied by much boisterous mirth' (says Archdeacon Gray, rather primly, 65–66).

warming to his task, listed 31 reasons why Schall should not be appointed superior, adding 12 more showing that to do so would have dire results. Opening his 43 points, Magalhães implies that Schall had imperilled his vows of poverty, chastity and obedience. For instance, not content with dirty songs and pictures, he was now ordering the performance of bawdy plays. In religious matters he was unsatisfactory, making such remarks as that the pains of purgatory were only priests' exaggerations and, Faust-like, had said 'leave me my cash and garden, and afterwards God can do what he wants with my soul'. He was also accused of gluttony and, for disgraceful instance, 'coming home at night drunk, swaying from side to side on his horse, and having to be held upright by his servant', or with the servant riding pillion, in the manner favoured by homosexuals. (14)

Magalhães now turned to that same servant whose two sons Schall called his 'grandsons'. This pair accompanied Fr Adam 'about the Jesuit residence, at the altar, always at table, and many times in bed with him'. (He was also said to have refused to eat with Frs Furtado and Longobardi, 'two dotards, it's like being tied to a couple of corpses'.) Fr-Visitor Simon da Cunha, to whom Magalhães was writing, was reminded how he himself had witnessed similar goings-on in Peking, where he had found 'a day in that house seemed like a year'. (15)

Others joined in. Magalhães's inseparable companion, Fr Buglio, complained to the general in 1660, reporting how a newly arrived German, Fr Bernard Diestel, thought Schall 'ought to be burnt on 24 counts'. (16)

Buglio expressed a constant anxiety: if the friars discovered what the Fathers were trying to hide, then the pope and all Rome would soon know everything. Magalhães himself believed the friars did 'know everything'. Navarrete however makes no specific mention of these particular scandals. On the other hand, the affair may explain his later threats to bring out more material if provoked too much. The friars certainly knew about Schall's adoption, for the Dominican Riccio referred to it in letters to the Jesuit general and to his own Manila provincial. There were few secrets in the mission, and Navarrete, for example, had somehow managed to get sight of the Jesuit annual reports for 1638 and 1640. (17)

Magalhães wrote again to the general in 1660. He rejoiced that provincial visitors, mandarins, merchants, and scholars could now see two Christian churches open to the public in the heart of Peking. When they returned home their reports would spread the news throughout the provinces, and protect missionaries and converts from local harassment. Magalhães advocated a policy of opening churches all along the main route from Canton to Peking. The moment was at hand, for the Tartars were still at war and could pay less attention to the missionaries' activities. So, little by little, and without their noticing it, the Christian message would be spread ('*sensim sine sensu Res Christiana propagabitur*'). He also urged that more mathematicians be sent, 'God apart, the Faith here depends on mathematics'.

But in the same letter Magalhães reverted momentarily to his obsessive theme, accusing the recent Fr-Visitor of favouring and flattering Schall and his 'odious' servant. In the midst of his Latin Magalhães suddenly excused himself, oddly, in Chinese, for playing his old tune again: 'I can't do other. May your Paternity forgive me, your wretched little son, my zealous love of the Society and the mission forces me on'. He also complained that in order to mollify Schall, the Visitor had commissioned his portrait in official mandarin robes. (18)

Schall of course had his defenders (Frs Gravina, Brancati, Smogulenski and Verbiest), one of whom recalled that in Spanish America 12 concurring witnesses were needed before a statement could be accepted as evidence. In the Middle Kingdom even greater precautions were required, for the Chinese were liars and scandal-mongers.[11] Schall also defended himself with vigour, sarcasm and contempt, making studied references to his theological studies, and once at least what could pass for a veiled threat. Though angered, as he was so easily, he felt no qualms of conscience, since he was innocent. He admitted that his own converts called him 'a fornicator, sodomite and superstitious idolater', but he knew they did not really believe it. The source of his troubles was Magalhães who, like other Jesuits, had taken a fifth vow: that of lying. And as for Frs Longobardi and Furtado, they were just a pair of 'Susanna's elders'. (19)

It would be difficult, if it mattered, to decide where the truth lay. Magalhães may have been unbalanced by his earlier experiences in bandit hands, but seems unlikely to have imagined for 12 years something wholly untrue, and to have found others on the spot to share his fantasies. More likely, his prudish temperament, affronted by Schall's breezy relaxed way of life, and jealousy of his standing at court, made him read too much, too readily, into the signs.[12] There is no proof that Schall was unchaste, nor does Magalhães say so unequivocally. He finds him guilty of giving scandal, and admits he was only an ear-witness. Possibly Schall did no more than linger imprudently near 'occasions of sin'. On the other hand not much can be made of an imperial decree of 1653 praising Schall's chastity, since he might well have asked the complaisant young emperor to issue it. (20)

Fr Longobardi (one of the two Susanna's elders), who in 1649 had been denouncing Schall's misdemeanours and 'the disorders of this house', demanding the dismissal of Schall from the Society, now suddenly in 1651

---

[11] In modern times he has been defended vigorously by Fr Brucker; learnedly by Fr Vaeth; sympathetically by Rowbotham, and clumsily by Fr Dunne who brushes the allegations aside brightly. An impartial study is in Pih's *Magalhães*.

[12] In 1661, believing he was dying, Magalhães made his will: 'I beg Fr Adam to pardon my impertinence and the troubles I've caused him; all came from my good will, not any evil intent. I promise him I'll be more help to him in the court of Heaven (where I believe, trusting in divine Mercy, I'm going) than I was in this earthly court'. But there is no specific retraction (RAH, Jesuitas 22, fol. 18v).

turned about-face, defending him and demanding the withdrawal from the mission of Magalhães and Buglio. He further stated that as Schall's confessor for the past four years he could swear to his sexual purity.[13] (The accusations of gluttony and drunkenness might arise from Schall's having to entertain the young emperor in fitting style. As another example, in 1656 a Dutch ambassador presented the emperor with European wines, which in turn were passed to Schall, who generously gave a lavish party for friends.) (21)

'Credo' does not mean 'I behave'. Schall was indiscreet, injudicious, and his own worst enemy. Never one to explain himself, he did, however, admit in his death-bed confession that he had been imprudent in adopting a grandson to whom he had shown such great partiality. His notorious sarcasm, sharp tongue, quirky humour, high-handedness (and freedom to indulge them all in those 'golden years') alienated the more thin-skinned Latins around him. Even those colleagues who defended him found him difficult, bad-tempered, guilty of 'extravagances and excesses'.[14]

Thirty-odd years of independence far from Rome's anathemas, faint whimperings by the time they reached his mandarin's yamen, did not help his commitment to obedience. He was playing for massive stakes on behalf of the Church, and hope of success made him impatient of the qualms of moral pedants. In those years, more accustomed to ordering than obeying, he caught from his lofty contacts an indifference to lesser mortals. Like some distant viceroy too long *en poste*, he could not easily be controlled. Rome might send out inspectors, but nothing could be done with one so experienced in the politics and silky sinuosities of that court, which was a world in itself.

Endlessly busy, distracted by imperial whims and tasks, it was presumably impossible to keep up the Jesuit's routine of daily mental prayer as a spiritual defence. His religious fervour could easily grow cold, even *ad maiorem Dei gloriam*, leaving him in danger of becoming the Père Gauchet of the Jesuit mission, sacrificing his soul in the interests of the order. A saint could resist the corrupting draught of power, but no one thought Fr Adam was a saint, not even the admiring Shun-chih, who in 1653 exhorted him 'from now on you should devote yourself more prudently to self-improvement and to the service of your office in order that your name may go down in Our History. Is this not a beautiful thing?' Not a plaster saint,

---

[13] A confessor's declaration of his penitent's innocence was not then unusual, though not permitted by modern canon law. Longobardi's *volte face* may be explained by his age; he was 92, and possibly confused, or easily influenced, though his hand writing is clear and strong (ARSI, JapSin 142, No. 29). Magalhães wondered if Schall might have omitted sexual matters from his confessions (Pih, 93–4 and cf. Sipe, 5, 73, 124).

[14] A priest living as a secular ran risks: in Elizabethan England Fr Gifford aroused suspicion by continuing to wear lay-dress even in the safety of the continent and 'he considered one of the marks of the gentleman was the use of the brothel' (J. Bossy in T. Aston, *Crisis in Europe, 1560–1660* (London, 1965), 240).

Schall is a reminder that the self is a cast of characters. One full-length portrait reveals a sad-eyed man with an anxious face, but a later one, by Fr Grueber, shows a severe, determined, sharp-eyed man with a lived-in face, much changed from the earlier picture. (22)

In 1660, when Magalhães had warned Rome that mathematicians were needed in China, he specified they must be men of solid virtue lest, puffed up with pride, they fall into Satan's trap. Twenty years later, Schall's friend Fr Verbiest wrote the same, warning general Oliva of the dangers of that mission to which only the most fervent spirits should be sent. And, he added, leaving men there for too long was also dangerous, for their zeal might gradually cool: *'timendum est ne paulatim animus illorum multum hic tepescat'*. Was he, too, thinking of Schall when he wrote those words? (23)

Some remarks by the late Jesuit General Arrupe might suggest what happened to Fr Adam. 'If a Jesuit drops personal prayer on the pretext that his apostolate leaves no time for it, refuses all spiritual direction, seeks worldly contacts and diversions while leading a completely secularized life without any apostolic purpose, it is not surprising that a day comes when in all sincerity he asks himself, "Why am I in the Society?" ' (24)

There were other, more marginal, results. Missionaries were observers rather than participants of society, but that was not true of Schall whose adoption of a grandson brought him into contact with his servant's extended family and thus into a world normally closed to foreign barbarians. Later, Protestant missionaries often felt that they were cut off from the vast secret life of those they were trying to convert: 'The very gravity of their character would prevent them from being eye-witnesses of many particulars of the interior conduct of the Chinese', as Thomas Percy puts it. That limitation did not apply to Schall. (25)

Protestant missionaries also found that homosexual 'crushes' could be a problem, and the Catholics were constantly on guard against 'particular friendships', which were more feared than particular animosities. This was especially true of the Jesuits who were proud of their record of chastity.[15]

It has been noted by a hostile writer that the Jesuits maintained a 'silence extraordinaire' about Schall who 'for 20 years was not mentioned in Jesuit published letters, despite his high position'. Yet this would be understandable: one has only to recall the distress caused in the world of anthropology when the publication of Malinowski's diary revealed him as a very human being. (26)

---

[15] A cypher key issued to Jesuit provincials in 1602 shows that '54' was to be used to report 'friendship with young men' (F. Zubillaga, *Monumenta Mexicana*, VII(1981), 770).

III

Magalhães's last delation to Rome was dated 18 May 1660. In the Jesuit curia it was stolidly docketed, and laid to rest with a laconic superscription: 'Not answered: the writer has been imprisoned by the emperor of China'.

Schall's political success story is reminiscent of the Old Testament tales in which Joseph in Egypt or Daniel in Babylon rise to power as chief ministers, and with new wisdom discredit the old royal advisers. But those advisers wanted revenge and in 1657 a group of mandarins memorialized the Shun-chih emperor begging him not to visit private persons, clearly meaning Schall. In that same year a Muslim astronomer, displaced by Schall, hoping he had caught out the Jesuit making an error in his calculations, laid a formal accusation against him. It was decided to hold a public contest in October that year to see which of the two astronomers, Jesuit or Muslim, was correct in a test forecast. Referees were selected from the mandarins, who, for the occasion, learnt off the position of the stars well enough to detect the Muslim in an attempt to deceive them. Schall had saved his face in the presence of the officials and sightseers who had gathered for the event. His accuser, having escaped the death penalty only because Schall had pleaded for him, was thrown into jail.

In 1661, however, the year of Navarrete's 'omen' the Jesuits suffered a loss in the sudden death of the 23-year-old emperor, who died with all the dignity of a Roman stoic. Schall had hoped to convert him, but the highly-sexed youth could not live without his concubines and, moreover, had latterly moved towards Ch'an Buddhism.

Since his successor was still a child, four regents were nominated to control affairs and Fr Schall was appointed tutor to the new emperor. It appeared that all was to remain much as before. But hostile forces were steadily gathering against the missionaries, although, such was the memory of the late emperor's regard for Schall, that it was not till three years after his death that anyone dared make a move against them.

When it came the move was sudden. In August 1664 Fr Fabre reported that attacks were being made on Christians in the provinces, but no one dared molest them in the capital. Three months later it was a different story, 'the enemy are powerful, affairs are delicate'. In September a formal indictment had been presented against the Jesuits by an almost professional opponent, Yang Kuang-hsien, who collaborated with the disgruntled state astronomers in an effort to disgrace the Fathers. The charges in the indictment were many: the missionaries had spread false doctrines, teaching that Heaven itself was not the First Cause, but was dependent, and, as it were, a slave of God. But the emperor was the Son of Heaven, *ergo* the Christians were implying that the emperor was the son of a slave. Christians taught that there was another life, which was manifestly untrue. They had no respect for ancestors, saying their God was born without parents. The early missionaries had not revealed the story of the crucifixion, because it went against their claims for Christ's divinity.[16] Christianity, alone of all religions, adored an instrument of torture as a sacred icon, and since holy men were never punished as criminals, Christ must have been the leader of a rebellion. Moreover, if the incarnation were true why did it happen too late to save so many ancestors?

One interesting accusation was based on something the Jesuits had once hoped might attract the Chinese, namely that since all men originated in Judea, the Chinese were, therefore, the eastern branch of this universal family, and Catholicism was simply a revival of the religion of ancient China.[17] Yang Kuang-hsien condemned this because it would mean that the Chinese were descended from foreign barbarians. The Riccista stratagems were beginning to boomerang. These accusations were reinforced by others less theological: allegations that the missionaries were spies, the scouts of invading armies hoping to gain control of China. Much more serious than any of these was an accusation that in 1658 Schall had deliberately chosen an unlucky day for a royal burial. Superstitious fears, and the coincidence that Shun-chih and his consort had died in quick succession, impressed the authorities, who took the charges seriously. (27)

The Jesuits' trial began. Schall, now in his mid-seventies, and paralysed by a stroke, could scarcely speak. Fr Verbiest therefore defended him, though as a comparative newcomer he was hampered by not knowing Chinese fluently. The preliminary examinations lasted from 26 September until 12 November 1664, when they were imprisoned, and 'bound in nine chains'. A petition was submitted to the regency council urging the destruction of all Christian churches. This was rejected, though it was decided to summon the missionaries in the provinces to Peking for examination. The trial of Schall and the others dragged on through the winter, and it was January 1665 before sentence was passed: Schall was condemned to death, but the supreme council proved reluctant to confirm the sentence. Fresh charges were brought emphasizing that the Westerners' mathematics were erroneous and their astronomy unreliable. Yet another contest was arranged to take place at one of the city gates and the three schools of astronomers were ordered to forecast the time of an eclipse due to take place on 16 January. The Chinese announced the eclipse for 2.15 p.m., the Muslims for 2.30 and the Jesuits forecast the hour as 3.00 precisely. On the appointed day, before a large crowd of witnesses, the astronomers took up their places, the Jesuits still in chains. An official called out the times, and excitement became intense as the moment chosen first by the Chinese and then by the Muslims passed without bringing the eclipse, which began

---

[16] Corroboration, from a strange quarter, of the friars' allegation.
[17] A theory published in 1663 by a Jesuit convert, Li Tsu-po (Young, 173–4; Gernet, *Chine*, 176; Hummel, II: 890 and especially Lo-shu Fu, 35).

precisely as the Fathers had forecast. Once again the Jesuits had triumphed, showing, they afterwards agreed, that their challengers knew as much about astronomy 'as do the gypsies of Europe'. (28)

When their enemies pressed the accusation that an unlucky day had been nominated for a royal burial, Verbiest retorted that Schall was only concerned with the movement of stars, and that choosing lucky days was not his province. It was then alleged that as departmental head he was ultimately responsible. Verbiest countered that if this were so, then Schall's judges were also responsible, for ultimately they were his superiors, as he was the superior of those working under his charge. But all argument was vain and the sentence came on 15 April: Schall was again condemned, to the 'lingering death'.[18]

What had happened so far might have come from the Acts of the Apostles, what followed seemed like one of the pious stories from the old, unreformed Roman breviary. The sentence was referred to higher authority for confirmation, and the following morning, Thursday 16 April 1665, as the matter was under discussion in the palace, an earthquake took place, causing injuries and damage. When the first fright was over, the officials turned back to their business, and again another tremor shook the city. Panic spread and the empress-dowager ran screaming through the palace. The collapse of one of the walls of Schall's prison seemed peculiarly pointed, since earthquakes, traditionally associated with miscarriages of justice, were commonly followed by amnesties. There was therefore general relief when it became known that the empress had intervened on Schall's behalf. A sudden outbreak of fire in the city was taken to be yet another manifestation of celestial anger. Schall's judges now made haste to become his defence counsel, refusing to ratify the sentence, declaring the selection of lucky days belonged to inferior members of the Board of Mathematics. They now remembered that Schall had repeatedly protested that his mathematics had nothing to do with such matters. Admittedly, he was wrong to allow his seal of office to be placed on the chosen day, and must be punished for it, but he was not to die, for he was an old man who deserved well of the empire. In the middle of May 1665 he was released.[19] (29)

---

[18] Described by Caballero (SinFran II: 559) and Gray (I: 59–60), the full horror of this form of execution can be seen in photographs of the process in the case of Pu Chu-li, condemned in 1905 for the murder of a prince.

[19] If these timely miracles in China proved the Jesuits right, others in France proved them wrong. The celebrated miracle of Christ's Thorn, when Pascal's niece was suddenly cured of a lachrymal fistula (1656), conveniently reinforced the Jansenist position against the Jesuits.

IV

The persecution began in the provinces and had been stimulated by an imperial order to send the missionaries to Peking for questioning. Reactions to these instructions varied, some local mandarins were well disposed, and treated the priests kindly. Others took the opportunity to indulge their hostility. Frs Gouveia and Costa were allowed to make their own way to Peking without guards. Frs Brancati and Fabre were left unrestricted in their church for some months, while the district governor, disbelieving the allegations, petitioned that they be excused the summons and allowed to stay there. Others, less fortunate, after seeing their churches despoiled and possessions confiscated, were handcuffed and despatched under guard.

The expenses of the journey lay on the accused, and for some this was a problem. Fr Canevari, an old man of 72, had little money and was sorely tried when, at one town *en route*, an officious mandarin detained him, hoping for a bribe. One of his guards, anxious to help the old Jesuit, and relying on Chinese inquisitiveness, struck on a surrealistic solution: he spread word that the foreign barbarian was 380 years' old. As he had foreseen, such crowds of sightseers 'came running and panting' to see the phenomenon that the mandarin, fearing a rebellion was about to break out, ordered the troublesome Jesuit out of his territory immediately, without insisting on his squeeze.

The Franciscan Caballero de Santa María heard the news on 16 January 1665, the day on which the Jesuits in the capital were forecasting the eclipse. That eclipse seemed to him the symbol of the fate of the Church in China; the only consolation he could see was that six Dominicans, being unknown to the authorities, had not been summoned to the capital, and were able to remain in hiding. Since one of them was the Chinese Friar Gregorio Lo, it was hoped that he would be able to help some of the converts who were suddenly left without priests. Caballero and the amiable French Fr Jean Valat were arrested on 20 January, and were unfortunate enough to be lodged in a special prison for the worst offenders. Conditions there were harsh, but they resolved to turn their trials to good account, so that when they were shown chains ('and not gold ones either') with which they would be shackled if they did not offer the warders a bribe, they astonished these by displaying not merely a willingness but a desire to be shackled. The jailers 'stood there with the chains idly in their hands, and never again tried to play the bogeyman with us'; but the prison was so crowded that they 'felt like sardines in a pannier'. There was no room to lie down, and sometimes they had to crouch Chinese-style for hours on end. The first night was spent in the only available space, a makeshift lavatory, to which prisoners came all night long tramping over the priests. Dawn found them 'sitting in a stream of urine, but nothing could make us fretful and even if we were still there we would rejoice'. Yet the lack of privacy was painful, for they had to perform their natural functions in public, and, though this did not seem to trouble the native prisoners, the missionaries found the 'mere thought of it an affliction and so we decided to eat and drink only just enough to keep ourselves alive', thereby reducing their body waste. During the first week Caballero suffered a looseness of the bowels which caused him intense shame, for 'there was nowhere even to spit out'.

Though ever more prisoners arrived, and few seemed to leave, the Chinese never lost heart. Indeed their very cheerfulness was an additional torment. The quieter ones ordinarily played card games, or dice, until dawn, but the majority passed their nights drinking, singing, shouting, until about midnight, when, drunk enough to begin fighting amongst themselves, they would leap upon each other with terrifying grunts 'gnawing and biting each other like piglets in a sty'. Special celebrations were even more distressing, and the two missionaries were shocked by the prisoners' way of welcoming the New Year. Their 'little feastings', accompanied by bawling and every kind of horseplay, quickly degenerated as they got drunker until the 'whole night became one long confused shout'. Worse followed, for, 'as the Chinese are addicted to sodomy', the prison soon became a 'living picture of hell in which not even the smoke was lacking', because earlier they had cooked their evening meal on a makeshift stove.[20] Eventually, 'just as the blacksmith's dog learns to ignore the smiting of the anvil', so friar and Jesuit, overcome by weariness, fell asleep. (30)

After 15 miserable days the judge sent to say that for a few *taels* he would remove them to a better place, to which they replied that even if they had 'golden millions' they would not give him a groat. The judge, after one more week, gave up in despair, and sent them on their way. To meet the expense of the journey they had to have their two small silver chalices melted down, although local Christians, who had remained faithful and fed them daily in prison, managed to raise a contribution. During their stay in prison they had the consolation of converting the local headman, who accompanied them to the capital, where, having completed his catechism, they baptized him on 18 March.

The Peking prison was worse than the previous one, but here also they were encouraged by the loyalty of the converts who sent food every day,

---

[20] Navarrete deplored what seemed a national tendency: 'In Spain we condemn sodomites to the galleys; the Chinese send them to the Great Wall, but if all the guilty suffered for it, China would be unpeopled and the Wall over-crowded'. Like others, he was deceived by his knowledge of Chinese living abroad without their own women, though Fukien had a reputation for homosexuality (Idema, 461, 466–7, 480–1).

visited them whenever possible, and bribed the warders to alleviate their conditions. When they refused to sign confessions they were threatened with torture and Fr Trigault, a spirited old Fleming, declared that he was no frightened child, and drew a hand across his throat to show he was ready for anything.

V

When the news of the arrests reached him, Navarrete was in Chin-hua, having just returned from Lan ch'i where he had retired to write. His experience was different from that of Caballero, for he found difficulty in persuading the authorities to arrest him. Despite this hopeful start he disagreed with those who thought that the persecution would pass quickly. His first reaction was to stop the printing of his Chinese catechism, suspecting that it would never be published, and seeing no purpose in wasting his dwindling resources.

He had ample opportunity to escape and could easily have made for the Philippines, but that seemed morally indefensible, since the local authorities who had treated him kindly would be punished. Then came news of Schall's arrest and, a month later, the order that all missionaries were to be sent to the capital. Next, Navarrete heard that two friars in nearby Lan ch'i had been detained. He immediately prepared for a similar fate, put his affairs in order, and spent the day waiting. When no news came he sat up all that night and most of the following day. To bring matters to a head he finally presented himself before the local magistrate, announcing formally that he was a Catholic priest. The only reply was that he should return home and await instructions. He then sent a petition to the magistrate saying he had heard that missionaries must report to the capital to stand trial, and that since he had no money for this journey he begged permission to sell some church property to pay the fare. Despite all this he was not arrested until February, and even then he was left in his own house and, although the front door was locked, the back was left open as a sign that he was trusted. At last he got his wish and was sent to Lan ch'i to join the two Dominicans there, the Sicilian Friar Domenico Sarpetri and Friar Felipe Leonardo, who had been treated harshly by the district mandarin. The three friars were sent to Hang-chou, arrived on 27 February and in prison met the local Jesuit, Humbert Augery. They were interrogated by the chief jailer, since the judge had a hangover, 'he had been to a great banquet the day before and was not yet come to'.

A hundred years later, Navarrete's description of Hang-chou prison aroused the admiration of the French physiocrat François Quesnay. But it would have astonished Friar Caballero, for it bore no resemblance to his prison experience in Tsinan. Navarrete described his prison as 'a well-governed novitiate-house, at which we were much amazed', and not even a stay of 40 days there diminished his admiration. Their prison, 'a well-run republic', was exemplary, like everything else in Navarrete's China: clean, with a well-appointed, much-frequented temple, it had shops, a laundry, and special married quarters. Poor prisoners received a daily rice ration, usually enough to leave some over for bartering. The most striking feature of all, however, was the behaviour of the prisoners. Although the men's and women's prisons adjoined, and had a communicating door, it was noticed with surprise and edification that the men kept to themselves and there was no impropriety: 'We noted with attention the courtesy, gravity and civility with which they dealt one with another and even with us also. This will seem incredible to our people at home. Suppose two Chinese went to one of our Spanish prisons — imagine what tricks would be played upon them by the other gaolbirds, what garnish they would be made to pay! Well, there's none of that there but always the same courtesy in everything as if we were great gentry. In this matter, as in much else, that nation, without any doubt, excels all others in the world'.

Yet Friar Domingo knew about the treatment of other missionaries, for he was to spend nearly five years in their company, and they often talked about the early days of the persecution. That he deliberately ignored the darker side shows once again that he was selecting his material to present a favourable picture to Spanish readers. His only criticism of the Hang-chou prison was of the overcrowding. The friars had only one bed between them and Navarrete volunteered to sleep on the floor beneath, letting the other two share the bed, but since it was a single bed and only made of cane, he passed anxious nights lest 'it should collapse and make a pancake out of me'.

On 21 April 1665, while Schall was alternately being condemned to 'the lingering death' and saved by opportune earthquakes, the prisoners were sent by river to Su-chou where they spent a pleasant few days entertained by five Jesuits who were still free, because the local mandarin had appealed on their behalf and refused to take further action pending a reply. After this respite they continued their journey. If there was a complaint to make, it came from Navarrete, who regretted that they had passed near Confucius's tomb without being allowed to visit it, although a siesta in Mencius's birthplace was some compensation.

On Saturday 27 June, an inspiring day, the vigil of the martyrs Peter and Paul, they reached Peking, with its fabulous Purple Forbidden City inside the Tartar City, already proverbial in Europe and soon to become for the 18th century what Babylon had been to the ancients. They travelled two leagues across the city to the Jesuits' east-end church, the Tong-t'ang, in Dried Fish Street.[21] Apart from this, they saw little, because during their three months' stay they were restricted to their house except when summoned before the Rites Tribunal, which, unfortunately for would-be sightseers, was only half a league away. But the prohibition did not prevent Navarrete from making one or two note-taking excursions into the city where he saw enough to fill several folio columns with the usual fervent

---

[21] Fr Longobardi complained that this church, established by Magalhães and Buglio, was in an infamous 'red-light' district (though not when they built it), and male converts visiting the church were pestered with invitations in no way connected with their devotions (Pih, 93).

praise and the warning, 'to read this is nothing; to see it is a marvel'. Like others overwhelmed by China, he frequently echoes the dying Marco Polo's protestation to his still incredulous listeners: 'But I haven't told the half of it!' Nor did this enthusiasm wane despite more severe treatment and the obvious contempt in which they were held by the court mandarins, who ordered that, when summoned for questioning, they were to walk behind the horse of the leading official, 'as though we were Blackamoors'. (31)

Fr Schall, together with his adopted son and fellow Jesuits, had already been released (on 17 May 1665), as had most of the Chinese involved with them, although five astronomers, all converts, were executed for having chosen the unlucky day for the royal burial. (32)

An uncertain lull followed, and when Navarrete arrived in the capital no one knew what might happen next. Missionaries continued to arrive from the provinces, until in the end there were 25 of them, not counting the four Jesuits on the staff of Schall's house. More than once they thought they were to be executed, and for all their desire to suffer some were afraid.[22] Whatever their fears, they decided that if the judges said anything against the Faith they would refute it, even if that meant death. Nor did they lose their sense of humour, especially Friar Caballero, who was easily amused, and who was kept awake one night laughing at the sight of Fr Valat trying to sleep on his feet in the crowded cell. They settled down, passing the time 'praying and studying, so that our life, which in the eyes of the world would seem sad and depressing, was good in the eyes of the Lord since we had lost our liberty for His cause'. They only dared to say mass on four or five occasions, and even then for safety's sake they waited until two o'clock in the morning. But after a few days their guards were withdrawn and, though their movements were still restricted, they managed to hear the confessions of some visitors and to baptize others. (33)

Caballero was loud in his praise of Schall, to whom he owed much, and his evidence shows a picture of Jesuit-friar harmony as rare as it was desirable. Even Friar Domingo had good to report of the Jesuits during this period, for the persecution had drawn them all together and enmity was temporarily forgotten. Navarrete had been impressed by the work of Fr Augery in Hang-chou and by the obvious affection of his flock for their pastor; in Su-chou he and his companions had been well treated by the local Fathers, and could only feel flattered when one of them, contrary to Jesuit practice, had allowed him and other friars to confess some of his parishioners. On 4 September 1665 Navarrete wrote from Peking to the Jesuit general expressing admiration for the Fathers' virtues, and gratitude for their charity to

---

[22] Twenty years later, the emperor visited Hang-chou and was greeted by Fr Intorcetta. When the emperor asked if he had ever been in the capital, the old priest's hands trembled as he replied 'once, during the persecution of Yang Kuang-hsien', but the emperor calmed him with kind words, 'there is nothing to fear now'.

him. Since this letter is still used against him as evidence of his changeableness and instability, it is worth considering what prompted it. Fr George Pray, one of the Jesuit historians of the controversy, writing a century later, commented that Navarrete praised the Jesuits while in China and attacked them only after he had returned to Europe. How he could have written a letter of praise to the general at that time, and yet reproached them in his later work, baffled Fr Pray, who confessed he found it an 'inexplicable problem' — as indeed it would be, had his version of events been correct.[23] (34)

Yet there was nothing contradictory in Navarrete's letter, which was inspired mainly by optimism. Certainly he never doubted that the Jesuits' calendar-almanac work had brought about the persecution, the evidence seemed irrefutable. He, and others, singled out Schall for blame, and a *bon mot* ran through the mission: 'the first Adam got us driven out of Paradise, and this second one, out of China'; other Jesuits parodied St Paul's 'we have all sinned in Adam'. Navarrete noted that Yang's accusations had all been made against Jesuits, not friars, and he cited unusual witnesses, such as a group of Dutchmen who had visited the capital shortly after the start of the persecution, and who also concluded that the Fathers were to blame. It was clear to him that the Riccista approach had failed completely. He noticed that many of Yang's accusations were the result of that method which the Jesuits claimed was so efficacious; for instance their holding back the story of the crucifixion in the early days. This seemed proof that trouble was never avoided by compromise and evasion, it was only postponed. This seemed so self-evident that he took it for granted that the Jesuits would now abandon the excessive accommodation policy which had been discredited by events, and some Fathers were indeed suggesting that there should be changes. But this group of Fathers was not influential enough, for Fr Verbiest, now the dominant personality in the mission, was against any change, and it was he who noted Friar Domingo as 'a trouble-maker with long ears, and a longer tongue'. (35)

But the determination to continue the old policy only became clear months later. Now, in Peking prison, in all the euphoria of that euphoric autumn, exhilarated by the unwonted brotherly love, first-fruit of their common trials, Friar Long-ears was full of hope. Interpreting the persecution as an expiation of past errors, he wrote to the Jesuit general to celebrate the happy sufferings of the Society, for although the trouble was of their own

---

[23] A few months later, Navarrete wrote a similar letter from their Canton detention. In quoting these letters Jesuit apologists behave like those theatre managers who clip isolated phrases, even from hostile reviews, to suggest unqualified praise for the entire performance. Navarrete's letters of recommendation may well have been solicited from him by Jesuits, who were more foresighted than he was. The Fathers used the same tactic against each other: Schall made a point of publishing that his adversary Magalhães wrote thanking him for help (*Hist. Rel.*, 194–5).

making, they were nevertheless to be congratulated that it had finally come. Persecution always indicated progress, and 'those who avoid it do so because they are not fighting the true fight'. This equation of persecution with progress, and of accommodation with apathy, was not peculiar to the friars. Years before, in Mexico, Navarrete had heard it propounded by Bishop Palafox. Domingo would have been surprised to learn that he was later to be called inconsistent and self-contradictory for praising the Fathers. He believed he was only encouraging change, and showing proper magnanimity and charity to crestfallen Jesuits in their humiliation. Others shared his groundless optimism. Friar Riccio wrote to the Jesuit general a little later, explaining Schall's tribulations, not very diplomatically perhaps, by saying that the Lord had permitted them, so that before his death Schall might cleanse the good name of the Society from the stain it incurred when he assumed heathen offices and dignities. He, like our first parent, had committed a *felix culpa*, a happy fault, destined to bring salvation for all.

In other words Navarrete's Peking letter, like that written a few months later from Canton, was the product of a brief honeymoon period before the old quarrels broke out again and the situation became painfully normal once more.

Events strengthened his opinion. Naturally the persecution brought apostasies, for the Chinese lacked the fierce courage of the Japanese, but the losses were balanced by benefits. Many, formerly cold in their devotion, were now inspired by fervour, and some of the lapsed were reconciled. Paradoxically, the imperial edict against the Faith even served to advertise it: the decree spread the knowledge of Catholicism to places where it was unknown until denounced. Once again Chinese inquisitiveness, one of the missionaries' secret weapons, moved many to investigate the proscribed religion, to which a number of enquirers subsequently yielded. One example of success in adversity was that of Friar Gregorio Lo, who had escaped arrest and continued working in secret. Unaided, and with everything against him, he had baptized more than three thousand converts 'without the protection of mandarins, without astronomy, mathematics, clocks or clavichords'.

As for the friars, even on the way to Peking they managed to continue preaching, and on a number of occasions during the journey Navarrete had gone about in a closed sedan chair hearing confessions.

Meanwhile, in the palace the tortuous intrigues continued. Schall's accuser, Yang, had lost much popular sympathy and his last book bore the defensive title of *Pu-te-i* ('I can't contain myself'). Not a qualified astronomer, he was alarmed when ordered to take over Schall's post. He tried to escape the responsibility, but in September 1665 was forced to assume office. The missionaries, aware of his ignorance, believed that his first mistake would be his last, and would save their reputations.

In the same month, as the hot dry summer came to an end, a decision was reached about their fate: the Christian churches throughout the empire were to be closed, and the 25 priests banished to Macao. Only Schall and his three colleagues Verbiest, Magalhães and Buglio, were allowed to remain.[24]

On 12 September the prisoners were brought before the council, where they were received with kindness. After reading the sentences the presiding mandarin warned their guards to treat them well at all times. Early on the following afternoon, after bidding an emotional farewell to the paralysed Schall and the others, the 25 exiles with 30 servants departed, surrounded by a clatter of soldiery. At first they were intended to travel on horseback, but, out of pity for their grey hairs and infirmities, they went by boat instead, 'safely, comfortably, even honourably', in three barges of the official fleet. Navarrete travelled with his friend Caballero and the other two Dominicans. To their surprise, the irascible Sicilian Jesuit Brancati, amiable now but later a bitter enemy, insisted on travelling with them. The journey was delayed because the water was low, following a drought that year. Then, they were held up when the canal froze over. This slowness had its compensations, since it gave an opportunity to give the sacraments to Christians whom they met on the way, and on the greater feasts they even managed to say mass for them, and give them communion. And they baptized more converts. One man who wanted to receive the necessary instruction offered himself to the sailors as an unpaid deck-hand so as to be able to remain in the priests' company. After ten days' mobile catechism he was baptized, resigned his temporary job and returned, a Catholic, to his own town, by then some 50 leagues back.

The journey to Canton took six months, including a fortnight at Nanking where, improbably, but according to Fr Intorcetta, the local viceroy lamented 'the folly of our empire which sends into exile these saints and sages'. Their guards scrupulously obeyed orders and 'offered not the least incivility, sometimes even helping us when we stood in need of it'. Navarrete as usual enjoyed the overland voyage and spent the time in delighted observation, marvelling at the abundance of shipping on the Grand Canal, its remarkable flash-lock gates and bridges, and such 'notable contrivances, peculiar to the ingenuity of the Chinese' as their fur-lined diving suits, brine-raising windmills, and piston-bellows. He did not, however, encounter any of the famous land-ships, or sailing chariots.

Others were less happy. Friar Felipe Leonardo slipped, broke his arm, and spent the rest of the journey in pain, and Fr Philippe Couplet, stricken with fever, was given the last sacraments, whereupon he recovered, much to his disappointment, for the friars were not alone in hoping for martyrdom.

They reached Canton on 25 March 1666, and were brought before the amiable governor, who told them that a dispute had broken out between him and the Portuguese in Macao, which, as a consequence, he was blockading.

---

[24] The Dominicans had to abandon 11 residences, 20 churches, and a number of village chapels.

Since the future of the port was now in doubt, the exiles would have to remain where they were for the time being. In fact, this was just as well, since there were already refugees enough in Macao. In December 1664 persecution had also broken out in Tonkin and Cochin-China, where 37 Christians died martyrs; their priests had been dispatched to Macao, and the Jesuit college was packed from cellar to attic with unexpected lodgers. The situation looked grim and many feared that the whole Church east of India was about to suffer the same fate as it had in Japan a few years earlier.

Yet despite his dispute with the neighbouring Portuguese, the governor twice sent them 250 silver ducats towards their expenses, 'Who would imagine a heathen should be so generous to us?'[25] With this donation they settled down to life in the former Jesuit church, although 'each of us had much ado to find his bits and pieces, and to compose ourselves to rest. There was neither fire nor candle, neither morsel to eat, nor drop to drink, and we did nothing but stumble and fall, yet we were very well pleased'. Jesuits and friars were, briefly, brothers in shared persecution. (36)

---

[25] The Jesuit order deposited 10 000 gold *pagodas* with the East India Company, arranging that 600 a year should go to support the exiled Fathers. For the *pagoda*, see Hobson-Jobson *s. v.*

6 A Dominican joins the Jesuits

Here all is amiability and gaiety, without the slightest discord, not the least contention of spirit, the greatest harmony reigns amongst us.
— Navarrete, Canton, 1666

I fled from them and the stones they daily cast at me.
— Navarrete, Canton, 1669

At times they were all honey one with another, and then again all turd. A strange rude life there was among them.

The time spent in the Canton house, as a member of the community of 19 Jesuit Fathers, was important for its effect on Navarrete. They, exposed to his candid-camera eye for almost four years, could not fail to drop their guard occasionally since they clearly underrated him as a potential critic, at least in the early years. So he lived with their natural, but very revealing, animosities and quarrels, and was allowed sight of their disunity over mission policy. Indeed, from time to time they involved him in their intrigues against one another, sometimes confiding to him their feelings and secrets. Not surprisingly, those years left him a changed man. After that experience there were no more letters to Father-General Oliva in praise of his subjects. He had come to know too much.

More positively, the detention gave him leisure to continue his Chinese studies since there were native catechists in the house. It was probably then that, according to Friar Varo, he had the opportunity to read 'well over 50 Jesuit works in Chinese'. He was also able to prepare the material which later formed his two books. And it was during this period that he made the startling discovery of the famous Longobardi treatise opposing the Riccista methods.

He divided their detention ('none of us called it imprisonment') into three periods. The first, which he dated from their arrival in March 1666 until June 1668, was the most severe. During that time they were subjected to roll-calls, forbidden to leave the residence and closely guarded; later these precautions were relaxed. The second stage dated from 24 June 1668, when they were visited by an official who promised them his protection, after which they had some freedom of movement and were allowed to go out, though they were suitably prudent. The third period dated from October 1669, when an imperial decree made clear that there was no possibility of their ever returning to their posts, but that they were free to cross to Macao if they chose. During this last period all official visitations stopped and they enjoyed more liberty. (1)

On arrival in Canton they reported back to the court Jesuits, informing them of the unexpected detention. The reply urged them to hold on discreetly, profiting by the happy accident of their detention; at some later date they might return to their stations. No one then guessed that they were to be there for five years in all. (2)

After the first four days the governor withdrew the guards. This left them unprotected, and they were harassed by hooligans who plastered defamatory posters on the church-house until the governor intervened. That apart, the only danger came from boredom. From the beginning they had the consolation of being able to say mass, but judged it wise not to keep a crucifix on the altar. In time, when conditions eased still more, local converts and fugitive slaves from Macao attended occasional, prudently conducted services. The internees' greatest trial was the knowledge that their flocks were unattended. The Jesuits in the capital could do little, and knowing that six Dominicans were secretly working among the Christians was no comfort to those who feared they would confuse Jesuit-taught converts.[1] The upshot was that four Jesuits, Brancati, Fabre, Ferrari and Gaviani, without confiding in the rest, attempted an escape so as to make their way back into the interior to work under cover. (3)

But the evening before their projected departure the missionaries were unexpectedly visited by a mandarin who checked their names in a roll-call. This brought home to the four the dangers inherent in their plan which was then dropped. But shortly afterwards, the impetuous Brancati set off alone one night, leaving behind a number of letters justifying his decision to Navarrete and some of the older Jesuits.[2] This caused consternation. It was decided that he must be brought back and Fr Manoel Jorge was sent after him. On the third day he caught up with the over-zealous fugitive and

---

[1] Friar Varo claimed that some converts thought God had deliberately allowed the imprisonment of the Jesuits, and freedom for the six friars, so as to 'clean the converts' of the superstitions allowed them by the Fathers.

[2] On 10 September Brancati wrote to Rome for permission to return to his converts: he would pose as a doctor, and had a way of reducing his beard to Chinese proportions (ARSI, JapSin 162, fol. 135).

persuaded him to return to Canton, where his indignant superior made him do public penance in the community refectory. News of the escapade leaked out, and brought a rebuke from the Peking Fathers. (4)

Friar Domingo sympathized with Brancati's desire to return to his converts. Yet the time was not entirely lost, for they were able to devote themselves to study. A member of each of the three orders, the Jesuit Costa, the Franciscan Caballero, and Navarrete, was elected to compose a joint refutation of the accusations of Yang Kuang-hsien. This would be held back until the appropriate time, for, as the Peking Fathers warned, 'no Christian apologia should be published until the emperor himself takes over the government from the regents'. (5)

Navarrete also used his enforced leisure to continue studying Chinese. He read a certain amount every day, calling on three native catechist detainees (Juan, Marcos, and Antonio Fernandes) to settle linguistic points. For greater assurance, he sometimes put the same problem 'through the sieve three times', taking it to each of the Chinese in turn, to establish a definition. The Jesuits also turned to study, and had part of the Macao college archives brought over to Canton. Following conventual custom, they listened to pious readings during mealtimes, although not all Domingo's reading matter was spiritual. When two Dutch ships arrived at Canton, the Flemish Jesuits begged newspapers from the sailors, in which they 'read a thousand things about the Jesuits in France — things of which I'd never before heard even a hint. But by then nothing surprised us!'[3] (6)

This period of physical inactivity explains how Navarrete appears to have written so much, so rapidly, when he reached Madrid.[4] Much of the material he then published, including his translations from the Chinese, was written in Canton. He also read histories of the mission, among them Jesuit writings, such as the manuscript of Fr Gouveia's still unpublished 'History', which Domingo was anxious to see in print, since, he claimed, it supported his case. (7)

News from Peking however was discouraging. Having recovered from their fright and the earthquakes, their enemies were busy again. Schall was recalled to face new charges. Still weak from his stroke, he was carried into the tribunal. A few days later, 15 August 1666, he died, after nearly 50 years' work in China. The news convinced the exiles that their chances of returning inland were poorer than ever, and since it seemed that they would have to stay for some time, the Jesuit Visitor over in blockaded Macao,

---

[3] Reports about the Jesuit-Jansenist battles, and the rumbling on of the affair of Pascal's *Provincial Letters*. Much 'news' was false, such as that the Japanese had stopped persecuting Catholics, and sent an embassy to Manila, appealing for priests (*Gazeta nueva*, 1661), and, in 1666, that 23 Jesuit recruits had reached China (Pandzic, 187).

[4] Varo, in enforced idleness in Moyang, up-dated Friar Morales' 'Relación'.

Fr Luís da Gama, sent an official rule of life for the community to follow. In effect, Friar Domingo had joined the Jesuits.

But the corner had been turned, and in April heartening news came from the capital: friends were whispering that things were looking up and would soon be as before. This forecast was correct. On 26 August 1667 the fourteen-year old K'ang-hsi dismissed the Regency Council, taking control into his own hands. Rumour alleged he was dissatisfied with the imperial astronomer, Yang. Such hopeful signs brought home to the detainees the need to compose their differences, and Navarrete, hearing that a French bishop had reached Siam on his way to Macao, wrote, in the name of the Dominicans, submitting a number of questions about future mission practice. The prelate, Pierre Lambert de la Motte, was fiercely anti-Jesuit, and Fr Gouveia warned his general that if he reached China all would be over.[5] But the bishop refused to intervene.

The incident was a reminder that the China mission problem could only be settled definitively in Rome, and later that same year, 1667, Navarrete wrote to his master-general and to his Manila provincial, requesting permission to return to Europe, taking the friars' problems with him. But Friar Varo hastily wrote off to Manila protesting that if the bishop did come from Siam there would be public debates in Macao between the missionaries of the three orders, and Friar Domingo, their heavy-weight, would be needed. He pressed further: when they regained their freedom they would need to deal with mandarins and literati, and no Dominican was better fitted for that task than Navarrete. Again, Christian books would have to be published in Chinese and Navarrete was not only a good theologian, but was well versed in Chinese. (8)

Varo's objections were theoretical, for there was no certainty that they would be allowed to return to their missions. Besides, Navarrete suddenly found plenty to do in Canton itself, for the Jesuits too were concerned about the future, and the need for unity, not only with the friars, but among themselves. For some time they had been holding private discussions, and they now called on the friar internees to join them in a conference on common problems, to be settled by vote. The suggestion left Navarrete uneasy, since there were 19 Jesuits in the residence and only four friars.

Nevertheless, and surprisingly, the friars agreed to join the discussions, for, as Navarrete wrote later, they believed that major theological issues would be avoided, since no one could suggest that they could be decided by a mere show of hands. He also relied on the traditional disunity within the Jesuit ranks to redress the balance in favour of the friars.

The conference began on 18 December 1667 by electing as secretary

---

[5] A devoted reader of Pascal, the bishop had earlier sent such an anti-Jesuit philippic to his Paris headquarters that they filed it away quietly instead of passing it to the addressee.

Fr Gianfrancesco Ferrari, a pleasant Italian whom the friars liked. Navarrete, as Dominican superior, spoke for his order, and Caballero de Santa María for the Franciscans. (9)

A number of the points discussed, though minor in themselves, caused dissension. For example, there was the question of the correct translation of the baptism formula; of the two versions in use only one seemed correct to Navarrete. This was not merely academic, for if the formula was invalid so too was the sacrament. Following his usual line of attack, Navarrete quoted dissenting Jesuits in his favour, and was successful enough to win over four of the Fathers, who voted with the friars. While it lasted the dispute was heated. Navarrete lost his temper, and was congratulated for doing so by one of the Jesuits, Manoel Jorge, who, in this matter shared his opinion. (10)

There was also hot debate over another question which at first seemed unimportant. In China, contrary to Roman custom, it was permitted to say and hear mass with the head covered, because, in Fr Semedo's words, 'Among the Chinese to uncover the head is not esteemed a courtesy but against good manners'. Accordingly, Paul V had agreed to allow Chinese men to keep their heads covered in church; the missionaries and their acolytes wore a special ceremonial hat six inches high, with four pendant flaps, both at mass and benediction.[6]

One of the Jesuits now denounced this custom, and four others agreed with him, against the friars and the rest. The discussion was protracted. Red herrings were dragged in by Fr Macret, who stressed the undesirability of variations in liturgical practice, and in particular complained of the Dominican mass-rite which was not the same as universal Roman usage. The red herrings were quickly caught and boned. Macret got the testy answer that the Dominicans' liturgy differed for the same reason that the Jesuit Constitutions differed from those of all the other orders.

Yet the opponents of the custom had their reasons, and they claimed it might be dangerous to introduce a detail of Ming etiquette into permanent religious practice. Supposing the new Manchu rulers abandoned this old Chinese usage, then the liturgy itself would have to be altered yet again to follow suit. If not, they ran the risk of seeming to register a protest in favour of the fallen dynasty.

Replying to this, Navarrete branded the five opposing Fathers as over-scrupulous on one count, and unjustified on another. The tradition went back to Ricci's day; and since the Manchus had consistently shown a wish not to alter any of the customs they found in China (apart from the symbolic imposition of their own hairstyle) there was no danger. On this point Navarrete was in the unusual position of appearing more liberal than the Jesuits; indeed the whole discussion had an ironical side which was not lost

---

[6] For consistency's sake, Chinese penitents bared their heads in confession, as criminals did when admitting their crimes.

on him, 'It was also noted what little reason the Fathers have for accusing *us* of interfering with civic customs. What a point on which to make a stand – to show their zeal for the Faith by knocking off a few bonnets!' Making the most of the situation, Navarrete added: 'It is good to introduce the customs of the Roman Church into new missions, but everything has its proper time and we must wait till then. As St Augustine says, "everywhere we must observe those harmless local customs which are not contrary to the Faith or morals".'

In the final vote, the Jesuits Grelon, Valat, Augery, Lubelli and Jorge, the Franciscan, and one Dominican, Leonardo, opposed the covering of heads. The remainder joined Navarrete in voting for the custom. He also claimed the right to count on his side the three Jesuits in the capital and the six Dominicans still out in the provinces. He was careful to give precise figures because this particular point, which at first it seemed so trivial, was later to cause trouble.

Despite the overwhelming number in favour of keeping the custom, the opposition were stubborn, and appealed in writing to Macao, to Fr-Visitor Gama. Navarrete, in the exhilarating position of spokesman for the majority of the Jesuits and friars, also submitted a memorandum on the subject. The incident shows his ability to compromise and to make Catholicism palatable to the Chinese wherever possible. (11)

Other discussions concerned the proper time to admit converts to Communion, the possible introduction of square hosts at mass, and Fr Fabre wanted to change the design of the chasuble, to make it more pleasing to the Chinese. Navarrete replied flatly, in a phrase he often used, 'let's not become chameleons', and no more was heard of the suggestion. (12)

The discussions lasted through December and into January 1668 and though they presumably followed an agenda, none is apparent, for they often discussed problems arising unexpectedly out of topical events. On 9 January, for example, in the middle of the session, the governor of Canton committed suicide.[7] This gave rise to a discussion about the salvation of unbelievers. (13)

Tempers flared again over a discussion of baptism methods. Navarrete, declaring himself shocked by Jesuit practice, accused them of 'rubbing and fretting the faces of women with their hands'. No wonder Chinese husbands were suspicious. The cause of the trouble was Jesuit inexperience. Spanish friars, he added, had rehearsed their lessons in the American missions, but raw Jesuits, Germans, Italians and Frenchmen, sometimes arrived in the East inexperienced in pastoral work, often without having baptized anyone before in their lives. And after this plain dealing he retired to his cell in some indignation until Fr Pacheco came to make peace. Even then Navarrete could not resist a last word, 'they should learn to baptize'. (14)

---

[7] At the same time ex-Governor Lu Hsing-tsu also committed suicide (NH cxiv).

The month-long conference had now debated 40 questions with varying degrees of acrimony and occasional harmony. On the morning of 26 January 1668 the only peaceful proposal was tabled: 'That St Joseph be named patron of the mission'. This was unanimously agreed and the conference seemed to have finished its business. But on that last afternoon, when the Jesuit vice-provincial routinely enquired for any other business, the Italian Dominican Domenico Sarpetri, to the consternation of his friar-colleagues, without warning, tabled a question on the rites. The friars were stunned when he went on to advocate the Jesuit line. The friars were thrown off balance not only by the unexpected departure from the tacit agreement to avoid major problems, but also because it came from one their own. Uproar followed.

Navarrete ought not to have been surprised, for the Italian had already shown himself a rebel. Indeed his earlier insolence to Navarrete, his superior, had been criticized even by the Jesuits. Now, after only a few years in China, he was setting himself up against his older, more experienced, colleagues. Friar Domingo found he was pious, but his theology was eccentric.[8] In the past he had been rebuked for unsuitable sermons to the Chinese, and Navarrete had warned his Manila superiors against ever putting him in charge of a church. The general had once ordered his withdrawal from the mission as 'unfit for service', but he had ignored the command, and 'since in this mission we can't take the stern measures we would at home, we're obliged to leave him there, out of necessity not desire'. Sarpetri's alignment with the Jesuits, and his advocacy of Martini's decree of 1656 permitting the rites (on the basis of Jesuit probabilism), was due to his general eccentricity, and his resentment of his colleagues' opinion of him. There was also another reason. Sarpetri was the devoted nephew of his Jesuit uncle Fr Francesco Brancati, there present in the Canton house. (15)

The Fathers, though earlier scandalized by Sarpetri's disobedience, did not disdain him as an ally. Indeed, doubtless coached by his uncle, he wrote an essay later published by them in Europe, since it put forward Jesuit-Riccista views under a Blackfriar's cloak. And, in a work published by their Roman agent, they cited him, implying that all the China Dominicans, except Navarrete, agreed with their policy. Later still, they played him off against Fr Longobardi, one of their own backsliders. In 1670, Fr Gouveia explained their tactic to his general, 'our best defence against Navarrete is the Sicilian Dominican Sarpetri who is writing to Your Paternity, to the cardinals of Propaganda Fide, to his general, and his superiors in Manila'. (16)

Sarpetri, in raising a thorny problem, went farther than some Jesuits, declaring that there was more than a probable opinion in their favour. It was the old quarrel over again, but for once the Jesuits presented a solid front,

---

[8] The aberration was temporary, for later Sarpetri fell back into line, but his theology was bizantine rather than Thomistic: as proof of Mary's virginity he cited the midwives' evidence (though he presumably got that from Clement of Alexandria's *Stromateis*).

supported by their single, new-found Dominican ally. For the friars this was the most dangerous moment in all the weeks of discussions.

That afternoon was spent arguing and at the end of the day the friars demanded time to prepare a written reply. The Jesuits refused: since majority decisions were being followed they would now submit the report to their Fr-Visitor in Macao. It is difficult to decide if all those present did sign the conference minutes, including the motion tabled by Sarpetri. Contemporary accounts differ, the Jesuits claiming that all the friars first signed the agreement, then wavered and later retracted. But even if the three friars (Navarrete, Caballero and Leonardo) did sign, and it is far from likely, they would have done so with reservations, for their subsequent conduct shows clearly that they disapproved of the contested proposal over which they believed there could be no compromise. As so often in the history of the mission it is impossible to parse the disagreements of evidence. Sometimes there are contradictory versions of the same interview between two persons, both certified as true 'on the word of a priest'. (17)

Navarrete, finding the Jesuits determined to send their report to Rome, tried to prevent the inclusion of the disputed question by complaining that he wished to submit a memorandum about it because the crisis had caught him unawares. His commentary took a month to write, so that not until 8 March did he hand it over to Jesuit Provincial Pacheco. Even a cursory glance at his essay makes mock of the claim that five weeks before he had reached agreement with the Jesuits, for the document is a spirited effort to show that for the Chinese masses the rites were superstitious. Here, as always, he insists that he is judging contemporary Confucianism, not what it may have been in ancient times. He concluded the memorandum with a personal appeal to the Fathers: the friars too had travelled thousands of miles, leaving home and motherland, to preach the Word of God. They were no less zealous than those whose opinions were contrary and, since all desired the same end, they must desire the means to reach that end. Nowhere is Friar Domingo's anxiety more apparent than here.

After five weeks, 18 April, the Jesuits replied. Through their vice-provincial they gave a firm answer. For them the question had been settled by the Martini decree; they regretted these new doubts about a point which was no longer debatable. Though they did not doubt Navarrete's good intentions, they deplored his reports, which would discredit the Society. They concluded by saying that since he had another paper to submit, they would reserve their final reply. Friar Domingo annotated this statement, accusing the Jesuits of avoiding the main issue, and then sent the whole with a covering letter to the Visitor Fr Gama, assuring him that he was not squabbling idly, and repeating his request for a straight answer.

Fr Gama had his limitations, but he could write a good letter. On 12 May he replied tactfully, urging the need for unity, begging the friars to embrace broader theological principles, ending with an appeal every bit as rhetorical as Navarrete's own to him. He enclosed a copy of a recent directive of the Dominican master-general (still unknown to Navarrete) urging harmony between the Society of Jesus and Order of Preachers. Navarrete, though touched by the letter, was cautious about the appeal: truth was indivisible, and not found by trimming; peace was desirable, yet not at the cost of truth.

Gama settled down to study the conference minutes, and to prepare a full reply. An uneasy lull settled over the residence, where the Jesuits, angry with Friar Domingo and the Franciscan for what seemed mere obstinacy, retaliated by sulkily refusing to speak to them for the next three weeks. The friars were in Coventry, rather than Canton. (18)

Community life is seldom easy, even for the saints, as is shown in the gentle autobiography of St Thérèse, *The Little Flower of Jesus*.[9] There were no saints in Canton and communal life there was no exception to the rule. There were tense, moody silences, sharp intakes of breath, pursed lips, and angry exits with slammed doors.[10] The detainees were old, or prematurely aged by hard work and the demands they made on themselves. Often troubled by illnesses caused by ignorance of the precautions proper to Europeans living in the east, when they fell sick they proceeded, in accordance with current practice, to bleed themselves into greater weakness. In addition, the months cooped up, believing that hundreds of converts needed their ministrations, brought tension and frustration. The little house, claustrophobic and oppressive, 'is so cramped', reported Fr Lubelli, 'that we can't breathe without our neighbour knowing it'. Hanging over all was the awareness of the ancient differences between Blackfriars and Blackrobes. On the one side, fears of moral laxity, expediency and opportunism; on the other, fears of rigorism, obstinacy and ignorance. The whole was so compounded by events in the mission, that harmony was impossible and friction inevitable.

'Even bishops are made of men', said Cervantes. So too are Jesuits, though they and their critics, for differing reasons, often forget it. Thus, 'not every Father in China is another Solomon', said Friar Caballero, nor of the calibre of Ricci, Schall and Verbiest. That trio of remarkable personalities, extraordinary by any standard, were the architects of the great enterprise. But it is often forgotten that the Society, too, had its share of run-of-the-mill hod-carriers, who basked vicariously in the glory of greater colleagues, hoped to be giants by association, and despised outsiders. Notoriously, the butler is a greater snob than his master.[11]

All this exacerbated the fresh quarrel sparked off by Sarpetri's proposal at

---

[9] 'Newman, touchy and neurotic, lived and ate with one young Oratorian in Birmingham for 20 years without a single word passing between them. Words, not always of an agreeable nature, *did* pass with others' (A. N. Wilson, *Belloc* (London, 1984), 18). See also Valles.

[10] For revealing instance, Navarrete relates one nervous outburst from an exasperated, but embarrassing, Fr Couplet, 'all heard him, but all kept quiet' (NC 329).

[11] The chronicler Fr Cordara heard of a brother who, visiting friars' houses, used to demand to be received with priest's status: a Jesuit-brother equalled a friar-priest (Mir, II: 518).

the end of the conference. Despite everything, Caballero, the gentle Franciscan, in his account of their life, described his fellow detainees as 'angels of virtue', and in the beginning Navarrete had concurred. But in suppressing the realistic side of the story, in the interest of edification, Navarrete laid himself open to accusations of changeability. He only once refers to any unpleasantness, and then in a unpublished work. Instead, it was a Jesuit critic, Juan Cortés Osorio, who later let the cat out of the bag when he revealed the 'cruel misunderstandings' of life in the Canton community. He showed, in unselfconscious but fascinating detail, how the Jesuit inmates made fun of Navarrete, 'Above all, in recreation periods, particularly on feast days such as Easter or Christmas . . . those [Jesuit] servants of God tried to hide their merriment with religious modesty, but couldn't repress the laughter that the fellow, Navarrete, caused them. It'd kill you to hear him holding forth in his mongrel oriental–scholastic Latin, misconstruing the elegant arguments proposed to him by our Fathers'. His over-seriousness clearly made him easy game, and so the Jesuits, with disguised merriment, teased him with absurd problems for his solution: 'may French soldiers serving in Canada take a second wife for sexual relief?'; 'Is there life on the moon?' Between that and their straight-faced 'praise' of his Dominican learning 'some little yarn or joke about Friar Navarrete was never wanting, and so the time passed merrily'. Not surprisingly, he came to see hostility all around him, and being trapped in that cloistered atmosphere could only increase his paranoia.[12] (19)

Fr Cortés's evidence is important. He must have obtained his information from his brethren in China, and it explains the otherwise extraordinary remarks attributed by Navarrete to some Jesuits. Whether he recorded these, naively and indignantly, because he failed to spot the leg-pull, or whether he was being disingenuous, cannot be decided. Sarpetri claimed the Jesuits believed Navarrete was arguing for mental exercise 'as lecturers do to fill up the time while waiting for the class-hour to end'. Either way, before long the 'servants of God in China' regretted this particular merry-making, for their biased Boswell forgot none of their incautious comments.

To bait him further, one Jesuit boasted of their power in Spain, especially after the Jesuit-courtier, Fr Nidhard, the queen mother's favourite, had become Spanish Inquisitor-General. A few years later that remark was to be recalled at a most inopportune time for the Society. Nor were all the comments light-hearted. Many Jesuits would have agreed with the one who told Navarrete that the Roman Congregation for the Propagation of the Faith

---

[12] Curious problems were sometimes proposed as debating exercises, as in the old moot courts: 'Since women are inferior, the Virgin Mary must have been a man in order to be worthy to bear Christ' (J. Lúcio d'Azevedo, *História de António Vieira* (Lisbon, 1918), I: 33). Such *quaestiones quodlibetales* ('If a child is born with two heads, which shall a priest baptize?' [Schons, *Censorship*, 40]) were usual as light entertainment at informal disputations.

was destroying the foreign missions. Not all the fake disputations were feigned for Navarrete's benefit only: sometimes the Fathers used him to hit at one another obliquely, and to pay off private scores against each other. (20)

Much later, Fr Verbiest lamented that Navarrete had unfairly published the Jesuits' careless remarks. He saw him not as the butt of light-hearted jokes but as an astute and treacherous reporter leading on the innocent and unguarded Fathers. He had 'as it were lain in ambush for them, curiously scanning and annotating their ways'. One can sympathize, but Verbiest did not know that his brothers had set their own ambush for themselves and had escorted Navarrete to his vantage point. They had only themselves to thank. Verbiest's complaints are better grounded where he remonstrates with Navarrete for taking literally 'and with raised eyebrow' everything he heard, and for censuring off-guard comments made in a relaxed mood during recreation periods, comments that 'must surely have made him smile, at least sardonically' at the time. Friar Domingo had indeed observed the normally discreet, reserved, even secretive, Jesuits going about their daily business with unbuttoned cassocks. He then behaved like a journalist at a private party who reports the gossip and private squabbles. In other words, he was no gentleman, but that does not necessarily make him a liar. (21)

Verbiest went on to draw an uncomplimentary parallel between bees and spiders.[13] Later apologists liked and copied it, but the comparison was not entirely accurate. The Jesuits had not gotten themselves a spider but a wasp, and in the end, their way of 'passing the time' in Canton proved costly.

Yet even in their view of Navarrete, the Jesuits were divided. Some liked him and were his friends (Fr Rougemont, was one) some respected him enough to consult him about serious problems; others even went so far as to choose him as a confessor. He was, admitted Sarpetri grudgingly, 'known for his talents and gifts'.

---

[13] The bee, producer of honey and wax, symbolized sweetness and light (Jesuits); the spider symbolized those spinning poisonous webs out of themselves (friars).

II

Where men of ten different nationalities and three different religious orders were cooped up together for years, quarrels were inevitable. Animosity between Spaniard and Portuguese was normal anywhere, at any time, but especially at that sensitive moment, for in February 1668 the Treaty of Lisbon saw the end of their 28 years' war and the defeat of Spain. The Jesuits' private letters from Canton show that Navarrete's account of some of the outbursts he witnessed is not over-coloured. The Portuguese Fr Gouveia was 'an insufferable old man', with whom he had one or two brushes, though 'I avoided him when possible, and when I couldn't, thought it best to hold my peace. The Portuguese are little-minded people raised in a corner of the world who, though they've seen nothing but Lisbon and Goa, lay down the law on everything'. Francesco Brancati, an Italian with no nationalistic axe to grind, but a very passionate Jesuit, gives interesting details in a confidential letter to the Jesuit general in October 1668: 'The spirit of nationalism runs rife in this house, and one Father in particular, our own superior, António Gouveia, talks of nothing but war, declaring publicly and repeatedly "Death to Spaniards, death to Castilians", with little edification, much scandal and offence to the Dominican superior [Navarrete] and three other Castilian religious exiled here with us for the Faith'. Navarrete, he added, had complained to him 'of the Jesuit superior's saying he wanted to see the Spanish nation wiped out, which', adds Fr Brancati mildly, 'is scarcely a religious sentiment'. Brancati added that his attempts to check Gouveia's harangues had failed, and that Friar Domingo, to avoid trouble, no longer attended community recreation. Worse, Gouveia's feelings often led him into other disloyal ways and he was denounced to Rome by Fr Ferrari, for his habit of stomping about the residence muttering, 'Oh, that Nickel, that wretched Nickel', referring to the former Jesuit general who was believed unsympathetic to the Portuguese *padroado*.[14] (22)

All this throws light on the exiles' life; and in this same light Fr Lubelli's remarks about Navarrete's character must be judged. For Lubelli found him melancholy, moody and not at all, one might think, the sort to amuse Jesuits relaxing after dinner. Of the many attempts to discredit Navarrete this is the most original, but no doubt Lubelli felt a special responsibility to compensate for his failure to keep Friar Domingo out of China a dozen years earlier. (23)

'Melancholia' covered everything from chronic glumness to clinical depression. It was often used pejoratively, as here, and the celebrated Fr José de Acosta had to defend himself against a similar imputation from his fellow-

---

[14] General Nickel (1652–61) was a rigorous and inflexible northerner.

Jesuit critics. Schall, too, was officially described as 'morosus'; however, as has been said, there were many cases of depressive illness in the missions and the term was not always used aggressively. (24)

That year, 1668, in which they finished their five weeks' conference and despatched their reports to the Jesuit Visitor in Macao, was eventful in other ways. Surprisingly, the new governor of Canton invited them to drink wine with him, but they sent only Navarrete and three others as representatives. Their situation was eased by local worthies who sent money to help with their keep. Then in June began the second period of internment in which they had more freedom and could leave the house, though discreetly. News from the capital was encouraging: the emperor was dissatisfied with his astronomer, and the Jesuits hoped for reinstatement. In Macao, the Fr-Visitor spent the summer studying the Canton conference minutes. In the autumn he sent his reflections back to the internees. They, however, had only intended him to forward the minutes to Rome, not to keep them for private study. But that was not Fr Gama's way, and his conclusions, upon arrival in Canton, excited universal hostility, at once exasperating his own subjects, and arousing the suspicions of the mendicants.

It was unfortunate that the Jesuit visitor at that time should have been Luís da Gama. He was devout, ascetic, narrow-minded, and an obstinate martinet. He himself obeyed the letter of the law and expected his subjects to do the same. He had served in Tibet, but knew nothing of China except the coastal town of Macao. He shared the prejudices of those Europeans whose only contact with the Chinese was with traders from Canton. For him the Chinese were 'smooth talkers, and poison-pill hawkers'. In short, Jesuit Fr-Visitor Gama was a stereotypical friar. Nevertheless he displeased the mendicants when he began tinkering with, even altering, some of the conference decisions. Simultaneously, he alarmed the Jesuits who were amazed that their own superior seemed to be taking the friars' part in some instances. The overall impression of Gama is that he was resolute about everything, but right about little. (25)

In October the conference secretary, the amiable Fr Ferrari, wrote confidentially to his general complaining that Gama seemed to side with the mendicants in condemning the rites as superstitious. December 1668 found Gama writing to Rome on his own account. So for the next year or so, letters from China poured into the Jesuits' Roman Curia and eventually even the Franciscan Caballero gave the Fr-General the benefit of his opinion. On 18 December a French Jesuit, Rougemont, wrote in strong terms: they were daily afflicted by this Fr-Visitor who interfered where he had neither experience, knowledge nor desire to learn. Instead, he had opposed Navarrete's proposal, adopted by the majority, to allow the Chinese to hear mass with their heads covered. Not even Navarrete, 'who defended this opinion, which is both his and ours, in a lengthy, learned memorandum' had been able to convince the Visitor of the desirability of this concession.[15] Rougemont warned that Gama's interference had destroyed hope of agreement with the friars, for Navarrete, their superior, had declared that he and his subjects no longer considered themselves bound by any of the terms of the conference. Gama, concluded Rougement, was following the frivolous reasoning of only four Jesuits, one Franciscan and one Dominican (Felipe Leonardo), against Navarrete and the majority of experienced men.

It was a curious situation. Navarrete, apparently no longer the butt of Jesuit jokes, must now be defended by them against a wilful and ill-informed Jesuit superior. Curious it may have been, but Gama was indifferent. Nor did he show any sign of being disturbed to find himself opposing his vice-provincial. Another correspondent, Fr Canevari, reported to Rome that Gama had demanded obedience in the matter of the covered-head problem: anyone disobeying him was to be punished and not even the superior of the house was excused. Gama had sharply, even rudely, reproved the vice-provincial, concluding with a remark which showed he was aware that his subjects were busily denouncing him: 'Let them who will write to Rome,' he had said, 'but in the meantime they will obey me'. And on 21 February 1669 he noted in his diary that he had ordered the vice-provincial 'to obey, and not to mention the matter again'. Fr Canevari, long ago an enemy of the friars, now, in common cause against his own Fr-Visitor, lamented that Gama could overthrow decisions reached by experienced veterans. (26)

Over a year later complaints were still being made, this time by Fr Gouveia: 'About Fr-Visitor Gama I shall make only one complaint, not that matter for others is lacking!' Things were serious when one Portuguese Jesuit denounced another but Fr Gama was grimly blundering into more dangerous fields. (27)

While Gama was busy upsetting the Canton assembly, in Peking the K'ang-hsi emperor had finally decided that his official astronomer was unreliable. The court Jesuits watched the situation closely, and when the emperor asked Verbiest's opinion, the Jesuit seized his opportunity, tactfully pointing out some 'errors'. An investigation resulted in the downfall of the old enemy Yang and the appointment of Verbiest as associate-director of the observatory. (28)

Joseph Needham shows that the Jesuits' subsequent calendar reform was unnecessary, due to their misunderstanding of the Chinese system, and that henceforth 'Chinese astronomy (in its pure state) descended into a limbo from which only the last century of study has resurrected it'. But the emperor, about to take over the government from the four regents, needed to

---

[15] Elsewhere Fr Pacheco referred to Navarrete's 'erudition', but the context required the praise which may have been merely diplomatic or expedient.

inaugurate a calendar-reform such as was customary at the start of a new reign-period. (29).

There was a close connection between the calendar and state power and Needham explains that 'New dynasties always overhauled the calendar and issued one with a new name, and this might happen even in successive reign-periods under the same emperor'. In this particular reform both emperor and Jesuit were using the calendar and each other, for their own ends. The Jesuit, having eagerly accepted the charge, started work by having the case against the late Fr Schall reviewed, and succeeded in having his name posthumously cleared. The omens, as Schall might have said, were good. (30)

The Jesuits' reinstatement came about on Christmas Eve 1668, and Fr Magalhães wrote from the capital on 2 January with words from the Christmas mass still fresh in his mind, 'Behold I Gabriel (not the Angel but a sinner) bring you good tidings of great joy'. He narrated recent events with characteristic but understandable excitement and rhetoric. He urged that volunteers gifted in mathematics and other skills be prepared for the mission, 'since Fr Verbiest will not live for ever. We also need one or two Fathers who know how to use a hammer and a file. And let not your Reverence despise these mechanical arts, nor shrink from the prospect of being a locksmith, since St Joseph, spouse of the Virgin Queen of Heaven, was himself only a carpenter! You should know that I rate files and hacksaws above mitres and crowns. Oh! great is my honour, great my glory, for I am God's locksmith, and Christ's journeyman.'[16] (31)

This call for divine drudges was soon answered by French Jesuits, and later even the skilled mathematicians and astronomers made a point of learning a trade before joining the mission. Frs de la Roche and d'Incarville spent some months as apprentices in a glass works and learnt copperplate engraving. Fr Bouvet arrived in France in 1697 seeking Jesuit watchmakers, musicians, and orchestra players. He enlisted Fr Parennin, a skilled 'trompette marine' player who introduced the instrument to the Peking court. (32)

Verbiest duly informed his superior, Fr Gama, of his return to imperial favour. The reply was not congratulations but a rebuke. Astronomy might seem their best hope to the courtier-Jesuits, but not to Gama. He forbade Verbiest to work in the observatory, even if the emperor himself were to order it, and he was no less opposed to mathematics, and requests for additional mathematicians were rejected. Gama had now alienated almost every one of the missionaries, Jesuit and friar alike. Fortunately for the Fathers, relief came from General Oliva, permitting Verbiest to work in the observatory, and overruling Gama, who, however, was not resentful, for he knew how to obey. (33)

None of this was lost on Navarrete who found life in a Jesuit community

---

[16] In 1670 alone Magalhães distributed 20 telescopes, 50 pairs of eye-glasses, 30 sun-clocks, and repaired the 80 clocks in the court (Pih, 220).

revealing. Gratifying though it might be to see them squabbling amongst themselves, their quarrels showed again the impossibility of reaching agreement with those who could not agree among themselves. This disunity fed the friars' own insecurity, which was now increased by an electrifying surprise.

The situation might seem lively enough, but Fr Intorcetta found things quiet, 'we were living in the greatest peace when suddenly the storm came'. The storm came because at that moment Friar Caballero showed Navarrete the treatise written 40 years previously (1623–24) by Fr Longobardi, the prominent dissident Jesuit. This denunciation of some of Ricci's stratagems was believed by his fellow Fathers to have been safely destroyed in a domestic auto-da-fé, because the vice provincial at the time, nervous that the first friars were appearing on the scene, had ordered the memorandum to be burnt. (34)

Caballero had met Longobardi twice in Peking during the 1650s when the old Jesuit was near death. The friar was greatly impressed by him, 'a holy religious, simple and guileless as a dove. When I saw him, although he was over 90, he was still thirsting to go back to his mission'. Caballero had had the treatise for years and why he did not show it to Navarrete earlier is a mystery, since it was startling evidence of the differences in the Jesuit ranks even in the early days. It was a weapon to use against them, and Fr Ferrari was right to see in this discovery another reason for Navarrete's hardening of attitude, for the effect of this revelation, a bombshell, on Friar Domingo cannot be overestimated. (35)

Caballero's copy of the notorious treatise was incomplete. It had been secretly leaked to the Franciscan by Jean Valat, the maverick French Jesuit always friendly to the friars. Navarrete, after his initial excitement, set himself to study it carefully, later publishing it in his *Tratados*. Henceforth Longobardi's essay was to be a constant sore to the Riccistas, and it weakened their position, particularly after its publication in Europe. Navarrete's purpose in publishing it was two-fold: it served to score a point, but it was also the perfect vade-mecum for future missionaries. Its source was irreproachable but it was in itself the freshman's ideal guide, the complete rapid-results course, the solution of so many of the problems encountered in China. As for Navarrete himself, he became the 'humble disciple of that great man Longobardi', and later, when he reached Rome, he was careful to present a copy of the essay to the archives of Propaganda Fide. (36)

In the background, Gama had more to say. Any agreement reached between Navarrete and the Canton Jesuits did not of course include the troublesome question raised by Friar Sarpetri at the end of the conference, for the friars had never wavered in their objections to that article. Now, just before the end of 1668, Gama ordered the Jesuits to compose suitable replies to these objections. Their theologian in the China mission, Fr Fabre, and their sinologue Fr Brancati, were ordered to take the field. On 21 March 1669 the first discharge came from the assembled Jesuit ordnance.

Fabre's reply, his *Compendiosa responsio*, is in the main an appeal to Navarrete to distinguish counsels of perfection from precepts of obligation, and added warnings against the heresies springing from excessive severity, and hinted at traces of Jansenism in the friars' thinking.[17] (37)

Navarrete, hurt by Jesuit sneers at his altar-boy's Latin, began his response with heavy irony, apologizing for writing in the vernacular: his poor Latin would make an unhappy showing beside Fr Fabre's, but, as Augustine said, a door can be opened by a wooden as well as by a golden key. What matters is to have the right key. Strengthened now by his recent discovery of Longobardi's essay, he emphasized his main line of attack: the Jesuits are unrealistic in basing themselves on theories about Confucianism as it used to be; they must judge it by what it is now; they are like men saying mass with vinegar instead of wine, on the grounds that vinegar and wine are essentially the same.

Fr Fabre had said that Chinese offerings of food to the dead was no more superstitious that the French custom of offering them food on All Souls' Eve. To which Navarrete retorted, 'Well, in that case, dear Father, off home with you, for apparently your preaching is needed there more than it is here'. As for the ancestor-ceremonies, one might as well declare that the idolatries of Greece and Rome were merely social and devoid of religious significance.

He reminded the Jesuits (hurtfully, for it was their boast) that they had no monopoly of the knowledge of China: and he made a pointed reference to Longobardi who, with his 57 years in the mission, could be expected to know what he was talking about. As for the appeal to avoid rigorism, Fr Fabre would do well to remember those heretics who had harmed the Church by their lax teaching; the Jesuits should take their eyes from Charybdis for a moment so that they might see Scylla. (38)

Suddenly the dispute was interrupted by death, for in May 1669 Caballero died. This was a loss to the friars, for Navarrete regarded him as 'zealous, tireless, diligent', though the Franciscan himself felt 'better suited to sweeping cloisters and brushing away conventual cobwebs' than to disputing with learned Jesuits. Caballero, hard on himself but loving to others, was a model of Franciscan humility, charity and simplicity, from whom came the few sweet notes in all the cacophonous repertoire of the early years of the controversy. Even as he lay on his deathbed, the Jesuits asked Navarrete, who was closest to him, to find out if he was still of the same opinion about the rites.[18] The dying Franciscan smiled at the question, and, after receiving the last sacraments, had the whole community assemble in his cell. He

---

[17] Fabre, who had studied a year's moral theology, used to discuss the subject with Navarrete, saying he was the only one there who knew any divinity, for as Fr Canevari put it 'The younger ones are only Goan theologs' and the rest 'greybeards who forgot their seminary studies years ago' (NC 317, 331, 424).

[18] The Jesuits had a reputation for collecting useful statements from the dying, and sometimes even from their own.

thanked them for their kindness to him (he had long since forgiven the Jesuit, Fr Schall, who had him kidnapped back in 1652), adding that he had nothing to change in his memorandum to Fr Gama, and reaffirming his opinion of the superstitions attached to the rites. (39)

He died on the 13th, and on the 20th was buried outside the city walls. Owning nothing, he had nothing to leave, but Navarrete got his old glasses in their tortoiseshell case as a last memento. Nine years later he was still using them.

The burial caused some distress. In his last agony, the dying man forbade the use of 'superstitious' Chinese funerary tablets at his funeral, as they had been at two recent Jesuit burials.[19] If they were, he threatened to rise from his coffin to destroy them. But the Fathers, in deference to the converts present at the funeral, ignored Caballero's threat on the grounds that, 'now in heaven, he'll understand better'. Navarrete saw them place the incense thurible in front of one of the tablets 'yet no incense was offered to the Cross, which grieved me much, but I held my peace'.[20] (40)

Controversy, like life itself, had to go on, so on 25 June Fr Brancati handed his reply to Navarrete in the form of a rough draft. Its title provocatively begged the question: 'An apologia for the Civil Ceremonies of the Chinese', and the tartness of its style made Navarrete say that it was written in a spirit of vengeance rather than of reason. Later, he regretted not keeping a copy of the vituperative original. Fr Brancati was not the best suited to convince Friar Domingo of his errors. Though zealous, distressed about the fate of his converts, and full of love for the Chinese, he was also impetuous, tactless, and irritable (he was a victim of gout). (41)

His reply to Navarrete he took a stirring if unfair text from Ezechiel 34: 'Woe be the shepherds of Israel. The diseased have ye not strengthened, neither have ye healed that which was sick, neither have ye bound up that which was broken and the sheep were scattered because there is no shepherd.' This, however, was rather offset by Brancati's manner in debate, which for him was all cut and thrust, and by his tendency to see everything as a personal issue. The controversy with the friars he saw in warlike terms; he wanted to inform the Jesuit general that in China his men were being provoked to battle on all sides, and 'not only by Tartars and other enemies, but by our fellow-soldiers and those of the same profession'. His 72-page reply to Navarrete was, he later explained, a blow for his 'Father and Mother, hoc est, the Society of Jesus and its glorious Founder'. Later, he dismissed the Dominicans' charges as the work of 'liars who are led by the Father of liars [Navarrete]'. He mockingly enquired how the friars, with a mere 40

---

[19] On the nature and function of the funerary tablets, see Ebrey.

[20] Caballero thought that 'Christ had died looking westwards, inviting missionaries to embrace the cross, suffering and death', but that at the Ascension he looked east inviting 'Jews, Muslims, even Chinese to the Faith' (AHSJ, I: 297).

years' experience of the mission, and 'only four or five books' to their credit, could know as much as the 60 Jesuits who had been in China for 90 years and had written 'three hundred books'. (42)

This was more than a Spanish Dominican could take from a Sicilian Jesuit. Infuriated, Navarrete demanded time to write a reply, but this was refused and he was asked to return Brancati's draft manuscript without delay. To play for time, he lied, saying he had burnt it, but after a few days' secret study he handed it back to the indignant Fr Vice-Provincial who, having believed him, had ordered Brancati to rewrite the treatise from memory. This second version, toned down by prudent Jesuit copyists, is the one most commonly found in archives. Toned down as it is, the memorandum makes lively reading, and Navarrete must have trembled with anger as he began his reply. Answering the appeal to 'make the Faith easier' his tone becomes shrill.

Brancati had defined the difference between them by claiming that the Jesuits 'made smooth the path to the Church'. In his retort Navarrete seized on that phrase, which he answered with a chant, set out as question and response 'What is their smooth path? It is the strangest mission ever seen in the Church since Christ founded it — that's their smooth path. To lament, even in this exile, that friars are confessing their parishioners — that's their smooth path; to refuse to receive duly appointed bishops — that's their smooth path; to send only a catechist to the seriously sick, so letting them die without confession — that's their smooth path; to keep the passion of our Lord a secret for years — that's their smooth path; to make the sort of reports to Rome that Fr Martini submitted — that's their smooth path'. The catalogue concludes with a warning, 'and if anyone ask me, I can easily write more to show the world the Society's smooth path'. (43)

Making a complaint, later repeated, about the Jesuits' published *Relations*, Navarrete asked, 'If they dare tell such lies to me who have the evidence here before my eyes, what will they not be capable of saying in Rome? *O bone Deus!*' (44)

Carried away by anger he jeeringly calculated that Brancati had spent 12 of his 34 years in China in bed (presumably with his gout), called him by his nickname ('The White Elephant'), and attempted to analyse both him and his nephew, Sarpetri, in terms of humour-psychology, finally deciding that Sicilian stubbornness explained everything.[21] (45)

Despite the tone of this counterblast to Brancati's broadside, Navarrete was said to have been impressed. Sarpetri alleged that when he first read the manuscript he declared that at last he saw a clear way, and wished he had done so earlier. If so, it is difficult to understand the warmth of his written reaction. But if so, it would be evidence of his objectivity that he could find

---

[21] He was following theories in the first-ever book on vocational guidance: Juan Huarte de San Juan's psychiatric manual *Examen de ingenios para las ciencias* (Madrid, 1575).

truth in so bitter a diatribe. Where his uncle is concerned, however, Sarpetri is a tainted witness, who possibly misunderstood what was intended to be irony. Friar Domingo was never subtle. But what he certainly did say was, 'I wish I could be proved wrong. How much easier life would be if we could all be friends, in harmony with Fr Brancati and his Society'. (46)

That was to day-dream. They were not friends, and his retort to Brancati is sharp and personal; it is also a display of his mental and nervous stamina. He was now conducting his battle on two fronts, for Fr-Visitor Gama, entrenched in his ecclesiastical dug-out in Macao, despatched to him in August a batch of letters about, as he noted in his diary, 'that long-standing business of his'. (47)

Despite what he saw as provocation, and despite his own tenacity, Navarrete made one more attempt to come to an agreement with the Fathers. On 29 September 1669 he approached the 'insufferable old man', Vice-Provincial Gouveia, to tell him that for 23 years he had heard talk of the controversies (now 33 years old). He admitted it might once have been possible to change his mind, but the last three years' detention with the Fathers and his reading of Longobardi had confirmed him more than ever in his attitude. Only a declaration by the pope could change his mind. Having made that clear, he went on to propose an *interim* working agreement. (48)

Gouveia asked for this proposal to be put in writing, and the guileless Domingo complied. Now he was caught. He offered on behalf of the Dominicans to adopt, as a temporary arrangement, the terms of an old, but little known, Jesuit conference held in Hang-chou in April 1642. On that occasion it had been decided to prohibit converts from praying to idols or their ancestors, and to persuade them that offering food or perfume could not benefit the dead. On the other hand salutations of respect before ancestral tablets were to be permitted. In the matter of Confucian veneration only the two solemn half-yearly ceremonies were condemned. In addition to accepting these terms Navarrete also agreed to accept the Jesuits' choice of word to mean 'God', and to follow their practice in all doubtful cases. But this was to be a temporary working arrangement, pending a final decree from Rome. (49)

Once again Navarrete had shown a desire for compromise. Once again he had made a tactical error. First the Jesuits disowned the alleged Hang-chou conference: even if it had taken place it was unofficial, at most merely a conversation between individual Fathers. When shown copies of the conference minutes they rejected these, again pressing the friars to accept nothing short of the Martini's decree of 1656. This was to ask for the impossible, but the Jesuits would settle for nothing less. And the naive Navarrete seems not to have realized that he had been outwitted.

On 4 October, Sarpetri wrote to Gouveia expressing delight at the prospect of peace. He added, unnecessarily, conscientiously, but usefully, that he had seen the proposal 'written and signed by Navarrete's hand'. There is something intriguing about the determinedly formal way in which the internees now began writing to each other from room to room on the topic of the proposed agreement. They summarized and restated the contents of letters received, carefully guaranteeing the authenticity of the handwriting and signatures of other people. The Jesuits realized that they had trapped Friar Domingo. But first they had to prove that he had indeed proposed such an agreement. Obviously, an affidavit would serve admirably if it came from a fellow friar, and for that purpose Sarpetri was ideal. He responded willingly. (50)

The Fathers rightly suspected that negotiations were about to break down, for the honeymoon was brief and troubled. Only three weeks later, 23 October, Sarpetri assisted the Fathers with another formal declaration that the letter of 29 September proposing his working agreement with the Jesuits was in Navarrete's hand, 'which I recognize easily, having received many papers written by him.'[22]

What had happened during those three weeks to make such guarantees necessary is easily established. Fr Brancati had intervened, blocking the mendicants' proposals, again demanding the impossible: acceptance of the Martini decree.

Navarrete had gone far (some thought too far) in his efforts to reach a working policy. Yet he had failed, for the Jesuits, after first having moved to meet him, not so much by making concessions as by beckoning him forward, had suddenly drawn back and demanded too much. Once a breakdown was obvious, the Fathers collected sworn statements from Sarpetri calculated to discredit Navarrete by proving he had agreed to follow Jesuit practice. His offer to Gouveia could be shown to be a volte-face, from his own position and, worse, a volte-face from which he later seemed to turn away, apparently changing his mind yet again.

Friar Domingo's mistake lay in not being as formal in retracting his offer as he had been, under Jesuit pressure, in proposing it. Failure to issue 'certified true statements' on his own behalf, offsetting his original letter, left the Jesuit party able to claim that after agreeing with them, he had unaccountably changed his mind yet again. The Jesuits took advantage of his strategic blunder, and he was therefore presented by later polemicists as unstable, shifty, and changeable.

Unaware that his position was weakened, Navarrete now made another decision which, more than any other, was used against him. He decided to leave secretly for Macao.

He had his reasons. In the first fortnight of October 1669 began the 'third period' of detention, when an imperial decree informed them that there was

---

[22] This policy of collecting friars' affidavits commended itself to Fr Verbiest who compiled and forwarded an anthology of them to his Roman headquarters 'for refuting Navarrete and his ilk' (*Corr.*, 377, 441, 462–8).

no possibility of a return to the interior. On receipt of the decree the missionaries held an animated gathering which was predictably divided over what to do next. Navarrete himself, and at least one Jesuit, Jorge, were convinced they would never be allowed back inland. Some wanted to go to Macao, others to remain in Canton in case the emperor relented. A vote proved indecisive, and the meeting broke up in noisy disorder. (51)

Navarrete now saw that it was futile to attempt a working policy with the Jesuits. The first time he tried Fr-Visitor Gama had ruined their hopes, the second time, Fr Brancati had dissented, overruling his companions. But, if there was no possibility of returning to China, where was the need of a temporary arrangement with the Fathers? What now seemed essential was a final ruling from Rome; clearly the rites controversy, already old, and daily more complex, would not be solved by letter-writing, especially when it often took four years to get a reply from Europe. To appeal to Rome, to throw the problem down 'at the feet of the Apostles', had never been far from Friar Domingo's mind and in answering Brancati's treatise he said longingly, 'let us go to Rome, and there, before his Holiness, verify the truth and make an end of all this'. (52)

They were now assured by a Chinese confidant that 'if they said the word' they could retire to Macao, but could not return to their old inland stations. To Navarrete the logical course seemed not to remain inactive in Canton, but to go to Macao to consult the Jesuit Visitor, then to Manila to his own Dominican superiors. (53)

Something else spurred him on. Some 12 months earlier, September 1668, the Jesuit internees sent Fr Intorcetta to Rome to present their case yet again, hoping to get confirmation of the disputed Martini decree, thus stifling opposition for ever. Navarrete had opposed this, realizing that the Jesuit's appearance in Rome, with no one to counterbalance his claims, could be fatal to the mendicant case. This was all the more likely since Intorcetta, bearing a mass of memoranda, was reinforced with the Sarpetri papers, which implied that the friars accepted the Jesuit viewpoint. (54)

Despite his objections, Intorcetta left for Rome secretly ('*furtim*' was Verbiest's word). Some Jesuits shared Navarrete's objections, though for different reasons. They feared that if Intorcetta's unauthorized absence was discovered by the local mandarin, things would go ill with the rest of them. A solution was reached by bringing in from Macao another Jesuit, Germain Macret, who took his place at roll-call. (The same was done a little later when Navarrete, following Intorcetta's example, also left secretly.) (55)

He now had the worst of both worlds. Having remained, in hopes of being allowed back to his church, he had allowed Intorcetta to steal a year's march on him. Yet he was now denied any hope of returning to his old post. He had earlier declared his wish to leave Canton, and had written to Gama to say so, but the Jesuits opposed this. When he tried to get formal permission for the journey from the mandarin in charge, they had again prevented him. Even an attempt to bribe his way out with 40 ducats failed. He now decided on another plan. (56)

For some months a Portuguese ambassador, Manoel de Saldanha, had been in Canton awaiting his license to go to Peking. The gregarious Navarrete made friends with some of his suite, especially with its secretary, Bento Pereira de Faria, who shared many of his opinions where Jesuits were concerned. Navarrete asked him to get permission for him to leave. It was, he claimed, a technicality, since the emperor's recent decree gave them implicit permission to go. Once again, however, the Jesuits foiled his scheme. (57)

In despair, he decided on boldness. On the night of 9 December 1669, he strolled out, saying he was going to visit the ambassador. He had confided his plan to the Dominican Leonardo, but told no one else, although he left explanatory letters in his cell. When these were read next day the Fathers deduced that after Macao, he would go to see Bishop Lambert de la Motte in Siam, so that, armed with his blessing, he could go on to Rome there to debate the Dominican case face to face with Intorcetta. (58)

It is difficult to decide if his departure did endanger the internees. They said it did, complaining bitterly of his 'flight'. That was understandable: they had to show him as a coward as well as unstable. Some of the more nervous Fathers were afraid that the mandarins might discover that someone was missing from the total of internees. Fr Lubelli's ambitions did not include martyrdom, and he thought they might be beheaded. In a letter to his general, Fr Gouveia denounced Navarrete for endangering them all and, worse, he had done so 'after eating here at our expense for four years'.[23] If he reached Rome he would make trouble, 'for he has with him his papers, presumption, and great lip'. (59)

In fact, the roll-calls had been gradually abandoned, although they might be started up again. On the other hand, European faces being inscrutable, the officials were content to find the required number of heads. And in an emergency any one of the Portuguese ambassador's entourage of 90 persons could replace Navarrete. Moreover, there were always Macao Jesuits awaiting an opportunity to enter China, especially to replace a meddlesome friar.

Friar Domingo's assumption was correct, for he was replaced by Fr Claudio Grimaldi, who 'eagerly seizing' the opportunity, took his place, adopting his Chinese name. As Friar Varo put it, 'the Jesuits have gained a mathematician for the court, we friars have lost a fine priest for the mission'. But others could argue that the Jesuits had gained more than the friars believed they had lost.[24] (60)

---

[23] Navarrete's bill (like Caballero's) was not forgotten (Ibáñez, *Cartas*, 82).

[24] Grimaldi, an incomparably greater man than Navarrete, wrote, 'I took to myself the name of that man who became my brothers' accuser, and who even after death still breathes threats. I took the Chinese name of Navarrete, *Min Ming-wo*, and have kept it till this day, thus

It was easy to bring over Grimaldi from Macao. A year earlier the Jesuit Rougemont had noted how easy it was to leave the residence, 'even for a whole day's journey if necessary'. Indeed people were now travelling freely between Macao and Canton. In September 1668, a year before Navarrete's 'dangerous flight', a Fr Pimentel made the journey, 'disguised as a gentleman' (noted Gama in an unfortunate phrase in his diary). This relative freedom puts into perspective the claim that Navarrete imperilled the lives of the internees. (61)

He made no attempt at a self-defence in his *Tratados*. It did not occur to him to be necessary, and it was not until he was writing the second volume, when criticism reached him, that he realised there was anything to excuse. He reminded his accusers that he could have taken flight at the outbreak of the 'persecution' when there seemed some danger; anyone who could escape when there was danger, yet stayed till it passed, could hardly be a coward. The case, he believed, was answered by the results: nothing had happened, though the Jesuits must have longed for such a useful weapon, 'I don't doubt they'd willingly give all the money in their provinces of Japan and China for that to have happened!' (62)

Later, the Jesuit critic, Fr Cortés, wondered at his reasons for leaving. Was it indiscipline, boredom and fear, or envy of Intorcetta, then on his way to Rome? Boredom and fear are odd bed-fellows, but whatever the cause, Cortés concluded that Navarrete was an deserter from Christ's salvation army in face of the enemy; such conduct had the hallmark of apostasy: Navarrete was playing the Judas to Grimaldi's Mathias.

For Friar Domingo, his years as a Jesuit had not been happy, and he was leaving Coventry as much as Canton, 'I left, fleeing from their daily shower of stones'. The earlier optimism had ended in desperate flight. (63)

Sarpetri apart, his colleagues believed Navarrete had acted rightly. And more significantly, Fr Gama made no complaint in his private diary, although, as Jesuit superior, he had had to nominate Domingo's replacement. Later, even the Spanish Inquisition, called in by the Jesuits to investigate, decided there was no fault to be found in his departure. All in all, it seems the much trumpeted perils were exaggerated.

Having left in Chinese dress, with two silver *escudos* as his only resources, Domingo went to a convert's house, where he was visited by friends from the ambassador's suite. He left at dawn with a guide, and by noon they were ten leagues out of town. To escape the local soldiery, they travelled by night, so that the journey took a week instead of the usual two or three days. They lived on scraps, suffered from cold and 'fear of tigers', and were alarmed by suddenly meeting the mandarin of Macao with a train of a hundred sedan

---

deceiving the Chinese, for whenever the emperor calls for *Min Ming-wo*, I play his role here on earth. I wonder if I'll have to take his place in Heaven too?' [Peking, 15 October 1705], (RAH, 9/2664).

chairs and a cavalry escort, 'though the days are short in December, this one seemed to me a year.' Not until the 18th of the month did they reach the town gates. Too late to go to the Dominican priory, they spent the night with sympathizers, doubtless recommended by Pereira de Faria. By next morning the claustrophobic square-mile-sized settlement was buzzing with news of his arrival. (64)

7 To the feet of the apostles

Ecclesiastical life is as much characterized by the spirit of conflict and domination as any battlefield.

— Luis Vives

The Jesuits had viewed Navarrete's arrival in the China mission with apprehension; now, at his departure, they were alarmed. He settled in Macao despite attempts to have him excommunicated as a deserter, and received two apparently amiable visits from Fr-Visitor Gama. Other callers, who brought town gossip, found a ready ear. Old Macao seemingly lived in a perpetual state of anarchy and has been described as a teacup of a place, a model for Lilliput – wracked by the rivalries, more spirited than spiritual, of its religious orders. Navarrete bears this out:

> It would take up much time and paper to write even a small part of the broils, uproars and quarrels that have taken place there. Amongst other things, some years ago [1623] the Jesuits and some laymen went with firearms against our Dominican priory there. The friars closed the doors, and to defend themselves exposed the Blessed Sacrament in a monstrance in a window overlooking the plaza. But when the attackers saw this they countered by giving the order: 'Genuflect and fire!'[1] (1)

His local superior, though a Portuguese, welcomed Navarrete warmly, asking the diocesan administrator, an Augustinian friar, to secure him a passage out. The administrator, more Portuguese than friar, refused to assist a Spaniard. He was further agitated by an appeal from the Canton internees asking him to prevent Navarrete's departure. The latter, however, found a protector in the local Captain-general, always pleased for his own reasons to vex the administrator, who next ordered the Dominicans to surrender

---

[1] An earlier proposal to establish a diocesan seminary there had to be abandoned; the young students would be exposed to too many scandals.

Navarrete, and was incensed by their reply that on the contrary they would defend him, if necessary with arms. Despite a threat of excommunication against any captain who allowed him to embark, he boarded ship on 11 January 1670, accompanied by a Chinese servant. He believed his troubles were over, though, as he was soon to find out, 'rough seas lay ahead of the prow'.[2]

A week later, the administrator, Friar Miguel dos Anjos, wrote to Canton excusing his failure to stop Navarrete's departure. He had 'turned cold at the news, for no good can be expected of the fellow'. On the other hand, he consoled his fellow Portuguese: there was no need to fear the 'low tricks of that Spaniard, for they've never yet got the better of a Portuguese'. (2)

Friar Domingo, on the high seas, was at the mercy of a pilot who was both a fool and obstinate. Yet they made good time, and by 1 February were in Malacca, where he hoped to find a ship to take him either to the French bishop in Siam, or to his headquarters in Manila. The ten days spent waiting there were useful, for there were about two thousand Catholics to be ministered to, though it was depressing to see Dutch 'soupers' bribing poor Catholics with food to attend their 'kirks'. There were also many native refugees from the Spanish Philippines. Predictably saddened by them, one day he burst into tears in public as he pondered their plight. (3)

Ships had always fascinated him (in Manila he had debated possible improvements in naval design, and even in the heat of later squabbles in Madrid, found time to read up the subject), and now in Malacca they showed him over an English ship which aroused his admiration: 'it would shine in any port'. It had cost less than 8 000 *pesos*, whereas Spanish ships built in Manila cost over 12 000, yet English vessels, here he agreed with Fr Vieira, were the safest. (4)

Sightseeing was not allowed to distract him from his purpose, and he decided to return to Europe, since he could not find transport to Siam or the Philippines. So when a vessel left for Goa on 11 February he joined it, having written to Manila to report this change of plan. This journey was slower. The whole of Lent was spent fighting adverse winds, but there were consolations, for the crew listened patiently to 19 sermons, besides attending his mass, which he managed to say on 30 occasions. (Though in rough seas he had to be content with a 'dry mass', in which there was no consecration for fear of spilling the Sacred Species.)

April 8th brought them within sight of Ceylon, and the following day they reached Colombo, where, since the Dutch refused to let priests ashore, the local Catholics went on board to make their confessions to him, and to have pious objects blessed.

He gave to travel the same intensity that he gave everything else, and not being allowing to land did not inhibit his interminable questions. As a result

---

[2] Intorcetta had left Macao on the same journey just a year earlier.

his *Tratados* contains a report on the island and he sent samples of the local coinage to the governor of Manila, suggesting that it was not necessary to rely on Mexican silver. (5)

A few days later they crossed over to the coast of India. At Madrastapatam he lodged with the French Capuchin friars whom the English governor had allowed to open a church there. As Capuchins these shared Navarrete's opinion of the Jesuits; as Frenchmen they shared his dislike of the Portuguese. Their visitor, therefore, found a warm welcome and one of them, 'though poorer than I, gave us something to eat, and to me he gave his hat, for I'd none'. Others had nothing to share but gossip, which they did not stint. An introduction to the celebrated Friar Ephraim, the centre of a recent public quarrel with the Jesuits, led to the recounting of further horror stories of Portuguese misconduct in India and Navarrete wondered, 'could the very Negroes of Angola do such things?' (6)

Unexpectedly, the ship's captain refused to go any farther. Navarrete, undaunted, decided to cross India on foot, aiming for Goa. He had two reasons: to save time, and to satisfy his curiosity. 'They gave me such a description of the road, that it would have put any man into the mood to see it, so I went to the English governor [of Madras] not so much to say good-bye as to beg an alms, and he courteously gave me five golden *pagodas* for the journey.' On 24 June he set off on the journey, which was comfortable, for there were good inns and such was the civilized behaviour of the Indians that it was possible to travel securely, 'which would be rare amongst Catholics'. There were, however, some trials: he was taken ill after drinking cold water, and suffered a grievous loss when fording a river where his papers and Chinese books fell into the water. Worst of all, his much-prized dictionary of 33 000 Chinese characters was ruined.

In Hyderabad he was consoled to meet a Spanish apothecary, whom he had known 24 years previously at home in Valladolid. His old friend, now an army surgeon, introduced him to the French East India Company factor, who offered him accommodation in a ship for Surat, provided he first returned with them to Masulipatam. On 28 July, therefore, they set out in a caravan like a royal progress, including five palanquins with sixty servants and musicians. Agog with enthusiasm he missed nothing: the grace of those 'mountains of flesh', the elephants, entering the river to bathe; the refreshing taste of coconut juice (which proved an inconvenient purge); the *pintados* (chintzes) on sale everywhere. All along the route they were entertained by dancers, not, he added primly, that he was present at their performances, though one could not help hearing their music and songs, which sometimes lasted for two hours at a stretch. Oddest of all were the snake-charmers, 'a strange way to get a living!'[3] (7)

---

[3] His is the only Spanish account of later 17th-century India, and affords a useful check on the accuracy of contemporary English, French and Italian travellers.

Despite the entertainments they travelled quickly, reaching Masulipatam in ten days where, lodged in the French East India Company factory, he was well treated, especially when he fell ill. But there was no time to be sick, for almost immediately they were involved in some dangerous excitement over an Armenian clerk, Makara, an employee of the French, who were taking him to Surat to stand trial on charges of embezzlement. During the ten days' journey he and Friar Domingo became friends. Claiming to be a Catholic, he put up such a display of piety that the gullible Navarrete grew well disposed towards him. Independent French and English assessments of him are unflattering; according to the latter, he was 'a fellow it doth appear of more subtlety than honesty and who had played his Game so sophister like'.

Makara, seeing little hope of escaping French justice, resolved to shift for himself, and on arrival in Masulipatam appealed to the native governor, Muhamed Beg, offering to turn Muslim if freed. His release was immediately requested and flatly refused. Negotiations went on for some days until 13 September, when, continued the English report, there broke out 'a mortall fray betwixt the French and Moores, there being slaine of the French Monsieur Fernardeen and of the others four, and seven mortally wounded'. Navarrete and the French, besieged in the factory, were virtually prisoners.

The English report, written in safety on the sidelines, described their position: 'those that remained [alive], though for the most part sickly and weake, yet appear with undaunted courage, resolveing not to deliver up Mackraw, though many tymes since demanded by the Moores, and truly wee are of opinion that they will persist in their denyall, whilst a man of them breathes'. But Muhamed Beg, a weak champion, was soon asking that Navarrete be sent out to negotiate. The French Company director, though seriously ill with fever, remained in command, and rejected this overture, replying that Navarrete, a Spaniard, had nothing to do with the business. But on the 28th, when the director died, a truce was arranged. Navarrete officiated at his funeral which took place with great solemnity, over a hundred servants carrying tapers in the procession. This put an end to the squabble for 'Mahomed Beague . . . haveing cryed pacavi [peccavi] for his rashness', lifted the siege and abandoned Makara to his fate.

The story allows an independent check on Navarrete's accuracy and shows that his account tallies in almost every detail with the contemporary report sent to London by the English factors; his statistics of dead and wounded on both sides are near enough the English figures, though sometimes he is more accurate than they, particularly in transcribing foreign names. (8)

Once the excitement died down Navarrete visited the town. The local English showed much interest in Catholicism, an interest for which they were denounced by their Protestant chaplain, who complained that many in India were being 'seduced into Popery'. Navarrete took the opportunity to have a long conversation with the governor, Sir Edward Winter, whom he found living quietly in retirement on his estates, after an exciting career during which he had set himself up independently of the East India Company. For three years he waged a private war against the officials trying to remove him from office. He still took a lively interest in affairs, passing on to Navarrete a rumour that the Indians were planning to attack Portuguese Goa simultaneously by land and sea, information which Navarrete promptly sent off in warning despatches. (9)

As soon as the *Couronne*, was ready, 20 October 1670, they set sail, attended by all the hazards that another bad pilot could provide. On the fourth day they sighted the coast of Ceylon, but a north-easter blew them out so far that they completely lost their bearings and spent the next 11 days trying to find the island again. All went well until they tried to round Cape Comorin, where they ran into fresh trouble. Friar Domingo, never slow to advise in nautical or any other matters, 'having seen so much of the sea, took upon me to play the pilot, and contended to have us get in under the shore. I argued, who would run upon an enemy's sword? The best is to attack from the side'.

This brought them to safety which they were so busy celebrating that they almost ran onto a reef. A boatload of natives nearby, astonished at the sight of an apparently unattended ship 'must have concluded we were either blind or mad'. Their cries of alarm saved the *Couronne*: 'God sent those Blacks, for had they not come we had surely ended our days there!'

For the rest of the journey Navarrete was busy consoling Makara, who, if he had earlier offered to turn Muslim, was now constantly to be seen telling his rosary beads, to Navarrete's great satisfaction. The French nevertheless treated him harshly, making him sign various confessions by 'holding four Pistols at his Breast', but, as he gravely explained to Navarrete, he always told them whatever they seemed to want to hear. (10)

The remainder of the voyage was quieter, though it was 14 December, and Friar Domingo had been travelling for a year, before they reached 'Golden Goa'. The sight of it delighted him, but his description of the great Portuguese city is singularly brief. He spares it only a couple of paragraphs in which he rebukes a 'certain missionary'[4] for his exaggerated account of the place. After two happy days, first resting at the Dominican priory, and then sightseeing, they embarked again for Surat.

In Swally, its sea-port, he met Francis Caron, director-general of the French East India Company. Caron was a Dutchman who, urged by ambition and helped by a staggering capacity for work, had risen from small beginnings to his present position. A staunch Protestant, he was no bigot, perhaps due to the influence of his Japanese mistress (a Catholic convert) who had borne him six children. After first working for the Dutch Company, Caron had transferred to the French. He had arrived in Surat only a short time before Navarrete, yet he had already set French trade on a satisfactory

---

[4] A 'certain person', usually means some Jesuit whom he is reluctant to name for some reason.

footing in India, and his employers were delighted with him. This meeting showed something of Navarrete's ability to charm, for Caron, at first unfriendly, was soon 'extremely loving'. He was interesting because he had been over 20 years in Japan, spoke the language fluently, and could answer many intriguing questions. Gossip blamed Caron for the persecution of the Japanese Catholics, and Navarrete asked for his version of the story. He was gratified to hear that, by implication, it had been caused by Jesuit imprudence. (11)

On 20 January 1671 he embarked for the Cape of Good Hope on board the *Aigle d'Or*. The following night, after a celebration supper with Caron, they set sail accompanied by farewell salvoes. Yet again they were unlucky in their pilot, through whose folly they nearly ran aground, to the fury of the captain, who was with difficulty prevented from shooting the man: 'Good God, what a wonderful confusion we were in!' However, they were back at Cape Comorin safely in 11 days, though on the way north the same journey had taken 49 days. Making steadily for the Cape they were fortunate in the weather, and mass was said almost daily as Navarrete found himself observing another Lent on the high seas.

Suddenly the weather changed. An unexpected storm carried off three of their sails, broke the rudder and buffeted the vessel until they believed she would founder. Every moment seemed their last. They could do nothing except roll themselves up in their corners and pray, while Navarrete sprinkled holy water over the sea. By this time they were approaching the Cape itself, and, knowing what lay ahead, prepared for the worst. The ship had already taken on so much water that the crew were constantly manning the pumps. They were making hardly any headway and sometimes for days at a stretch the ship stood to in contrary winds. Then, when they finally reached the southernmost point, the dreaded 'Needles' a few miles short of the Cape, they ran into another storm which drove them down to the 42nd degree of latitude.

The sea 'appeared full of whales on the surface of the water, and they would play round the ship to the terror of us that beheld them'. To this was added the awesome sight of St Elmo's fire hanging over the mast 'like altar candles', arousing much discussion, for 'every man spoke his mind'. Friar Domingo, always determined to check mere report against experience, even forgot the storm to study the new phenomenon, 'I having read something of it, was very curious in making particular observation of it'.

They returned to the Cape, but after marking time for a month, were still unable to round it. In despair, it was decided to make for Madagascar. 'What we endured all this time is not to be writ, though God and I know it. Often the sea, beating on the poop, frighted us, and ran so high that I'd not the courage to look at it. How many nights I spent clinging to a brass gun, how many more sitting by the bittake. Amidst the foul weather, and the discontents betwixt the captain and the pilot, we at length arrived at

Madagascar'. And there, on 29 May 1671 they dropped their only remaining anchor. (12)

His enforced visit to Madagascar was no waste of time, for there he met the influential François Pallu, Bishop of Heliopolis, principal founder of the Paris Foreign Mission Society, who had also been delayed there on his way east. Pallu was lodging with the local community of Lazarists. These belonged to yet another of those French congregations, whose establishment was further evidence of the shift in missionary influence in Asia from the Iberians to the French. Pallu had already been in the east, where his experiences convinced him that God was calling the French to put right there what the Spaniards and Portuguese between them had bungled. He had returned to Paris to seek help and found no one more generous than Louis XIV, who saw in him a means of extending French influence in Asia. (13)

Bishop and friar remained firm friends to the end of their lives. Pallu shared something of Friar Domingo's feelings about the Jesuits, and these feelings were later strengthened by the Fathers' antagonism towards him and the other French bishops sent to Asia. More positively, Pallu, as his letters reveal, felt a lively concern for the China mission, which fell within his jurisdiction, and the meeting (in his view, an act of divine providence), enabled him to discuss its problems with one who knew them at first hand.

A voluminous letter-writer, Pallu poured out a stream of enthusiastic memoranda to Rome and Paris praising Navarrete, who 'deserves the title of Apostle far more than many others working in the East. I can scarcely describe what pleasure I've had from talking to him, an expert on Chinese affairs'. Pallu's letters also reveal that Navarrete did not publish everything he knew. It is from the bishop that we learn how the Portuguese, for their own reasons anxious to kidnap a French priest, Antoine Hainques, out of Cochin China, tried to lure him on board a ship where, they said, the dying Navarrete was asking for the last sacraments. The plot failed when Hainques was warned off by an informer.[5] (14)

Pallu had already heard of the missionaries' detention in Canton but knew nothing of events there. He now compiled a report for Propaganda Fide outlining the conference discussions as seen by Friar Domingo. One discussion concerned the need to create a native clergy. This was one of the principal aims of Pallu's Society, as it had been of the former Secretary of Propaganda, Francesco Ingoli. He, visualizing indigenous priests working under his direct control, had already urged the bishops newly appointed to Asia to seek suitable candidates. Navarrete was able to show how the Dominicans had forestalled them all by ordaining the Chinese, Gregorio Lo, and how their policy had been amply justified by Lo's work during the recent

---

[5] 'Sub specie sacramenta Navarretto jamjam morituro ministrandi' (Pallu, Lettres, II: 40). And though Domingo does not say so, it appears he was in Siam in December 1670 (AME, vol. 858, fol. 194).

persecution. Navarrete went further, persuading Pallu to recommend that Friar Lo be made bishop of China, as he was in 1685. (15)

Pallu was not the only one to benefit by this 'providential encounter', for he too had news to pass on, and the sort of news that Friar Domingo would have wished for. In Mexico, 30 years earlier, Bishop Palafox had shown him Fr Morales's treatise on the rites controversy; then in Canton Friar Caballero had shown him Longobardi's banned treatise. Now Pallu revealed how two indiscreet French Fathers, Tissanier and Albier, had once leaked news to him of a secret Jesuit conference in Kiating in 1628. This had been called by the then Fr-Visitor, Palmeiro, at a time when the controversy among the Jesuits was most acute, just before the coming of the friars to China. Fr Longobardi had been at that meeting, and in several cases his viewpoint had prevailed. The Visitor seemed to be won over, and many Fathers advocated an approach nearer to what was later proposed by the friars. After the conference Longobardi set himself to write his thesis.

All this is what Navarrete had in mind when urging the Jesuits to follow the policy of their own 'veterans': he meant the Fathers of the 1628 conference. And although Navarrete had hitherto refrained from criticizing Schall's work in the calendar bureau, after seeing the Kiating minutes his attitude changed.

Nothing was settled at Kiating, but the Fathers kept the uneasy discussions to themselves. Pallu's Jesuit informants begged that their revelations be kept secret. And so they were, until Pallu met 'the learned expert, Navarrete', the first person he felt justified in talking to about the matter. He even gave him a copy of the conference minutes. Since no friar had heard anything of all this, he published the document 'so that it may be seen plainly what disunity and doubt there is within the Society, though they try to give the opposite view in their writings'.

Why the Jesuit pair chose to reveal this information to Pallu, a man known to be unfriendly to their Society (though his brother Jacques was a Jesuit) might puzzle some. But Navarrete saw it as the will of God. For the Jansenists it was 'a sort of miracle'. More prosaically, it was probably done out of the fellow feelings of two Frenchmen for another. (16)

The talks between bishop and friar were frequent, long, and harmonious and Pallu persuaded Domingo to change his plans and to visit Paris before Rome. He prepared the way for him by writing another batch of letters for Europe: he ordered his Paris headquarters to receive Navarrete, and 'since he is extremely poor, take care of his needs, and when he leaves for Rome give him an alms'. He wrote much the same to the Duchess d'Aiguillon, Richelieu's pious niece and, aware that the news from China would interest the politicians, despatched a summary of Friar Domingo's news to Louis XIV's minister Colbert, for the king's attention, hoping that Navarrete would be given an audience on arrival in Paris. (17)

Pallu left Madagascar in August 1671, continuing his interrupted journey east, carrying letters from Navarrete to his old Dominican colleagues. By then the bishop had been completely won over to the friar's viewpoint, though not all the talk had been critical of the Jesuits, for Navarrete had praised the three Peking Fathers, and had spoken well of some the French Jesuits whom he know. This was not simply a gesture to capture Pallu's goodwill, because in detention he had become friendly with some of the Frenchmen. (18)

Towards the end of October, as the weather became warmer and the winds died down, preparations began for a second attempt on the Cape. They set sail on All Souls' day and this time luck was with them. The only annoyance on this journey was not being able to land at the Cape, for he was never satisfied to be told 'here be elephants'. Besides, having heard strange stories of the Dutch settlement there, he was curious about their excellent, well-armed fort. He did however see some marine ducks: 'feathered fish. God alone knows how they laid or hatched'. Apart from this, there were the usual arguments with the crew about politics and there was always information to be picked up, information which must be sent to the right quarters in Madrid: that, for example, the French had recently sent a spy to Mexico who, after three years studying harbours and defences, had submitted a report to Paris.[6] (19)

Seven weeks' sailing brought them to St Helena, a traditional stopping-place between Europe and Asia, where they spent Christmas, though initially the governor showed them no welcome. Richard Cony had a reputation for being aggressive to visitors and a few months earlier the islanders had denounced him to London as hostile even to English captains, 'threatening to beat some of them . . . takeing another of them by the Coller, telling them in common they had nothing to do ashore, and might goe back on board and finish their Prowleings'. Their litany ended with the reflection that 'never were Company and people soe gen'lly slighted and abused since St. Hellena was St. Hellena as they have bin by this Govr. to this day'.

Undismayed by the prospect of a chilly reception, Navarrete called on Cony who, surprisingly, was soon won over. Breaking his own rules, he insisted that his visitor spend the night at Government House. This was at odds with his more normal practice of overcharging strangers. Not that the islanders fared much better, for he 'would not let them have soe much as a little butter and cheese or milk from the dairie, for their tender Babes, though he would sell abundance to the portugalls and other foreigners to his own profit'. (20)

Navarrete was as unaware that he was in a lion's den, as Cony was unaware of his guest's temper. This mutual ignorance led to a moment which could

---

[6] Fr Pierre de Pelleprat, a French Jesuit accused by the Mexican Inquisition of spying and map-making, was deported to France.

have been embarrassing. After supper, his host invited him to join in a little psalm-singing, pointing out knowledgeably that he might legitimately attend, without actually joining in their devotions: it would be simply 'material attendance'. But where Jesuit casuistry had failed, the 'little governor' was unlikely to succeed, and his invitation was firmly rejected with a reference, apposite but tactless, to Tertullian on the impropriety of joining in infidels' prayers out of friendship. (Recalling the incident later, Navarrete recommended the maxim to the Jesuits.)

Cony was keenly interested in religious matters, especially in the theory of the transmigration of souls, and he had a fair opinion of himself as a metaphysician. Friar Domingo's comment 'to say the truth he was an ingenious man' was high praise, especially after the two had spent some time together, and had 'discoursed upon several subjects, and he put to me three problems concerning baptism'. Cony had few friends on the island, 'not above three or four ever cared for his company', and he was at that very time in the middle of a bitter quarrel with his chaplain, Mr Noakes. The two were busy denouncing each other to London, and soliciting signatures from other residents to support the charges each made against the other. According to the governor, chaplain Noakes was a 'person scandlous to ye Ministry in his life and conversation and a seditious troublesome person' who had 'preached treason, sedition, schisme and Heresy in a certain sermon'. To make things worse, he was 'a non-Conformist to ye Church of England though a parson yt doth baptize, burry, marry, but ye Govr. having pressed him severall times to administer ye blessed Communion to ye inhabitants he declared yt ye inhabitants of ye Island were not capable of receiving it'. Mr Noakes and his supporters answered with brisk counter-charges, both general and particular, accusing the Governor of pocketing official funds, suppressing the liberty of the islanders, displaying 'insolence and opposition to, and derision of us, both in words and farago after ye Spanish mode'. Furthermore, 'he hath lett fall dangerous expressions and withall is very careless of the safety and defence of ye island'. (21)

On Christmas Eve, at the request of Catholics in the ship's crew, Navarrete said a midnight mass and two more at dawn. Then, early that evening they set sail for France. The last part of the journey began pleasantly, and the crew, in good humour at the prospect of reaching home, neglected none of the traditional crossing-the-line ceremonies. But optimism was unjustified, for the weather suddenly turned, it became bitterly cold, and they made little headway. They were running short of supplies. A strange sickness broke out and carried off a dozen or so sailors. Navarrete was kept busy attending those who could not help themselves, and in seas so heavy that sometimes he had to be held steady by two sailors while he gave the last sacraments to a third. (There were other perils, beside those of the deep. One morning a French traveller was found dead: 'He liv'd like a beast and drank like a madman, so that I took him for an atheist rather than a heretick. One night he got up to drink, but instead of the wine laid hold of the ink-bottle of which he drank mightily.')

The ship's plight became critical when contrary winds suddenly drove them so far north that they found themselves in the English Channel. Now abandoning all hope of making a French port, they turned south for Lisbon, and so Bishop Pallu's recommended visit to Paris never took place. But still their troubles were not over, and they did not enter the harbour until 19 March 1672, so that the journey from Macao to Lisbon had taken well over two years. Navarrete, reflecting on it later, concluded that a man who puts to sea is a fool, unless it be in the service of God.

As soon as they docked, Navarrete, dressed in Chinese clothes, landed and went to the Dominican priory.[7] The war with Spain had only just finished, but Lisbon was seething with rumours of yet another. The Dominicans, traditionally mistrusted for their partiality towards Spaniards, had been unpopular during the war, because they alone did not preach in favour of the Portuguese.[8] Despite the double disadvantage of being Spanish and Dominican, Navarrete was welcomed by the Inquisitor-General, who questioned him closely about affairs in the East. He passed on to the secretary of state the warning he had already sent to Goa about the danger of an Indian attack upon the city.

The Dominican rule forbade friars to go to Rome unless summoned by the master-general. Navarrete therefore wrote for permission to report there and while waiting for a reply, he stayed in Lisbon (except for one brief visit to Seville) indulging in some inevitable sightseeing. Of the Portuguese he had little to say, beyond reaffirming their narrow-mindedness and those delusions of superiority which led them to boast that 'even their wines were better than those of Spain'. In a regrettable access of prudence he hints that he heard other, more serious gossip, 'which I think should lie buried in oblivion, so that future ages may not have cause to condemn this one'. (22)

Mid-May found him on the road to Madrid, travelling from priory to priory for 11 days. On arrival there he found letters from Cardinal Barberini demanding information about the missions, and he replied with a brief despatch. Finally, the Dominican general's summons arrived, and in September 1672 he set off, travelling, for safety's sake, in the official retinue of the Duchess of Osuna, wife of the governor of Milan, since Valencia was notorious bandit-country. (23)

It was early December 1672 when 'alternately stumbling and rising again' he entered the Eternal City where the atmosphere seemed propitious. The 83-years-old Clement X was well disposed to the Jesuits, but he had been so

---

[7] The Jesuit Boym's 'tendency to dress in Chinese clothing must have further increased his curious aura in the eyes of the Venetians' (Mungello, *Curious*, 140).
[8] Whereas the Jesuits, for mysterious reasons of their own, supported the Portuguese movement for independence from Spain (Boxer, *Salvador*, 142–3).

ill for so long that affairs had passed into the hands of the cardinal-regent, Paluzzo-Altieri. The Romans, typically, had a suitable saying: 'Clement is pope in name, but the Cardinal is pope in fact'. Clement regretted it, 'at this time when we wish to be an eagle, our health impedes us more than ever'. For all his years and ailments the old man struggled on, to the surprise of all and the disappointment of some. On occasion he looked so well that gossip said he gave himself a healthy colour by washing in Greek wine. His ups and downs were confusing. In May 1673 his health was such that the 81-year old cardinal who hoped to succeed him felt able to encourage his supporters. Yet in the following October Clement was not only better, but, according to his Carmelite astrologer, was not yet likely to gratify those who wanted to see the papal chair vacant. Altieri had the same reassurances from his own astrologers whom he consulted daily, 'as one might the physician'. Reassured he might be, but the cardinal-regent had to keep alert, for the old man's memory often failed, and as he caused embarrassment by sometimes promising the same favour to different people, his audiences had to be discreetly curtailed. Nevertheless, Altieri allowed Friar Domingo two interviews from which he came away 'edified by the pope's humility and the poverty of his little room'. (24)

Navarrete, lodged in Dominican headquarters on the Minerva, immediately began 16 months of vigorous activity, lobbying cardinals such as the scholarly Bona ('the Fénelon of Italy'), the pro-Dominican Casanata, the anti-Jesuit Ottoboni, and Puertocarrero of the Spanish faction. He was disappointed that Intorcetta, his fellow internee in Canton, had already left Rome, for the friars hoped for a confrontation between the two in the presence of the cardinals of Propaganda. But on his way south Navarrete had visited the Jesuits in Genoa, where apparently he spoke too freely and believed that as a consequence Intorcetta had fled Rome, after hearing that he was on his way. Had the two met the result would have been lively, since Intorcetta's report to Propaganda gave Navarrete plenty to quarrel with, and the Jesuit might have profited from a public clash with Navarrete, for he made little impact on Rome, a failure over which he brooded for years.[9] (25)

Navarrete's first move was to translate relevant Chinese texts into Latin and to make fair copies of the material to be submitted to Propaganda. This kept him busy until September 1673. Friar Francisco Varo, in a favoured metaphor, used to describe the pope as the one true pilot, alone able to sail between Scylla and Charybdis: 'and this holy navigator in negotiating the seas of this China mission is guided by the rutters and charts drawn up for him by the ministers of that mission'. Navarrete therefore determined not to stint information. He translated the Chinese ritual that laid down

---

[9] In 1681 Verbiest wrote from Peking to his general that Intorcetta had depression. It started in Rome, and he brought it back with him, 'I beg Your Paternity to console your afflicted son with a little note (*scripto verbulo*)' (Verbiest, 351).

regulations for the performance of the various rites and he supplemented this with illustrations, no detail being omitted to make the case clear, for if there was one Jesuit maxim that he approved and obeyed it was that prayers are never enough to gain one's ends. A mortuary tablet, which the Chinese venerated, was produced and explained to the committee of cardinals, 'with all its shape, form, longitude and latitude and profound mystery'.[10] He quoted to his own advantage the writings of the unfortunate Fr Roboredo who, long before in Manila, had rushed into the fray with more energy than knowledge. He submitted Friar Caballero's more recent treatise on the rites, written in Canton for Fr Gama, and he added copies of letters now reaching him in Rome from the friars still in China, together with a brief history of Dominican achievements there. There were also his two trump cards: the dissident Longobardi's treatise, and Pallu's report of the hitherto unknown Kiating conference in 1628. After he had finished the translating and editing he prepared a list of 119 questions for Propaganda to answer. Behind his phrasing of these there can sometimes be detected an attempt to suggest a favourable answer; sometimes he drops a hint of which way the wind ought to blow. This formidable list of questions did not satisfy him, and he prepared more, which he did not in the end submit, partly because he feared to exhaust the cardinals, and partly because of sudden illness. (26)

His basic aim was the annulment of Martini's decree, for while the two contradictory decrees of 1645 and 1656 stood together there must always be stalemate and confusion. The Dominican Polanco had made an earlier effort in 1669, but the answer he received, as we have seen, was that both decrees were valid in their different ways, and both were to be obeyed according to circumstances. Legally, the cardinals' reply was shrewd – it could not be faulted; administratively, it was convenient – it allowed the issue to be evaded; practically, it was useless – it confused everyone and satisfied nobody. Patient rather than ironical, Navarrete explained his failure to force a decision out of Propaganda: 'I desired a fuller answer, yet it was not given me. In Rome they are governed by more elevated causes, and I do not question that they are just and right, and though neither I nor others comprehend them yet our duty is to respect their commands'. (27)

His efforts were watched. The Dominicans of course encouraged and helped their champion; the Philippine provincial wrote from Manila urging him on, expressing the hope that he would return to East Asia as soon as his business was concluded. These were sentiments that the Jesuits could not be expected to share; alarmed by his activities, they lamented that his evidence seemed to be accepted as irrefutable. (28)

Yet it was not easy for him. Rome had had to listen to more than enough about China during the 30 years since Friar Morales had brought an apparently simple case for solution. There had been a series of supplicants

---

[10] Described in Dyer Ball, 31, and see Ebrey.

since then: the Jesuits Semedo, Boym, Martini, and Intorcetta; and from the Dominican side Morales, Polanco, and now Navarrete. All brought accounts which, when not flatly contradictory, were confusingly different. Varo's 'only true pilot', the pope, was bewildered by the number and variety of theological sea-charts being thrust into his hands by missionaries who had navigated those stormy waters, each to his own satisfaction. Little wonder that the 13 cardinals of Propaganda had a reputation for not reading the memorials rained upon them for scrutiny and answer; little wonder either that Propaganda was sceptical about missionaries' reports in general. A confidential report to Innocent XI (which got unfortunate publicity) confessed that 'in the opinion of Propaganda little credence is to be given to the missionaries' relations, letters and solicitations. Hence the usual answer of the Congregation is to ask for further information, which often proves useless'. The China business was obviously more involved than had first appeared, and dangerous too, particularly after Pascal had given it a new and alarming dimension. And the theological problems, complex enough, were entangled with power politics, especially since Propaganda's decision to send out its own bishops had infuriated the Portuguese, who saw their old patronage privileges in danger.

The shrewd agents of the Paris Foreign Mission Society noticed that Rome was reluctant to be too precise: 'the Holy Office follows the maxim that "definitions are dangerous" '. Indeed there is a note of more than usual Roman caution in the replies to Navarrete's 119 questions: some answers were laconic, some were not answers at all, and some almost rebukes. But he obstinately persisted. Cardinal Casanata, Assessor of the Holy Office, Dominican ally, known for his opposition to religious novelty, ought to have been tireless in his cooperation with Navarrete, but even he lost his temper. Rounding angrily on him one day, he told him that the Holy Office was not there to answer every conceivable problem; it was there to guard the Deposit of Faith: other questions were to be settled by following 'the best opinions'. But this was the exasperation of anxiety, not indifference. (29)

It was now June, and since the cardinals of Propaganda did not normally meet during the summer, Friar Domingo realised the need for haste. He urged the setting up of a 'Particular Congregation' (an *ad hoc* working party) to study his reports. But Propaganda parried that by falling back on the oldest bureaucratic defence of all, 'passed to higher authorities [the Holy Office]'. However, exceptionally, on the last day of July, in the stifling Roman summer, the cardinals met again to discuss mission problems, in particular the sending of French bishops to the east. This was a question 'in which the Society is as involved as is Portugal' noted António Vieira, then in Rome.[11] He reported that the cardinals' meeting took place on the feast of

---

[11] They did not meet. Given the smallness of Rome, and their common concerns this looks deliberate; but we cannot say. Vieira's comments would have been revealing: professing a

Ignatius Loyola, who had worked a 'great miracle' in favour of his Society, for the sudden illness of the pro-Jesuit Cardinal Albizzi was happily balanced by the equally sudden illness of the anti-Jesuit Baldeschi. Consequently no decisions were taken that day, although there was talk of summoning Friar Domingo and the Jesuit general jointly to give evidence before the committee. (30)

While the cardinals were debating (or deferring), Friar Domingo spoke to the Secretary of Propaganda, urging a papal confirmation of Urban VIII's decree 'empowering missionaries to go to Japan and China from all parts, and by all routes'. Just before Christmas he had the satisfaction of obtaining this, which was another significant step in the gradual pruning of the *padroado*. Some Jesuits detected the unfriendly influence of Cardinal Altieri in the use of the pointed phrase 'including the Society of Jesus' (*etiam Societatis Jesu*) in the address of the decree.

As a result of this move China was no longer anyone's ecclesiastical monopoly. [12] The Dominicans claimed that this confirmation of Urban's decree justified Navarrete's visit to Rome and crowned his work there. It may have been a victory for him, but it brought him into conflict with the Portuguese ambassador, Gaspar de Abreu, who, ruthless in defending the old *padroado* rights, planted spies to get at the congregation's decisions, and bought up stolen copies of the minutes of the cardinals' confidential meetings. [13]

In December 1673 Navarrete, encouraged by his success, submitted 14 more points to Propaganda, at the same time reminding them that he was still waiting for answers to his earlier questions. (31)

His visit had coincided with another gratifying event: the banning of the so-called 'Jesuit Relations'. As the Anglican Bishop Burnet observed, 'Priests, and the Men of the Religious Orders, write larger and more particular Letters than any other sort of men'. This was certainly true of the Jesuits, one of whose skills was the sophisticated use of techniques of communication. From the beginning Loyola had regarded letter-writing as an apostolic task, to be undertaken in an apostolic spirit. It was as though every Jesuit was given a pen on his profession in the order, much as a medieval knight was given his sword. Frequent correspondence enabled the general to direct his men more closely. It was also a means of mutual encouragement between individual Fathers, of fostering psychological union,

---

judicious affection for the Dominicans, he was anti-Spanish. One of his sayings gives some idea of the man: 'Not even Jesus Christ, for all his miracles, succeeded in curing a fool of his folly.'

[12] In December 1673 two papal decrees stripped the Portuguese of their privileges, stressing that the Propaganda bishops (Vicars apostolic) were independent of Portugal.

[13] The atmosphere of intrigue in Rome is excellently conveyed by Bruno Neveu's *Sébastien Joseph du Cambout de Pontchâteau* (Paris, 1969). Pontchâteau, a Jansenist, had to adopt a false name and move about after dark. Finally, trapped by informers (1680), he was expelled.

and of spreading knowledge of Jesuit achievement. The Fathers were ordered to report regularly, and in detail, to their superiors, sending not only personal information but precise accounts of the new countries they entered. In the early days the letters from Brazil and India were to give particularly close detail.[14] The prescriptions for writing these letters were typically thorough, nothing being left to chance: handwriting was to be clear, margins enough to allow the recipient's annotation; no unusual abbreviations were to be used; secret and non-secret matter were never to be written in the same letter; the calendar date was to be used and not that of the religious feast of the day; two, three, up to five copies were to be despatched by different routes, according to the importance of the contents. Replies were not to be expected. In addition, the Society's rules, as has been said, allowed every Jesuit direct access to his general over the head of intermediaries: this made the individual Father conscious of the power of his letters. These reports arrived steadily in Rome from all parts of the world, and were an exchange and mart of knowledge and gossip. By 1679, when there were 17 000 Jesuits, divided into 35 'provinces', the general regularly received an extraordinary amount of information, making his position unique in the Europe of the time. And that is what Pierre Bayle had in mind when he complained that 'the Jesuit general rules everywhere from Paris to Peking'. (32)

After due censorship, selected letters received in the Roman headquarters were published as works of edification and to attract alms, sympathy, prayers, and vocations. Even today, no other order devotes so much manpower and resources to publicizing itself and compared with them the friars' efforts make a poor showing: it has always been one of the differences between the two groups. Following a looser tradition of government, the mendicants were remiss in keeping in touch with Rome, and although the Jesuits' example made some of them aware of this failing, they did little to correct it. As early as 1609 the master-general expressed amazement that no news came to him from his Philippine subjects, and he wrote begging for a letter 'at least once a year'. This carelessness was general and the China friars were often left without news from their Manila headquarters, and sometimes did not even know what new superiors had been elected 'as though we here were not sons of the same Province'. This was an old problem: from Peking in 1305 Friar John of Montecorvino wrote 'Charity demands that those who travel for Christ should be consoled by letters. I have often wondered that

---

[14] In 1553 Ignatius demanded from Fr Nóbrega, in Brazil, reports written *distinctius et exactius* of the 'region, climate, longitude, latitude, native customs, dress and houses, and this not out of mere curiosity (legitimate though it be) but that, should the need arise, Fr-General can take decisions in the full knowledge of the situation.' This accorded with contemporary business practice: for example, the Fuggers, the German merchant princes, requested their foreign agents to report local gossip and rumour as well as facts (Ambrosini, 181–88, 360-61).

until this year I never received letters or good wishes from any Brother, so that it seemed to me that no one remembered me'.

The secretary of Propaganda, Monsignor Ingoli, rebuked Friar Morales when they met in Rome in 1643 because the Dominicans, who had then been in China for some years, had never reported their progress either to him or to the pope, and it was an Augustinian who 'by chance, and casually, between the lines of his own report, had informed Rome that the Dominicans had managed to enter the China mission'. 'I do not praise or approve such silence', said Friar Domingo, for that was not his way.[15] Other Dominicans would have agreed with him; the mendicant historian Fernández de Plasencia, for example, thought the Jesuits' diligence in writing was as praiseworthy as the friars' negligence was blameworthy.

The different orders of friars did, of course, produce chronicles and histories, gathering statistics and assembling annual reports, but none was as systematic and sustained in the work as were the Jesuits. Once, in a burst of enthusiasm, the Spanish Dominicans commissioned the dramatist Lope de Vega to write a history of their martyrs in Japan which was published as the *Triunfo de la Fee* (Madrid, 1618). But, that was a flash in the pan, and some friars were out of sympathy with the aims of such chroniclers, believing they would be better employed saving souls than in recording how others did so. It was Samuel Purchas's opinion too: 'In some there is a want of History of their Severall Acts, who sought rather to write Christ's Passion in the hearts of others, than their owne Actions in books: to produce deeds not wordes, and monuments of Divine, not their owne glory'. (33)

The Jesuits' *Relations*, though successful, were criticized, and in the 17th century complaints of their exaggerations were frequent. One Franciscan, inspired to volunteer for the Canadian missions by his pious readings, looked in vain for the many converts he had read so much about. Feeling deceived, he exclaimed indignantly, 'Is it possible that this pretended prodigious number of Savages should escape the Knowledg of crowds of French Canadins, who go abroad every Year from home at least three or four hundred Leagues. How happen'd it that these devout churches disappeared when I travelled through these countries? Would to God that all those Churches spoken of in the *Relations* were as real as the people of Canada know they are chimerical.'

Others noted how even Jesuits who knew only the *Relations* and nothing of the private letters reaching Rome from the missions, were often similarly grieved and disappointed when they went overseas. 'The *Relations* ought not to be read as though they tell the whole story', warned one Father writing to

---

[15] Navarrete, given his pretensions, would have been gratified by the praise of a modern historian: 'There is nothing in Dominican mission literature faintly comparable with the informative Jesuit Letters, except a few works like the racy *Tratados* of Fernández Navarrete' (Boxer, *Fidalgos*, 190).

Rome, and in Siam in 1666 the unsympathetic Bishop Lambert de la Motte noted how eager Jesuits often arrived there only to find themselves 'face to face with the other side of the coin'.

As an Englishman, Bishop Burnet was in a position to draw comparisons between the reality and the *Relations*, and his condemnation was forthright. 'The Extravagantly vain Letters that they write to Rome from England, are such contextures of Legends, that ever since I first saw them, I know what value I ought to put on their Letters that come from the Indies and other remote Countrys, for when they take so great a Liberty where the Falsehood is so easily found out, what must we think of the Relations that come from places at such a distance, that they may lie with more assurance and less hazard of discovery'.[16] Other Englishmen were equally cynical. 'This is Jesuits' news; dare not say it is Gospell', wrote one from India in 1671, passing on shaky information about the Dutch in Ceylon. In 1616 Samuel Purchas, sharing an attitude common among the members of the Royal Society later in the century, warned his readers that 'in relating their Success remember that they are Jesuits: in other things which are not serviceable to Rome, we will heare them as Travellers, when lying doth not advantage them, nor hurt us'.

The *Relations* came into disrepute partly for their frequent accounts of miracles. The Jesuit *Constitutions* had warned against this (*pro miraculis non ponantur quae miracula non sint*), to little avail. It was to this tendency that Navarrete objected. He could have quoted the words of Gideon (Judges 6: 13), 'where be all the miracles which the Fathers told us of?', but instead he noted that 'here in Europe I've read much about miracles in China which are unknown to those working there'.[17] Fr Magalhães, for instance, produced some pious nonsense in his 1641 Annual Letter, with yarns about a convert's dead son who appeared at night surrounded by angels; another dying convert saw Christ judging the souls of a thousand recently dead Christians, of whom only one went to heaven, two to purgatory, and the rest to hell, to be tortured by wolfish devils for all eternity. However good the intention behind this Navarrete saw the result must be harmful. 'They give grounds

---

[16] 'In their Annual Letters, the Jesuits supply endless statistics, no doubt intended to impress the General and hence as flattering as they could honestly be. In 1624 the London Jesuits record 65 conversions, including (and such cases always delighted the fathers) a man of high position and noble birth' (B. Basset, SJ., 193). Cf Gibbon: 'The only defect in these pleasing compositions is the want of truth and commonsense'.

[17] Cf. John Donne's 'their greatest miracle is that they find men to believe their miracles'. Even the K'ang-hsi emperor was intrigued: 'I told Fr Fontaney that I would gladly witness some of the miracles they talked about, but none was forthcoming' (Spence, *Emperor*, 84). In 1743 John Lockman published a two-volumed edition of the 34 volumes of these *Edifying Letters* by omitting the accounts of miracles as being 'insipid and ridiculous to English readers'.

for mockery to many, nowadays there are no miracles as there were in former times. What's needed now is peace among the missionaries'.

He suggested some Jesuits were embarrassed by these effusions: 'Fr Matias de Maia wrote an Annual Letter full of such Romances, that those of his Society would not allow it to be read in the presence of us friars [in Canton]. Yet at home its contents are doubtless looked upon as an oracle. This is to deceive Europe, as Fr Adam Schall said once.'

Navarrete was therefore gratified when on 16 April 1673 a papal brief (*Creditae nobis*) prohibited over-optimistic mission reports as *'falsa et inepta'*, offensive to pious and learned alike. He claims no credit for this decree, but if Propaganda Fide believed his description of how the *Relations* were written, they could not have acted otherwise. (34)

Yet the *Relations* were popular and postulants multiplied after 1545 when Xavier's first letters from Asia were printed, and Jesuit schoolboys made to turn them into Latin as translation exercises. Many, such as St Aloysius Gonzaga, joined up as a result of reading them. Obviously, the enthusiasm engendered by heroic readings was not limited to Jesuit pupils, and even Newman said that reading Wellington's despatches made him 'burn to be a soldier'. The Jesuits, Christ's new salvation army, knew that fable has a place in military history, and at least one soldier, the 19th-century Prussian general von Moltke, agreed that it is a pious duty to publish 'certain traditional accounts, if they can be used for inspirational ends'. Such procedures have been called 'authentic fraudulence'. (35)

II

In his lobbying of the influential he had made friends with some cardinals, especially with Brancacio, regarded as a likely successor to the pope. Lobbying cardinals was strenuous, even unnerving, for some were hostile to the friars, whom they dismissed with bitter recriminations, denouncing them for upsetting the peace of the China mission and disturbing Rome — that is, making work for cardinals. Some flatly refused to receive friars. Barberini was the official cardinal-protector of the Franciscans, but one friar found he could never get an audience with him, even after spending whole days waiting in his antechamber, whereas groups of Jesuits glided in and out of his apartment without an appointment. In the end, even Franciscan patience could stand it no longer and the petitioner began to shout abuse at the cardinal's servants at the top of his voice, until his eminence rushed out in alarm to see what was wrong. The Franciscan, by then thoroughly worked up, turned on the aged prelate, accusing him of neglecting a member of the very order he was supposed to patronize. From that day on he had no more trouble in being admitted. (36)

Navarrete was more fortunate in his interviews. The priests of Bishop Pallu's Paris Mission Society, natural allies of the Dominicans, had a vast experience of Rome to share and showed him the memorandum of advice and warning ('List of those to see in Rome') compiled for friends from home engaged on business in the curia. It was, for instance, useful to learn that the Cardinal-Prefect of Propaganda, the anti-Jesuit Pietro Ottoboni (later Alexander VIII), was fascinated by oddities of scientific information, and to be warned that it was 'a good thing to keep up one's sleeve for him something or other that has not yet appeared in print, nothing pleases him more'.[18] Few people could satisfy him more than Navarrete, who now found a use for the notebooks he had been filling for years and shouldering for miles. Who else could tell the cardinal about the tree whose fateful fruit Adam and Eve shared in the Garden of Eden? (Of course, it grew in China, was beautiful, and its leaves provided a garment from neck to ankle, even for a tall person.) He could relate how the emperor of China had a precious ointment which, applied to the wrist of a concubine, revealed if she had been unfaithful, an ointment which Navarrete wished was in general use in Europe. From a priest in the Philippines he had heard of the famous 'woman-fish', the dugong, thought to be either a mermaid or one of Homer's sirens; its bones were used for making rosary beads. In Acapulco 30 years earlier, he

---

[18] Some popes and prelates 'were friendly to the new science' (W. E. K. Middleton, 'Science in Rome, 1675–1700', *British Journal of the History of Science*, VIII(1975), 138–54); on 'scientific' thought in the 17th century: Atkinson, *Horizons*, 50ff.

had seen the iron-pecker bird, which could eat its way through metal – now he regretted not having tested its powers by covering a nest with a sheet of iron, 'but I was alone, without ladder, help or iron plate, so couldn't'.[19] (37)

Ottoboni, presumably delighted with these 'pièces de science', was soon urging that Navarrete be appointed the first bishop of China. The honour was declined, and the cardinal insisted. Navarrete resisted, and the cardinal threatened. The friar explained that he no longer had the energy to bear the wrangling and disputes of the mission. At this Ottoboni 'raised his eyebrows', and Navarrete, emboldened, added that even if his eminence himself were to go out there he would not escape great difficulties – a prophecy later dramatically fulfilled in the person of the papal legate, the Cardinal-Patriarch Tournon, who died in confinement in Portuguese hands in Macao. Navarrete, skilfully following up his point, added that even if he were prepared to return to China, how was he to re-enter the country? Did they suppose in Rome that the Portuguese would allow a Spanish friar-bishop to pass through Macao? Cardinal Ottoboni conceded, but the conversation enabled Navarrete to suggest (as he had done earlier to Pallu) that Friar Gregorio Lo was the person best suited to be bishop of China. When finally the cardinal agreed, it was a triumph for Navarrete and his order. For the Jesuits it was the realization of one of their greatest fears, the appearance of a mendicant-bishop on the China scene. (38)

Navarrete's success with Ottoboni was overwhelming. It amply demonstrated the advantage of having shrewd French allies who knew their way about Rome, could point out the short cuts, and reveal a cardinal's weaknesses, especially if he were to become the next pope.

Nor did French resourcefulness stop there, for they had more advice to give: in Rome it was necessary not only to know whom to see but whom to avoid, or at least when to avoid them. For example, Cardinal Deccio Azzolini, a prominent and attractive member of the 'Flying Squad' (the elite corps of intellectual reformers in the College of Cardinals) was interested in everything from alchemy and engineering to zoology, and was close (some said too close) to Queen Christina.[20] In addition, he was 'a veritable father to the missions', yet for all that 'one should never dare call on him after dinner'. (39)

But Roman cardinals were easily managed after Chinese mandarins, and Navarrete's tact and ingenuity became known to his superiors as well as to the Paris Foreign Mission priests. In time, both turned to him for help with

---

[19] This, like much early popular knowledge, is half right: he is describing an insect or beetle with an exo-skeleton so hard that it can gnaw wood and soft metals such as lead and copper.
[20] Christina, interested in China, owned books about the mission, e.g. Gouveia's *Innocentia victrix*, which she left to the Vatican Library (AOPM, 'Ritos chinos', Trats. breves, 1702).

delicate tasks. When Propaganda refused the Dominican general access to its archives because 'there is much material there which, if published, would be of little honour to Religion, and of small edification to the world', it was to Friar Domingo that his general turned for help. Navarrete, by now no stranger to Roman archives, knew the best tactic for getting through the doors of Propaganda: 'be sure to make friends with the little secretary'. (40)

Cynical French help was useful, but the Spanish connection was not naive. One contemporary manuscript discusses 'whether it is permissible to dissimulate when in Rome', and warns Spaniards to be on guard, for the Romans, 'an artful people, reckon that patience and composure are the chief virtues in business dealings. Straight lines are shorter, but the Romans consider oblique approaches to be surer, so never relax your guard when dealing with the papal court'. (41)

Not only his own brethren but influential layfolk were impressed. The Countess of Oropesa wrote to his general praising him, and hoping his merits would be rewarded. The more practical Duchess of Osuna, sent him 'considerable alms'. The cardinal-regent discussed with him the Armenian Christians of Persia, and when two Dominican envoys arrived to report to Clement X, Navarrete read the letter from the Armenian Archbishop. There were other important and demanding tasks, such as helping a young friar who had fled the order and now, repentant, needed help; or else trying in vain to restore to reason a half-crazed but allegedly successful Portuguese alchemist. (42).

But whatever distractions presented themselves, it was never long before he returned to his favourite subject. He knew how to profit by every moment, which was easy in Rome where, said a contemporary English traveller, 'the conversation is generally upon News of Europe, together with many speculations upon what passeth. There is more News in Rome than anywhere else'. And Navarrete, in some palazzo awaiting an audience, always found time to discuss affairs with fellow petitioners, and to take down the inevitable sworn statements about Jesuit misbehaviour for possible use later. It was a strenuous but satisfying life. Now 56 years old, and officially 'elderly', he was awarded the honorary title of 'Master', given to distinguished religious in their later years. (43)

As 1673 came to an end, prospects seemed bright. Rome itself was in jubilant mood at the news that the Turks had been defeated at Khotin by the Polish leader John Sobieski. On 15 December the pope celebrated the victory with a high mass in St Peter's, where Navarrete, overcome by 'the beauty and greatness of it all, found my heart rejoiced within me'. In addition, news came that all was well in China, the persecution was over, and the missionaries back in their churches. Moreover, his propositions were being studied by Propaganda and the success of his work seemed assured enough for him to make plans to leave. In January 1674 he volunteered to return to the

China mission, and his offer was accepted by Propaganda, who ordered that first his papers were to be placed in their archives. (44)

But his own superiors had other plans. The news from China meant that there would be a need for more missionaries, and he could be useful in Spain, managing the affairs of the Philippine province, and recruiting. So he was sent to Madrid with orders to edit and publish Friar Riccio's history of the Dominicans in the East Asia. On 21 April he performed his last duty in Rome by attending the Provincial Council in the convent of the Minerva. The following day the two consultors of Propaganda who had studied his submissions signed their answers, the majority of which were in his favour. All seemed settled, and when he left Rome he went in high good humour. With his departure, the friars virtually withdrew from the front-line of battle and were replaced by French missionaries from the new congregations. (45)

In fact, the consultors' answers were never confirmed by Propaganda. Once again, the curia would not commit itself, and the Portuguese ambassador blocked any decision that might harm the *padroado* privileges. Consequently, the decisions given in his favour never came to have the force he had hoped for, although, as Bishop Pallu emphasized, they were important, for they showed the mind of the Holy Office and as such were worthy of study and obedience.

Navarrete's Roman *démarche* is sometimes written off as a failure, as though he had made no more impact on Rome than Fr Intorcetta. Of course, had that been true, there would be less hostility towards him. He certainly failed in his main purpose: the annulment of the 1656 decree. But he had successes in which he took pride: 'I was the chief and first cause why all came to agree that the "King of the Upper Region" is not our God. That alone sees all my labours well rewarded'. And his contribution to Propaganda must have helped turn the official tide against the *Relations*, the banning of which was an indirect result of the rites controversy. In more general terms, the China controversy only warmed up after the 1670s which coincided with his return to Europe to tell his story. Soon after that, studies multiplied, and by 1690 the quarrel was at its most violent. (46)

When he set off, Navarrete suspected nothing of this. Had he done so he would probably have remained in Rome to press his case further. Instead, confident that there was nothing more to be done, he found time for a final bout of sightseeing, though the eyes that had seen Peking found few great things to remark in the Eternal City: 'it is not necessary to set down what things I saw there, they may be supposed'. There was little noteworthy in Rome other than the indecency of the public statues; but at least they served to remind him of the modesty of the Chinese.

He had other complaints. Officious Roman customs-men had demanded duty on the 3 000 medals, and the relics given him by the pope and Cardinal Puertocarrero. Only threats to report them to the cardinal-regent saved him. But in Spain Altieri's name was no password and payment was ruthlessly exacted. He gave what he could towards the total, making up the rest with an indulgenced medal, while noting with disgust that it seemed they would have preferred the money, 'though I had nothing but medals, papers and two dirty old shirts. Good God! What people these are. And then they call the Chinese covetous!' (47)

8 Madrid entr'acte

When the kingdom is in danger, nothing should stop a faithful counsellor like Mao from crying out a warning . . . But where can we find a Mao for our own times?

— Navarrete

When I read certain passages of these great men I can hardly refrain from saying, 'St Socrates, pray for me'.

— Erasmus, *In Praise of Folly*

His optimism and good humour did not last. Two years earlier, returning home, Friar Domingo had been shocked by the widespread poverty. Now, in 1674, he found the picture no brighter. It was symbolized by a village near his birthplace, which was now reduced to a single household. 'I was amazed to see so much desert-country, so bare of food we could scarce get bread'. The province of Alicante made a depressing contrast to Chinese agricultural life with its neat husbandry and industrious people: 'there's not a foot of waste land in all the country, not a horn, bone or feather, but what they burn to make ashes to manure the ground'. (1)

By the time he reached Madrid on 24 June, he was in no mood for argument. He presented himself as the new procurator of the Philippine province at the court of Spain, but the incumbent, Friar Pedro Díaz del Cosío, refused to relinquish office. Without protest, Navarrete immediately left, retiring to St Paul's priory at Peñafiel, where, 40 years earlier, he had entered the order. He had reason to go there, since at his final audience with the pope he had been granted privileges and relics for his old mother-house. The grateful community, proud of their much-travelled brother, promptly elected him prior. For the next few months he lived there quietly, reminiscing, doubtless boasting, and certainly discussing Asian drugs and plants with the local physician, Dr Requena, who had once been given some ginseng by an English visitor and must have have been intrigued by Navarrete's eulogy of it as 'the medicine that raises the dead, for it strengthens the body, inspires new spirits, and helps those indulging in sensuality. I could say more on that score', but he doesn't. (2)

Retirement ended abruptly on 14 December. Rebuked from Rome, he left his old community a stipend for masses for his soul, 'when they hear that I am dead', and returned to Madrid, taking over from his much-chastened predecessor, who had been forced to resign by the formidable Master-General Rocaberti.[1] The close of 1674 found Navarrete established in St Thomas's priory. Rocaberti changed his mind about the plan to have him edit Friar Vittorio Riccio's history, written in Manila in 1668. Instead he was to pass the manuscript to a Friar Lorca (who lost it) and to write a history of his own. (3)

He began by discussing the rites controversy, until someone pointed out that China was still an unknown world to most Spaniards and without knowledge of the context his book would not be fully appreciated. He therefore suspended work on what was to be his second volume, and turned to write his *Tratados historicos, politicos, ethicos y religiosos de la monarchia de la China* as a background to his main story. The book would also be an opportunity to celebrate Spanish religious work in Asia, too long neglected at home. Such indifference had 'for years pierced my heart like a nail', declared Friar Juan Francisco de San Antonio, in words which others echoed. (4)

Though he insisted that his book was merely a brief description, the *Tratados* is a lover's account of China, 'for there my thoughts always return'. It includes translations of maxims of Confucius and Mencius, and of the 'Precious Mirror of the Soul' (the *Ming-hsin pao-chien*),[2] an equivalent to Aquinas's *Catena aurea* ('golden rosary') of edifying passages from various writers. At the master-general's suggestion he added Fr Longobardi's long-suppressed memorandum (itself a time-bomb). This was followed by an account of his own travels. Finally, he appended an anthology of papal decrees relating to China, which gives a useful survey of the official moves in the controversy up to 1675. These writings, instrumental in opening the second phase of the rites controversy, may also be seen as one of the many draft obituaries of the old Jesuit Society.

The *Tratados*, though not primarily concerned with that controversy, contains enough on the subject to startle the average reader, for the troubles of the mission were obviously uppermost in his mind while he was writing.

---

[1] Rocaberti had a sharp pen, no-nonsense manner, and great ambitions for his order, which he nearly bankrupted in achieving the canonization of the Dominican nun, St Rose of Lima. Transferred to the archbishopric of Valencia, he left behind debts of 25 000 escudos.

[2] 'The first translation into a European language ever made of a Chinese book, [Friar] Cobo's [*Ming-hsin pao-chien*] commands respect' (Van der Loon, 19, referring to an earlier version).

The missionaries had now been allowed back into China and everywhere there was excitement and false rumour. From Rome, Fr António Vieira reported that the missionaries were being returned to their old churches at imperial expense, and added wrongly, that in Japan a pardon had been declared for Christian converts. All this made it seem imperative that recruits be prepared for the beliefs, customs and problems of China.[3]

But he had yet one more reason for publishing the *Tratados*. He agreed with the Chinese sages that 'History is the Mirror for Everyman'. He quoted a 7th-century emperor, T'ai Tsung, 'By using a mirror of brass you may adjust your cap, but by using the mirror of antiquity you may foresee the fate of empires'. Logically, the history of moral and civilized peoples was the most efficacious. His French contemporary Fénelon took ancient Greece as a model and as a vehicle for exhortation and veiled criticism, and now in much the same way, Navarrete took China since 'the Chinese are the Athenians of Asia, and as Cicero said, "where there are Athenians there is civility, and humaneness"'. (5)

The task seemed urgent when he regarded the state of Spain. Thirty years earlier, setting out, he had been disappointed by the failure of Philip IV, the dandy of disaster, to fulfil the hopes that accompanied him to the throne. But that was long ago when, though there was cause for alarm, there was no need for despair. Now the times had changed. The Spain he left in 1646 had been limping; the Spain of 1676 seemed a crippled giant. The deterioration during those 30 years, less obvious to those surviving in that slowly mouldering world, had been a painful revelation for him, whose eyes were sharpened both by absence and the utopia he had experienced in China. From an alleged paradise of paternal government he had returned to royal anarchy. The impact of this may be seen in the *Tratados* which, written immediately on his return home, has a different tone from the the *Controversias*, where the problems discussed are theological, and pastoral. The *Tratados* must be read as a tract for the times. His generation suffered from the *preocupación de España*, and he shared the same fears for the nation's welfare as did Francisco de Quevedo, the Jesuit Baltasar Gracián, and Saavedra Fajardo. Less profound than they, his lamentations and prescriptions are just as passionate and as anguished. (6)

The 1680s showed signs of national recovery, and led to the 18th-century revival. Monetary stability, for instance, was achieved in 1686. Fresh attitudes can be dated from 1682, when it was decreed that ownership of a

---

[3] Navarrete, as procurator, had to find recruits for the Philippine mission, then greatly depleted, with only 64 Dominicans there. By 1677 the king had authorized 60 more Dominicans, a considerable coup for Procurator Navarrete, since they would be financed from royal funds.

factory did not deprive a nobleman of gentle status, 'provided he does not work therein with his own hands'.[4] Three years later the Minister Oropesa attempted reforms after the manner of Colbert by trying to bring in foreign artisans and Manuel de Lira revived an earlier suggestion, asking the king to open the American colonies to Jews and Protestants. Spain was beginning to intone her *mea culpa*.

The latter half of the century saw the birth of Spanish journalism. During this period Castilian editions of Amsterdam newspapers were helping to break down the *tibetización* of Spain. Significantly, a small group of scientists began reading relevant European publications. This was a tacit derogation of Philip II's decree (1558) prescribing the death penalty for unauthorized publishing. In 1687 Crisóstomo Martínez, a Valencian surgeon, made a breach in the wall surrounding Spain when with a royal subsidy he went to study in Paris. This was the first official reversal of Philip II's decree (1559) forbidding study abroad.[5] In 1682 Juan Cruzado was sent on a European tour to buy mathematical books and instruments for the Seville Board of Trade. If we can believe Núñez de Castro's *Sólo Madrid es corte* (1669), the modern courtier had to have a knowledge of history, and be able to hold his own in 'cosmography, geography and hydrography'. This, not mere elegance, distinguished the gentleman from the plebian, for ignorance condemned a man 'to much silence, or many gaffes'. (7)

The central figure in all this was the royal bastard, Don John of Austria, elder half-brother of the King, Charles II. Don John took an active interest in science and technology, and financed the innovators (*novatores*). Keenly interested in chemistry experiments and anatomical dissection, he had his own instruments made for these purposes. He studied Tycho Brahe and, more daringly, Copernicus and was interested in military science and environmental problems (he planned street lighting for Madrid). His hobbies embraced music and carving, and his mechanical inventions included a Cupid who fired his arrow to point out the time on a clock. His experiments made a break with the old abstract theorizing. Out of the meetings of like minded amateurs were to emerge the academies and scientific societies of 18th-century Spain. Friar Domingo hovered on the fringes of this movement, so coming into contact with Don John, to whom he dedicated his *Tratados*. The prince's standing with the group may be surmised from

---

[4] Spanish attitudes to work and status did not differ from the French or English: cf. the anecdote of the English gentleman who repaired the stage-coach when it broke down. Thereafter the other passengers, genteel rather than grateful, refused to speak to him.

[5] Spaniards living abroad were thenceforth 'foreigners and aliens to these kingdoms, to be deprived of their titles'. Similarly the Chinese disowned all who, abandoning the Middle Kingdom and their family tombs, went overseas.

other works dedicated to him: the *Architectura civil* of Juan Caramuel Lobkowitz, or the *Discurso físico* of the Milanese Juan Bautista Juanini.[6] (8)

Don John was involved in the establishment of the *Gazeta nueva* (1661), and used the press to circulate his manifestos, reaching illiterates through public broadsheet readings (*relaciones para leer*). He gathered about him a posse of secretaries (public relations men), chief of whom was Francisco Fabro Bremundán, his foreign language secretary, who in 1676 became Spain's first *gacetero*, or state journalist. (9)

Yet when allowances have been made for exaggeration, rhetoric and revisionism, there remains the irreducible fact that Navarrete's contemporaries saw themselves as living in an age of recession. Its cause, and uniqueness, were academic questions to those living through it. They wanted only to end it. The decline was not merely economic, it was also moral. There was a sense of spiritual loss, the new Chosen People had lost their way in the wilderness. The resultant bewilderment was harder to endure than mere poverty.

Those biased gossips, the Venetian ambassadors, gratified to see nothing now left of Spain's former greatness but her name, are guilty of inaccuracies and slander. Yet they were not alone. One English ambassador set the tone for subsequent despatches, 'I hold this to be one of the most confused and disordered states in Christendom'; and Louis XIV's envoy found it difficult to describe the situation on his arrival there in 1688. The secret suffering of the poor-but-proud *hidalgo* set high standards, even for Santa Teresa's ascetic Reformed Carmelites, one of whom, dying of stomach cancer, bore her pain so stoically that, with a strange reversal of values, they congratulated her on being like those gentry who would die rather than complain.

Mere ineptitude could not account for the nation's woes. Nature with all her malice joined the conspiracy: the 1670s and 1680s saw a series of catastrophes and disasters. In John Lynch's words 'Spain was visited by every conceivable adversity and by scourges of biblical proportions'. Failed harvests left few crops, and what survived were preyed upon by locusts. To complete the picture, 1680 brought the notorious comet, followed by an earthquake, bubonic plague and cholera. (10)

In 1618, the year of Friar Domingo's birth, Spain was drawn into the Thirty Years' War, and from then till 1714 the country remained almost permanently at war. During that century there occurred a chain of defeats which sapped Spanish might and spirit. The battle of the Downs (1639) saw the end of Spain's sea-power, and four years later came the loss of her military prestige in the Netherlands at the battle of Rocroi. When one more effort was made to regain Portugal, it failed at Montes-Claros (1665). The Spanish rout 'makes this nation look very blue' reported the English consul from

---

[6] Juanini, the prince's doctor, achieved the rare distinction of being translated into French (1685). His *Nueva idea physica* (1685), which opens with a eulogy of Don Juan, also quotes Navarrete's *Tratados*.

Cádiz. That last blow broke Philip IV's heart. He died a few weeks later, and was succeeded by the child who was to be Charles II, the last of the Spanish Hapsburgs. (11)

The Spanish rosary had snapped, for the shift in the balance of power was reflected even in religious affairs, and those years saw the founding of French religious corporations which, as has been said, eventually took the East out of the Iberian sphere of influence.

The state bureaucracy was disorganized. One ambassador noted there were officials receiving an annual salary of two thousand *escudos* for administering half that amount. An unfortunate Englishman in Madrid in 1681 to collect a debt, found that, though armed with 'the Royal Firm' in his favour, no one would pay him. After waiting long enough to translate Gracián's classic *El Criticón* into English, he abandoned his mission, 'better to have an interest in an English Farm than be a Creditor of the most Mighty and Potent Monarch of the Indies'. (12)

The king, a permanent invalid, suffered from depression, which was treated with exorcisms, hence his nickname, 'the Bewitched'. Near feeble-minded, he 'moved like a clockwork ghost'. This valetudinary monarch, the outcome of a series of family intermarriages, united in himself all the weaknesses of the Spanish Habsburgs. Louis XIV, with an eye on the Spanish throne, wondered if Charles would ever produce an heir. To answer his question, the French ambassador somehow got hold of a pair of the royal drawers, and had the embassy doctors examine them but, typically, they could not agree in their prognoses. (13)

The situation was diagnosed by economists, satirists, philosophers, and *politólogos* whose collective concern was expressed in tracts, theses, plays, poems, ranging from stoic cliché to roll-calls of past heroes. The treatise writers theorized while the biographers narrated lives of patriarchs (Job), emperors (Justinian), and kings (Ferdinand the Catholic). The satirist Quevedo preached lost virtues in fantasy fiction; the poet Góngora presented an innocent community guided by nature; Saavedra Fajardo and Caxa de Leruela interpreted emblems; Bishop Gaspar de Villarroel found lessons for kings and counsellors in the Bible, and the Jesuit Pedro Motezuma wrote a strange novel featuring model Aztec rulers.

Friar Domingo's contribution to this mirror-for-princes literature was deliberate. 'I was moved to publish some passages culled from Chinese history, which I was wont to read in order to learn about that empire, and to improve myself in the language. I now offer these useful documents on good government which can be found in the index. The lesson of this book is political and moral, with sayings and anecdotes of emperors and magistrates of Great China.' (14)

Others before him had praised the Chinese. As early as 1585, González de Mendoza had described China as one of the best governed states in the world, commended the emperor's paternal care of his people, and praised the people's skills. But Friar Domingo differs from his predecessors, for where they make isolated comments he maintains a consistent, all-embracing praise of the empire: 'I'll repeat it a thousand times, that nation surpasses all others in the world'. His model world citizen was a noble Sage inhabiting a paradise, 'In truth that whole country is a beautiful garden', ruled by a most benevolent despot and by philosophers as wise as any in Plato's dream.[7] Here, as Gregory Blue has pointed out, Navarrete and Fr Le Comte share the same view of the Chinese state, and both relate similar uplifting anecdotes.

This idealized picture became commonplace in the next century. In the words of L. A. Maverick, 'In the period 1669–1700 began the movement urging Europeans to study and imitate the Chinese government and institutions. The greatest name involved is that of Leibniz. But he had two contemporaries, John Webb and Domingo Navarrete whose *Tratados* is at once an early and the most significant Spanish contribution to European chinoiserie'. (15)

In his last will, Philip IV had expressed the vain hope that his successor might be inspired by reading history. Friar Domingo knew that 'Great men don't like to hear naked truths', and that those around the king kept him ignorant, preferring that he 'remain blind and not know the house is falling down until it be upon his very head'. Charles, however, heard some warnings and in 1686 the papal nuncio saw him listening 'with a melancholy air and slightly astonished expression', to a Carmelite friar's sermon. The king was urged to take the emperor Charles I as his model, and reminded of the fate awaiting oppressors of the poor, who are guilty of one of the 'Sins crying to Heaven for Vengeance'. Preachers, like writers, ran some risks, and two friars were banished for over-obvious allusions in sermons. A Trinitarian was punished for a homily in the Chapel Royal on Christ the King, crucified between thieves. Even the royal confessors suffered occupational hazards, sometimes dying of 'confessoritis' (*achaque de confesor*). In April 1677, for instance, the king's confessor, Friar Ramírez de Arellano, was suddenly and inexplicably dismissed, giving rise to gossip of the sort that at the French court was reserved for the discarding of a royal mistress. (16)

Navarrete hoped, naively, to escape such troubles, by disguising his criticism as innocent praise of benevolent emperors, who were likened to 'the holiest saints, popes or kings'. To those who thought it unnecessary to bring such obvious truths back home from China, he retorted, 'Then let's practise them as do the Chinese, whose government fulfils Aquinas's precepts, and then indeed it'll be unnecessary to bring them back!'

Friar Domingo quotes Mencius on the ideal relationship between a ruler and his subjects, 'If the king rules by punishments and penalties, he will be

---

[7] Some (Ricci, Valignano) found the laws of China so praiseworthy that 'if Plato were to return from Hades, he would admit that everything he had designed for his Republic was practised in China' (Dainville, 78–9).

obeyed out of fear, but such government is not lasting: if he rules virtuously and with love, then he will cause his vassals to obey him willingly and be ashamed to do wrong'.[8] On taxation he asserts that the monarch's own needs alone never justify heavy increases, 'the king is made for the kingdom, not the kingdom for the king'.

China, as construed by Navarrete, was an agrarian wonderland presided over by paternal emperors passionately interested in farming and the welfare of the peasantry.[9] There was, for example, the inspiring generosity of Shun-chih, who when the harvest was poor, suspended all taxes, while another ruler,[10] used to take his sons to see the peasantry working in the fields saying, 'note the pains these poor men take all the year to maintain you and me. I have always been careful to favour them, because without their labour and sweat, there would be no empire'.

The number of Navarrete's emperors who show this particular form of generosity is significant, but he singled out for special praise the imperial custom of guiding the plough at the start of the spring tilling: 'An emperor instituted this ceremony which still continues. He would plough the ground and sow corn; when it was ripe, he would reap and carry it in. He commanded his sons and the nobility to do the same. It were good to bring this ceremony to us here in Europe, that great noblemen might have compassion on their vassals'.[11]

Of all the beneficient activities attributed to the Chinese emperors this picturesque ceremony was the most romantic, and attracted comment from Diderot, Montesquieu and Voltaire. Raynal hoped it might replace 'those religious feasts invented by idleness to make the country a barren waste'. So enthusiastic was Raynal's account that he felt constrained to warn, 'it is not to be imagined that the court of Peking is actually engaged in the labours of rural life'.

Occasionally, however, even China fell under an emperor less conscientious than the model rulers. But providence arranged for zealous ministers to offset this, again making a contrast with Spain.[12] Navarrete had once been present in Madrid when a state counsellor was asked why he and his

---

[8] His translation of Mencius, the first in a European vernacular, was accompanied by a venture into literary criticism: Mencius is 'verbose, fluent and satirical' (NC 405, NT 231). On Mencius: Needham, *Science*, II:16 ff.

[9] These passages influenced François Quesnay (leader of the physiocrats), who quotes Navarrete when presenting China as an examplar of his economic theories in his *Despotisme de la Chine* (1767).

[10] He can be identified as Hung-wu, a ruler of the Ming dynasty, 1368–98.

[11] Huang Ti, the 'Yellow Emperor', one of the legendary rulers

[12] The censorate was intended to draw a ruler's attention to provincial misgovernment; its functionaries had no immunity, and often suffered ruin or death. An old custom allowed a commoner to 'knock at the palace gate' to point out dangers to the state. It was revived by Yang Kuang-hsien (1661) to denounce Schall. To discourage the frivolous a complainant had to suffer thirty lashes in advance of his petition.

colleagues did not protest against misrule. The answer was, 'First put a coach-and-four at the gates, for the result will be immediate banishment!' Matters, of course, were different in China, where an emperor, rebuked by Mao, a minister, seized a sword to kill him. Whereupon Mao calmly removed his mandarin's cap, awaiting the blow. The emperor, ashamed, pardoned his boldness. Pondering this example, Navarrete wondered, 'Where can we find a Mao for our times?' But Mao was not unique. Mencius reproved his emperor for keeping 'fat cattle and fowls in the kitchen, and full-fed lusty horses in the stables, when the people are starving'. Another minister, when taken by Prince Yuan Ch'i to visit his newly-built 'Mount of Pastimes and Diversions', exclaimed that it should be called after the sweat and blood which had paid for it: 'In Europe, too, many a building might be razed for the same reasons'.

After hints to royalty Navarrete comments on the behaviour of those nobles who 'think themselves fine Catholics', yet are sinning against the Natural Law by owning large idle estates, which are forbidden the poor, who are prohibited from fishing, hunting, or woodcutting. Passing to criticism of the clergy, Navarrete condemns superfluous churches, 'There are two churches: one made of living stones, I mean the poor, and another, made of dead stones, that is, mere buildings. To neglect the first in order to build the second is plainly a sin.' (17)

In China, others, besides ministers, took it on themselves to educate the ruler. Emperor Kuang, returning from hunting, was refused admission to his palace by a sentry, who was later rewarded for reminding him that his 'ancestors had not spent their time in hunting, but on the affairs of state. Yet here the very preachers will not dare to say so much'. This clear criticism of Charles II's fondness for hunting, is too harsh, for the wretched king had few pleasures.

Comparisons between parallel counsellors led to parallel lives: those of Charles II and his half-brother, Don John. The king had succeeded to the throne at the age of four under the guidance of the queen-mother, Mariana, acting as regent. Friar Domingo would have preferred to see Don John ruling instead of the simple-minded boy. There would then have been no need for a queen-regent acting, under Jesuit guidance, on behalf of the infant king.

Such sentiments were dangerous, even when hidden behind three confusing Confucian parables: one wise emperor (unlike Philip IV) left his throne to an older prince, rather than to his own infant son; an empress (unlike Mariana) lamented that an empire fallen into a child's hands is in peril; and a young prince (unlike Charles II) in his humility, yielded his inheritance to a better brother. Navarrete, to cover himself, adds a sly but unconvincing rider: 'This cannot be done everywhere, and in our own day we have seen great monarchies left to infants: Spain to our own Charles the Second whom God preserve; and China to the present Emperor K'ang-hsi, who succeeded at five years of age, and took over the government at thirteen, and in my time ruled to the satisfaction of all'.

After rulers, regents and women, the *Tratados* turns to royal favourites. Much of this section would be stimulating to contemporary readers, for Charles too had fallen under the domination of Fernando de Valenzuela, a typical prince-pleaser who ingratiated himself with the queen-regent's confessor and political adviser, the Austrian Jesuit Eberhard Nidhard.

In the usual guise of an example from the Chinese, Navarrete launched an oblique attack upon this pair, Valenzuela and Nidhard. The emperor T'ai T'sung was warned by a censor that 'a ruler who listens to all men is safe from deception, or flattery. But he that gives ear to only one man cannot govern well, because favourites tell the prince only what he wants to hear, concealing the subjects' grievances, even though they be starving'. The words may refer to a long-dead Chinese emperor, but they also applied to Charles. Another observation, 'bad aristocrats govern better than do the ambitious poor', was aimed straight at the backstair-climbing Valenzuela. (18)

Navarrete's attitude to Nidhard was linked to the old Jesuit-Dominican animosity. He remembered how the Canton 'Fathers had boasted of Nidhard's power over the Spanish government, and how they now exert influence over all the Catholic monarchs', for this was the era of the great Jesuit courtiers. Nidhard, as the queen-regent's confessor, clearly had immense influence. 'A Spanish ruler without a Jesuit at his elbow is beef without mustard', said one contemptuous Englishman, who should have held his peace, for his own James II had two of them in his Whitehall palace. Elsewhere, too, there were Jesuit confessors, in France Frs La Chaise and Le Tellier; in Portugal, Fr Manuel Fernandes; in Bohemia, Fr Frederick von Wolff; and in far-away Peking, Fr Schall had sometime dreamt of a such a post, but had to settle for that of astronomer royal.[13] (19)

Eberhard Nidhard arrived in Spain in 1649 with Mariana when she went to marry Philip IV. After the king's death (1665) she, as queen-regent, began to rely openly on Nidhard. In 1666 she appointed him a state councillor. So began his years of power as her political and spiritual director. She had him naturalized, hoping to forestall criticism at a foreigner's rise to eminence. But in that she failed. The chauvinistic outcry following his appointment to the privy council was slight compared to the uproar a few months later, when he was appointed him Inquisitor-General. (20)

Navarrete did not hesitate to invoke xenophobia. He named no names, because there was no need, but he quoted the Chinese sages who constantly warned that 'Princes should not prefer foreigners to places of trust, as

---

[13] In all, Charles II had nine confessors. In nowaday terms the royal confessional was akin to the post of presidential psychoanalyst or astrologer. Some thought that these Jesuit-Dominican struggles over Nidhard's post were endangering the state itself (M. Danvila y

ministers or council members, because they are ignorant of the constitution, have no love of the country, and, moreover, because the commons will resent it'. Some Spanish Jesuits feared Navarrete might be right and that these appointments would bring grief to the Society. Memorialists begged the queen-regent to reconsider. Old friends and new enemies sent warnings to Nidhard. One Jesuit urged him to moderate his style, 'In times past, members of the mighty Gonzaga and Borgia families joined the Society to renounce their worldly riches, but he seemed to have joined for profit and advancement'. There were more official complaints and the universities of Alcalá and Salamanca were petitioned for their opinions. Did the law allow the office of inquisitor-general to be held by a foreigner born of heretics, and a Lutheran until the age of 14? And would the Jesuits use their new Inquisitor for their own ends, such as imposing their peculiar moral theology, penalizing any who differed?

Nidhard was unmoved by pleas and undisturbed by criticism: 'like cats, we Jesuits have nine lives', he reassured a nervous colleague. He was now entitled to be addressed as 'Your Excellency', and his insistence on this honour scandalized the papal nuncio. He could be insolent, and to a dignitary who demanded from him the customary obeisance, he replied that the roles were reversed: respect was due to him, for 'I daily have your God in my hands, and your queen at my knees'. All this might have been condoned had his reputation as a political adviser been high. Unfortunately it was not. Some, the Earl of Sandwich for one, dismissed him as 'of small skill in politics and sillogistical in argument'. Yet in fact he tried to right some of the wrongs he found about him: he tried to introduce the German tax system as being cheaper to administer and less of a burden to the people: 'But, to my grief, I could not accomplish it'. (21)

Spain was divided into 'Nidhardistas' and 'Donjuanistas', for the king's brother was the Jesuit favourite's chief enemy. When finally, in 1669, the queen-regent was obliged to dismiss her inquisitor, she sent him to Rome as her ambassador.[14] There, his former indocility still rankled and he found Clement IX cool and his own general harsh. But Clement X, elected in 1670, was better disposed, and the queen managed to have Nidhard made archbishop *in partibus infidelium* (where some thought he belonged). Two years later she got him into the purple. Not satisfied, he demanded to be made a member of the Roman inquisition on the grounds of his Spanish experience, but this was denied him. (22)

Collado, *Reinado de Carlos III* (Madrid, 1893–96), II: 540). 'Instrucciones' for Spanish royal confessors are in BNM Ms. 5758.

[14] As a sop to criticism, she ordered Nidhard not to attend the regency council, but he demanded admission in his role of Grand Inquisitor (A. Paz, *Voto de la verdad* (Saragossa, 1669), 12). NC 620 has dark hints about chocolate-covered gold bars smuggled to Rome, apparently with Nidhard, but Saint-Simon has the same story about other Fathers; it was a common anti-Jesuit canard.

To keep him busy in Rome (where he received a salary of 4 000 *livres* as 'ambassadeur capon'), Mariana instructed him to work for 'the defence of the great Mystery of the Immaculate Conception', dear both to Spain and the Society. A task close to his heart (he had already written on the subject), Nidhard managed to combine it with the theory of probabilism, and his attempts to convert Dominicans into probabilists amused Pierre Bayle. Rome politely considered his various proposals, but kept him at arm's length. Indeed, he was not a success there, though he impressed his brother-Jesuit António Vieira, who praised his modesty and was edified by his wearing his simple Jesuit gown over his newly-acquired purple. (23)

Mariana, deprived of his support, became a reformed woman. For a time she worked in collaboration with the Council of State until, apparently unable to manage without more personal advice, she found the cardinal's successor in Fernando Valenzuela, whose rise was rapid. In 1671 he was given the habit of the Order of Santiago; two years later he became master of diplomatic ceremonies, surveyor-general and chief equerry. Eventually he was ennobled as Marquis of Villasierra. Resentment towards the parvenu was intense, and he was accused of everything from simony to sexual impropriety.[15]

It was this last which Navarrete had in mind when relating another of his Chinese parables:

> A certain emperor, having succeeded as a child, had two counsellors to govern for him. For twenty years they went constantly into the inner palace, discoursing with the empress and her ladies, yet there was never the slightest suspicion of them as regards the women. Indeed, during that employment, one of them never lifted his eyes from the ground, or looked the ladies in the face. These were heathen Chinese, yet some look upon them as Barbarians! According to legend, Blessed Aloysius Gonzaga, who for two years was a page in the service of the empress María, never once looked her in the face. That, too, was great modesty but comparing all the circumstances, it cannot be compared with the modesty of the two Chinese counsellors.[16] (24)

Valenzuela's real crime was his humble origin, and when he was made a grandee, there was a virtual revolt of the aristocracy, who were said to have felt his ennoblement more keenly than the loss of a dozen provinces. But that same year, 1675, was also the year of which Spaniards had great expectations, for it saw the coming-of-age of Charles II on 6 November.

---

[15] 'Rumours began to circulate, chiefly from the pen of the archbishop of Toledo, that Valenzuela's relations with the queen were sexual; this was certainly untrue and, in Mariana's case, out of character' (Lynch, *Habsburgs*, II, 241).

[16] St Aloysius, patron of youth, so modest that 'he never looked at any woman, and would never stay alone with his mother in her chamber' so that she did not know his eye-colour (Butler's *Lives of the Saints*, though modern editions omit, and modern Jesuits disown, this once-popular portrait).

The year began badly, and ended worse. In Madrid, Friar Domingo witnessed the struggle for power, verging on civil war, as the queen-regent and her favourite fought to keep their hold over the young king and to prevent Don John from seizing control. Almost inevitably, Jesuits and Dominicans were on opposing sides. The former supported the queen-regent, because their man Nidhard had been virtually her prime minister. Dominicans supported Don John, some because he patronized their order, others because they saw him as the country's only hope. His anti-Jesuit feelings may largely have been due to his hatred for 'the poisonous basilisk', as he called Fr Nidhard. But other Jesuits had alienated him, too, and in 1668, safe under Nidhard's wing, they had imprudently criticized Don John in sermons which he neither forgot nor forgave.

When eventually the prince seized power, the Fathers were apprehensive. Nevertheless, in presenting their formal compliments to him, they assured him that they had longed for his coming to which he replied that the information surprised him: 'though we hope for our salvation through Jesus, we do not look to the Society of Jesus for it'. The Fathers learnt to fear his sharp tongue and when other preachers were pouring out extravagant eulogies of the prince, it was noticed that the Jesuits were ambiguous in theirs. Navarrete, inevitably in these circumstances, was a natural ally of the prince and his entourage of *novatores*. (25)

In 1675, on the royal coming of age, an attempt was made to overthrow the queen-regent and Valenzuela. The coup misfired but the unrest continued until January 1677, when Don John's army entered the capital to a warm welcome. The queen-regent was forced to retire to Toledo, and Valenzuela fled to the Escorial for sanctuary. On Saturday, 23 January, the prince took charge and there were excited hopes of reform. Navarrete's account of these 'miraculous' events is rapturous:

> The whole city was in confusion, then, just as affairs were at their worst, behold, in the east a planet stirred. It was a Saturday, the day dedicated to Mary, Star of the Sea. And there was made a great peace. [17] The heavens cleared, the clouds dissolved, the court was quieted, hearts were calmed. There's matter here for a great book, but my pen is too rough for such a subject and thus I leave this point to others more gifted. (26)

Not everyone was so content. Eager for revenge, the reformers confiscated Valenzuela's fortune and annulled his nobility. Then towards the end of the month they made Don Quixote's mistake and fell foul of the Church. Having bribed the apothecary's boy in the Escorial to reveal Valenzuela's hiding-place, they forced an entry into the monastery and, violating sanctuary,

---

[17] 'Saturday, our Lady's day', refers to the day when Don John entered Madrid. Civil war was feared, so that his peaceful entry delighted all. Navarrete's praise was written a few months later, when hopes of the prince's ability to save the country were still high.

arrested him. An immediate outcry from the clergy followed, and to appease them Valenzuela's death-sentence was commuted to exile in the Philippine Islands, Spain's most distant colony.[18] (27)

Violator of sanctuary or not, Don John remained a hero for some months, and even when the price of food rose the populace tolerated it, 'Let it rise yet again, but let Don John remain!' Stories of his efficiency and devotion to duty spread abroad. (28)

In the end, however, the prince failed and soon the tide turned. Some began to look back to Mariana's regency with nostalgia. The task had proved too heavy, and in 1678, the year following the coup, Fr. António Vieira reported, 'Poor Don John took on his shoulders what not even Hercules himself could bear in the present circumstances'. The following summer, 1679, after less than three years in the unequal struggle, the prince's health declined. and the enemies he had banished returned to court with confidence. His condition worsened and he made his will. On 16 September, he entered the last agony and was given the viaticum. He died next day, aged 50, a disappointment to all, including himself. Navarrete had lost his protector and patron. The Spanish Jesuits breathed more easily. (29)

Years earlier, hearing a rumour of the prince's death, Pepys had pronounced a premature obituary: 'there's a great man gone'. Now, hearing the sad news, Vieira confided to a correspondent that Don John had not died of bodily illness but of anguish of soul, for he could not bear what he saw and heard all around him: it was an affliction that Vieira could appreciate, for he too suffered from it. The statutory rumours of poisoning were not supported by the post-mortem and, given the state of contemporary medicine, were superfluous. (30)

The queen-regent returned to power and, said one bitter report, 'triumphed over his ashes by persecuting his friends'. The king quickly forgot the last lecture given him by the dying Don John, and spent most of the rest of his life hidden away in his palace, surrounded by women, dwarfs, and animals, indifferent to the state of his dominions or to Europe itself.

Navarrete had completed his book and left Spain before the prince's death. This explains the optimism in his writings. He still believed that under the young and energetic Don John there would be reforms perhaps in accordance with his Confucian prescriptions.

Since 1675 he had been procurator of the Dominicans' Asian province, as we have seen. It was a daunting task because at the same time he was under orders to continue his writing. This double burden proving too much, he was instructed in June 1675 to concentrate on writing. Hampered by lack of

---

[18] His exile was not severe. In Manila he befriended both Jesuits and friars, read mission history, acquired a name for generosity, left his house to the Dominicans, and endowed annual masses. Eventually allowed to go to Mexico, he died there in 1689 (Maggs's Catalogue 442 (1923), iii, 192; Castro, *Osario*, 335).

source material, he applied to Rome for copies from the Dominican archives, but was told that no one there had time to devil for him. In the same letter he was pressed to make haste: 'the work,' wrote the master-general, 'will be greatly to our credit'. Make haste he did. His first volume was ready for the printer within a matter of weeks. (31)

The Madrid priory was not an ideal work-place. Other friars lodging there complained of the superior's harshness and that, although the house had never been richer nor the guests poorer, the prior had just increased the rent. Nevertheless, he pressed on, and by that autumn of 1675 had worn out his secretary, who fell sick. By the end of the year Navarrete himself was ill. It was a frightening time to be unwell, for the plague, raging in the nearby provinces, was daily moving nearer Madrid. But his morale was high, for he received word that in 1674 his Chinese writings had been published.

He now finished the manuscript of the *Tratados*, the first draft being submitted to the censors of his order in June 1675. In six months he had edited over 300 000 words. Although much of the work had been written during his enforced stays in Canton and Madagascar, or in diary form *en route*, it was a remarkable feat of editing. (32)

The next six months were spent arranging approbations and licences. First, the Dominican censors passed the manuscript, extolling in ample prose the simplicity of Navarrete's own. In November 1675 the diocesan censor gave his approval, adding that in his opinion 'every phrase in the book is afire with zeal'. In January 1676 permission to print was granted by the last censor, whose approbation was a eulogy, fortified with 19 quotations ranging from Demosthenes to Denis the Carthusian. His enthusiastic remarks about Friar Domingo's style give grounds for suspecting that he had not read beyond the title-page. On the other hand, he was the only official reader to perceive the book's political purpose, 'this book for rulers, full of moral disquisitions for the information of kings and princes'. His conclusion was lyrical, 'now that we have seen what the author offers in this first book, the tedious slowness of the printer in giving us the second will be a torture and frustration to the mind'. (33)

This particular reviewer shows more enthusiasm than talent, for Navarrete wrote in an authentic 'missionary style'. Never totally incomprehensible, he can disconcert, halting in a dramatic account of his arrest to discuss Chinese 'kidney-bean paste, why there are even people who'll leave pullets for it'; or he suddenly launches into a Shandyesque digression on the properties of Chinese medicine. Many of these digressions, particularly in his translation of the *Precious Mirror of the Soul*, are misplaced footnotes. Often aware that he was meandering, he is sometimes rueful:'I've deviated too much, yet never upon frivolous matters, so I can be excused'. He can show a Spanish indifference to his readers' comfort. 'This should have been said earlier, but it doesn't matter, it's a diversion, and change of subject. Sometimes though wine is advertised, 'tis vinegar that's sold, and so everyone should look to what he buys. After all, no bookseller forces anyone to buy, so if any have deceived themselves in buying my book, the fault's theirs that bought, and not mine that wrote'. (34)

Impatience caused much of his disorder, leading him to drag the magnificat into matins, and giving an oddly stream-of-consciousness effect to his narrative. Large bridges remind him of large alligators, so they are described together. Presumably this rambling, garrulous prose was an escape from the corseted thought-patterns of his scholastic theology.

His writing has much of the strange charm of some English contemporaries, among whom he most resembles John Aubrey, many of whose characteristics, interests and curiosity he shared.[19] But in 17th-century Spain published diaries and autobiographies were rare.[20] One explanation is suggested by the reaction to the *Tratados*. The swiftness with which he was denounced to the Inquisition, and the way his remarks were twisted, show that in Spain frankness could be dangerous. Yet, riskily, the *Tratados* has some of the characteristics of a diary, and sometimes he even refers to his *diario*. There is internal evidence occasionally where the writing consists of journal entries, or a passage in the past concludes with a change of tense to express a hope for the future. And his interpolations ('As I was writing this, Brother Antonio[21] came in and . . .') lend weight to some of his remarks, suggesting they were taken down in evidence at the time and are not an old man's colourful recollections. (35)

Many of his notes are like Pepys's *Contraries* and *Extraordinaries*. Chinese bells, thimbles, roads, students, and rivers, are all compared with those of Europe. Out of his inquisitiveness come the notes on winds, temperatures, positions of islands, the depth of bays, constipation in sea-farers, native dress, mourning customs in Indonesia, homosexual goldsmiths in Macassar, and the need for different diets in hot and cold climates. Sometimes he seems unwittingly to be following James Howell's *Instructions for Forreine Travel* (1642): 'The traveller must always have a *Diary* about him, when he is in motion of Journeys, to set down what either his eares heare, or his eyes meet with and let him take it for a rule, that he offends less who writes many trifles, than he who omits one serious thing. For the Pen makes the deepest furrowes, and fertilizes and enriches the memory more than any thing else'.

The *Tratados* offers some praiseworthy if rudimentary ethnography, and for the prospective traveller there are useful hints in this haphazard Baedeker ('at Tenasarim there are always vessels to go over to Coromandel, Bengal and other parts; this is a convenient way for those without much baggage') with

---

[19] In Spanish his style is reminiscent of Las Casas and Oviedo; among his missionary contemporaries he is similar to Le Comte.

[20] English Low Church movements (Methodism, Quakerism) stressed individual feelings, stimulating conversion stories. Catholicism, on the other hand, dubious about unsupervised introspection, did not encourage 'funny inside feelings'.

[21] Macanese Jesuit and fellow-detainee in Canton.

advice on, for instance, where to buy your elephant: 'Burma elephants are cheaper than those of Ceylon, but not so noble'.

There is a similarity between his writing and that of the modern gossip-columnist, for it combines awareness of his readers with a lack of concern for those he is discussing. He offers his readers copies of documents and relevant material if they write to him, but it seems not to occur to him that he might embarrass some of those quoted: François Caron or Bishop Pallu, for instance, not to mention the Jesuits. These two traits suggest that he had no conception of writing for a wider public and that subconsciously he regarded himself as writing a form of newsletter for a minority group. In part this explains his highly personal style, as well as his apparent lack of scruple in relating anti-Jesuit gossip. His prefacing some items with a 'reliable source states' has a familiar ring, and more than once he strikes a penny-a-liner note ('the following will serve to fill up another chapter'). Some of his more amiable critics interpreted this modest style as a mark of humility, or as a deliberate avoidance of the fashionable 'gongoresque' style of the day. Navarrete has no such rhetoric, and, as a good Dominican, shuns 'too preened a way of writing'. His style is a journeyman's: flat, almost devoid of imagery, with only the most banal of metaphors ('the ship of state'). Aiming at simplicity, he is sometimes ambiguous and his letters earned him a rebuke from his master-general who was irritated by his way of referring to 'a certain person': 'If your Reverence won't tell me clearly and without pseudonyms what you require, I'll not be able to oblige, for I can't guess your meaning'. (36)

Navarrete could have defended himself against critics of his style by quoting a contemporary Dominican who warned his readers: 'If it's style and grand words you're after, you'll find them in the thousands of novels and plays at your hand, but if you stop to examine their quality you'll find they're like counterfeit coins compared to money, dross dolled up with fancy verbiage'. (37)

Or, he could have cited three eminent Jesuit contemporaries who emphasized how little time missionaries had for polishing their prose. Francisco Colín prefaced his *Labor evangélica* (1666): 'The style is unaffected and unstudied, as befits a work on ecclesiastical history which is not meant to entertain or gratify mere curiosity, but to offer spiritual teaching, consolation and edification to the religious reader. This is especially true of us who write in the remote Indies, where, since the harvest is vast and the labourers few, we must work fervently rather than write with dainty rhetoric'. Fr Le Comte claimed 'we ought to be allowed the privilege of writing ill, for after we have cut the line [e.g. crossed the equator] four or five times methinks our stile should not be canvas'd by the criticks, and, for aught I know, politeness in a missionary would be less edifying than negligence'. And Fr François de Rougemont thought a rough style was a guarantee of sincerity. Moreover, Friar Domingo had spent 24 years studying foreign languages, and seems to have been far more interested in acquiring an elegant style in Chinese that in Spanish. Among themselves, or in conversation with other Europeans, the Asian missionaries used Portuguese as a common language, and consequently many of them found they were forgetting their own language, as Friar Riccio explained in a letter to his brother, excusing his poor Italian.

Friar Domingo has so many critics that it is worth noting some of the modern specialists who speak well of him. Blair and Robertson, the historians of the Philippines, find 'the *Tratados* is a rambling, gossipy account with much entertaining information. It contains matter of considerable value not found elsewhere, and it is from relations of this sort, and on account of these characteristics, that the student gains additional and valuable sidelights on the history of any time or country. The narrative, although rambling and sketchy, is fresh and picturesque, and indicates a keen, shrewd observer, and a man intelligent, enthusiastic, outspoken and humane'. Denis Twitchett concurs: 'it is a treasure house of minor observations and details'. Otto van der Sprenkel is more precise: 'Even the "Rites Controversy", with its disastrous repercussions on the mission itself, was productive of "source books" of major importance, outstanding among which are Navarrete's *Tratados*'.

For Joseph Needham, Navarrete 'is one of the most interesting characters among the Europeans who worked in 17th-century China. One of the cardinal figures in the lamentable "Rites Controversy", sinologists are not inclined to smile upon him or his brethren. Nevertheless the paradox remains that on the personal side he was a distinctly attractive character and never dull for a moment. Though he disagreed with the Jesuit "geometers", he fell completely in love with the Chinese and with their civilization. His narrative preserves for us many fascinating details of life in China in the years 1658 to 1670. The good order in China amazed him and he contrasted it bitterly with the savagery of Europe, and Spain in particular. One reads his account and feels as if one had stumbled across old Domingo himself in some tavern or coffee-bar'.

And Lo-shu Fu, citing Navarrete's account of the suicide of the viceroy of Liang-kuang, adds 'contemporary Western sources can help Chinese historians to reconstruct Chinese history. The death of Lu Hsing-tsu is a good example. No Chinese official source gives any clue about Lu's suicide'. Few things would have pleased Navarrete more than knowing that he had made some contribution, however minute, to those Chinese historical studies that he admired so much. (38)

Navarrete must have decided early on to write an account of his travels, for he had discussed the matter years before in the Philippines with the Dominican Bishop Juan López, who warned him against recounting the more bizarre features of Asian life, which would not be believed by home-bound readers. (39)

Anxious to be believed, he distanced himself from the errors of earlier writers in criticism which incidentally reveals the range of his reading. Among others, he examines the work of Frs Colín, Nieremberg, Kircher, Trigault, Bartoli, and Friar González de Mendoza.[22] He clinches his remarks on the celebrated Martini's work by recalling how in Canton he overheard two Jesuits disputing which book was the more fantastic, Martini's or Marco Polo's. Recalling that 'tall yarns and long journeys go hand in hand', he distinguished what he had seen for himself from what he had got from others. He therefore hoped to be believed, and would have endorsed the words written a generation later by the English interloper, Alexander Hamilton: 'if any Things are mentioned that may seem dubious or fabulous, the best Way to cure your Doubts is to take a Trip to those Countries from whence they come and inform yourselves better than I have done; some amuse the World with florid Descriptions of Countries they never saw, yet, since their stock of Knowledge is all on Tick, the want of being Eye and Ear-witnesses very much depreciates their Accounts'. Sir Walter Raleigh had earlier defended the friars' narratives in much the same way: 'If any man object that they have certain incredible relations, I answer that many true things may to the ignorant seem incredible'. (40)

Domingo, as has been said, had something of that scientific curiosity then beginning to manifest itself even in Spain among the *novatores*. Yet, a child of his age, he may be found resorting to 'unicorn skin' as a cure, in obedience to time-honoured prescriptions. His most farfetched story, that the leaves of one Filipino tree turn into living creatures, was a favourite with many writers, and he was not the last to repeat it. The Italian Gemelli-Careri reported it later, 'the most wonderful thing of all, is that the Leaves of some Trees, when they come to a certain pitch of Ripeness become living Creatures, with Wings, Feet and Tail, and fly like any Bird, tho' they remain the same colour as the other Leaves.' Gemelli, wiser than Navarrete, backed his account with sketches and affidavits.[23] (41)

Fr Verbiest described the China mission in theatrical terms, speaking of his role in the play, and of how one day it could become a tragedy. The *Tratados* gives a glimpse of that drama from the wings, a glimpse which, if less edifying than that presented by more conventional mission-histories, is none the less valid for being entirely human. Homespun as it is, we are grateful for the omnivorous, chatterbox sweep throughout this extended newsletter. (42)

As autobiography the work is not a success, for Domingo presents a scant

---

[22] His reading also included Spanish classics: Guevara, Granada, Huarte de San Juan and Ribadeneyra.

[23] The story appears in Kircher and Argensola. *The Encyclopedia Britannica* (11th ed.) cites Navarrete's account of the tabon to show how apparently fantastic travellers' tales, disbelieved at the time, were later proved accurate. On leaves and unicorns: Atkinson, *Nouveaux horizons*, 50–51.

curriculum vitae, and apart from his intellectual liveliness and over-earnestness, it is not easy to form a rounded idea of him. One of his few personal remarks is that he did not believe in the nonsense of unlucky days: 'for me every day in life has been lucky, beyond what I've deserved'. Nor does the evidence of others help much, since his Jesuits inevitably make biased witnesses. Fr Lubelli's description of him in Canton as morose and moody was not only due to the Jesuits' need to discredit him, but also a likely consequence of four years' detention among companions who for much of the time were nagging him to abandon his stance on the rites. In later life he became, at least for some, a boring 'Old China Hand', and he reveals himself as something of a show-off. (43)

He was a good mixer, interesting to such diverse personalities as Sir Edward Winter and François Caron in India, Bishop Pallu in Madagascar, Governor Richard Cony in St. Helena, and Cardinal Ottoboni in Rome, all of whom found him amusing and agreeable. His lawyer's mind approached problems with a set of precedents and authorities, and in the Spanish manner, he tended to strain at gnats. Unlike the more imaginative non-Iberian Jesuits, he worked on a detailed canvas, and often failed to appreciate the broader strokes of others. Yet, though his background and training disposed him to narrowness, experience broadened his vision and deepened that concern for social justice which was characteristic of his masters, the Dominican humanitarians. He saw qualities in strangers that others missed, and was sufficiently a 'relativist' to protest that cultural differences must not be held against 'The Other'. He realized that 'barbarian' is a sliding term, adaptable to the user's needs.

> In Europe we often declare other peoples to be barbarous merely because they don't observe our ways and customs. The Chinese and Japanese are not barbarians, for they live ordered and orderly lives, and are governed by rational laws. Nor ought any nation to be called barbarous merely because it has some customs that are against reason, as we see with the Japanese, who regard it an honour to slash themselves with their swords, for if we assert that, then no nation will be exempt from a share of barbarity. Other European nations regard our bull-fights as barbarous, thinking it a barbarity for a gentleman to fight a mad bull. And how can duelling, so common between persons of quality, be exempted from barbarity? (44)

Theological differences apart, he was fair, even kindly, in his dealings with others. On his way home he left his Chinese servant in Goa, 'rather than see him suffer any more from the sea, for I lamented his woes and illnesses more than my own.' Not a natural ascetic, he was scrupulous in religious observance. Once, crossing the date line, when he 'lost' a day, he carefully but unnecessarily read the breviary prayers prescribed for that day. He was something of a handyman, able to make his own Chinese robe, hence perhaps his appreciation of Chinese round-eyed needles. He combined shrewdness in judging people with the gullibility that allowed him to be deceived by the hypocritical Armenian Makara, whom he defended against his French masters. Behind his severe countenance[24] lay a love of beauty, not for its own sake, but as a mark of God's goodness; similarly, animals, of which he was fond, reminded him of man's relationship to God and the sight of a deer, grateful for being fed, moves him to exclaim: 'O God! The very wild animals teach us gratitude'. (45)

---

[24] 'De aspecto grave', says the Vatican *Processus Consistorialis* 81.226/4.

II

By June 1676 the *Tratados* was printed. In July the master-general was demanding his copy, and urging Friar Domingo to hurry the second volume. The book was well received, not only by the *novatores*, but by the reading public at large (one of his defenders found it in 'all the most prestigious bookshops'). He received encouraging letters from people 'of all states — the great, the learned, the informed, the dispassionate'. But none of these compared with the gracious words of Don John, who in April 1677 (four months after his *coup d'état*) found time to grant him an audience and to tell him that the *Tratados* was the book he most valued in his library. This flattering exaggeration was backed by a letter in the same vein, of which Navarrete confessed, 'I guard it as a precious jewel'. (46)

In fact, it must be doubted that Don John even glanced at the book, for in that spring he came to power, deposed Valenzuela, and found the 'Herculean tasks' lined up for his attention. But Don John would have heard of it from his friend Juanini, who read and quoted it. Other readers included the Jesuits, who expressed their opinions with fervour, though in a different tenor. Far from rejoicing that their enemy had written a scroll, they hastily demanded the suppression of this 'hotch-potch of sugar and gall, honey and vinegar, of ambrosia and poison'. They went farther, declaring that the *Tratados* was 'one of the most dangerous books ever published in Christendom, were it not that the bad style and disordered arrangement make it wearisome to the reader'. (47)

Navarrete was now about to test the truth of an old proverb: 'one should fear the nib of a Jesuit's pen, more than the point of an Arab's sword'. His mischievous treatment of the delicate subject made the rites controversy available to all. As such it clearly required an equally popular antidote. To provide this, the Spanish Jesuits turned to Fr Juan Cortés Osorio, a satirist known for his attacks on Don John. Celebrated by his friends as 'the Juvenal of our day', he was dismissed as a 'Don Quijote moderno' by those who shared Navarrete's view. Father Juvenal's first attack, his *Memorial apologético*, came in the autumn of 1676. (48)

9　The *Controversias*

The reception by the clerical world of my book [on the Dead Sea scrolls] was for me an educational experience: I gained from it more understanding than I ever had before of the attitudes of the various religious bodies. One is surprised by the lofty tone, combined with complete lack of scruple, which the apologists sometimes adopt and the devices to which they resorted.

　　　　　　　　　　　　　　　　　　　　　　　　　　　　　－ Edmund Wilson (1969)

Navarrete did not wake up one morning in the fall of 1676 to find himself notorious. Fr Cortés's attacks were not as effective as that, even in the ecclesiastical cockpit of Madrid. Nor were these the first attacks, for earlier attempts had been made to discredit him by spreading allegations that he had deserted his post in China, or that he was not the official procurator of the Philippine Dominicans, as he claimed. To counter these, the royal confessor was ordered to read out publicly an official Roman denial of these and similar rumours. Then, shortly after the publication of the *Tratados*, came Cortés's *Memorial apologético*, the first edition of which was followed in 1677 by an enlarged version, the *Reparos historiales*. Both appeared anonymously, but Navarrete quickly discovered the author's identity. (1)

Fr Cortés had not been to the East, but he was in no way inhibited: 'we Jesuits in Europe know more about China than Navarrete, even though he's been there!' He relied on Jesuit letters, and the published works of Frs Herdtrich, Rougemont, Gabiani and García, and declared confidently that Confucius had foreseen Christ's incarnation and passion. In the main however he contented himself with an attempt to discredit Navarrete's honesty and commonsense. Most of his criticisms of the *Tratados* are lightweight: Navarrete had quoted sailors' language, worse than the oaths in Pedro Calderón's *Mayor of Zalamea* (1641), which had driven 'decent men from the

215

theatre in horror'.[1] He was accused of snobbery, of selling indulgenced medals to customs-men, of describing Indian dancing-girls, of corrupting youth with a lascivious account of the mermaid-fish [the dugong].[2] Slightly hysterical now, he complains of Navarrete's observations and experiments, accusing him of lingering salaciously over matters that are only mentioned to one's doctor, in a low voice – all this in a so-called travel book. In how many convents and novitiates would superiors, misled by its title, order the *Tratados* to be read aloud in community refectories, thereby harming their innocent charges? The book should not have appeared in the vernacular. In short, Cortés concluded that Navarrete's only prudent act had been to refuse the China bishopric offered him by Cardinal Ottoboni. (2)

Denouncing Navarrete's apparent reluctance to believe in miracles, he reminded him how in Macao in 1638 an Italian Jesuit (known to Navarrete) had cast out a devil which confessed to having stirred up the English Civil War, and that it had hoped to destroy Catholicism in China. This story was typical rather of the Spain of Charles II, with its royal exorcisms, than of the Jesuits in general. Cortés next accused him of spreading false dogma by detailing, but not refuting, 'the false sects of China', thus exciting religious doubts. Less dangerous, but equally offensive, was Navarrete's constant exaltation of the Chinese. In short, this scandalous book would depress the missionaries, discourage vocations, scandalize the laity, and encourage the enemies of the Church. (3)

Anxious to enlist allies where he might, Cortés also denounced the book on political grounds. Plainly subversive, it would reveal Spain's weaknesses to her enemies, and its comments on government ministers were those of a 'beetle-like censor, not a bee-like historian'. In his allegations of mistreatment of the Filipino natives, Friar Domingo showed the same 'misguided zeal as Las Casas, who had discredited the Spanish nation in the eyes of the World'.[3] (4)

Action was demanded: 'quite apart from religious questions, his comments on political affairs demand that this book be prohibited and its author given his due punishment.' Finally, Cortés called on the Conde de Villaumbrosa, president of the supreme council of Castile, a Jesuit sympathizer and foe of Don John, to intervene. (5)

These proposals, and the allusions to the Inquisition, were not lost on Friar Domingo. He had expected criticism, for he had noted earlier that defenders of the Indians soon found themselves in trouble, and critics of the Jesuits were never allowed to rest in peace: the Fathers must always have the

---

[1] Navarrete had quoted such bizarre oaths as 'By a ship-load of consecrated hosts', and, like Vieira, had praised the Calvinists and Puritans in comparison with Iberian Catholics.

[2] Surprisingly, his denunciations of such 'lurid' stories were repeated by a more sensible Jesuit, Murillo Velarde: *Geographia* (Madrid, 1752).

[3] A reference to the Dominican Las Casas, whose denunciations started the 'Black Legend' of Spanish genocide in America: Cummins, 'Las Casas'.

last word. His reply was forthright. He admitted complaining about ministers of the Crown, but only of bad ones; he had exposed evils for the very reason that a hydrographer charts the sandbanks on a pilot's map: not to lure him onto them, but to warn him off. Changing the imagery, he enquired was it not a duty to warn the farmer of foxes in the vicinity? As for the state of Spain: 'What nation does not already know it well enough?' Nor had he written anything more subversive than could be read in such contemporaries as the Jesuit Baltasar Gracián or the satirist Francisco de Quevedo. (6)

His book had all the normal censures and approbations, and moreover he had personally handed a copy to the inquisitor-general asking him to condemn anything offensive to faith or morals.[4] Had there been anything to merit the attention of the Holy Office, his own order would have denounced him, and would not send him off to foreign parts to escape trouble, something he had seen done in 'certain other' orders. (7)

He remained firm over his defence of the Amerindians, whom he compared with the suffering Jews in the period of their captivity, and the Holy Innocents, 'whose only crime was to have been born'. This last, taken from Las Casas, leads him on, 'My attitude is in line with our kings' compassion. They, seeing their Indian subjects as their children, have daily repeated orders for their welfare. Yet all these pious and merciful royal orders have had little effect. So those wretches though several times redeemed still remain in slavery'. (8)

The Jesuits began to suspect that their defence counsel was not up to his charge, and were dismayed to hear that Navarrete was working on a second volume. There was even talk of a third. On 3 September 1676, as Cortés Osorio's damp squib was being fired off, they therefore submitted the first of a series of denunciations to the Inquisition. (9)

The opening move was made by Fr Francisco Miño, the provincial of Toledo, who delated the *Tratados* on 23 counts: 'the whole book is stuffed with calumnies against the Society so that to the diligent reader it will seem that the author's sole object is to discredit the Jesuits, for he loses no opportunity to do so, even if he has to drag in an excuse to do so. Where other orders are concerned he is silent about the bad; where we are concerned he is silent about the good'. Such accusations, complained Miño, ought not to be spread abroad. If the author sees any necessity for complaint he should submit a memorial to the proper authorities instead of making the ignorant public a judge of what it does not understand. (10)

Responding to this appeal the Inquisition called in the *Tratados*, submitting it to consultors for a preliminary report. The news reached Navarrete who, for the first time, wavered. Once before, arguing with a

---

[4] It was not unusual to pre-empt denunciation by taking one's manuscript personally to the Inquisitors (A. Bell, *Luis de León* (Oxford, 1925), 178).

'heretic', he had praised the Inquisition's discretion, piety and compassion. Now it suddenly appeared in a different light and he hurriedly wrote to the master-general, asking whether it might be wiser to desist from continuing the *Controversias*. (11)

In Rome they had a proper opinion of the Spanish Inquisition; 'whose severity', the secretary of Propaganda had once explained to Innocent XI, 'is such that the Holy See never need take action in that country'. The confident Dominican general replied pressing Friar Domingo to continue his work, adding the pious hope that this time the Jesuits might stick their necks out too far. The letter was reassuring, and then Christmas 1676 saw the fall of Valenzuela and the rise to power of Don John, in whom he had a protector and the Jesuits an enemy. (12)

Subsequent events proved that he had no cause for concern. Within a few months he was to see Cortés rebuked for his tone, first by his general, Oliva, and later by the Holy Office itself, for the Inquisitorial consultors took exception to Fr Juvenal's bitterness, his 'foul-mouthed taunts' and habit of giving jeering nicknames to Friar Domingo. The Inquisitors finally recommended the condemnation of his earlier *Memorial apologético*. (13)

All that, however, was still to come. Meanwhile the consultors debated throughout the winter of 1676. The following spring they handed over their findings. One consultor was critical of the *Tratados* fearing it might be harmful to the peace of the Church, and therefore should be banned. Others felt that certain statements about individuals might be prejudicial to the Society and recommended that some anecdotes be omitted from future editions. Allegations about the Jesuits' rich way of life in China might well be amended, and it was suggested that Friar Domingo be more circumspect in writing his second volume.

These rebukes were implied rather than expressed, and the verdict lenient – not to say partial – for with the one exception the consultors saw no reason why the book should not continue to circulate, especially if amended as recommended. They rejected complaints about the Palafox scandal and, as for China, Navarrete had written with all due reverence of Jesuits in general, criticizing only those dabbling in politics who, mainly French and Portuguese, were anxious to keep Spanish missionaries out of the Chinese empire. It was noted – they did not question his veracity – that he scarcely ever made an allegation that was not backed by a quotation from one of the Jesuits themselves. As for the differences over evangelical methods, these needed to be settled, so that the converts might know the pure truth, retaining nothing of their former superstitious errors. In conclusion the consultors sounded a warning: they had noted that some of the Fathers' accusations were irrelevant and hoped that those Inquisitors finally appointed to deal with the matter would use all proper care in doing so. (14)

By March 1677, in the heady spring of Don John's coup, Navarrete had handed over the manuscript of his second volume to the printers, having negotiated the usual battery of censors. It was a remarkable achievement, given the circumstances, because, even unfinished, the *Controversias* runs to 668 folio pages and nearly 700 000 words. The *Tratados* had frequently touched upon the friars' differences with the Fathers; this second volume dealt with almost nothing else. It, too, was edited from notes made during the four years spent cooped up in Canton. Those circumstances did not make for an impartial tone. Moreover he was stung by Cortés's attacks. And, as he was preparing the book, news arrived which kept his resentment warm. First, he heard of the arrest in Manila of Bishop François Pallu, his old ally from Madagascar. At the same time disturbing letters reached him from friar colleagues still in China.

It was during the summer of 1676 that he became involved in the Pallu affair, which called for someone with a knowledge of the Philippines, and the ability to present a case in Madrid. What had happened was that Pallu, after leaving Madagascar in 1671, reached the Philippines in 1674 when his ship was driven ashore. The Spanish authorities there regarded him, a French bishop, as a possible spy and probable Jansenist, and an outlandish rumour that with Dominican help he planned a native rising was believed.

He was arrested on 27 October, his papers were seized and handed to a Flemish Jesuit for translation. The Fleming did more than translate, he talked. The bishop, unfortunately for himself, was carrying incriminating documents, including a letter from the celebrated Dominican theologian Juan de la Paz, criticizing the governor of the Philippines. There were also some letters which upset the local Jesuits, who forwarded a catalogue of them to Rome. Pallu loved secrets and they found on him a cypher key in which the Society of Jesus was defined as 'Berenice'.[5] His known antipathy to the Jesuits, and their hostility to him (as one of the new papal vicars-apostolic who were taking over the missions), led many to suspect that the Fathers were behind the arrest. Certainly the bishop himself thought so, and for Navarrete, of course, it was the old story, similar to that of Palafox in Mexico, though in minor key. (15)

The governor reported the arrest to Madrid. The news simultaneously reached Rome, where it caused a flurry of activity. In July 1676 the Dominican master-general and Propaganda Fide ordered Navarrete to act on Pallu's behalf, but because of a diplomatic break between Spain and France, Madrid had no French ambassador, and the whole burden of negotiating the affair fell on him. Pallu had befriended him in Madagascar, and his French colleagues had helped in Rome: now both favours could be returned. He bustled about Madrid, seeking audiences, lobbying support, delivering

---

[5] She was Herod's mistress. Others, too, used cyphers: the Jesuits, particularly when sending mail on Dutch ships. Fr Anthony Thomas sent the Duchess of Aveiro a key in which he was 'Paulus Brabant'; the royal confessor: 'Gabriel Fernán' and Christians were 'merchants' (Maggs's *Catalogue* 455 [1924], 79).

messages from Paris and Rome. He conferred with the royal confessor and the nuncio, made reports to the president of the India Office, Count Medellín, and pointed out from personal experience the dangers of the Manila coast, and how easily a ship might be driven to seek shelter in its harbour without any ulterior motive. (16)

The news, and indignation, spread. When on his bishop's behalf Louis XIV wrote to the pope and Jesuit general, the Spaniards suddenly realized how much trouble they had stirred up. At once everything was done to placate the prelate. He was returned to Europe, arrived in Cadiz in November 1676, and reached Madrid on 18 January, a week before Don John's triumphal entry. He was greeted with apologies and showered with presents. Friar Domingo waited on him, together with the Nuncio and Count Medellín. There were letters from Rome, two hundred *pistoles* from Paris and three hundred *escudos* from Propaganda.

The embarrassing affair was quickly smoothed over. Within a short time Pallu informed his Paris headquarters that the incident was closed. Indeed so diligent were the Spaniards in pacifying him that the pope, who had issued a brief rebuking the Manila officials, was also obliged to issue another thanking the king for his kindness. Pallu himself bore no resentment, and tried to please the Spaniards: when they insisted on taking him to see the Escorial he felt obliged to go 'more to content my hosts, than from any desire on my part'. (17)

He remained in Madrid for three months, giving Navarrete an opportunity to renew an old friendship and to hear more gossip. (The bishop, on his unexpected arrival in Manila, had been able to tell the local Dominicans of his meeting with Navarrete in Madagascar, giving them their first news of him since his departure from China.) On 31 January 1677 he convened a series of conferences in his lodging, the Calced Trinitarian friars' convent, to discuss mission problems. (18)

The Pallu incident had repercussions for Friar Domingo. As the agent of Propaganda, of the Paris Foreign Missions Society, and the master-general, his services brought him into contact with influential people. In a delicate situation, a moment of political crisis, he had shown resourcefulness, and they were to recall his name a little later, when they were looking for a man of resolution and energy.

Nevertheless, dramatic though it was, the Pallu affair alone does not account for the tone of the *Controversias*. A more potent cause was the news from China, where the Jesuits, in defiance of papal decrees, were still maintaining their private apartheid and trying to keep friars out of the mission. Friar Varo, writing from the Philippines in 1671, had called for more volunteers for the China mission. His letter would have gone straight into the hands of Navarrete, one of whose duties as procurator was to find recruits. But, having asked for new men, Varo had to admit that he doubted if they would be allowed into China, for 'though the door is open to the

Jesuits, the Macanese keep it barred to everyone else'. In February 1673 Varo wrote direct to Domingo, and part of the letter was printed in the *Controversias* (presumably without permission and to Varo's surprise). Varo recounted how, after his release from detention in Canton, the Chinese ordered him to share a house with the Jesuit Gouveia, a situation which pleased neither of them: 'He grieved that I remained, and I, that I could not leave'. The Jesuit had refused to let him catechize the locals or administer the sacraments. Others found obstacles in their way. The outspoken Franciscan Buenaventura Ibáñez had arrived in Macao with four friar companions, assuming that under the new papal dispensation the Portuguese would allow them passage through the city into mainland China. But not so: 'they turned the archives upside down until finally they came up with an out-dated decree forbidding the entry into China of all religious, unless by way of Lisbon, so that having waited here for a year, we have now been told to return to Manila, willy-nilly'. Two other letters from Ibáñez stressed that the Franciscans had received every kindness from the heathen. Their only trials came from the Portuguese and Jesuits. To Propaganda, Ibáñez made further accusations: some Jesuits would rather let their converts live without priests and die without sacraments than that missionaries of other orders should administer to them. (19)

The travellers' old problem of being believed was given a new twist by these despatches from the battlefield. Ibáñez feared his account would not be believed in the calmness of Roman headquarters: 'In Roma hoc erit incredibile omnibus'. But he was writing to the 13 case-hardened cardinals of Propaganda, who must have been difficult to surprise.[6] A little later he reported that the Jesuits were 'waging war' against the friars, and in October 1673 complained that recently the Fathers had reported the presence of friars to a mandarin. To the Franciscans' surprise, the official was obviously aware of what was afoot and unwilling to play the Jesuits' game: 'Your accusers have evil intentions, but I will not expel you'. (20)

Navarrete could not believe the Jesuits were motivated by genuine fears of confusing the converts, nor believe that for them the ecclesiastical civil-war was just and justifiable. Carried away, he lashed out wildly at times, finding other motives. They wanted to be alone in China, safe from witnesses, so as to maintain the 'fictitious conversions' claimed in their *Relations*. He rehearsed old accusations, including the Fathers' initial slowness to preach Christ's passion. Another complaint was about the Jesuits' trading activities. This must have been one of the first accusations he had heard against the Fathers, for years earlier his namesake, Baltasar Navarrete, Dominican prior of San Pablo in Valladolid, had denounced them for 'marrying holy

---

[6] Riccio reported the same in 1673: 'Will it be believed in Europe that Jesuits denounce other gospel ministers to heathen judges to get them arrested and thrown out of the empire?' (SinFran VII, (i) 68).

poverty with worldly riches, and destroying the beauty of the Church by trading'. (21)

Rather unkindly, Navarrete took a phrase from the Jesuit apologist Diego Morales who had described their Macao College as 'a house of learning, garden of holiness, and school of apostles'. Indeed, was the retort, this apostolic school was well stocked, since it contained no fewer than three Judases, whose names he supplied. But Morales's description of the College did not go far enough; he should have said it was 'a trading post, a supermarket and bargain centre'.[7] (22)

Some of these attacks are unfair as, for instance, his reference to the Jesuits who apostatized under torture in Japan.[8] Disingenuous too was his reference to Fr Sall (1612–82), the Irish Jesuit provincial, who had turned Protestant a few months earlier. This shows him keeping abreast of Jesuit scandal on all fronts.[9] He avoids mention of Dominican misdeeds, and in the *Controversias* selects his evidence as carefully as he does in his idealization of China in the *Tratados*. Thus there is no mention of the English Dominican Thomas Gage de Santa María, whose apostasy had far reaching effects since he helped to bring about the loss of Spanish Jamaica to Cromwell's forces. Nor does he say that in 1672, when he travelled across Valencia on his way to Rome, the province was living in terror of a friar-turned-bandit, who with his gang was ravaging the countryside. Had this been a fallen Jesuit he would have received adequate publicity, for elsewhere he had declared sententiously, 'Every historian has to relate those excesses that have taken place, no matter how grave they be, for history is the study of evil'. He fortified himself further with a quotation from Cicero: 'The first rule of History is that no one shall dare to speak falsehood, and the second that no one shall shirk the truth'. (23)

Friar Domingo's declared aim was to show religious superiors the need to examine carefully volunteers for the missions. Another preoccupation was to prepare those future evangelists for the special difficulties of the China mission. He was a military engineer in the army of the Church Militant, 'My aim is to undeceive Europe, to prepare Christ's Soldiers, to remove obstacles that would delay the gathering of the fruit of conversion. I play the part of those who level the roads for an army, so that its soldiers may travel more easily and fight more spiritedly'. He insisted that he was not judging the

---

[7] For the Jesuits as 'spiritual' traders under Christ the 'sovereign merchant of the gospel', see Brading, 172).

[8] 'Oh my God! Had they been friars, how they'd have been written up, and what slings and arrows would have been hurled at us in every line and page.' (NC 476).

[9] Sall's apostasy made a stir: Lord Longford thought him 'the considerablest convert from Rome'. By June 1680 Sall had preached in Irish to '100 Papists', though there were fears for his safety since the living consisted of 'mere Irish'. Unfortunately for him, his new brethren, having recruited him, seem to have neglected him (*Hist. Mss. Commission, NS. Ormonde, Kilkenny*, V: 227, 334–5).

issue, he was simply posing questions to those qualified to answer. He was governed by no party spirit, there could be neither victor nor vanquished in this quarrel in which both parties sought only the truth.

The *Controversias* carries all the statutory protestations. He is not opposed to the Jesuit order in general, indeed he expresses admiration, even affection for the Society, recalling how during the persecution he had written from Peking to their general, congratulating him on his men, and later had written again from Canton, claiming that between them there was union of hearts, if not of doctrine. He insists he is not attacking the Society, only individual members of it, 'only some of the China Fathers'. (24)

The sincerity of his disclaimer was borne out later, when, as archbishop of Santo Domingo, he could have dealt harshly with the Jesuits in his diocese had he looked for mere personal revenge, as they feared he would. Instead he earned their fervent praise. This is where Navarrete differs from the Jansenists and other anti-Jesuits who, not content to attack individuals, prided themselves on condemning the Society as a whole.

Navarrete makes no reference to Schall's alleged conduct, possibly because he found it too frightful to mention. Yet sometimes he felt something akin to guilt when he reflected on how much he had left still in the inkwell. Towards the end of the *Controversias* he made a threat which he might have carried out had things gone differently: 'I'll stop here, trimming my pen in case more be demanded of me. In five years I've taken in a lot, and I'll bring it up, rather than die of indigestion'. But it was unlikely to worry the Fathers. They were as determined as he, and in the end they won, for circumstances played into their hands, and as a result the *Controversias* was never published. The Jesuits had the last word.[10] (25)

---

[10] For the self-righteous protests of some anti-Jesuits, see Ronald Knox (*Enthusiasm*, (Oxford, 1950), 198) where the Jansenist Arnauld, 'upon the mention of the Jesuits, breaks out into the astonishing phrase, "Si j'eusse eu la moindre animosité contre cet ordre . . ." obviously in all sincerity, so strange are we, so delicately fashioned'.

10   The Battle of the Books and after

No other dispute over mission policy in the entire history of the spread of Christianity was so intense over so prolonged a period as that over the Chinese rites.

— Kenneth Scott Latourette

Worship God and practise justice – this is the sole religion of the Chinese literati . . . O Aquinas, Scotus, Francis, Dominic, Luther, Calvin, canons of Westminster, have you anything better?

— Voltaire

Their complaint to the Inquisition rejected, their apologia condemned, the Jesuits were obliged to bide their time. But they were pleased by two events which now took place. First, Friar Domingo was promoted to the American archbishopric of Santo Domingo and departed for his diocese in 1677.[1] The promotion was regretted by his friends, for it deprived them of an ally. For that same reason it was welcomed by the Jesuits, except by those stationed in Santo Domingo. Second, the Madrid Fathers were encouraged by the decline in Don John's popularity, and a few months later by news of his ill health.

In May 1679 they were spurred into fresh action by an informer's report that in spite of his departure, Navarrete's *Controversias* had gone to the printers. This gave the Fathers an excuse to approach the Inquisition once again. They declared that they had now heard of a second volume which continued the calumnies made against them in the first. (Here they were begging a question which the Inquisitors had not conceded: that there were calumnies in the *Tratados*.) In June their 'mole' supplied stolen sheets from the second volume, and these they submitted to the Inquisition,

---

[1] The promotion, suggesting Don John's patronage, was also interpreted as a sign of royal benevolence towards the China mission and its mendicant staff, to which Charles made occasional donations (Friar Alvaro Benavente, Lilly Library, Phillipps Ms. 8469, fol. 251v).

accompanied by a new delation consisting of thirty complaints. They pointed out that these came from the few pages they had seen, so it was obvious what the completed work would be like. The printing was almost finished, and swift action was necessary to prevent its appearance. They supplied the name and address of the printer, 'a Frenchman named Anisson'. (1)

The Holy Office at once set up an investigative committee consisting of Friar Joseph Méndez de San Juan, a Minim, Friar Juan de Heredia, a Carmelite, Friar Basilio de Zamora, a Capuchin, and Dr Juan Benítez Montero, Dean of Granada Cathedral. On 27 June they stopped the printing of the second volume, and recalled any copies in circulation. They next elected the Carmelite Heredia to draw up a preliminary report. This he submitted on 21 August. Heredia himself must have been unsympathetic to the Jesuits, for it is difficult to understand how else he could have written so leniently of the *Controversias*. For instance, Navarrete's 'dangerous and scandalous accusations', Heredia found explicable: they were 'not made against the whole Society, nor even against all the Jesuits in China, but only against a minority group there'. Nevertheless Friar Heredia wished to show himself properly attentive to the demands of the Holy Office, and he therefore listed 39 points from the *Controversias* which might be dangerous. It is obvious that this was a mere formality, a cockshy erected to be knocked down, for in the end he found nothing objectionable in the book. He concluded by admitting that Navarrete did show bitterness when answering the Jesuits' *Memorial apologético*, but even here an excuse was found: he was only replying in the vein in which he had been attacked. (2)

The Fathers were put out by this unhelpful report. They were especially sensitive to criticism in Spain, where they were still trying to live down the Fr Nidhard affair. And from Rome the news was worse: for the first time there were rumours of machinations to suppress the Society: 'not a few cardinals, if they could find a decent means of bringing it about, would gladly do so. One is the [Franciscan] Cardinal Laurea who glories in being our enemy'. There was other disturbing news from Rome. A papal brief had been issued against those Jesuits who continued opposing French bishops (such as Pallu) sent east by Propaganda, and that loyal Portuguese Fr Vieira thought its stipulations 'the most terrible and dreadful ever seen'.[2] (3)

Vieira prayed God to forgive whoever was to blame for the fact that on all sides the Society was now held in such little respect.[3] More depressing to him was the further news that even the Lisbon Junta of Foreign Missions had

---

[2] He cheered up on hearing that the Viceroy of Goa had threatened to hang any such bishops venturing there 'even if Propaganda declares them martyrs' (Vieira, *Cartas*, II: 354, 554).

[3] But others feared them. In 1671, John Beale estimated there were 100 000 Jesuits in 1 000 colleges with 'the best share of gold and silver in both the Indyes. They are sd. to double their numbers and wealth, every seaven yeares'. (Oldenburg, *Corr.*, ed. Hall (London, 1971), VIII: 139). In reality, there were only 17 655, in 35 'provinces' (1679), of whom 7 870 were priests.

agreed that Spanish Dominicans from the Philippines might enter mainland China through Portuguese Macao. This concession had been granted at the request of the Dominican archbishop of Evora.

Against this sensitive background, Navarrete's works took on a greater significance for the Jesuits than might otherwise have been justified. While the preliminary examination of their complaints against the *Controversias* was still in progress, the Fathers created a diversion in the form of a new delation of the *Tratados*. In this they adopted fresh tactics, putting heavier emphasis on the book's political content and its inherent dangers, 'because it contains irreverent propositions against popes, emperors, and kings . . . and against the ministers of his majesty and the Spanish and Portuguese nations'.

The Chinese, continued the Madrid Jesuits, were materialists who 'regard the foul pleasures of this mortal life as the greatest happiness' and yet ignorant European readers were told by Friar Domingo that China is 'the most excellent nation in all the world, in the justice of its government, the reasonableness of its laws, the discretion of its manners, the modesty of its armies, the upbringing of its youth, the maidenly shyness of its womenfolk, the diligence and disinterestedness of its mandarins. Is it not certain from this that in the weakness of their minds, readers will suffer dangerous upsets in their estimation of our holy Faith'.

This was a reasonable fear, though curious in a Jesuit, for they usually complained that the other orders underestimated the Chinese. The Spanish Jesuits, however, felt they had their backs to the wall, and had to resort to any tactic they could. Yet the tactic itself is revealing. It shows the conservatism of the Iberian Jesuits compared to their foreign brothers. No French Father would fight with such weapons. Tactics or not, the passage makes amusing reading, for during the next decades no one did more than the Jesuits to elevate China in European eyes, as Navarrete was now doing in the 1670s, apparently too early for comfort.

These new accusations were not limited to politics. The book was now seen as dangerous because it 'gave aids to atheism' by explaining Chinese religions and superstitions in the vernacular. Similarly, the missionaries' controversies had already been discussed in Rome by the competent judges, and no good could come of making them known to the uninstructed public. For as the Jesuits saw, Navarrete's crime was his bringing the quarrel before a wider public. As Fr Bernard-Maitre puts it: 'it was almost exclusively due to Navarrete that Europe came to learn of the Rites Controversy in East Asia'.

The Jesuits' report failed to impress the inquisitors, who replied on 10 November that they had already given their verdict about the first volume, and since in their opinion nothing fresh was raised by the new delation, no action was needed. They remarked, with evident satisfaction, that this denunciation was more restrained in tone than the earlier *Memorial apologético*.

Later that month a meeting of the appointed examiners considered the allegations against the second volume. Giving their decision on

29 November, they once more showed themselves favourable to Navarrete. They rejected the points raised by the delators, sometimes out of hand, sometimes giving reasons. To the complaint that he had accused the Jesuits of obstinacy in their opinions, the inquisitors replied that if the Fathers were, as they admitted, holding probabilist theories, it was difficult to see what calumny there could be in saying so. Navarrete, they agreed, had made terrible accusations against the Society's methods in China, but since this was the core of his book it seemed more reasonable to suppose that at least some individuals had committed such faults, than that he had invented a tissue of lies. The inquisitors absolved Navarrete from any blame for his remark that the Society had never been the same since the death of its founder, and that it was now too devoted to trade and merchandise. Again, the consultors took this to be reasonable in that it might apply to individual Jesuits. In any case, they pointed out, the remark was a quotation and writers frequently cited others in this way without being denounced for it, nor was the Holy Office accustomed to punish them for it. As for the accusations that some Fathers had apostatized and married in Japan, the inquisitors found that this might apply to individuals and was no reflection on the Society as a body (although, they added, carefully placing their dart, the allegation might usefully serve Jesuit superiors by showing them the need for a careful selection of volunteers). Some other complaints were rejected with a rebuke, two or three were dismissed as untrue, others were thrown back as being themselves calumnies against Friar Domingo. The consultors made it clear that the Jesuits had only themselves to blame if he had repeated some of the lighthearted leg-pulls made in Canton. The point was that, jokingly or not, the remarks had in fact been made.

Having dealt with the Jesuits' complaints they next turned to the observations of their own examining member, Friar Heredia. They dismissed the 39 points he had raised, adding that Navarrete's sharp style had been provoked. Their report ended with general remarks of small comfort to the Fathers, including the comment that Domingo's works might usefully serve for the true Christianizing of the East.

The Jesuits were not routed. Two years later, 1681, they were still urging the prohibition of the *Tratados* and the *Controversias*. Exactly what did happen is not quite clear. The *Tratados* was not condemned, though the projected second edition did not appear. The fate of the *Controversias* was more curious. The book was not printed beyond page 668, which had been reached when it was seized by the Inquisition. The few remaining, unprinted pages of Friar Domingo's manuscript are bound into the copy in the Biblioteca Nacional in Madrid. In the Bibliothèque Nationale in Paris there is a draft of the title-page and a manifesto by the publisher suggesting that the confiscated copies had remained in the hands of the Inquisition. The publisher seems to have considered the possibility of bringing out a Paris edition of some copies that apparently he had not surrendered. But in the end he presumably thought better of it. His draft suggests that no formal Inquisition order was ever issued against the work. Yet the allegation that the *Controversias* was 'suppressed by the Inquisition' is frequently repeated without evidence.[4]

It appears that Spanish lethargy overcame inquisitorial zeal, and that the book lay forgotten in the archives. The publisher's preface to the projected pirate edition shows that it was to have been produced as it stood, 'crippled, without title-page or frontispiece, without its due and proper prologues, approbations, licences . . . but you must not blame the author, nor me, for the fact that the book comes to you thus halt and lame'. The publisher explains that the death of Don John, to whom it was to be dedicated, together with the departure of Navarrete for Santo Domingo, had left the work at the mercy of his enemies. (4)

The incomplete, partially printed, *Controversias* survives in five libraries: in Rome, Madrid, Valladolid, London and New York. Undoubtedly there are others. A third volume, left in manuscript on Navarrete's departure for America, is extant. Its contents are unknown and there is a puzzle about its ownership. A fourth volume has been surmised but if any such exists it, like the third, is unknown and in private hands. (5)

The Spanish Jesuits finally saw that they could not enlist the Inquisition to fight their battle. They needed what lawyers call 'further and better particulars' concerning the background to the quarrel described by Friar Domingo. Convinced that his allegations must be false, they set the machinery of the Society in motion to defend their reputation. It was no novel task for them, and the necessary machinery was well prepared: 'I fear the Jesuits', wrote Montesquieu. 'If I offend a powerful person he will forget all about me, and I him; or I can go to another province or kingdom. But if I offend the Jesuits in Rome, I'll find them awaiting me in Paris; they're everywhere, surrounding me on all sides. Their habit of endlessly writing to each other feeds their hostility. A man who makes an enemy of the Jesuits is like one who makes an enemy of the Inquisition itself – he runs into their familiars everywhere'. (6)

Galileo, too, had been warned that 'to take on the Fathers would be never ending: they are so numerous that they can face up to the whole world. Even if they're in the wrong, they'll never admit defeat'. One Father admitted, 'if Galileo had only known how to keep the Jesuits' goodwill he would have been spared his misfortunes, and he could have written what he pleased about everything, even about the motion of the Earth'. (7)

---

[4] For example, *New Catholic Encyclopedia* (New York, 1967), X, 283. In fact, no Spanish Index was issued between 1632–1707: 'The preparation [of the 1747 Index] had been committed to two Jesuits, without supervision, who abused their position by gratifying the interests of the Society through including a large number of authors who had never been condemned' (Lea, *Inquisition*, III: 495–6).

Diderot, sending Sophie Volland the 'obituary notice' of the French Jesuits when they were banished from France, added with relief: 'This rids me of a great number of powerful enemies'. In 1686 Antoine Arnauld wrote to the Landgrave of Hessen-Rheinfels that 'the bishop of Namur, appointed judge [in an ecclesiastical dispute] by the papal nuncio, is reluctant to accept, so great is the fear the Jesuits stir up . . . their power is such that one cannot get justice against them in this world'. The Conde de Linhares, Viceroy of Portuguese India, informed the king in 1635 that his predecessors always courted the Fathers, partly to get them to send home favourable reports of their tour of office, such was their influence in Lisbon official circles. And where their betters were circumspect, lesser colonists worked on the prudent principle that it was wiser to mollify the Jesuits rather than the Viceroy, for, in the words of the 17th-century Goan jingle,

One by one Viceroys go,
But the Fathers? Never! No!
(*Vicerei va, vicerei vem*
Padre Paulista sempre tem.)[5] (8)

Navarrete, as a member of a powerful religious order, was in no danger from the Jesuits, but a private person, such as Pascal, believed he was taking a risk.[6] In modern terms some comparison can be seen in the dangers courted by an individual flouting a government agency in a dictatorship, or in the risks of retaliation run by a public critic of a multinational corporation. In this respect the modern Society bears no resemblance to the awe-inspiring organization it was before its suppression. (9)

---

[5] Boxer, *India*, 19. The jingle owes something to Ecclesiastes I: 4.
[6] Pascal cited Jesuit theories that 'A religious is permitted to kill a slanderer who threatens to publish scandalous charges about his order' (*PL*, VII).

II

The opening moves in the final campaign against the *Tratados* came when the Spanish Fathers despatched copies to their colleagues in China, urgently demanding a refutation. In February 1680 the book reached its destination via Manila. Reaction was sharp. Gabiani, the Jesuit superior, ordered the Peking Fathers to give their opinion. If necessary a team might be set up to scrutinize the work. Every mistake was to be ferreted out, documented, and then in a joint denunciation, exposed to scorn. 'He who strikes the Society' was to be crushed. It was, after all, no more than they would have done to one of their own.

Jesuits in the provinces were circularized for material towards this composite reply. With the usual admirable speed and efficiency, replies came back. On 21 March Fr Lubelli, although his own knowledge of Chinese was poor, replied to the Fr-Visitor that he would content himself with accusing Navarrete of knowing little of the language, since that was obviously the root of the trouble. Indeed, after seeing the book he had lost what little opinion he had previously had of his knowledge of Chinese. Fr Grelon was more outspoken: only a depraved conscience could tell such shameless lies, 'grave statements are made against us and if they were true . . . the entire Society should be exterminated . . . and if Friar Navarrete were our judge, as he is our accuser, I don't doubt it would be done in a very short time'. Fr Mesina declared that Navarrete must be mad, a conclusion somewhat weakened by his confessing that he had read the critics rather than the text. Like Lubelli, Fr Filipucci limited himself to quarrelling with Navarrete's Chinese, submitting seven pages of corrections. Distasteful as it was for him to have to dispute with Navarrete, it was necessary for the Society's good name. He had strong opinions about the friars who, he said, had only gone to China to censure the Jesuits and in all their half-century there had not managed to convert more than a hundred natives. Having denounced Navarrete, he added, 'For our own justification it's also high time we took measures against Friar Antonio de Santa María and his successors, to show how little Chinese they know'. (10)

From the replies drafted by the Peking community Fr Verbiest compiled his *Responsum Apologeticum*. A man of impressive gifts, Verbiest was a brilliant controversialist, and Navarrete's inferior powers of sarcasm were no match for his. Unfortunately Verbiest did not see the *Tratados* for himself, but only the selected passages sent up to Peking for comment. He was therefore at the mercy of those who chose what he should reply to, and the result is disappointing, for too often he was asked to answer trivial charges instead of major ones. His defence in the main does not concern itself with the rites, but with the reputation of the Society, so that where one would prefer a statement from Verbiest on such problems as religious syncretism, there is instead a rebuttal of some item of gossip. Verbiest makes some telling points, routing Navarrete sarcastically where he has jumped to conclusions, denouncing (what he presumes is) unfair reporting of Jesuit ways in Canton; pleading that the statements quoted by 'Friar Long Ears' be taken 'in the favourable and wholesome sense' in which they were made at the time. (11)

True, Friar Long Ears' straight-faced publication of the Jesuits' leg-pulling proved that he had little sense of their humour, and lacked French 'joliez'. It also reveals a lack of tact and charity, but it does not necessarily make him 'a shameless liar'. Understandably, Fr Verbiest fails to make this point.

The joint answers were despatched to Europe, but arrived too late to be effective, for in the meantime a change had taken place. The number and persistence of the accusations of so many were proving corrosive, and suspicions were being strengthened not only in official Rome but among the general public. Friar Domingo had suddenly emerged upon the scene as the most vocal opponent of the Society's China policy, and it is in part due to his activities that the atmosphere in Rome was less favourable to the Jesuits. Modern Jesuits, such as Fr Bernard-Maitre, see him as the one who reopened debates which should have been settled 20 years earlier, when Fr Martini secured the papal decree of 1656. That is to oversimplify, for during those intervening years there had been no peace, since the friars had never accepted the validity of that celebrated decree. (12)

Friar Domingo had no hesitation about publishing his *Tratados*. Indeed, he believed he had no alternative. He held to Schall's maxim that scandal published is better than truth abandoned, which was 'why Paul withstood Peter to his face'. Navarrete was not one to see many moves ahead. Had he been able to do so he might have taken fright at the prospect, for with his accusations he laid and lit the train of gunpowder leading straight to the barrel. (13)

Years earlier in Canton, Jesuit Brancati had warned that a war of words could be as bloody as a war of arms and as morally devastating. He was right. Pulpits fulminated, presses groaned and poured out a flood of books, reports, memorials, pamphlets, theses, open-letters, even poems, as both sides charged and counter-charged with accusations ranging from ignorance of Chinese to forgery. John Locke, keeping an eye on it all, heard in 1701 that the more the contestants wrote, the more entangled the problem became. (14)

The earliest of the more formidable Jesuit replies to Navarrete came in 1687 when Fr Le Tellier published his *Défense des Nouveaux Chrétiens*. Five years later the opposition produced its *Histoire des Differens entre les Missionaires*, and in 1699 the *Apologie des Dominicains*, followed up this attack. Between them, blast and counterblast fill 55 columns of Henri Cordier's *Biblioteca Sinica* and the titles speak for themselves: *Censure; Apologie; Eclaircissement; Difesa; Il Disinganno contraposto; Dimostrazione della Giustizia; Dubitationes gravissimae; Réponse aux remarques; Contra-risposte;*

Innocentia Victrix; Imposturae detectae et convulsae. By 1700, when the battle was at its height, the paper involved must have aggregated several tons.[7] The tone was bitter. Charity, justice, and truth were sacrificed to party interests. Some titles can mislead. *Lettre d'une dame de qualité a une autre dame savante* proves less demure than suggested. The ladies, for all their quality and learning, were capable of surprisingly robust language, and Archbishop Fénelon, despite his sympathy for the Jesuits, 'wished to God that they and their adversaries had never published such writings and that Religion had been spared such frightful scenes'. At about the same time Cardinal Tolomei noted that 'this business started badly, continues worse, and will end fatally'.

Others were more light-hearted. Fr Mesina wrote from Manila in 1680 to his colleague Fr Grelon reporting that a Dominican had left for Europe, 'I suspect he's gone to take Navarrete's place, but for all their comings and goings these friars may bark away, but they've no bite!' (15)

Books from both sides went out to the missions, causing fresh distress, disturbance and intrigue, which in turn provided material for even more pamphlets, and kept the wheels turning. Yet the contestants were painfully aware that they were providing arms for 'the heretics of Europe', and in 1692 a Manila friar informed his superior that 'It's beyond belief what has been written and sent to France and Rome this past year. All Europe must be sighing!' But not all Europe was sighing, much of it was laughing, especially in France. (16)

The uproar spread and the Mexican Inquisition became involved in a denunciation of the Spanish edition of the Jesuit *Défense des Nouveaux Chrétiens* [of China] which contained 'calumnies of the living and dead', including their late Bishop Palafox. The *Défense*, a 'pernicious mishmash, deserved silence rather than bell-ringing, and certainly ought never to have been paraded through Spanish plazas by its misguided translators'. Then, in 1699, the Dominican general complained of a new Jesuit work, offensive to his order and the memory of the late Friar Navarrete. A century later, and 16 years after the Society had been suppressed, Fr George Pray was still vigorously carrying on the fight in his *Historia controversiarum de ritibus sinicis*.[8] (17)

With the cry of 'Jesus, and no quarter!' each side closed ranks, taking stern measures when troubled by an occasional dissident sharing the opposition's view. The Dominicans, initially pleased with their Chinese friar, Gregorio Lo, later detected his deficiencies when he was caught temporarily wavering towards the Riccistas. Similarly, the Fathers sought to

---

[7] Yet John Aubrey thought manners were milder and in 1690, discussing a disputatious old-timer, remarked, 'It was an epidemick evill of those dayes which is now out of fashion, as being unmannerly and boyish [childish].'

[8] Pray was outspoken: '*O! prolixa garrulitas tua, te theologum desultorium, lepidissimum caput*' (to an unhappy priest of the Pious Schools order).

discredit Fr Longobardi, belatedly discovering that he was no great theologian after all. Against him they deferentially paraded their friar-ally Sarpetri, as a skilled witness and an expert in Chinese, though his own Dominican brethren deplored his bizarre theology and general incompetence. (18)

Rome, after moving with the usual professional slowness, finally made a decision. In 1704 the Confucian rites were condemned and the term *T'ien chu* ('Lord of Heaven') was declared to be the only acceptable expression for 'God'. The decree was sent out to China with a papal legate, Charles Maillard de Tournon, who was to supervise its observance.[9]

Sincere and earnest, Tournon was young, and his personality was neither tactful enough to soothe, nor strong enough to crush opposition. From the start he met trouble. Permission to enter China had not been requested from Lisbon by the Holy See, and this was regarded as an infringement of the Portuguese *padroado*. Consequently the Jesuits in Peking, where he arrived in 1705, were cool towards him. Indeed, according to Fr Sebes, the French and Portuguese Jesuits even sank their differences in order to oppose him. The emperor, initially well disposed, turned against him, and banished him from the empire. Inevitably, the Fathers were blamed for this, especially when the K'ang-hsi emperor decreed that missionaries who wished to remain in China must obtain an imperial preaching licence (*p'iao*). Newcomers to the mission were to be examined as to their fitness to have this *p'iao* granted them, and only those following the Jesuit line were to be licensed. (19)

The legate was on his way out of China when he heard this. He imprudently countered with a decree opposing the emperor's ruling, demanding obedience on pain of excommunication. In other words, missionaries had to choose between obeying the emperor or the pope. When Tournon reached Macao the local Portuguese refused to recognize his powers, placed him in virtual arrest, and fired off sundry accusations and interdicts. They kept him in detention, even after the pope, outraged at the affront to papal dignity, granted him a red hat. Papal support for Tournon angered both the Portuguese and their Jesuit allies. In 1709 Fr Arxo told the Duchess of Aveiro that the Portuguese agent in Rome 'in a tigerish rage had bawled at the pontiff' during an audience and threatened that the Portuguese would 'go to Europe' [i.e. the universities] for a decision, if necessary withdrawing their men from China, abandoning it to Dutch Protestants. (20)

His red hat did not save Tournon, who, for all that he was now a Cardinal-Patriarch, died in Portuguese detention. Pastor's Jesuit collaborators admit that he did so with courage and dignity. Indeed, they say of him that 'he may

---

[9] Even minor ceremonies were found superstitious by 'contamination'. In 1684 Verbiest had attempted some indirect lobbying, reporting how a papal document had been received by the converts on their knees, laid on a table and solemnly venerated with incense. This seems like purification of the rites by analogy (*Corr.*, 459).

almost be styled a martyr for the prerogatives of the Holy See, and he himself was conscious of being such'. The 'martyrdom' was seized upon for fresh anti-Jesuit publicity, and the British press did not miss its chance. *The Postman* (2–4 October 1711) made his death front-page news, reporting his 'very long Confinement and many Hardships through the Interests of the Jesuits in that Country. That Prelate is very much lamented, and after the cruel treatment he has received there, 'tis believed few will be willing to go thither upon the same [papal] Errand, though the [non-Jesuit] Foreign Missionaries represent the necessity of sending another Prelate without any delay to put an end to the Idolatrous worship practised and taught in that Country by the Jesuits, who have framed a new religion there made up of some Doctrines of the Holy Scriptures, and some Tenets of Confucius and other Heathen Authors.'

The Tournon story echoed around the world. It reached Brazil, and the Dutch carried it into Japan, the 'Closed Country', where the event was not without interest, for though the Japanese had cut themselves off from the outer world, they kept a keen eye upon it.[10] (21)

To the Jesuits the papal decision of 1704 was untimely, as in 1692 K'ang-hsi had issued an edict tolerating Christianity.[11] This was a reward for the Jesuits who had served him during recent negotiations with the Russians. Now at last Matteo Ricci's strategy seemed to be succeeding, and Jesuit hopes of a Chinese Constantine leading East Asia into the Church, nearer to fulfilment. But the Fathers were over-optimistic. The friars, who saw more hope of conversion through martyrdom than mandarinates, would not have accepted this view. In their opinion the Church always has more to fear from Constantine than Nero.

Not all Jesuits were optimistic and Fr Noel noted that 'despite his benevolence, the emperor does not appear to wish to become a Christian, nor do any of the court nobles'. K'ang-hsi's 'toleration-edict' meant only that Catholicism was seen as offering no danger of rebellion. It was the Fathers' knowledge of astronomy and their abilities as artists, diplomats and ordnance workers which accounted for his tolerance of their religion. 'Astronomy', said Verbiest, 'introduced and established Christianity in China and with good cause she leans on the arm of Astronomy'. (22)

In 1700, the Jesuits, having secured the toleration-edict, hit on an apparent master-stroke. They appealed to K'ang-hsi to define the nature of the rites, admitting that, as outsiders with little knowledge, they did not know if their interpretation was correct. In Chinese terms this was the equivalent of asking the pope to define Catholicism. The emperor graciously

---

[10] Robert Browning noticed Tournon, who was also celebrated in a contemporary poem (Gripswaldia, 1709), beginning '*Adspice, Roma, tuos, in praelia cruda ruentes*' (Pritz, *Relatio*).
[11] This was seven years after the Revocation of the Edict of Nantes. Bayle noted how the Chinese emperor was granting freedom to Catholics while Louis XIV was enforcing religious conformity through dragonnades.

replied guaranteeing the rites were not religious but civic and social. But he was bound to say so, for, as a ruler of the alien Manchu house he could not permit a foreign cult to interfere with the traditional Chinese system he had inherited. At the same time not even an autocrat, such as he was, could purify the rites of any religious content. Nonetheless, the Jesuits were delighted. They now had the backing of the highest authority in the empire, the imperial head of the literati. (23)

K'ang-hsi's infallible declaration *ex cathedra* was printed in Rome and 700 free copies were distributed throughout the city in an effort to give it the widest publicity, as though it were a papal bull in danger of neglect. (24)

The Jesuits' opponents always saw this as the most tragic moment in the controversy. The move was seen as premature, since in 1700 the matter was still *sub judice* in Rome. The Jesuits' appeal to K'ang-hsi was designed to cut the ground from under the opposition, but served only to bring pope and emperor into direct conflict. The latter was scornful of the pope's attempt to decide something beyond his experience ('after all, they know only a fraction of what I know'). And Clement XI was taken aback by the emperor's pretensions to legislate on Catholic theology, equating on his own authority the Christian God with *Shang-ti* and *T'ien*. Foreign missionary and native convert alike were now obliged to choose between two opposing decrees. Hostile eyes were only too ready to see the Jesuits as more inclined to follow the Son of Heaven than the Vicar of Christ. In the end their appeal to the emperor only worsened the situation. (25)

The Fathers nevertheless insisted that the controversy could not be settled in Rome, but only in the east, and under Jesuit influence the king of Portugal was to demand a Vatican Council in India to discuss the rites.

Their enemies made much of Jesuit resistance to Roman decisions, giving wide circulation to the proposition, reputedly put forward by a Fr Louis Porquet in 1706, that the pope could not define infallibly in the Rites Controversy. Some time later, in a moment of panic, a Jesuit denounced two friars to the local mandarin because they, obeying pope rather than emperor, had not obtained an imperial preaching licence. Although on second thoughts the Father withdrew his denunciation, the story was widely circulated. (26)

Yet the Jesuits could see no other course. They were honestly convinced of their opponents' bad faith. In 1709, that Aragonese chatterbox Fr Arxo, busily writing to the Aveiro duchess, complained that 'even if an angel revealed to Rome that the rites were purely political they would still want to ban them, for the hostility is not directed at the rites, but at us Jesuits'.

Generally however the Fathers were patient and optimistic. Some thought their attitude smacked of the 'There'll-always-be-another-pope' approach. They pointed out that though Innocent X had disapproved of the rites, his successor Alexander VII had differed, so whatever was now decreed by Clement XI might well be reversed later by a 'better informed pope'. This might be especially true, said Fr Arxo, of the present pope, Clement XI, 'a man of quick impressions, both muddled and muddling, always painting himself into a corner and then can't see his way out. He lives in perpetual hesitation'. Typical was his hasty promotion of Tournon, without waiting for the result of his legation. Now, having elevated him, he is obliged willy-nilly to defend him, despite the harm that policy does to the Church. But, Fr Arxo told his duchess, 'we're all, even the pope, only men in the end', and he recalled how Pope Siricius had nearly signed a decree favouring the Arian heresy but was saved at the last moment by the hand of God. Such ruminations spread, and from time to time the mission itself was swept by reports which raised false hopes, such as that the pope had died, but that before doing so had revoked all his decrees referring to China. The rumours inevitably produced panic reactions, and fresh ammunition for the ongoing battle. (27)

Muddled or not, Clement made a attempt in 1711 to force obedience to the decree of 1704. On 11 October, through the Holy Office Assessor, Antonio Banchieri, he wrote to the Jesuit general, Michelangelo Tamburini, declaring that he must put an end to all perverse (*sinistras*) interpretations of the pope's mind, such as that the second half of the papal decree nullified the first half. Clement stressed that the decree of 1704 was not to be considered as conditional, or patient of individual readings. Exact obedience, nothing less, was demanded, under pain of excommunication. Enclosed with this letter went yet another papal decree on the subject and, Banchieri added pointedly, 'since this is the day the mail leaves, let Your Reverence take the opportunity to despatch copies to your subjects in China. His Holiness fully expects complete observance of this decree without any delay whatsoever'. (28)

Tamburini was stung by this, and on 20 November he made a solemn profession of 'blind obedience' to the pope in the name of the whole Society.[12] In particular the decrees of 1704 and 1710 would be 'inviolably obeyed'. He presented his memorial in person, accompanied by his five assistants and the proctors of 20 Jesuit provinces.

But there was a problem. The melancholy truth was that by now the Fathers' reputation was such that when they explained or defended themselves, even reasonably, they were not believed. 'Docility', remarked Benedict XIV, 'is not a Jesuit quality', and their sudden new spirit of resignation seemed at odds with the subtle evasions of the recent past. Tamburini showed himself aware of this. He sounded desperate, he pleaded to be believed, he wished he could think of a form of words more forceful, clear and unequivocal with which to express himself, and he hoped that the

---

[12] *Sanctae Sedi reverentissimam submissionem et obedientiam caecam'* (*Synopsis*, 282).

words he was now using might have an unmistakable meaning. He went on to pledge that the Society rejected in advance any Father who should put a different interpretation on his submission to the pope. (29)

The pope now fulfilled Fr Arxo's expectation of him. Reacting to Tamburini, he got the impression that all was well: the problem was over. But his mood did not last long. In 1715 he issued the apostolic constitution, *Ex illa die*, to stop 'subterfuges, pretexts, delays, interpretations, tergiversations and disobedience'. With this in mind the papal document was meticulously worded; indeed it is remarkable for the care with which it was prepared. Every possible resource of the curial style was brought into play to prevent evasions and casuistical interpretations, and Pastor mentions no less than three drafts, each with the pope's own corrections. The decree reaffirmed earlier rulings, and demanded that all the China Jesuits sign an oath of obedience.

This put the Fathers in yet another quandary. They had had to sign a deposition that they would follow the Riccista line in order to get K'anghsi's *p'iao* to stay in the mission. Now they had to sign Clement's oath to the contrary in order not to be withdrawn from it. The emperor, irritated by the papal decree, made a marginal comment on the translation prepared for him by the court Jesuits: 'After reading this I can only say that the Europeans are small-minded people'. On another occasion, he concluded 'such dissension cannot be inspired by the Lord of Heaven but by the Devil, who, I have heard the Westerners say, leads men to do evil'. (30)

For all its careful wording even *Ex illa die*, too, left the door open for the more loyal of the Jesuits and they began publishing their famous *Lettres édifiantes* and Fr du Halde's *Description de la Chine* (1735), which were later seen as an underground movement, a clandestine defence, in which they avoided dangerous topics, being content to canvass opinions with an air of openness and simplicity, for they still hoped to dispose the pope in their favour, and to educate at least French public opinion. (31)

In 1713, two years before *Ex illa die*, Clement XI had issued another bull, *Unigenitus*, condemning a hundred Jansenist propositions. This bull also started another long and impassioned conflict. But it was the Duke of Saint-Simon who first drew a parallel between these two papal rulings, a subject to which he devoted some of his most scathing and graphic pages. The Jesuits hoped to hide their defeat over the Chinese rites behind a smokescreen of anti-Jansenist activity, piously demanding that *Unigenitus* be unconditionally obeyed. They brushed aside the Jansenists' distinction that the propositions condemned by Clement were indeed rightly condemnable – that was a matter of *law*. But since Jansen had never held any such theories there was no case to answer – and that was a matter of *fact*. Distinctions between *fact* and *law* were a lawyer's not a theologian's, but that apparently deterred no one.

Yet, even as they were hounding the Jansenists into submission to the pope, Saint-Simon observed that they themselves were using similar tactics over the Chinese rites. The anti-Jesuit Cardinal de Noailles pointed out that in spite of their much-vaunted fourth vow of obedience to the pope, the Jesuits were still demanding further explanations, drawing distinctions, querying meanings, and deftly side-stepping inconvenient rulings in a manner matching that of the Jansenists over *Unigenitus*.

The Jesuits, for instance, agreed that idolatrous rites were to be condemned – that was a matter of *law*; but the Confucian rites, not being idolatrous were not condemnable – that was a matter of *fact* – and a fact on which the pope was not properly and sufficiently informed. The spectacle of Jesuits picking and choosing which papal bulls to accept and which to question, delighted the freethinkers. Broadsides, songs and *libelles* soon appeared, drawing attention to this double-standard policy and one pamphlet sold at the Frankfurt fair in 1716 was entitled *An Essay on the Necessity of Accepting Papal Bulls in France, and of Rejecting them in China.*[13] (32)

It should be emphasized again that the Fathers' resistance was based on their conviction that they alone understood the language, literature, culture and religions of China, and that the Holy See was misled by the ignorant and malicious. They also believed that the condemnation of the rites would lead to the collapse of the China mission. The arrival in China in 1720 of another papal delegate, Mezzabarba, who, hoping to ease the situation, issued eight interpretations of the decree *Ex illa die*, thereby giving rise to fresh uncertainties.

Wearily, almost despairingly, Rome examined the whole issue once more. The result was the bull *Ex quo singulari* (1742). This solemnly forbade the rites and, picking up an Augustinian phrase, declared them 'not evil because forbidden, but forbidden because evil'. Direst censures were threatened against anyone contravening this latest papal decree. The new pope, Benedict XIV, the 'pope of the enlightenment', demanded the recall of recalcitrants and threatened the generals of the orders that failure to comply would result in a ban on their ever again sending men to the East. He also prescribed a new form of oath of obedience to these papal rulings. (33)

Ex quo singulari narrated the history of the controversy step by step and repeated, within itself, the full text of its ineffectual predecessor, *Ex illa die*. It had been hoped, said Benedict pointedly, that 'those who boast of how implicitly they obey the Holy See would have done so in this matter'.[14] But,

---

[13] 'The general public, largely unfavourable to the Jesuits, followed with amused interest this stage of the Controversy. The memoirs and histories of the time show what a large place they occupied in French minds; popular ballad- and street-singers took up the hue and cry' (Guy, *Image*, 48).

[14] '*Ex illa die* refutes those who think the papacy is Jesuit-dominated. Alas, it also shows that the Holy See has not always been implicitly obeyed by Jesuits. If this was disobedience, it was a grievous fault, and grievously did the Society expiate it. Thirty years of persecution, at home and abroad, and then suppression' (Fr Rickaby, SJ., *Month*, LXXIII (1891),74–6).

instead, 'certain persons' had tried to evade their duty by seizing upon the word 'precept' in the preamble to *Ex illa die*, misusing it to find a way around those carefully worded rulings.[15] Benedict solemnly reaffirmed the decree of his predecessor Clement, in every sense and 'as far as in Us lies'. The bull concluded with an exhortation to obedience, and the 'harsh phrase' *etiam Societatis Jesu* occurs 12 times in the text, showing how keenly the Roman drafters felt the need to block further evasions. (34)

Thirty years later, when Clement XIV issued the brief suppressing the Jesuit order (*Dominus ac Redemptor*, 1773) the Chinese Rites affair, not surprisingly, figured in the catalogue of reasons justifying that drastic, incredible action. (35)

Roma locuta est, causa finita est. Contrary to its proud claim, Rome was forced to utter no less than five times before this particular case was closed, and a hundred years had passed since Friar Juan Bautista Morales had expressed his misgivings to Urban VIII. Yet some think that not even *Ex quo singulari* would have succeeded had K'ang-hsi still been alive. His successor was less well disposed to the Fathers which, writes the Dominican González, 'was a blessing for the Church in China'. But the final settlement came too late, for the controversies had had a fatal effect upon the mission. (36)

Other reasons help to account for the decline of the mission but, said Clement XI, 'From this [Controversy] most of all . . . the losses in the China Mission have unhappily come'. Yet some friar-historians believed that the loss was preferable to a Chinese variety of Gallicanism. (37)

There the controversy rested for the next two centuries, until the question was examined again by Rome, following representations made by the mission hierarchy. But the problems presented to Rome in modern times were simpler than those raised three centuries before. The decline in religious belief in the West was paralleled in China not only officially but also among the masses. The intellectual renaissance following the 1912 republic seemed to have dethroned Confucius, and the classical texts had lost their canonical character. In 1935, therefore, the Holy See felt able to declare the rites were no longer superstitious. They had *absolute nullam religiosam indolem*: they had become only signs of respect, comparable to that paid to the cenotaph in the West.[16] There could be no conscientious objection by the time Pius XII issued his 1939 decree noting that 'It is a matter of common knowledge that some ceremonies common in the Orient, though *in earlier times connected with rites of a religious nature* [my italics], have at the present time, owing to changes in customs and ideas in the course of centuries (*mutatis saeculorum*

---

[15] Had *Ex illa die* been only a *praeceptum*, it would conveniently die with the pope who issued it. This attitude made Benedict think of *Confucius Loyola*: 'They fight for Confucius as if he had founded their order'(*Corr.*, ed. Morelli, I: 20).

[16] Rituals and taboos outgrow their origins. No British sailor could now object to saluting the quarter-deck on boarding a naval vessel, for the crucifix that once hung there disappeared long ago.

fluxu moribus et animis), no more than mere civil significance of filial respect for ancestors, or of patriotic sentiment or of social amenity'.

As such, Navarrete would have welcomed that decision, which summed up his own words, 'the past is gone, it is the present generation that concerns us'.[17] (38)

This last Roman ruling has been interpreted by some as a reversal of the old decision and as 'the Church coming around to the Jesuit viewpoint'. A moment's reflection, or even a reading of the decree, suffices to dismiss that as unhistorical. A more loyal and logical view was that of Mgr Adrian Languillat, Jesuit Vicar-Apostolic of Nankin. At the First Vatican Council, anti-infallibilists asked him how he could reconcile papal infallibility with the condemnation of those rites tolerated by his Society. He answered that the assistance of the Holy Spirit had never been more clearly shown than in that matter, where the popes might easily have made a false step and permitted the rites to converts.

To quote Fr Rickaby once more:

> It is not difficult to justify on historical and critical grounds the [earlier] action of the Holy See in forbidding the rites . . . even if the loss of China had resulted . . . the end does not justify the means, when the means are evil . . . The question was examined and re-examined at Rome during more than forty years, under six Popes . . . Chinese witnesses and Chinese documents were consulted in abundance. Every facility of representation was allowed and taken advantage of. The last Pope who examined the matter [Benedict XIV] was a man of prodigious learning, the best canonist of his age, and had, in various subordinate official capacities, followed the question from the first. Yet Benedict XIV took exactly the same view as Clement XI. Certainly the argument from testimony is very strong.[18] (39)

The development of Benedict XIV's thought on the subject can be traced in his secret week by week correspondence with Cardinal de Tencin. In the end he concluded that 'where the First Commandment is involved, *tutiorism*[19] is the only acceptable course', thereby accepting the friars' caution as reasonable, and rejecting Jesuit accommodation as risking syncretism. (40)

---

[17] Pius also stated that the former missionary oath 'is today superfluous as a disciplinary measure. The old controversies regarding the Chinese Rites have died down. The missionaries no longer need to be *forced by oath to render prompt and filial obedience to the Holy See*' [my italics] (*Acta Apost. Sedis*, VII (Rome, 1940), 24–6).

[18] Rickaby's opinion was later validated as 'impartial' by Jesuit colleagues: *Month*, CLXI (1933), 420.

[19] Tutiorists practise safe morality and for them the course of moral safety always comes first in cases of conscience.

III

The 'theological gladiators' (Fr Murillo Velarde's phrase) disputing in the European arena attracted an amused audience. The controversy grew more intense as it spread, and at times the original issue, the salvation of souls, seemed forgotten as the battle ranged over the whole field of theology, ethics and religious politics. Probabilism, Jansenism, Quietism, Gallicanism, Deism, Atheism and Figurism: the 'isms' merged like words written on damp blotting paper. As Voltaire saw, it was 'no longer a mere monks' squabble; it had become a philosophical question'. From a paragraph in mission history, the controversy developed into a chapter in the history of the universal Church and of European intellectual development. As Joseph Needham has pointed out, it cannot be ignored by historians of science.

The later struggle was concentrated in France, where the Jesuits found fresh opponents in Pallu's Foreign Mission Society, whose members supplanted the friars as rivals of the Jesuits in the East. They enjoyed some official support, and it was they who involved the Sorbonne in the controversy later in the century.[20] They eagerly read Navarrete's work, whose stance they shared, and whose friendship with Pallu they remembered. In his writings they found ammunition for their assaults on the Jesuits – assaults so violent as to surprise even the Jansenists. One Father complained that these attacks were compiled of 'scraps of Navarrete', whose work had become 'a sort of Fifth Gospel'. (41)

The Fifth Gospel found equally avid readers among the Jansenists. They combed it for suitable quotations, and their task was not arduous. The *Tratados* had little of interest for them, but somehow or other they managed to get hold of a leaked copy of the *Controversias*, then still held 'under arrest' by the Spanish Inquisition. The leading Jansenist, Antoine Arnauld ('The Great Arnauld'), drew heavily upon this copy when composing part of the *Morale pratique des Jésuites*. In June 1689 he took up the study of Spanish so as to read the original for himself and was soon reporting good progress. As a Spanish primer the *Controversias* has its drawbacks, but Arnauld was undeterred, and by November had made it his daily diet. He found 'admirable points and capital things' there, such as the documents referring to poor Fr Roboredo's rash intervention in the dispute and his wild admissions of long ago. (42)

So heavily did Arnauld rely upon Navarrete for the sixth volume of the *Morale pratique* that when negotiating its translation into Spanish he was able to point out that the task would be light, because of its many quotations

---

[20] Trouble with that Institution was no novelty for the Jesuits. As early as 1612, St Francis de Sales wished some 'pious and prudent prelate might be able to bring about union and mutual understanding between the Sorbonne and the Jesuits'.

from the original. His only regret was that he could not get hold of a copy of the mysterious third volume which had been left in manuscript: 'no price would be too great to pay for it'. It mattered to him because for years the Jansenists had accused the Jesuits of corrupting morals in Europe. Now they believed they could point out what happened when the Fathers, unsupervised, were allowed a free hand in the foreign missions. (43)

The Jansenists, said the Jesuits, were 'Calvinists who say mass'. They were alarming not least because, an ecclesiastical Fifth Column, they were difficult to identify. 'A Protestant', wrote de Maistre, 'is a soldier who openly and in broad daylight marches on the fort I'm defending, but a Jansenist is a soldier from a mutinied garrison who stabs me in the back while I'm on duty in the fort'. In their nervousness, and with some paranoia, the Jesuits saw them everywhere. Both Pallu and Navarrete were suspects. When the latter told Cardinal Bona that the Paris Foreign Missioners were said to be Jansenists, the saintly Bona lost his temper: 'To be poor, prayerful, and live exemplary lives, preaching like apostles, well, if that's Jansenism, then I wish we were all Jansenists'. But any ascetic group risked the nickname, and even though Innocent XI condemned such unjustified labelling, the practice continues, and has been recently rebuked as contributing to the linguistic dissipation of our time.[21] (44)

The Jesuits' opponents were also denounced for arming the enemies of the Church. The answer was that there was no alternative, since it was better for Protestants and Deists to witness quarrels about religious purity than that they could point to Roman toleration of idolatry or superstition. The Jesuits forgot that they too had contributed to Voltaire's armoury, and that, for instance, when La Mothe le Vayer discussed Confucius ('The Chinese Socrates'), he cited Frs Ricci, Trigault and Borri as his sources.

Though Navarrete helped to spread this quarrel, he was not the first to do so. Before the *Tratados* appeared, knowledge of the controversy was limited to the professionals, and only the very watchful saw how things lay from the papal decrees of 1646, 1656 and 1669. More publicly, Francisco de la Piedad had published his *Teatro Jesuitico* (Coimbra, 1654) which devoted over 60 pages to 'The Preaching of the Jesuits, and how they adulterate the Word of God in Japan and China'. The following year there appeared in Cologne the *De martyrio Fidei* of Thomas Hurtado, which achieved some notoriety when cited by Pascal.[22] In 1656 A. M. Verricelli published his *Quaestiones morales* which relied upon the work and personal advice of Fr Martini. In the

---

[21] 'The state is not usually interested in theological error, and so to alarm the authorities catchwords are used. In the Middle Ages the most frequently used was "Manichaean" ' (S. Runciman, *The Medieval Manichee* (Cambridge, 1988), 4). The same now happened with Jansenism. For a suggested link between Jansenist theology and modern structuralist theory, see P. Thody, *Faux Amis* (London, 1985), 142.

[22] It drew an intemperate retort from a Fr Raynaud whose *Missi evangelici ad Sinas* (Antwerp, 1659) ended with the alarming warning *Cave thoracem* ('Have a care. Watch your back!').

following year the *Catenae moralis doctrinae* of Pedro de Tapia, Dominican archbishop of Seville, also referred to the rites question.

Navarrete's *Tratados* (the last significant work from the period of Iberian patronage of the China mission) differs from its predecessors, for it was addressed to and reached a wide readership, in extracts or in full translation. In this way it spread news of the controversy, shifting the centre of action from China to Europe, precisely when the Jesuits were trying to confine it to the east. Just as Pascal took the Jesuit-Jansenist quarrel out of the Sorbonne and into the salon, so Navarrete brought the rites controversy home from the missions into the plaza. (45)

IV

The rediscovery of China affected the West in many ways. One of these was the undermining of the Christian faith. A disturbing discovery came from an innocent, almost accidental, source: Chinese chronology. This threw doubt on the dating of the Old Testament. In 1654 Archbishop Ussher's researches had fixed the date of the first Creation on Sunday 23 October, 4004 BC, and the second (after the Flood), he had fixed at 2348 BC.[23] This was now about to change, for four years after Ussher had comfortably settled the matter, the Jesuit Martini published his *Sinicae historiae decas prima* which outlined the official version of Chinese history. Martini accepted that this went back to 2952 BC, over 600 years before the Vulgate date for the Flood. This translated the cradle of civilization from the Middle East to Asia. Martini's book caused a commotion, but he was undismayed. A reporter, not an apologist, he left the solution of the problem to others. (46)

The Old Testament now began to look like local history, and the 'universal' Flood as no such thing. Once again, the Jesuits were in a dilemma. To accept the Chinese dynastic histories meant denying Genesis. To reject the histories meant doubting that culture which, for political purposes, they were extolling at home. Happily, they hit on a solution. They abandoned the limitations of the Vulgate bible, adopting instead the more expansive Septuagint version, which gave them another thousand years to play with, allowing them to fit the Chinese tradition inside the Christian framework. This manoeuvre was necessary since no convert would dare adopt a religion whose sacred books, unable to accommodate the historical records, denied the existence of the earliest emperors.[24] Septuagint or not, some people were troubled, and Pascal wondered 'which is the more credible, Moses or China', and Navarrete was denounced by Fr Cortés for putting the Chinese annals before the scriptures. In fact chronology in itself did not much interest Navarrete. He cared only to protect the Faith, for as Owen Chadwick has said 'the coming of the "age of reason" during the last quarter of the seventeenth century had thrown into disrepute every form of authority except the Bible'. Thus Navarrete denounced those Jesuits, as usual they were divided, whose speculations seemed to him to be so dangerous. (47)

More bizarre problems were raised by a small group of Jesuits, the theological-symbolists or 'Figurists', who discovered fragmentary remains, foregleams of Christianity, in the ancient Chinese classics. In doing so they

---

[23] Overall's *Dictionary of Chronology* (London, 1870) gives 140 dates for the creation; see also J. Finegan, *Handbook of Bib. Chron.* (Princeton, 1964); for Ussher: James Barr, *Bull. of the John Rylands University Library of Manchester*, LXVII (1985), 575–608.

[24] Thanks to some missionary indiscretions, the Chinese had discovered this discrepancy and exploited it (Gaubil, 355, 943). K'ang-hsi, for instance, was surprised to hear that the Vulgate and Septuagint bibles differed.

were following tradition, for reading pagan literature in a Christian sense was justified by Paul's quotations from Aratus, Epimenides and Menander. And the opening words of St John's gospel may be plausibly represented as the use of the pagan classics to attract the Platonizing Jews. (48)

In China the movement began early (in the 1640s Fr Diego Morales had found 'guardian angels' there), was nourished by Fr Martini, and flowered under Fr Bouvet, who spent 20 years in creative interpretation, discovering benevolent meanings in early Chinese literature and legend. Once gripped by this enthusiasm, ideas came fast, and the Figurists' inventions aroused both the envy of the like-minded and the alarm of the conservative, once more splitting the Jesuits into two divergent groups. (49)

Ignoring the post-Confucian exegetes, the Figurists went directly to the original sources, including that most enigmatic of the classics, the I Ching ('The Book of Changes'), which for Confucius was the repository of quintessential wisdom. For the Jesuit Enthusiasts the I Ching played the role of the sibyls in the pagan world, and they hoped to find there, as a subtext hidden in coded messages, the 'Ancient Theology' awaiting fulfilment through Christ. In other words, they proposed to explain to the Chinese the inner meaning of their classics by revealing to them a double-voiced narrative, understood in a vulgar sense by the uninitiated, and in a symbolic sense by those possessing the secret of Christian Revelation. (50)

In their rambles in these byways of theological speculation, the Figurists found evidence of a Judaeo-Christian influence fitting the theory that one of Noah's children took the Old Law to the East. The theory brought bonuses: it explained the disturbing similarities between Catholicism and other religions; it suggested that the Christian god was universal, and had at some time been known to all humankind. It also absolved the Almighty from the charge of abandoning certain peoples without hope of salvation until the arrival of the latter-day missionaries.

Though they were the heirs of a respectable if exotic tradition, the Figurists aroused hostility, even among many of their own brethren, for stolid Dominicans were not alone in protesting against claims that the Chinese classics contained allusions to the immaculate conception, Adam's fall, and purgatory. Fr Prémare, for example, dowsing in the 'Book of Odes', found a reference to a lamb whose skin had been pierced five times, and interpreted it as Christ 'the Paschal Lamb' with his five wounds. Later critics complained that if a Figurist came across any reference to a 'mountain', it had to mean Calvary, and any eulogy of an emperor was taken to mean the Saviour.[25] (51)

---

[25] Less imaginative is Rev Pakenham-Walsh's *Preparation for Christ in the Chinese Classics* (London, 1921) which detects in Mencius the Psalmist's prophecy of the Messiah. Simone Weil's *Intimations of Christianity among the Ancient Greeks* (1957), in the same spirit, is original rather than convincing.

In time, and after many battles, Figurism seemed discredited and died away. Then suddenly, if belatedly, the movement appeared to achieve respectability with the publication of Fr Prémare's *Some Chosen Vestiges of the Chief Dogmas of the Christian Religion extracted from the Ancient Books of the Chinese* (Paris, 1878), with an enthusiastic preface by Pope Leo XIII.

But a modern Jesuit, Fr Damboriena, dismisses it harshly. 'The praise with which Pope Leo prefaced the edition does him little credit, that is if he actually saw the text of his preface, or personally saw the contents of the book'. The same critic is equally severe on his long-dead Figurist brethren, dismissing their works as 'a few truths mixed with wild imaginations and strange delusions', and denouncing their 'obsessions and infantile exegeses'. Fr Damboriena clearly thinks this is the realm of theological-fiction. (52)

Others too had complained in their day. Yang Kuang-hsien thought Figurism especially dangerous and Navarrete, while not going as far as Fr Damboriena, was suitably indignant. For him, the theory was perilous and bizarre: 'though there's not a word about the Trinity in the whole of the Old Testament, yet these speculators find it revealed to the Chinese ancients'. (53)

The Figurists are important in the history of the Controversy for a number of reasons. First, they show how the China Jesuits continued to be divided even into the 18th century. There were now two groups of Fathers in the mission: the Figurist theological-symbolists who, inevitably in so subjective a field of research, often differed from one another within their own sub-group; and on the other hand there were those Jesuits who regarded the Chinese records as historical documents, not as allegories with hidden meanings and sub-texts. Another, third, group consisted of those Paris-based Fathers charged with the task of publicizing the work of their China colleagues. This burden fell mainly on Fr du Halde who, censoring and bowdlerizing the more bizarre reports from the mission, harmonized the differing views submitted to him. His efforts were published so as to smooth over the disagreements and tensions. China, and the mission there, were displayed with a calm smiling face.

Second, Jesuit boldness begot more nervous caution in Rome where sharp eyes detected continual if gradual concessions to Confucianism, despite the Fathers' claim that they were only continuing the Riccista methods. Ricci's final judgment of the Chinese rites had been careful if hesitant: 'certainly not idolatrous and perhaps not even superstitious'. That 'perhaps' indicates calculated risk. But 'perhaps' is a dangerous word with a tendency to get lost, for as Bayle's *Dictionary* warned 'it is a very common fault to change into an affirmation what an author had qualified with a *perhaps*'. That was now happening to Ricci's *'forse anche'*, which first became 'probably', and then, by an inconspicuous transition, sometimes even 'certainly'. Unsurprisingly, suspicious Roman minds felt faced with wild speculation as well as obstinacy. (54)

Some Jesuit apologists give the impression that 18th-century Rome stubbornly and belatedly condemned Ricci's tentative suggestion. But nothing could be farther from the truth: what was finally judged in 1742 was not Ricci's tentative approach of a 150 years earlier, but its apparently wayward evolution. Lactantius had already received Hermes Trismegistus into the Church in the fourth century, and it seemed superfluous for the Jesuits to admit him again the 18th, even under the Chinese name of Fu Hsi.

In short, much of what the Jesuits were advocating, though not new, seemed excessive, and Figurism is a reminder that religion is one of the strongest of all the intoxicants.

V

Towards the end of the century French Jesuits played into their enemies' hands, starting yet another battle, in the course of which the Sorbonne buried Confucius in unconsecrated ground, a free-thinker canonized him,[26] and the Jesuits 'invented' a new sin.[27] (55)

It all started with two new Jesuit publications. First came the *Confucius sinarum philosophus* (1687), edited by Fr Philip Couplet. This composition was prepared in the Canton detention centre by the Jesuit internees who worked on it so intensely that Fr-Visitor Gama feared they were harming their health. Clearly a labour of love, it was in a good cause, and 'we are convinced', wrote Fr. Rougemont, 'that this book will please Europe, Catholic and heretic alike'. But that proved over-optimistic.

Couplet seems to have regarded his work as a *Festschrift*, celebrating the Jesuits' entry into China a century earlier. His preface explains Ricci's policy: faced with an ancient, xenophobic and conservative people, how else could he hope to make them believe anything at first sight so incredible as a Man-God, and Him crucified? But the book goes farther, for it turned what had previously been a debate over ecclesiastical discipline and missionary methods into a controversy over doctrine and dogma. The Jesuits, however, were content with a flank attack, and there were no denunciations of '*frayles idiotas*'. Instead there was an apparently impartial account of Chinese religion. Yet underneath lay a disguised apologia for Jesuit strategy, and they were very satisfied with it. In January 1688, Fr La Chaize wrote to Verbiest that this would be the final solution to their problems. (56)

Though impressive, the book did not please everyone.[28] In Canton, discussing the composition of the work with Navarrete, Fr Gouveia grumbled that his colleagues were making a prophet of Confucius 'without sufficient vouchers'. Others too found the book audacious, believing that taken to its logical conclusions it would make Catholicism superfluous. No one was vulgar enough to say so, but the Jesuits seemed intent on putting themselves out of work. The modern Jesuit, Fr Damboriena, complains that Couplet's collaborators were 'obsessed by the wish to free the Chinese of all idolatry or superstition', and he regrets their use of 'language to which Ricci

---

[26] La Mothe le Vayer's '*Sancte Confuci, ora pro nobis*', was in the tradition of Marco Polo, who declared that had the Buddha been a Catholic he would be called 'saint'; as indeed was done when Cardinal Baronius unwittingly admitted him into the 1586 Martyrology as 'Saint Josaphat', and as such he is still venerated on his feast, Nov. 27 (*Polo*, ed. Yule-Cordier, II: 326–28).

[27] A Fr François Musnier (Dijon, 1686) maintained that no action was mortally sinful unless the agent was actually thinking of God at the moment of committing it (Kirk, 119).

[28] But it received a respectful review (which noted the troublesome discrepancy between the Chinese and Christian chronologies) in the Royal Society's *Philosophical Transactions* (1687), 376.

would not have subscribed. What that venerable pioneer put forward tentatively, Couplet was flatly stating to be without doubt, and parts of the work were exaggerated, if not heterodox'. Fr Couplet's enthusiasm is understandable, however, for he had already found the conversion of China predicted in Isaiah.[29] (57)

A still greater furor greeted the second publication, the *Nouveaux Mémoires sur la Chine* (1696) of Fr Le Comte. This work, in French as opposed to Couplet's Latin, brought China before a wider public, and helped to spread sinophilism throughout Europe. Its popularity was immediate and it rapidly went through three printings. But from the Jesuits' viewpoint, it proved unfortunate, for it gave still more weapons to their enemies. As a result of the consequent controversy the religion of China came to be closely associated with Deism, belief in a God but not in a revealed religion.

This was not apparent at first. The *Nouveaux Mémoires*, behind a modest facade, naturally made much of Jesuit achievements. But its main purpose was to describe the religion of the Chinese, and once again Ricci's qualifications were pushed aside in favour of certainty. The first emperor had sacrificed to the Almighty, the third emperor had built him a temple and 'although the temple in Judea was more magnificent, and was hallowed by the presence of our Redeemer, it was no little glory to China to have sacrificed to the Creator in the oldest temple in the world'. European readers were told, once more, that 'for two thousand years China had the knowledge of the true God, and practised the purest morality, while Europe and almost all the rest of the world were wallowing in error and corruption'. This, in other words, was the high-water mark of praise for Confucius. (58)

Some of Le Comte's certainties have embarrassed another modern Jesuit, Fr Bernard-Maitre, who laments 'how different all this is from the restraint and reservations of our pioneers in China'. Le Comte's contemporaries were more outspoken. Bossuet denounced the book to the Sorbonne, and a commission of inquiry was set up. The 160 members sat through the summer and autumn of 1700, holding 30 stormy sessions. Tensions were understandably high and some discussions ended in fisticuffs.

The Sorbonne condemned Le Comte's book as 'false, temerarious,[30] scandalous, erroneous and injurious to the Christian religion, rendering the Passion of Christ superfluous'. The decision, regarded as a triumph for the anti-Jesuit faction, finished off the 'Ancient Theology' in France, though not the publication of a flood of books on the subject. Bayle noted gleefully: 'At this time (I am writing in November 1700) all Europe is ringing with their

---

[29] In 1765 the *Confucius* converted an English cobbler who, capable of skipping Christmas dinner to afford a book, bought the *Morals of Confucius* which 'made a very deep and lasting impression on my mind' (James Lackington, *Memoirs* (London, 1791), 97). Navarrete would have been astounded to learn that four Spanish 'Confucianists' registered in the 1877 Spanish census (A. Machuca Diez, *Council of Trent* (Madrid, 1903), 551–553).

[30] 'Temerarious': a technical term meaning 'rash but not heretical'.

disputes. They accuse one another at Rome to the Congregation of Cardinals, and to the Sorbonne. Princes and authors are all in a ferment.'[31] Louis XIV banned all writing about the debate, but what could not be published in Paris could find a printer in Amsterdam. There were other ways of avoiding the censor: Bayle took flight down a bewildering rabbit-warren of footnotes; and Diderot's subterfuges included the wickedly effective use of ironical cross-reference. For the rest of the century free-thinkers taunted the orthodox with the 'argument from the Chinese', who apparently were so good and happy that Christianity was unnecessary for them. (59)

Those busily condemning Le Comte failed to notice that many of his propositions were also presented by Navarrete who was equally entranced by Confucius's 'Catholic' precepts, but had learnt that it was unwise to cite them in sermons, as it were.[32] (60)

The Sorbonne theologians feared the trends they saw spreading about them, for, even as they debated, Thomas Hyde in Oxford was conferring the status of Chosen People upon the primitive Persians, as Le Comte had done for the ancient Chinese.[33] This meant robbing the Jews of their unique privilege of alone having known the one true God. The pious soon began enquiring whether all the ancients were to be converted into Chosen Peoples, and whether the Church was to become all things to all gods? Other conclusions were being drawn, and Leibniz declared that 'it seems to me that we need missionaries from the Chinese who might teach us the use and practice of natural theology just as we have sent them teachers of true theology'.[34] (61)

Ironically, then, missionaries who started out to convert the heathen ended by undermining Religion at home. Navarrete himself does not escape, and his work was sometimes quoted against himself. Matthew Tindal's *Christianity as Old as the Creation* (1730), the 'Deists' bible', denounced the idea of a God granting the truth only to Jews and Christians, thereby damning millions of morally superior Chinese: 'Navarrete, a Chinese missionary, agrees with Leibniz and says that 'It is God's special Providence that the Chinese did not know what is done in Christendom, for if they did, they'd spit in our faces'.[35] (62)

---

[31] Yet the ever-cheerful Fr Arxo told the Aveiro duchess it was all a lark: *'parece esto una comedia'* (Ms. owned by C. R. Boxer); and so too did Navarrete, *'entremes parece'*, NC 239.

[32] Some Jesuits had done so until they found that converts took it as evidence that Christianity had to turn to him for examples.

[33] 'Fr Le Comte, who has been blamed for asserting that the true religion has lasted in China for ages, will find an assistant in this learned Oxford Professor's *History of the Persians*' (Bayle, *Dict.*, 'Zoroaster', note 'G').

[34] A wish now fulfilled. As Jesuits were accused of smuggling Catholicism, cloaked with Renaissance science, into China, so Transcendental Meditation, proposed as a species of mental hygiene and psychological welfare, has been denounced as veiled Hinduism.

[35] Navarrete's most celebrated remark is still repeated (L. Stephen, *History of English Thought in the Eighteenth Century* (London, 1963), I: 144).

However, there was no great danger of that. The missionaries tried to prevent the Chinese from learning about the darker side of life in Europe. Navarrete had wondered what would happen if they heard of the wars, revolutions and treacheries of Christendom, and Fr Giulio Aleni tried to make sure they did not. His geography for Chinese readers suppressed any disturbing references. The life and ascension of Christ were included, but not the crucifixion; Europe was shown as prosperous, socially stable, and morally superior and 'This idealized world appealed to many disillusioned Ming literati as the alternative for which they were searching'. (63)

It was less easy to hide the truth at home in Europe, where religious folk suspected the thin edge of a dangerous wedge. Reaction spread, and in 1721 Christian Wolff, 'the model German professor', after lecturing on the high ethical character of the Chinese was obliged to flee Halle, suffering persecution for Confucius's sake. Elsewhere too, embarrassed Christians doubted the missionaries' veracity. 'Have we been given Chinese Tales without sufficient vouchers?' asked John Wesley who was displeased by 'the whole laboured panegyric on the Chinese and the Peruvians. Is it not a blow at the root of Christianity, insinuating all along that there are no Christians in the world so virtuous as these Heathens?' There seemed no end to it, and in his journal for April 1778 he wondered 'Oh, when will even the Methodists learn not to exaggerate?' Ten years later, reading Ely Bates's *Chinese Fragment*, for which Navarrete was a main source, Wesley was still unimpressed, dismissing the *Fragment* ('that odd book') and, as for the Chinese, 'I account the contrasting them with the Christians, to be a mere pious fraud'. He added, 'Father du Halde's word I will not take for a straw'. By then it was too late. (64)

VI

Chinese-inspired fantasies were not limited to theological speculation, for the controversies served other, unintended, purposes. In the words of Etienne de Silhouette, 'they gave rise in the minds of everyone to a desire to know China', and not only introduced Europe to the religious and philosophical exoticism of the Middle Kingdom but widened horizons generally in art, architecture, agriculture, economics, geography and science. Above all they made a lasting impact on the study of history and languages. Serious Sinological research dates from this period.[36]

In 1681 it was still possible for Bossuet to write a 'universal history', limited to Europe and the Mediterranean world. Less than a century later, China was 'better known than some provinces in Europe'. John Evelyn heard a sermon in St Martins-in-the Fields where the preacher denounced those foolish moderns who were ever 'curious to know the places, cittys, rivers and geography of China, whilst ignorant of their owne Country'. In 1700, while the Sorbonne was coming to blows over Jesuit eulogies of Chinese virtue, a contemporary declared that 'everyone is forced to admire this people, as old as it is wise and as preeminent in religion as in wisdom'. So the missionaries' filtered presentation of China led to its acceptance as a moral and political model for the wider world, and permitted coded criticism of one's home government.

Travel literature had affected European thought from the first. The rediscovery of China enabled reformers (who previously had to urge the imitation of a legendary golden age) to show Europe that Paradise did still indeed exist. Just as Navarrete had urged reform upon Charles II of Spain, so a contemporary revealed to Charles II of England that a 'golden-mine of learning' was to be found in China, and urged him to follow the example of the ancient Chinese emperors and become 'religious, wise, victorious, beloved and reign happily to eternity, and your kingdoms will enjoy wealth and prosperity throughout the ages'. Charles of England took no more notice of this than did his namesake in Spain, though for different reasons. In France when Louis XV complained of the evils of the times, his chief minister replied that the country needed to be 'inoculated with the Chinese spirit', and it was to China that Quesnay and his physiocrats turned for a solution to contemporary economic problems.

Sinomania spread widely. Chinese-style kiosks, paintings, fans, porcelains, wall-papers, hangings, screens, became the rage. In England, a mistaken belief that the Chinese preferred 'beauty without order' brought about a revolution in gardening. Regular, geometrical gardening patterns (sometimes seen as a symptom of Deism, an act of co-creation with the

---

[36] T. H. Barrett's *Singular Listlessness* (London, 1989) gives an amusing account of the progress of English Sinological studies.

Divinity) were rejected in favour of what Sir William Chambers's *Dissertation on Oriental Gardening* (1772) described as 'the variety which causes astonishment and prevents a state of languor in the beholder', for it was believed that in Chinese gardens there was to be found 'the pleasing, the terrible, and the surprising . . . and nothing is forgot that can exhilarate the mind'. For a time this novel 'parkomania' became popular. Fashionable folk, bored with the linear formalism of their classical gardens, took this escape route into a fantasy world thought more charming, rustic and natural, and designed in accordance with the (entirely fictitious) principles of Chinese *sharawadgi*. (65)

The Chinese virus affected both the Americas. Thomas Jefferson joined the chorus: 'I would wish our States to practise neither commerce nor navigation, but to stand, with respect to Europe, precisely on the footing of China. We should thus avoid wars, and all our citizens would be husbandmen'. On his return home the first American envoy to Peking built a house near Philadelphia called 'China's Retreat', hired a Chinese coachman, and praised George Washington by comparing him to the paternal rulers of the Middle Kingdom. (66)

In north America admiration for China survived the end of the 18th century, but as trade with China increased, so too did antipathy towards its people, for the merchants seldom shared the missionaries' idealized view; instead they made China the scapegoat of the nations. Before long, travellers and traders were complaining that Europe had been misled. In 1794 the Dutch ambassador, Isaac Titsingh, indignant when the emperor sent him a 'dish with bits of game, looking like remnants of gnawed bones', found that the incident 'furnished conclusive proof of Chinese coarseness and lack of civilisation . . . From the reports with which the missionaries have deluded the world for a number of years, I had imagined a civilized and enlightened people. These were deeply rooted ideas and a kind of violence was necessary to eradicate them'. The reaction was understandable, for the later Manchu emperors differed from Navarrete's models and, in any case, by then much of Europe advocated not paternal monarchy, but liberty, equality and fraternity.

In England, too, complaints were heard. In 1758 a writer in the *Gentleman's Magazine* objected to 'those romantic accounts of the first emperors of China'. And a little earlier, a new programme was suggested in the London publication, *The World*: 'As the Chinese and Gothic spirit has begun to deform some of the finest streets in this capital . . . an anti-Chinese Society will be a more important institution in the world of the arts, than the anti-Gallican in that of politics'. In time China came to be condemned for the qualities that had once earned it praise, and Coleridge, for instance, saw it was nothing more than a 'permanency without progression'. (67)

In the formation of the Chinese cult, a preparation for Romanticism, Navarrete accidentally played some part, although he was dead by the time the movement was launched. His *Tratados*, translated or summarized in English, French, German and Italian, was widely known and appreciated at a time when travel and religion were the two most popular topics, and led to the *Collections of Voyages* by Churchill, and others. Louis Hennepin, the Franciscan author of *A New Discovery of a Vast Country in America* (London, 1698), declared that 'The World, tho' unjust in most cases, do however Justice to Travellers, and the Accounts of their Voyages meet, generally speaking, with a more favourable Reception than any other Performances. This is a kind of Reward to Travellers for the unspeakable Fatigues they have suffered'. Travel literature also served a double purpose, for as the editor of Fr Semedo's *History of China* (London, 1655) remarked, it 'happily united, with the truth of History, the delight of a Romance'. (68)

VII

The first partial translation of the *Tratados* allegedly appeared in the *Mercure Galant*, in November 1684.[37] In 1693 in Parma there appeared a brief, discreet summary, 'a work full of curious information, very learned and most useful to missionaries'. In 1704 an English translation of the complete work appeared as the first item in the Churchill brothers' *Collection of Voyages*. This was the result of pressure from John Locke, one of Navarrete's earliest admirers.[38] It is not known how he came across him, but in 1698 he was recommending the *Tratados* to his French correspondent, Nicholas Toinard, whose interests included travel and exploration. In August that year, Locke wrote urging him to translate Navarrete '*en langue chrestienne*'. He returned to the topic the following year: '*c'est un livre curieux, je serais bien aise de le voir traduit en François*'.

Another Englishman interested in Navarrete's writings was Francis Atterbury, Bishop of Rochester, who discussed the *Tratados* with Bishop Francis Gastrell of Chester, 'the Design of the book is so remarkable, that No body who had once seen it, could well forgett it: 'tis an account of the Antient Chinese Principles in matter of Religion, given by a Dominican Missionary, who understood the Language & their Books perfectly well, in order to show, that the Jesuits representations of their Doctrines were all false, and deceitfull; that the Antient Chinese had no true Notion of a Deity, and that their Philosophy was a Scheme of Atheism'. (69)

Thomas Astley included excerpts in his *New General Collection of Voyages* (London, 1746), on the grounds that the *Tratados* was one of the best of the friars' accounts. But he had none of the Churchills' detachment, and could not refrain from sniping at the author from the trenches of his editorial footnotes and carrying on a harrying action throughout such pages as he includes. When Domingo uncharitably remarked of a Dutch 'heretic' that 'he died and went to hell', Astley warns his readers that they can expect no better from 'a Dominican, who is of a more hellish Order, if possible, than the rest: Witness, the *Inquisition*, or Hell in Miniature, of which they are the Managers; and their Founder Dominic, (he should have been called *Demoniac*, for he was a Limb of the Devil)' (III: 512). In England, therefore, Navarrete was known, quoted, used (*Universal History*, 1759), and rated highly ('no man wrote better concerning the affairs of China', declared the English edition of Voltaire's *Essay on Manners*).

He is quoted on occasion in the *London Magazine* (1732, 1735), and the *Gentleman's Magazine* (1732) cited him as a witness against an allegation that adultery and sodomy were tolerated in China. The outraged writer declared that 'All creditable Accounts of China averr the contrary. Navarrete says

---

[37] I have been unable to see this version.
[38] He cites Navarrete twice in his *Essay on Human Understanding*.

"The Chinese so far excelled the Christians in all kinds of Moral Virtue, that the Jesuits were forced to conceal from them the Vices of us Christians" '.[39]

In France he was probably less well known than in England despite exploitation by Arnauld, mention by Bossuet, Voltaire, Quesnay, Rousselot de Surgy, and inclusion in Volume V of the *Histoire générale des voyages* of the Abbé Prévost d'Exiles. Fourmont (*Meditationes Sinicae*) and the *Biographie Universelle* quote Navarrete as one of the missionaries who did most to make China known. A partial translation, based on Prévost, appeared in German in Volume V (1749) of Schwab's *Allgemeine Historie der Reisen zu Wasser und Lande*, but long before that Leibniz had been obliged to Navarrete for rescuing and publishing the Longobardi treatise.

In his own country, Navarrete's work was scarcely known.[40] This is no surprise, for the Dominicans are notoriously indifferent to their own history, and the Spanish were formerly neglectful of their writers. Even among the publicity-conscious Jesuits, the Iberians are less known than their French and Italian brethren. The 19th-century Spanish writer Juan Valera regretted it: 'It's a shame that we Spaniards don't collect such books, and that no one devotes himself to study them. You'd never guess that St. Francis Xavier was a Spaniard, or Friar Navarrete either, though the latter was the first to give us a detailed account of the Chinese literati. Scaliger's words are always ringing in my ears, "The Portuguese have some pretensions to learning; but few Spaniards do" '. (70)

Seventeenth-century Iberians sometimes displayed less curiosity about foreign parts than did other Europeans.[41] The pious reader would remember uneasily that Navarrete had once been scrutinized by the Inquisition, and his praise of China would be regarded suspiciously by readers who knew the use made of it by the Church's enemies.[42] Navarrete's admiration for China offended many Spaniards (like Fr Cortés Osorio) who in their way were as proudly xenophobic as the Chinese themselves. And even at the height of the European *rêve chinois* some Iberians still regarded the Chinese as savages.

Since Spain never had more than a veneer of neo-classicism, there was not the same reaction against it there as elsewhere. The few Spanish pre-Romantics, seeking relief from neo-classical artistic restraints, turned not to the *goût chinois* but to the vogue of the 'Sentimental Moor', a theme linked to their own national history, and rich enough in exotic oriental overtones to

---

[39] But other travellers were shocked too: Protestant pastor Olof Toren, in 18th-century Canton, complained that Jesuit accounts had not warned him of the many homosexuals there: 'not choosing to discredit the nation' (P. Osbeck, *Voyage to China*, I (London, 1771), 238).
[40] An exception is Luis P. Alvarez y Tejero's *Reseña histórica de la China* (Madrid, 1857) which refers to Navarrete's *two* volumes, and quotes him, without acknowledgement.
[41] In 1678 Vieira complained that a Jesuit had arrived at the Portuguese court from Asia, and 'no one asked him a single question, even out of curiosity' (Vieira, *Cartas*, III: 324, 333).
[42] In the 1780s it was rumoured that Aranda, Charles III's chief minister, planned to engrave Confucius's name on the front of every Spanish church.

satisfy any craving for colour and relaxation, though there is one Spanish work, Forner's *Los Gramáticos, historia chinesca* (1782), which presents in oriental disguise an account of the author's parochial squabbles with fellow writers.

Historically the *Tratados* was significant. Until its publication, the 17th-century Jesuits had been considered the only authoritative writers on China. Navarrete's account was the first to break this cultural monopoly. As has been said, it was also to be the last important work on China written while the East was still within the Iberian sphere of influence. Had the *Tratados* been written 20 years earlier, it would have made a greater stir, but in 1676 it was too late to interest seriously an age already growing news-conscious, and it was soon replaced by the spate of French Jesuit literature, especially by du Halde and the 30 volumes of *Lettres édifiantes*, which swept the field and put previous accounts out of date. So that in the end, the Jesuits, who had fought hard and long to keep China as their mission monopoly, succeeded in doing so on paper if not in reality.

VIII

For many, the conversion of China remains one of the 'might-have-beens' of history, and they are quick to blame the friars for this failure. But the harsh truth is that both groups, Jesuits and friars, were destined to fail. The matter was summed up by an 18th-century Chinese emperor, 'In China, the teaching of the sages has always enlightened us. Who among us will destroy our dead parents' tablets, and discontinue sacrifices to their ancestors, and pay the same homage to the [Catholic] Lord of Heaven as they did to their own parents and ancestors? This is their first Commandment, yet it would be the first obstacle to our adopting it'.

Douglas Lancashire ponders whether Ricci's policy of 'completing Confucianism' by grafting Catholicism on to the Chinese tradition could have succeeded if there had been no rites controversy. He concludes that there were two major obstacles to Ricci's dream. Catholicism would have had to replace both Buddhism and Taoism; and it would also have had to influence Confucianism, which ultimately, Catholics would have to eliminate.

In human terms this was impossible, all the more so when the heralds of the Faith, the Jesuits, seemed to be yielding to the notorious syncretistic 'pull' of Chinese culture. Kenneth Scott Latourette agrees, 'it is by no means certain that had Rome taken the opposite position and sanctioned the Jesuit accommodation to Chinese culture Christianity would have made more headway'. Even Fr Pastor Gutiérrez admits that, praiseworthy though it might be, the Jesuits' policy brought dangers with it. René Laurentin has shown how Nestorian Christianity was impregnated with Buddhist, Taoist and Confucian elements, and Tridentine Catholicism could not hope to escape.

Owen Lattimore finds in politics a third example of this absorption and transformation of foreign teaching: the Chinese take-over of communism. In China Marxism-Leninism-Stalinism was reworked, suffered a sea change, and emerged as the 'Thought of Chairman Mao'. Lattimore goes on to ask this question, 'If Rome had accepted the Jesuit contention that the veneration of ancestors was not a pagan worship but an admissible respect for genealogy in a family-grouped civilization of high quality, would the outcome have been the Christianization of China in a desirable form, or the Sinization of Christianity to an unacceptable degree?' The unanswered question remains, but there is no doubt of the reply.

Blame for failure in China cannot be neatly apportioned. In any case, it seems as though the Middle Kingdom was beyond conversion except through revolution. The Chinese Rites Controversy was only a 17th-century version of an old phenomenon. The adaptation of Buddhism to Chinese taste has already been noticed, and sometimes the failure of the Nestorians is linked to the policy of accommodation:

Apparently the mistake made by the Nestorian preachers was that of being ashamed of their faith, and trying to recommend it merely as a branch of Buddhism. There is always a danger in Mission work, a temptation to soften down the edges of our faith, to represent it as what is already known; such a policy may avoid immediate difficulties, but afterwards it tends towards defeat; the Christianity which has conquered has been that which is urged with distinctness amounting to harshness. It seems as if the compromising nature of Nestorianism was the reason why, when Buddhism fell, it was entangled in that fall and then forgotten.[43]

In the rites controversy it is misleading to divide the parties into 'Europeanizers' and 'Sinicizers' *tout court*, for that makes a general problem merely provincial, and limits a situation which is both ancient and modern, and knows no boundaries. What is at issue is not the need for compromise, but the degree of that same compromise. The difficulty is to discern where accommodation slides into sycretism and at what point it leads to deformation of the Message.

In their imaginative gamble, the Jesuits staked all and lost everything. But their less adventurous opponents, the friars in particular, were aware that one can only relax one's grip after having taken hold, not before.

The problems of that mission were not peculiar to the time or place, then, for it was simply a variant of an ever recurring discussion in the Church: *aggiornamento*. To that extent the rites controversy continues.

---

[43] The Reverend Lord William Gascoyne-Cecil (in P. Y. Saeki, *The Nestorian Monument in China* (London, 1928), iii).

Epilogue: Death comes for the Archbishop

There's a cure for everything, except death.

— Spanish proverb

Friar Domingo does not reveal his reactions to his appointment as Archbishop-primate of Santo Domingo in the Caribbean, 'the American Mediterranean'. He would have found significance, and taken pleasure, in that having begun his career where his hero, Las Casas, had died, he was to end his days where Las Casas had started his life as a Dominican. The See had a distinguished history. Created by Julius II in 1511, it was described in 1669, 'The Archbishopric has a prelate's income of two thousand ducats, and a cathedral Chapter consisting of sixteen clerics. It has four bishoprics and two abbeys suffragan to it'. (1)

The reality proved different. By the 1670s Hispaniola was verging on ruin. The salary was academic, and clerical parlour gossip already knew the mitre was 'not coveted, because of its poverty'. As the empire spread westwards the island, from being the original centre point, had become a mere staging-post. Few colonists wanted to remain there as farmers while the Main offered the possibility of quick returns for no effort. Thomas Gage had summed up the the situation neatly but wrongly: 'there being no Jesuits in Hispaniola is a sign of no great treasure being there either'. It was difficult to maintain an adequate population, 'if a hundred men come from Spain, two hundred leave, with or without permission' and in 1679 Navarrete noted that 53 men left on one ship alone: 'By 1700 there will no Spaniards left'. (2)

During the early years of the 17th century the Spanish India Office was concerned by reports that the islanders on the north-western coast were secretly trading with foreigners. Anxious to put a stop to this, the Office took the extraordinary decision to evacuate the zone, whereupon French buccaneers moved in as squatters. This zone, eventually occupied by the

French as Saint-Domingue (Haiti), was recognized by the Spaniards in the Treaty of Ryswick (1697) and so the strategy of Ferdinand the Catholic, of Charles V and Philip II was undone: foreigners had established themselves within the empire.

Political blunders and economic decline were accompanied by other trials, and in 1666 a smallpox epidemic carried off so many that even a century later it was still talked of as the 'tragedy of the sixes'. In the next decade many townsfolk abandoned their homes and took to the backwoods rather than be seen in their poverty. Others lacked the energy or the vanity to leave, and were to be seen naked in the streets, 'like so many new Adams and Eves'. (3)

Spain supported the economy with an annual subsidy to pay resident officials and clergy. But this *situado*, on which they depended like so many remittance-men, arrived irregularly. In the decade 1660–69 it came only three times, with the result that by 1669 the soldiery, 'now barefoot', mutinied. (4)

Even the Church suffered. Navarrete's successor, Archbishop Carvajal, was plainspoken to the point of disrespect, 'read this letter slowly, and note what I say', he ordered one Minister, 'the churches here are shacks, hovels, dumps' and divine service there the most indecent he has seen anywhere. Usually the Church survived such crises, since the clergy's many acquisitions were neither unprotected in life, nor dispersed at death. The Santo Domingo Church had from the beginning represented the spiritual power of Spain in the Americas. This 'first See in the New World to send souls to Heaven' (said Navarrete proudly) had been favoured in its early days and been the recipient of the first relic in America: a fragment of the true cross. (With characteristic curiosity Navarrete was tempted to open the reliquary, to discover what tree the cross had been made from.) In the early days a series of cultured prelates turned the episcopal palace into an intellectual centre, and Paul III established a university there in 1538, entrusting it to the Dominicans.[1] (5)

Diocesan affairs had further deteriorated under Navarrete's quarrelsome and violent predecessor, Archbishop Juan Escalante. From time to time disturbing reports of his conduct reached the India Office which decided in 1677 to translate him, archbishop though he was, to the bishopric of Yucatán. (6)

The vacancy in the See coincided with a special conference in Madrid to discuss the island's problems. Repopulation was urgent, and it was decided to transport families there from the Canary Islands. Negro slaves were also to be imported. It was hoped that these regulations would ease the situation, but 'the remedy is to find good officials . . . they must be sought out'. (7)

The choice of Navarrete to replace the bullying Escalante is not surprising, for under Don John he had acquired powerful friends, and had enhanced his

---

[1] Inevitably this later became the cause of a dispute with the Jesuits: C. de Utrera, *Universidades . . . de la Isla Española* (Santo Domingo, 1932), 234.

reputation during the embarrassing scandal that followed the over-hasty arrest of Bishop Pallu. They also had his conscientious report on the activities of French spies in Santo Domingo, about which he had learned on his journey home to Europe.[2] (8)

On 29 March 1677 (as his *Controversias* was being handed over to the printer), Count Medellín, a man well disposed towards the Dominicans, proposed him as one of the statutory three names offered to the king for selection. On 5 May, the list came back with the the royal nomination: 'I name Friar Domingo Navarrete'. For the second time in his life Navarrete found himself offered a bishopric; and for the second time he refused the honour. He was following Bishop Palafox's advice: 'There's no greater folly than to accept a bishopric cheerfully'. This time, however, his objections were overruled and he had to accept (9).

The Spanish Jesuits saw the promotion as due to their enemies' machinations rather than to his worth. In Santo Domingo the local Jesuits received the news of his appointment with foreboding. His friends saw themselves deprived of an ally and Pallu, writing from Rome, warned his Paris Foreign Mission Society of their loss and urged them to make new arrangements for liaising with the Dominicans. In Madrid, certain tongues (no one knew whose) spread a rumour that he was fleeing the clutches of the Inquisition. Navarrete dismissed the gossip airily, explaining that his haste to leave had been in obedience to standing orders which required that priests promoted to colonial Sees should depart forthwith. Within a few days of acceptance he was petitioning, vainly, for his passage money. By 22 May he was on the road to Seville to speed up the formalities there, but there were delays at every stage, and he did not reach Santo Domingo until 20 September.[3] (10)

Any ideas about a peaceful and dignified future were quickly dissipated. For one thing, his predecessor was unwilling to leave, and went about the town giving himself the double style of 'Archbishop of Santo Domingo and bishop-elect of Yucatán'. A list of complaints against him was submitted to Navarrete: allegations that a royal grant of 1600 *pesos* for cathedral repairs had disappeared; misappropriation of two chalices for which he had paid only half the value, not in cash, but 'in wax so inferior that it harmed the mass-book, and in wine so far gone as to raise doubts about the validity of the masses where it was used'. When the nomination to his new diocese was received, he forced the canons to record their regret at the departure of their 'Good Shepherd', and made the lower clergy sign undated letters of

---

[2] He continued to be an ecclesiastical private eye: 'I've secretly investigated the number of troops here. At present there are 330 infantrymen divided into four companies and 39 artillerymen under a captain' (To the India Office, 4 April 1679: AGI, Santo Domingo 93).
[3] He was permitted an official 'companion' (Friar Joseph de San Juan) and a page. Unable to raise the fare, he travelled on charity in the *N. S. de Aranzazu*, in the Armada of the Windward Fleet commanded by Admiral Antonio de Astina.

recommendation, the contents of which, he explained, were not sufficiently important to require their reading them. (11)

A prelate given to such behaviour needs a forceful character, and Escalante was not lacking. When one of his canons attempted to remonstrate with him 'he reminded him of how one archbishop of Mexico had dealt with unsympathetic priests, some of whom lost their lives, others only their teeth'.[4] To emphasize the point, Escalante 'accompanied his words with unbecoming gestures, and expletives better deleted'. (12)

This situation called for tact. During his first three days in the island, Navarrete sent to Escalante asking permission to pay his respects, and begging his guidance. These overtures were received with hostility, and therefore on Saturday 25 September Navarrete decided on resolute action, sending his letters of presentation to the cathedral Chapter and taking formal possession of the See. (13)

No one dared to break the news to the bishop, who that same night sent menacing messages to Navarrete's lodgings, warning him not to attempt to take over. This was followed up at dawn by threats of penalties, censures and violence. This message was delivered by a party of six, who on their way met a priest whom they pinned against the wall, and, since he was unable to read, they forced him to listen to the decree. Apparently dissatisfied with his reception of this document they attempted to carry him off to the bishop's presence, a prospect which so terrified the prisoner that he struggled enough to escape. Rushing to the cathedral, he warned the dean and Chapter, then assembling for high mass. (14)

The Chapter then went in a body to the Dominican convent to report to Navarrete, and to the municipal president who tried to placate Escalante, whom he found muttering that 'he would give that friar a good hiding'. Ignoring this threat, Navarrete visited the bishop and made a number of concessions. Things settled down momentarily but suddenly a new storm arose, for Navarrete, unable to overlook the tangled state of the diocesan accounts, sent for the records. Escalante refused to surrender these, daring 'that friar' to come for them himself. (15)

Escalante had few supporters in Santo Domingo, but among them were the local Jesuits. Before Navarrete's arrival they had written a letter presenting the bishop's case for him, warmly praising his zeal in 'shepherding his flock with remarkable constancy, even though this zeal had only served to arouse the blind anger of his enemies . . . who had stoned his palace for many nights running'. Once again, the Jesuits and Navarrete found themselves in opposing camps, with stories to tell that in no way tallied. (16)

---

[4] A later archbishop of Mexico, quarrelling with a priest (the scholar Sigüenza y Góngora) struck him with his walking-stick, smashed his spectacles, covering his face with blood (Robles, *Diario*, 11 October 1692).

By October all was quiet. Escalante departed, accompanied by a heartfelt godspeed for their 'Right Reverend Father in Christ' from his relieved Chapter: 'Thank God we now find ourselves freed from all oppression, and consoled by the very different character of our new Archbishop Navarrete whose manner is reassuring in comparison with his predecessor's'. His arrival, accompanied only by a chaplain and a page-boy, reflected on Escalante, who had landed with a train of 21 attendants, many, by general agreement, of doubtful character.[5]

Not for the first time, Friar Domingo was welcomed by those who saw his arrival as 'a disposition of Providence and a cause of universal consolation', in the words of the island's royal attorney, reporting to the king on 4 October. For the moment, Navarrete was high in the favour of all, cleric and layman alike.

In view of later events it is interesting to note this enthusiasm and in particular the Chapter's grateful report to Madrid that their new Archbishop was 'of benign disposition, 'loving', 'peaceful', 'mild natured'. The report was confirmed by individual canons. (17)

---

[5] Escalante's end was dramatic, if we can believe the story that in 1681 he was poisoned by the Franciscans in his new diocese. His death certificate, however, records only that his death was violent.

II

To be poor was no novelty, and now, as Archbishop, he found himself little better off than in those days in Indonesia when he had been driven to steal food. Within months the Chapter was writing to the king on his behalf pleading that it was impossible for a prelate to live in fitting dignity on the small stipend.[6] Their new bishop was as poor as any unfortunate on the island. To see him saying his mass 'with only one candle on the altar brings tears to the eyes'. The church vestments were worn and torn, and some sets did not match in liturgical colours, so that a green chasuble might only have a red maniple. Sometimes mass could not be offered at all, for lack of hosts or wine. The municipality added their collective voice, warning the king that the day would come when no one would accept the See. As for Friar Domingo himself, they continued, during his first year he had had to sell his few possessions in order to support himself, and his chaplain had sold firewood to make ends meet. Most of the churches were in a state of disrepair and open to profanation by man and beast. The cathedral itself, little more than a shell with broken windows, had no carpets, bell, or even oil for a sanctuary lamp. At Candlemas there were no tapers, and it was the same in Holy Week, when imitation ones had to be concocted. And everywhere else, the story was the same. Inevitably he thought of China. He recalled the temples there 'how numerous, clean, beautifully adorned they are. I write this for our confusion and my own shame. I am powerless to remedy affairs, but helplessness is no consolation'. (18)

He had no possibility of collecting tithes and came to depend on the charity of better-off colleagues, such as his suffragan bishops. He showed some enterprise: since peacocks were plentiful in the west, near the town of Azua, he sent some as a present to the bishop of Caracas, and received in return flour and leather which he sold. In 1683 he summarized his poverty, 'I am still using the dogskin shoelaces with which I left Spain'. Yet poor as things were, no one was safe from plundering pirates. Frequently reports came that somewhere along the coast a wretched parish shack had been burnt, its pitiful 'treasure' rifled, his priests murdered. (19)

He may have felt inadequate but he was also restless, and at the first opportunity he embarked on a tour of the island. Travel over the rough, roadless terrain was not easy for a man nearing seventy, riding from town to town, always pressing on to a new destination, plucking and eating an orange without dismounting, since there was no time to rest. Leisure was a jewel he never had. (20)

By the end of the first year he had carried out a visitation of the dangerous western zone, much of it in the hands of the French buccaneers, and

---

[6] It was 2 000 ducats a year but did not arrive regularly. For comparison: in 1630 that of Jaén was 40 000 ducats, Pamplona 28 000, Cádiz, 12 000.

elsewhere great tracts of depopulated land were reverting to wilderness. And he travelled in the knowledge that at his next chapel he would find only a handful of souls, all with the same story of distress and want. (21)

His judgments were sometimes harsh. Much of the prevailing poverty was due to laziness, which he could never understand, 'he who goes through life with one hand resting on the other is not a man', he informed the king.[7] A year after his arrival he added, 'Every day I understand these people less . . . the poverty here comes from lack of desire to work'. The land itself was among the best anywhere, and needed only to be planted. The locals, who had 'the sea within their house as it were', were too idle to fish, some even demanding dispensations to eat meat on abstinence days. Poor as they were, the townsfolk still arranged frequent bullfights, until the king, reacting to Domingo's complaints, had them reduced to four per year.[8] Theatrical performances, however much he deplored them, continued 'usually as late as nine o'clock at night. No good can be expected of such gatherings'. Hand in hand with idleness went pride. Since 1625 it had become customary to celebrate mass after dark because 'some would rather miss Sunday mass than be seen in their rags, and so every holy day has its midnight mass, as though it were a perpetual Christmastide', said an earlier archbishop. (22)

On arrival Friar Domingo had begun a stream of letters to the king reporting on all aspects of local life, and since there was no formal postal service the letters were written in advance to await a ship to carry them to Spain.

Then, in 1681, after visiting the whole diocese he wrote a more formal *Relation of the Cities, Towns and other Places in the Island of Santo Domingo*, which has earned him a mention in the slim history of the colony's literature. This account gives population statistics and other detailed information, in particular on the island's defences which were in a poor state, the money for their upkeep having been misspent or misappropriated. 'They built a wretched bit of a fort near here. Common opinion is that it's unnecessary, majority opinion that it's useless, my own is that it's a hazard to ourselves. In my time I've seen many a fort, and examined them carefully, so I may be allowed to raise my voice in this matter'.

References in this work again show his wide reading: the chroniclers Bernal Diaz del Castillo, Agustín Dávila Padilla and Juan de Solórzano. His reading was surprisingly up-to-date, and he even quotes the 1681 edition of the *Code of Laws for the Government of the Indies* by which he clearly regulated his conduct as archbishop. (23)

He insisted that free trade was vital to counter smuggling. This economic

---

[7] Laziness, slowest vice to leave Pandora's box, finding no room in Europe, settled in America (Baltasar Gracián, *El Criticón*, ed. Romero-Navarro, I: 380).

[8] They could no longer afford the luxury of the earliest colonists, who amused themselves in the evenings by driving wild horses into the sea to watch the sharks devour them.

heresy shocked the India Office, anxious to protect the merchants of Seville, and the suggestion brought a royal rebuke, 'We are surprised at your proposal, especially as it comes from so zealous a prelate'. But economic problems were only one concern. There was, for instance, the state of the clergy. He had reported earlier on their illiteracy and 'great aversion to study . . . few ever look at a book'. (They might have retorted with Dr. Johnson that 'a man doubtful of his dinner is not much disposed to abstracted meditation or remote enquiries'.) Attempts to establish seminars in theology and competitions in literary subjects failed. Yet so calamitous was the shortage of priests that despite their incapacity, he had to tolerate them. In 1679, three out of the nine parishes in the island were vacant, and the remaining six were supplied by clerics who were 'reverend ministers only from necessity – it cuts me to the soul'. But there were limits. Two years later he was obliged to suspend certain clerics until they had first taken a course in moral theology. Earlier he suggested that Spain would be better off with 'fewer priests, and fewer hungry soldiers'. He knew that the 'Golden Age' was over, 'this present differs from the past as does the sitter from his portrait'. For all that, it is unusual to find an archbishop hoping to God that he would be required to ordain few, if any, priests. (24)

The clergy had other faults. Some cathedral canons were failing to declare additional income from personal stipends. When he reported this they objected strenuously, and before long he was complaining that he lacked the equipment necessary for his task: 'I have neither prison, shackles nor chains with which to remedy the faults in my clergy'. (25)

There were three orders of friars on the island, Dominicans, Franciscans, and Mecedarians. As was natural, he turned first to his own. Here he got the greatest shock of all, for the Dominicans were poorly educated and generally indifferent. Discovering that they were granting degrees to unqualified people, he promptly turned upon them, complaining to Madrid twice in 1679 that priests looking for a ready-made degree went to the Dominicans' university. It was quite unlike the Chinese whose 'examinations are rigorous, and circumspect in all particulars'. (26)

The Dominicans fought back but got no hearing in Madrid, or Rome either, for their master-general was firm in dealing with academic irregularities.[9] Friar Domingo got leave to apply for two more Dominicans as assistants, and in 1681 he petitioned for four more, men of 'maturity, piety and learning'. Before his death he was gratified to witness improvements: standards were higher and literary *actos* were being held. (27)

More surprising were his relations with the Jesuits who had only settled

---

[9] Seven years after his death, they were still justifying themselves. There was no attack on him, merely a catalogue of their good works as unpaid military and naval chaplains (some had been captured by pirates etc), and they also stressed their university work (Barcelona Univ. MS. 968/13, fols. 10, 15).

there in 1658, and were still not permanently established. News of his arrival had caused gloom and despondency but their fears were unfounded, for under Archbishop Navarrete a new and favourable chapter in their history was to open. (28)

At a glance he saw they were everything that his own Blackfriars were not. They were zealous, energetic, well-trained, exemplary in every way. As such he took them into his confidence. if not to his heart. They, reacting to the situation quickly, co-operated with him to the full. Like him, they also had assessed the situation on their arrival and reported back that the only efficient cleric they found there was a mulatto secular priest, 'a good theologian and preacher, and as unique in this as he is in his colour'.[10] With characteristic industry they began an Annual Letter from the island, attempting, more stylishly than Navarrete, to make sense of the place, 'reducing the measureless Polyphemus of Hispaniola into the small space of a clear, if brief, description'.(29)

Soon he found he could not manage without them and by November 1683 was writing to the king, 'It's true that I can't feel affection for them and I wouldn't die for them!' but 'I've often told you, Sire, how useful they are to this community'. He had lost, or put aside, all fear of Jesuit probabilism and laxity, for he went on 'I've entrusted the teaching of moral theology to them and they're doing it marvellously. With their preaching and continual hearing of confessions . . . they relieve me much in my work . . . In all conscience I'm bound to beg your majesty to grant them licence to establish a college; the whole city is deeply interested in this, because it is beholden to them. If your majesty concede this boon you will be doing a service to God our Lord. It is absolutely necessary that the Jesuits take charge of studies here. There is no other way. I'm looking to the common good, not to any love I bear the Society'. (30)

This was the burden of his letters and reports as year after year he praised the Jesuits' efficiency and energy, urging the king to see that they must stay there. In 1679 he appointed them to teach humanities and theology, and soon they were earning 'universal applause'. A confidential postscript ('This is in my own hand') repeats the old refrain. Many seculars are so illiterate that they cannot be trusted to administer the sacraments, but as always, the Jesuits are rallying round. Three of them alone do more than all the priests in the city, 'the Father Rector [Francisco Moreno] is never wanting in the work'. He made a point of always saying mass for them on St Ignatius's day. They realised what they owed him. Another report to headquarters, with some fine Livian flourishes, acknowledged their debt. '[He] treated us with extreme and singular kindness, and extraordinary charity. We had from him all the favours to be had from the most loving of Parents. His love for us and

---

[10] Tomás Rodríguez de Sosa, a former African slave who became a theologian and renowned preacher.

veneration towards our Society inspired him, so that he did nothing without our advice. He is anxious for us to open a college, and if his income were not such that he can scarcely support himself, he would finance this venture for us.' (31)

There was an extra irony here. The Jesuits' superiors on the mainland did not want them to stay in Santo Domingo, concluding, on the basis of earlier erroneous reports that they were not needed. The Father Provincial could never be persuaded otherwise, and he therefore repeatedly summoned the group back from the island. Navarrete as repeatedly fought to keep them there. It was a wholly unexpected tug-of-war and one that ten years before would have seemed unbelievable. (32)

In 1682 the governor informed him that the Jesuits, could no longer put off their superiors, and had applied for visas to leave. Navarrete in an impassioned memorandum expounded in detail the reasons why they must stay, concluding his appeal by urging the governor 'to use the gentlest possible means to dissuade the Fathers from their petition'. He appealed to them to reconsider their decision, claiming that if their general were aware of conditions in the colony he would order them to stay. (33)

Zeal or instability? Devotion to duty or erratic behaviour? Navarrete would have argued that he was being consistent, that he took the Fathers as he found them, that he would subordinate any institutional rivalry to the welfare of the Church. This was not the first time he had put broader issues first. In the Philippines he had protested at the removal of Jesuits from an area where they were doing excellent work and, notoriously, had praised them twice to the general, from Peking and Canton, though admittedly in the euphoria of common persecution.

Nor was he assuaging guilt for past accusations. The very letters of praise contained a confession that he could never love them. Moreover, at this same time he was planning a second edition of the *Tratados*, and composing his 'Ratificación', the final defence of his attitude in the rites controversy. Yet that final affirmation itself praised the Jesuits in Santo Domingo, as distinct from those he had known in China. This is remarkable when it is realised that the very Jesuit industry and tenacity he was lauding, were, he knew, elsewhere denouncing him to Rome, the Inquisition and even the Holy Roman Emperor.

'Hang a Jesuit and he'll take your rope!' True to that old Spanish saying, some critics twisted his words into a tacit withdrawal of his accusations against the Jesuits in China. Disingenuousness could hardly go farther. The two situations were entirely different. Archbishop Navarrete's diocese was half a world and a quarter of a century away from the mission field that Friar Navarrete had known in China. (34)

In the end, one suspects that his claim to take the Fathers as he found them was not without some truth. Occasional Jesuits thought the same. Fr Cahour, for instance, declared that Navarrete in Santo Domingo had shown 'a zeal for souls and a love for the Church which overcame every other sentiment in his apostolic heart'. (35)

That his mind was still held by China is amply documented. He could not have avoided it, for information from the mission continually reached him via Manila and Mexico. When he heard that Sarpetri had died at Easter 1683 he composed a generous obituary, claiming that he was an innocent whose soul had never been soiled by sin, which suggests he had been his confessor.

He also remained in touch with Pallu, and the controversy was kept fresh for him by reports of the Jesuits' continued manoeuvrings in Peking and Madrid. 1679 found him writing the 'Ratificación' and refuting, to his own satisfaction, the criticisms of Cortés Osorio.[11] Returning to the subject was no waste of time, 'if the wound's still open, good medicine cannot hurt; if healed, no harm's done'. (36)

These last unpublished writings have notes on flora and fauna (grapes, peacocks, and different types of mahogany). He does not stay in the island for his comparisons and recommendations: 'In Puerto Rico on my way here I saw yet another use made of the palm tree mentioned in my *Tratados*'. He then describes how to make a palm net into a sieve for straining cassava juice. Again, in Terra Firma he noted how the local Indians planted rice grain inside a sardine head for the necessary nourishment: 'This is like the Chinese, who plant rice inside a ball of pig hair'. (37)

However, there was little time for hobbies in Santo Domingo where there was work for a bench of bishops. There was as also much to do outside the ecclesiastical sphere, from the reforming of the hospitals to the founding of new towns.

The hospital of San Andrés, founded in 1512, had not been a success. It had a history of maladministration, and as a result rich endowments had been lost, but he soon arranged accommodation for eight persons. The second hospital San Nicolás, was in a worse state, and those who held the records refused to produce them. Two other local communities needed help, the black slaves, and the Canary Islanders brought in to re-populate the island. Friar Domingo found in them an outlet for his compassion. The Canary Islanders had been happy to escape the sufferings of their homeland, desolated by plagues, tropical storms and droughts. They were hardworking, reliable, honest and only wanted the opportunity to improve their lot. Yet when Navarrete reached Hispaniola he had to report that of the first hundred families sent there most had died, because they had been settled in an unhealthy area. Friar Domingo's last months of life were consoled by the sight of a new town being built for them. (38)

The black slaves raised more complex problems. They had replaced the

---

[11] The 'Ratificación', signed 5 May 1680, is in BNM Ms 7522. A report (1693) claims that another two autograph notebooks are in the Dominicans' Manila archive, and 'Far from withdrawing anything, he added more' (AOPM, vol. 275, fol. 91).

delicate aborigines who quickly died out after their first contact with the Spaniards, as a result of violence, overwork, but above all from unknown European diseases for which they had no natural immunity. These black replacements were brought in on such a scale that Santo Domingo was 'an image of Ethiopia'. Spanish treatment of them was severe, but conditions under the French may be judged by the large numbers who fled into the Spanish zone.[12]

On his arrival in the colony Friar Domingo made no distinction between French and Spanish slaves: 'It's a point of conscience to take care of slaves. The Chinese outdo Europeans in looking after the poor wretches both in sickness and in health'. (39)

Within his first few months he commandeered land for a new town for blacks and started what became San Lorenzo de los Minas.[13] He petitioned the king to provide for their education. By April 1679 he was reporting that he had 70 of them under his care. His worries were increased by the islanders who constantly shipped slaves off to the mainland for sale. Hardly a ship left without blacks, and, worse still, many of them were married men separated from their families. For Navarrete this was too much: 'this is a grievous matter', he complained to the king, 'ever since this came to my notice I have fought against it'. (40)

That same summer of 1679 found him fighting on this new front, demanding a royal protector for the blacks, as had been done for the Amerindians, 'without any Spaniard ever being allowed to interfere with them'. Letters, written every few months on the same theme, in time were rewarded. Orders came from Madrid that the refugees were to be left free and unmolested, so that by 1685 his black community numbered 150 adults. The action from Spain came late, and gratitude later still: a royal commendation of his concern was useless, for by then he was dead. (41)

During the first years he remained 'archbishop-elect', and not until 1682 did the papal fiat arrive from Rome. Then he had to find a bishop to consecrate him. Puerto Rico was near, but *sede vacante*; the next nearest was Santa Marta (in modern Colombia). Still he had to wait another year to raise the fare and to find a ship to take him. Early in 1683 he arranged to be consecrated in Santa Marta on 4 April by Bishop Diego de Baños y Sotomayor. The return journey lasted three months, and took its toll, for as soon as he arrived back in Hispaniola, in mid-summer, he fell seriously ill. (42)

By August, he was home again and busy once more. One of his first

---

[12] 'Monseigneur, I am reluctant to carry out your orders, for slaves are human beings, and should not be reduced to a state worse than that of cattle', protested the French governor to Colbert in 1672 (Mims, 322–3).

[13] His successor Archbishop Carvajal, a racist who would only ordain whites, wanted San Lorenzo destroyed, 'it consists of unteachable black barbarians' (1692).

achievements after his consecration was to hold a diocesan synod in accordance with India Office standing orders. The diocesan records were in such chaos that there was nothing to show if a previous synod had ever been held, so that though there had already been five, no one was aware of them. In November 1683 therefore Friar Domingo convened the sixth diocesan synod under the impression that it was the first. Its report was published later and, like much else connected with him, it aroused controversy, for it provided the first written evidence of the islanders' belief that Columbus was buried there. Friar Domingo himself accepted local belief: 'Columbus's bones lie in the presbytery in a lead casket according to ancient tradition'. (43)

During the Synod, Navarrete touched off another, more immediate, reaction when he remarked adversely upon certain local deviations in liturgical practice, ordering that in future universal Roman usage be followed. For him in Santo Domingo, as in China, conformity in ritual symbolized unity of thought, action and belief. Some of his new rules are revealing. Mass is not to last less than 15 minutes, nor more than 45, celebrants must not take snuff or smoke tobacco beforehand, and since mass at night is unavoidable, it must finish by eight o'clock.[14]

The cathedral canons were resentful, objecting that they were following custom, and they rejected ten of the synod's ordinances. Friar Domingo, obedient to his consecration oath that a bishop must perform his duties without fear or favour, dismissed their objections. In October 1685 he called a second synod. He referred the dispute to the India Office, who, two days before his death, decided in his favour. But in the end the Chapter triumphed. Taking advantage of his death they quietly buried the second synod along with their archbishop, and a conspiracy of silence saw to it that its rectifying clauses remained a dead letter, and unknown to the minor clergy. (44)

Initially, the canons had welcomed Navarrete as an escape from Escalante and were charmed by his humility, which they mistakenly attributed to weakness. When he showed his mettle they were indignant. They felt deceived, but rallied quickly, for Hispaniola had another tradition which was not common to universal Roman usage. This consisted in reducing its bishops to despair through psychological terrorism. Escalante had been obstinate, but in the end had been beaten. Others, less aggressive, had surrendered, sometimes beseeching the king to let them leave the diocese. Archbishop López Dávila, for instance, had begged that grace, twice in the same year. Navarrete's successor, Carvajal, made a more dramatic exit. In 1692 he was plotting a secret flight – in disguise – via Jamaica. That failed, and the following year he attempted escape from what was 'worse than captivity in the hands of the Moors of Algiers'. That too failed. In January

---

[14] Printed synod rulings, though commonly neglected, can often be a source of local social history.

1698, however, after lulling suspicions by making a series of apparently casual trips out of the city, he made off in a foreign ship which took him to France. From there he crossed into Spain, flatly refusing to return to his See and eventually resigning the mitre. (45)

In time Navarrete too felt the strain. In the first few months his relations with his Chapter were cordial and his reports optimistic: 'In the midst of many trials it is a consolation that there is peace, agreement and unity in the city'. One suspects that if this were so, it was because he held his hand.

The first clash between Navarrete and his canons came after he had disciplined a young but well-connected cleric for some giddy behaviour. There followed resentment, complaints, threats. He hastily warned the king to expect denunciations, and urged that they be ignored. He was right in his forecast, for the Chapter complained that he was excessively severe, and more so since his consecration: 'He has reduced the authority of your cathedral Chapter to such an extreme that the prebendaries can barely be distinguished from the lower clergy'. Nor was that all, for he was guilty of that most heinous of crimes in Spanish eyes: he was introducing novelties. When he walked in procession to the cathedral he was attended by more than one candle-bearer. This, they admitted, was in obedience to government standing orders, but it contravened local tradition.[15] Moreover, he had forbidden municipality members to wear their swords when taking communion, which was customary in Hispaniola.

But they found an excuse for him, ascribing his innovations and deviations to 'his lack of experience of the proper government and ceremonies of cathedral churches, for he was brought up as a friar in the Order of Preachers, and while still young went to the remote provinces of China where until 1671 he was an Apostolic Missionary'.

Perhaps they were weary of the strange enthusiasms of a tiresome old man, forever lauding China, 'the blessedest country that ever yet was seen'. This was their revenge. His proudest experience was an excuse for his shortcomings. Of this, however, he probably knew nothing, for the Chapter went on to ask the king not to mention their grievances in his reply. It would suffice to issue a decree in their favour which they could brandish to their bishop at some appropriate moment in the future.

There was another, understandable, grievance. He had bored them. Once, in another context, he had remarked 'It is towards China that all my thoughts are always bent. I cannot chose but return to it'. His very sermons were full of China, if we judge from his writings. Doubtless he had taken copies of his *Tratados* with him to his diocese to press upon his canons which may explain his early complaint about their reluctance 'to look at books'. The local Jesuits do not comment on it, but they too must have had to tolerate

---

[15] A custom observed for at least 40 years is given legal force in Canon Law, even if not expresssly codified (M. Davies, The *Liturgical Revolution* (Chumleigh, 1976), I: 69).

stories of their erring brothers in China, stories which they received politely, as from their bishop, though with incredulity as Jesuits. Even the soil of Hispaniola, rich as it was, could not compare with that of China, which reminded him of Deuteronomy's 'land of brooks of water, of fountains and springs, flowing forth in valleys and hills. A land of wheat and barley, and wines and fig trees and pomegranates, a land of olive trees and honey'. Admittedly, olive oil and vineyards were lacking in China, but there were 'a thousand other' compensations.

Friar Domingo, like all old, reminiscing travellers, ran the risk of becoming eccentric or boring. John Aubrey knew one of Raleigh's veterans who was sober, learned, even a good mathematician, yet if you happened to mention Guiana he would be strangely passionate and fall to mumbling of the brave designs of yesteryear. And James Howell's *Instructions* offered advice to those who had managed safely to 'hoyse [hoist] sayle and steere homewards'. They must beware lest 'all their talke is still Forraine, magnifying other Nations, and derogating from their own, nor can one hardly exchange three words with them at an Ordinary [inn] or elsewhere but presently they are t'other side of the Sea, commending the Wines of France, the Fruits of Italy or the Oyl and Sallets [salads] of Spaine relating strange wonders, and they usually present them to their Hearers though multiplying glasses', like those 'hyperbolizing Spaniards' who fetch tales back from China where everything is ten thousand this or ten thousand that. (46)

These, then, were his faults. They were almost flattering. Many a bishop would have sighed with relief that this was the worst a prosecuting Chapter could allege against him. And the India Office saw through their design, 'the Chapter's complaints against their prelate arise because he wished to make them attend choir, fulfil their obligations and do their duty'. The Office may have been swayed by the declarations of the island's governor, Andrés de Robles, and of the municipality, who reassured the king that Navarrete 'has not given the slightest cause for complaint to the city or to any person whatsoever . . . while he is here all will continue in quietness, on account of his gentleness, and the calmness of his Christian character'. That a bishop – even a colonial bishop – should have a Christian character might seem tautological, but in Madrid they knew otherwise, and valued the reassurances all the more. (47)

The Chapter thought him too scrupulous, but he himself feared he had been too easy-going: 'I've behaved with overmuch smoothness, the better to avoid grief; and I fly from disputes as much as possible, although for that very same reason a man finds himself entangled in them'. It was almost an epitaph. (48)

III

He was now an old man of 68, but his health was good. Nevertheless, sometimes it seemed impossible to continue. Before his consecration as archbishop, he made three separate appeals to be released from his appointment, claiming that he was unworthy of it: 'for me the best thing would be a friar's cell in which to die in peace and calm'. Later he again ordered his Madrid agent to negotiate his retirement, but the attempt failed. In November 1685, he wrote on his own account asking to be allowed to resign the See:

> With all humility I beg royal permission to return to my Cell so as to finish my life quietly, otherwise I shall die disconsolate here where daily I receive grief, where I had hoped for gratitude. I have fallen into disgrace with these people, and especially with my Chapter, only because of what your majesty can see in the two synods I convened. Nor does the progress made in the Church here work in my favour. With tears in my eyes, and on the knees of my heart, I beg you, Sire, to grant this favour. (49)

The king was not ungrateful but reliable servants were too few to be spared. They must continue working *en servicio de ambas Majestades* ('In the service of both Majesties: God's and our own'). As for Navarrete's trials, he was to regard them as 'fit rather to be despised than considered'. To hearten him, the royal letter ended with a note of gratitude for eight years' faithful service. (50)

The exhortation was unnecessary, the congratulations late. In January of the new year, 1686, two months after writing his appeal, he had set off on a pastoral visit to the town of Santiago. The journey of some 30 leagues was strenuous, and a few days after his arrival he was suddenly taken ill. The local hospital had only two beds, and there was no room for him, so he was lodged in the house of an old friend, Pedro Morel de Santa Cruz. There he was granted what the king could not spare: time to prepare for death. With characteristic obstinacy, he held out for a month but in the end was defeated. During the morning of February 16 he died. It was a Saturday, our Lady's Saturday, and in the words of that day's mass the priests throughout his diocese were – or should have been – praying, 'Grant, Lord, thy servant to enjoy the happiness of eternal life'. (51)

The body was dressed in full pontificals, and laid out in a coffin lined 'with China silk'. On his head was placed the mitre of the Indies, in his left hand his pastoral staff. At two o'clock in the afternoon the notary public, Joseph García Garses, came to do his duty, but since the cause of death eluded them, they recorded that he 'seems to have died naturally'. It was reminiscent of Fr Antônio Vieira's earlier verdict on Don John, 'he didn't die of any bodily illness, but of frustration of soul, worn out by work and anguish'. (52)

Long before, lying in the Swally Road, off the coast of India, he had written longingly in his diary, 'May Almighty God grant us a place to rest for a little while'. But leisure, the jewel he never had, was something that only death could grant — death, the cure for everything, even for itself.

There is no mention of his burial-place, for his exasperated canons refused to register his death in the cathedral records, or to acknowledge that he had been their Archbishop. Even his epitaph was not written till 1950, but the delay is compensated by a fulsomeness of 18th-century proportions. It reads, in part, 'Archbishop Friar Domingo Fernández Navarrete del Rosario, tireless prelate, co-founder of the cathedral, restorer of ecclesiastical disciple, rejuvenator of clerical studies, codifier of the duties of his Chapter and canons, he was diligent in stirring up the drowsy priests in the negro parishes — if only he had not been so opposed to the Immaculate Conception movement in our Lady's honour!' (53)

Friar Domingo, it will be seen, remained a loyal Dominican to the end.

References

The references listed below are presented in an abbreviated form. For full details, see the Bibliography, p. 304.

Chapter 1

1 Knowles, 'Portrait', 151–3; Tugwell, *Early Dominicans*.

2 Lemoine, 73–86; Knowles, *Pachomius*, 51.

3 Smalley, 'Novelty', 102; Knowles, *Religious Orders*, I: 150–61. On the Dominicans' tendency to theological conservatism: Ernst, OP., 145, and Borges, OFM., 163.

4 Hamilton, *Inquisition*, 37. Richards, *Sex, Dissidence and Damnation*, 53.

5 Hay, in Hamilton, C. D., I: 317.

6 Flew (ed.), s.v. 'Scholasticism'; Schurhammer, I: 170; Kristeller, 1–55; On the early decline in the friars' standards: Coulton, *Failure*.

7 Curtius, 553; Gibbon, *Vindication* (1779), 132; Purchas, I: 55; Cano, *De locis*, IX: 1, 2, 6, 7; XI: 6.

8 Alonso, 170.

9 Ledóchowski, 493.

10 Lemoine, 121–160.

11 Guibert, 393n.

12 Ledochowski, 850. On Jesuit obedience: Espinosa Polit; Arrupe, ISJ, V (1973), 241; Ribadeneyra, *Tratado*, ch. 25. On military sense: Schurhammer, I: 37, 463. On nuns: Ribadeneyra, *Tratado*, ch. 37; Ramière, *Compendium*, 461. On Dominican influence; Hsü.

13 Clancy, *Introduction*, 45–116; Mir, I: 423–4; Coemans, 327, 364, 375. Macaulay, *History*, II: 287–95; Lebégue, 'Les ballets', 325.

14   Cohen, 'Why', 245–46; Basset, ch. 9.

15   Wedgwood, 45; Fr Cordara quoted in Mir, II: 517.

16   Benedict XIV, ed. Heeckeren, II: 505.

17   Passman, 86. Terrien, *Historical Inquiry*; *Imago*, 649; Koch, 1759.

18   Mariana, *Obras* in BAE, XXXI: 597, 617; Cohen, 'Why' 247, 257; Brodrick, II: 42.

19   Cistercians: Southern, *Western Society*, 253–61; Edwards, *History Today*, 274.

20   Brodrick, II: 415; Quarrels: Camden Society, LVI, 1–62. Redondi on 'the Jesuits' marked vocation for cultural controversy', 169. Adam's rib: Domınguez Ortiz, *Sociedad*, II: 112.

21   Ledóchowski, 93, 245–5, 336, 578; ISJ, V (July 1973), 171.

22   Molina, *Concordia*, ed. Rabenech and Molina, *Concordia*, Pt IV, ed. Freddoso. General study: Zagzebzki, *Dilemma*.
On the Dominican side: Serry, *Historia congregationum*; Mortier, *Hist.*, VI; Aelred Whitacre, in Hastings *Encyc. Religion and Ethics*, 774–77.
On the Jesuit side: Meyere, *Historiae*; Bellarmine in Le Bachelet, 1–200; Schneemann; Astrain, IV;
Impartial accounts: Cayré's *Manual*, and Stewart's introduction to Pascal's *Letters*. Acosta in the 'Aids' affair: Mustapha; Molina in Browning's poetry: Verbrugge.

23   Anscombe, *Collected Papers*, II: vii. Mariana in BAE, XXXI: 599. Huerga, 'Escolástica', *Diccionario*; Fr Crehan, *Cath. Dict. Theology*, II: 304.

24   NC 238.

25   Serry, 303–4, 377; Bonet, 137; Stewart, 266; Mortier, VI: 93; Garrigou-Lagrange, 83; AFP, I (1931), 118; Astrain, IV: 385; Meyere, II: 372.

26   Wicks, 243.

27   Harnack, *Dogma*, VII: 109. For the 'probably probable': Lea, *Confession*, II: 334.

28   On probabilism: Mortier, VII: 176 ff; Pastor, XXXI: 246–52; Astrain, VI: 129 ff; *Enciclopedia cattolica*, X, 57–61; Ceyssens, *Bulletin*, XXXIII, 329–410; Pastine, *Caramuel*, 298–312; Bishop Kirk's *Conscience* quotes typical condemned propositions. A learned but hostile review of Jesuit casuistry in the *Quarterly Review* (1875) was answered in the *Month*. There is an impartial study in Jonsen & Toulmin. On probabilism and royal confessors: Lea, *Confession*, II: 447. Macaulay, *History*, II: 291.

29   On Tirso González: Mortier, VI: 183 ff; Pastor, XXXII: 624; Hoàng Manh Hiên, J.M.-M. OP, *Thyrse González et le Probabilisme*; Mabillon, *Corr.*, I: 60n; Hillenaar, ch. 3, passim. On Dominicans reject opportunism: Knowles, 'Portrait', 152.

30   Lea, *Inquisition*, III: 596–612.

31   Bellarmine in Le Bachelet, 626 ff; Kendrick, 71–86, 162; Canal, 142.

32   Bayle, *Dict., s. v.* 'Lugo'; Canal, 141; Serry, 635; Ford, I: 399.

33   Colín, I (Introducción): 238.

34   Domínguez Ortiz, *Golden Age*, 211; Domínguez Ortiz, *Sociedad*, II: 97–99; Serry, 635; Vranich, 'La guerra mariana'.

35   Kendrick, 90–92.

36   Mss: TCD, K3. 20, fols. 486–7; AGN, Inquisición 485: fols. 11–12; AOPM, vol. 353 (1635); Gage, 177; Carreño, 171, 183, 435–6; Schons, *Notes*, 26; Serry, 636; Ribadeneyra, *Tratado*, Preface fol. 3v, fols. 2, 61.

37   *Guia: Mss. da Ajuda*, II (Lisbon, 1973), 582; Muro Orejón, I: 241–2; Canal, 156; Domínguez Ortiz, *Sociedad*, II: 198.

38   AOPM, unclassified mss: 1649, 1688; Canal, 131; F. de Quevedo, *Verso*, (Madrid, 1943), 1506.
      NC 2, 13; Mortier, V: 314, 449; VII: 15, 83; Silva Rego, V: 177; Pastor, XXIV: 308, 364–5; Domínguez Ortiz, *Sociedad*, II: 112; Lapide, 186; Ramière, 460, 509; Ribadeneyra, *Epistolae*, II: 370; RHE, LXIX (1974), 764; ARSI, XLV (1976), 251–260; ISJ, VI (May, 1974), 136–7.

39   Mss: TCD, K3. 20, fol. 497v; AGN, Inquisición 1548: fols. 79, 87, 125; BNP, Mss. esp. 381: fol. 341; (Barcelona, San Cugat): Pastells Mss: LVI: fol. 92. Saint-Simon, *Memoirs*, I: 409; Murillo Velarde, *Historia*, 371. Santillana, 296, 320; Wedgwood 119, ISJ, V (May 1973), 130; BR, XXV: 246–50; XXVI: 61, 91; XXXVIII: 81 ff; L: 138–9; Thwaites, II: 413, 587; *Spectator* (ed. Bond), IV (Oxford, 1965), 449–453.

Chapter 2

1   Background: Lach, I (i), 30–48; and Needham, *Science*, I: 225 for early east-west contacts, and the connection between the crusades and the voyages of discovery. Bataillon, *Annuaire* (1951), 257; Pinot, 18; Etiemble, 67; Dawson, *Mongol*, 222.

2   *Gentleman's Magazine*, XL (1770), 68.

3   Harris, *Mission*, 82–5.

4   Chinese view of Ricci: Franke, *Studia Sino-Altaica*, 72–5; *Chinese Recorder*, XX (1889), 82. On Ricci's perfect Chinese: Needham, *Science*, I: 149; Harris, *Mission*, 40, 43, 47.

5   D'Elia, *Fonti Ricciane*, I, 369; Schall, *Hist. Rel.*, 7; Ambrosini, 290; Verbiest, *Corr.*, 442.

6   Xavier's unhappy choice of a Japanese term for 'God': Elison, 33, 36, 401–2; Bernard–Maitre, *Hist.*, II: 30–31 and 'Dossier', 54.

7   Bernard-Maitre, *Concilium*, 43–44; *Hist.*, II: 331, and 'Dossier', 38; Dehergne, *Répertoire*, 328–9.

8   AOPM, vol. 87, fol. 30v; and *ibid.* Unclass. mss: Lubelli SJ, letter of 1681.

9   Rosso, 65.

10 ARSI, JapSin 112, fols. 3–4 and 162, fol. 41. AOPM, vol 6: Court of enquiry evidence (Manila, 1649); Furtado (to Vitelleschi) *Informatio*, 16. NC 40–50, 79, 155, 182, 232, 288, 363, 433, 464–66, 485, 507, 510–11. Metzler, I (i), (Rome, 1971), 181; Verricelli, 30–37; Tapia, II: 27–32; D'Elia, *Fonti Ricciane*, II: 225n; Gernet, *Chine*, 81; Ohm, 86; Streit, V: 826–7; Maggs's Cat. 455, 20.

11 AOPM vols. 6, 8. NC 66, 425, 479, 542, 543, 546; *Morale pratique* (1716), VII: 62–3; Semedo, pref.; Candidus, *Tuba magna* (1713), 78; Biermann, 17, 27; D'Elia, *Fonti Ricciane*, I: 232; II: 637; SinFran II, 320; III: 91; AFH IV (1911): 35–6, 495–6; VIII: 588–89; AIA, XX–XXIII (1918), 130–31. On Friar Ignacio de Loyola, See Tellechea Idígoras in *Salmanticensis*.

12 Díaz, 739; Ocio y Viana, 33.

13 Purchas, V: 586; Pascal, *Letter No. XI.*

14 Ledóchowski, 717. Bernard-Maitre, *Aux portes*, 104–5; Boxer, *Race*, 22.

15 NC 168, 408, 516; Bernard-Maitre, *Hist.*, II: 34; id. 'Dossier', 49–51; Rosso, 107–8; *Apologie des Dominicains*, 130–31; Ruthven, 7–8; Idema, 460.

16 Gutiérrez, 511–73; AFP IV (1911), 54–55.

17 Poor or rich converts: NC 53, 92, 116, 428; Acta Cong., 20; Elison, 65; Boxer, *Christian Century*, 235, 339; Pérez, *Cartas*, III: 2; Maas, I: 76–77.

18 AFH, IV: 52.

19 NC 46, 332, 446; AOPM, unclassified mss: Varo's letter of 5 December 1667 and Lubelli's 'Survey of the Rites Controversy', Macao, 24 April 1681. Bernard-Maitre, *Hist.*, III: 31 and 'Dossier', 39–52; D'Elia, *Fonti Ricciane*, I: 117; SinFran III: 402; Bontinck, 22–25, 60. Schall was doubtful about the rites in the beginning: Biermann, 174. Lobo: NC 84–5; AFH, VIII: 584–5.

20 NC 32, 400; Benavente, 'Itinerario', 363. Boxer, *Christian Century*, 234.

21 Apartheid in Japan: NC 447, 470; Boxer, *Christian Century*, 418.

22 NC 538; Voltaire, *Louis XIV*, chap. 39.

23 Biermann, *Anfänge*, 47, 151. NC 507. Gernet, *Impact*, 170, 283.

24 ARSI, JapSin 164, fols. 15, 56, 117; *Collectanea SCPF*, I (1622–1886), (Rome, 1907), 43; Codoin VI (Madrid, 1845), 178–80; Melo, 32; Gutiérrez, 519–20; Harris, *Mission*, 29–30, 49, 55, 70; Boxer, *Christian Century*, 241; Guibert, 285; Pandzic, 179, 193.

25 On the Portuguese *padroado*, see *New Cambridge Modern History*, V, 408 and background: 398–416. The 'Memento': Pérez, *Cartas*, III: 255; *Cartas selectas* 45, 75, 135–149.

26 Boxer, *Fidalgos*, 162.

27   Astrain, IV: 314.

28   Palafox, *Obras completas*, IV, 529.

29   Lo's warning: AGI, Fils 305: letter of 20 June 1683; Vieira in *Corpo Diplomatico Portuguez, Actos xiv*, ed. Freitas Moniz, 132; 'German Indies': *Mon. Historica. SJ.*, XXVII: 214–5; Ricci's dream-vision: NT 3; Zeuli, 64.

30   Lewis, *Missionaries*, 105–7; Farmer, *Technology transfer*, 1–21.

31   D'Elia, *Fonti Ricciane*, II: 315.

Chapter 3

1   ARSI, JapSin 163, 9.

2   AGI, Fils 86; SinFran VII (i): 94; Cordier, II: 869–70.

3   NC 150, 165, 335–37; Intorcetta, *De cultu*, 178, 223, 297, 303. Bernard-Maitre, 'Dossier', 51.

4   CASA, 1070, fol. 2; AOPM, 58, fols. 129ff; 275, fols. 80–81; BNP, Mss. esp. 155, fol. 212; Biermann, *Anfänge*, 63–4.

5   APF, Acta 15: fols. 173, 328–9; 108, fol. 164; AOPM, 223: fol. 26; BL, Add. Mss. 16933, fols. 248–9; Fernández, *Dominicos*, 4–6; Bernard-Maitre, *Hist.*, II: 341, and 'Dossier', 52.

6   BL, Add. Mss. 16933, fol. 256; Piedad, 314.

7   APF, SRCG 108: fol. 161; 193: fol. 200. Acta 15: fol. 443. AOPM, 58: fols. 10–11, 130; 275: fols. 16–18. AGI, Fils 5, 81, 86; Contaduría: 373A, 373B; the unpublished 'Hechos' of Vittorio Riccio, chapters 31, 32; Pastells, IX: 30–31.

8   VAT, Proc. consist. 81: 228v. AHN, Clero 1118: 270. BL, Egerton 406: fol. 170. NT 436. NC 426. Carro, *La teología*, II, 380. Herrero, *China*, 8.

9   CASA, 1074: fol. 191. On the reputation of the Philippine province within the order: Juan de los Angeles's MS 'Historia', (AOPM, 305: fols. 416, 631). NT 290, NC, 426. Mortier, V: 30; BR, XLIV: 114. On the selection of recruits for the Philippines: Master-General Gillet OP, RHM, XVI (1939), 2 ff. On the concept of missionary vocation: Hillenaar, 23; NCE, IX: 920 and Eliade, XV: 294–6.

10   List of friars sailing: BR, XXXVII: 84–5; Biographical sketches: Ocio y Viana, 455–78; Nominal rolls, licences and other documentation: AGI, Fils 81; Fils 330A; Contratación 5539; Indiferente general 2873.

11   Benavente, 291–364; and Aduarte, 'True report of the difficulties': BR, XIV: 90–108.

12   NC 507.

13   On Cypriano: NC 12, 435. Aduarte, *Historia*, I: 66 for Friar Baltasar's gloomy diatribe.

14   On Palafox: Arteaga, *Una mitra*; Brading, 228–51; Israel, *Race, Class*, 202–47. On the Jesuit view: Pastor, **XXX**: 207–13. See also Hillenaar, 149, 175, 178.

15   BL, Add. Mss. 16, 933, fol. 260; CASA, 1074, fol. 127.
AOPM, Ms. 'Tratados' (17th century), fols. 42–47; APF, SRCG 145: fols. 297, 311; AGN, RC 52, fols. 153–4. For Morales, see Bernard-Maitre, 'Dossier', 52.

16   NC 332, 339, 468–9, 616, 665; Cummins, 'Palafox and China'.

17   APF, SRCG, 145, fol. 311; 193, fol. 209; Biermann, *Anfänge*, 85; Pastells, IX: No. 15761.

18   Brou, RHM, XI (1934), 202; Pastor, **XXXV**: 411; Mir, I: 321, II: 21. BR, **XXIV**: 267–71.

19   AOPM, 6: fol. 372; 58: fol. 123; 305: fols. 416, 631. BL, Add. Mss. 16933: fol. 229. APF, SRCG, 193: fol. 204. Biermann, *Anfänge* 85, 88.

20   Capillas: APF, SRCG 193: fol. 204; Santa Cruz, 172, 259. Tagalog studies: NT 306, 431; Colín, III: 718. Nominal roll of proficient friars: AGI, Fils 81. Navarrete as Notary Apostolic: AOPM, 570 (Libro de consejos de la provincia, at 20 Jan 1657). Dominicans' intellectual work in the Philippines (500 books before 1800, not including those published in Spain): BR, I: 78–9.

21   AOPM, VI: fol. 372. SinFran II: 380; III: 24–9, 75 ff; VII (i): 35–37. Maas, I, 24. Jesuits oppose friars entering China (1649–1662): MEP, mss. 423, fols. 137–47, and Fr Damboriena (133n) lists 20 Franciscan allegations of opposition.

22   Canevari's illness: SinFran II: 380. Santa Cruz (149–50) is sensible on 'scruples' [anxiety neurosis] and 'melancolía' [depression]. See also BR (XLIV: 83–5), Castro (217–8, 281), Costa (24–5), Basset (143), Ledóchowski (586). Salazar's life: Castleton, 'Domingo de Salazar'.

23   NT 113, 305, 331, 372, 426. NC 622.

24   Navarrete in Philippines: *Acta capitulorum*, 232, 243. Conditions in Manila: Riccio to Gen. OP (1649): APF, SRCG 193: fol. 210, and Ocio, 30.

25   Circular to the province 1689 (AOPM, Mss. sin clas.).

26   NR 12, 68. NT 314, 325, 377.

27   NT 307–33. Trials of missionaries' ship-board life: Plattner, *Jesuits go East*, 29, 58–61; survey in Standaert, 'Jesuit presence in China: statistical approach', *S-WCRJ*, XIII (1991), 4–17. Macao Dominicans: Hugo Brunt, *Journal of Oriental Studies*, IV (1957–8), 66.

28   Friar García (to Manila HQ), 29 Sept 1659, Mss. AOPM, Mss. sin clas. NC 328–9; *Collectanea*, 42; von Mosheim, *Memoirs*, 19; Mortier, VII: 282. Pastor, **XXXI**: 167–9; Chappoulie, I: 400; Biermann, *Anfänge*, 95; Brou, *Les Jésuites*, 360. Pascal and the Chinese rites: Pinot, 81. Martini's journey: H. Bosmans, RQS, LXX1 (1912), 211–12; his anti-Portuguese remarks in Macassar: Boxer, *Figueiredo*, 102–3; alleged Jesuit discontent with Martini's

decree: NC 319; though justified on grounds of probabilism: Intorcetta, *De cultu sinensi*, 312.

29   Navarrete's account of Macassar is of interest because there are comparatively few other accounts from the period but see also the papers in AGN, Inquisición 446: fols. 349–90, 525–603.

30   NR 6. NT 334. NC 22; Lubelli at AHN, Inquisición 4440. 13, fol. 16. SinFran III: 398.

31   ARSI, JapSin 162, fols. 35, 71. Aduarte, *Hist.* 414.

Chapter 4

1   For Navarrete's account of this period, see NT 330–43.

2   Boxer, *South China*, 14–15; NR 28. Negroes in Fukien: Boxer, *Church Militant*, 102.

3   'Plowmen speak like Courtiers': Knox, *Historical Relation*, 168.

4   Mendicant 'ignorance' of Chinese: Fr Magalhães to SJ general in ARSI, JapSin 162, fol. 56v. Jesuit praise of friars' linguistic abilities: Colín, I: 359 and for unusual Jesuit praise (possibly compatriotic) of Navarrete as sinologist: Heras, I: 409. On Manila sinology: Biermann, *Neue Zeitschrift*, VII, 18–23. BR, XXX: 234; XXXII: 30, 31; LII: 333. Manila language studies were relevant since the Philippine Chinese came from Fukien where the Dominicans were based, but Navarrete (NC 51) claimed to know both Mandarin and Fukienese. For Varo on Navarrete's knowledge of Chinese: CASA 1070, fol. 5; vol. 58, fol. 134 and AOPM, vol. 58, fol. 121. NC 55–6, 90, 102, (430 catalogues friars' Chinese publications). NC 430 finds some Jesuits were excellent sinologues. Sensible remarks on the Jesuits' Chinese: Vaeth, 243. Not all were equally accomplished: Fr António de Gouveia, a poor linguist, made up for that by cribbing Friar García's Chinese catechism and publishing it as his own work: Biermann, *Anfänge*, 210–12; NC 87, 181, 186, 245, 356–7, 390, 427, 430, 431. A Jesuit who learned his Chinese from a friar was Foucquet using Varo's *Methodus*. Official Spanish interest is signalled by Charles II's decreeing in 1698 that a school of Chinese studies be opened by the four relevant religious orders (SinFran, V: 363).

5   Salazar in Castleton, 137. On Jesuit study of Chinese in Macao: *Acta Cong.* 78.

6   Magalhães, *New History*, 77–8. NC 68, 87, 186. On modern Jesuit attitudes to Chinese studies: Ledóchowski, 688, 713–18.

7   Needham, *Science*, II: 458, 490.

8   Cranmer-Byng, 233–4 (slightly elided).

9   On convert scalp-collecting: Furtado, *Informatio antiquissima* I: 18 (Biermann, *Anfänge*, 188).

10   On the Chinese as atheists: NT 80; NC 147, 149, 153, 321. Needham, *Science*, II: 500, 581; Coronado in CASA, 1074, fol. 32.

11   Navarrete makes Lao Tzu rebuke the probabilism of the Jesuit 'noveleers' in NT 207. NC 275, 285, 318. Varo in BL Add. Mss. 16933: fols. 232, 247; Intorcetta, *De cultu*, 303.

12   Lubelli in AOPM vol. 58, fols. 161v–162r. Jesuit disunity: Varo to OP provincial (1667): AOPM vol. 28, fol. 83; NT 249, 250, 262, 279, 356; NC 20–22, 106, 116, 123, 129, 150, 162–66, 173, 249, 325–6, 517, and mss additions to NR 44r–44v, 51v.

13   NC 90, 186, 214, 424, 432. Simón: SinFran II: 171–2.

14   On the mendicants' American experience: Cummins, 'Two Methods'; and for the 'Chinese Rites Controversy' in South America: Duviols, 330.

15   Chan Wing-tsit, 193.

16   Allegations regarding syncretizing converts: NT 357, [cf NH, lxix]; and NT 82, 283, 286, 287, 340; NC 240, 347, 350, 387, 517, 530. On the Chinese converts' need to learn religious intolerance: Boin, *Itinerario*, VIII: 71. For the classical Catholic view of syncretism: McHugh-Callan, I: 823–4. On modern Catholic anxiety: *Puebla*, 86, 100.

17   Pollak, 78.

18   ARSI, JapSin 162, fol 35r. NC 39, 52, 292; Le Comte, *Memoirs* (1738), 46; Fr Thomas, *Carta circular*, 10; Focher, *Itinerarium*, 37; Schurhammer, II: 205; Godwin, *Kircher*, 10. Elison, 55; Maas, I, 68; Cammann, *China's Dragon Robes*. The friars' habit as symbol: Galbraith, 184.

19   Ripa, 128; D'Alembert, *Sur la Destruction* (1766), 199.

20   Varo on friars' policy change: BL Add. mss. 16933, fols 239, 248; SinFran III: 422–23, 491; Gutiérrez, 564. Schall in AFH, VIII: 589. Semedo, *History*, 246. On dangerous sea-travel as bait for Jesuit volunteers: Verbiest, 250–53 and Maldonado in Bosmans, *Analectes*, XXXVI, 59–60. Fu, I: 155; Masetti, *Lettere Edificanti*, 70. Magalhães: Annua 1641 (Ajuda 49–V–12/33).

21   Elison, *Deus*, 41. SinFran III: 433; VII (i), 141; AOPM vol 28 (letter of 5 Dec 1667); CASA 1074, fol. 33.

22   Letter of 14 Nov 1668: ARSI, JapSin 162; Caballero on ideal vocations: Pandzic, AFH, LXI, 194.

23   AOPM, vol. 305, fol. 437; ARSI, JapSin 162, fol. 57–60; Maas, II: 21; SinFran II: 484; III: 280, 282, 432, 478, 595; IV: 21–22. Verbiest, 242.

24   On Cobo: van der Loon, 2, 18–9. Muñoz as mathematician: San Cugat archive, Pastells transcripts LII: fols. 119–120; Aduarte, I: 129; Chirino on Rada: BR, XII: 179; Zaide, I: 183–204; Ribadeneira, 48. On friar-builders: Castro, 177; and engineers, Fernández, *Dominicos*, 134, 135, 182, 272, 343, 505, 671; on fencing-masters: Boxer, *Christian Century*, 235.

25   Rosso, 84, after Shryock, *Origins*.

26   Needham, *Science*, I: 243; II: 294, 351–59, 383–85, 496; III: 52, 114, 258,

379, 437, 447, 449, 450, 583; IV: 509; Needham, 'Roles', 13; Needham in Iyer, *Glass Curtain*, 280. Young, 183; Fu, I: 340; II: 589–90.

27   Maritain, *Peasant*, 54. Needham, *Science*, V (3), 225–7 (here elided), following the LEC. For Parennin profiting by earthquakes: Pfister, I: 510.

28   D'Elia, *Fonti Ricciane*, I: 182. Attiret and Castiglione: Sullivan, 67–77. Jesuits as 'honourable galley-slaves': Ripa in Rowbotham, 216. Gaubil in LEC, IV (1843), 87, and *Corr.*, (ed. Simon), 131. Gemelli-Careri in Churchill, *Voyages and Travels*, IV, 318.

29   For Verbiest: See Bosmans in RQS, 71 (1912), 232.

30   D'Elia, *Galileo*, a Jesuit self-defence. Needham, *Science*, III: 438–450; Schall in Sivin, *Isis*, LVI, 201–5; Santillana; Blackwell, *Galileo*, ch. VI.

31   NC 549. Duyvendak, *T'oung Pao*, XXXIX (1949–50), 193–4; Boxer, *Christian Century*, 204, 235, 359. Elison, 208. On role of metal tools in Spanish missionary success: A. Métraux, *Diogenes*, XXV (Spring, 1959), 28–40.

32   Castro, *Osario*, 162; Meersman, *Studia*, 148–9; SinFran II: 378–80 [a friar-medic attends the sick Fr Canevari]; III: 20, 22, 129, 133, 174, 196, 237; IV: 293, 444, 493; AIA, XXXIV–VII (1931–37), passim; BR, XXX: 202, 213, 214, 305; XXXI: 133, 208, 291; LV: 730. Pastrana, Ms. 11–2, fol. 29r.

33   NT 346; NC 54, 254, 534; SinFran III: 433, 478, 491–2, 535; IV: 276, 281; Visitor's complaint: Boxer, *Christian Century*, 479.

34   On curiosity as a mission-aid: Price, 567.

35   Acosta, *De procuranda*, II: 9/2.

36   ARSI, JapSin 162, fol. 1; BL, Add. Mss. 16933, fol. 236; Riccio: AROP, X: 2569; NC 53–4, 103, 289, 495. SinFran III: 172, 472; IV: 96, 266–67, 281, 405–6. On the Jesuit mission in late Ming Fukien: Zürcher in Vermeer, 417–57.

37   Varo in CASA 1074, fols. 291; NT 98, 342; NR fol. 15. Lo in Manila: BR XLII: 253. SinFran IV: 96, 268, 281, 405. Boxer, *Christian Century*, 460. Converts' lists of Christ's precepts neglected by Christians: Price, 125.

38   CASA, Ms. 1074, fol. 33. Boxer, *South China*, 286. NT 28, 98, 125, 192.

39   Based on Gernet (*Chine*, 240) and Lancashire (*Church History*, XXXVIII, 231–2). For Xavier's surprising harshness towards dead pagans' salvation: Schurhammer, IV: 445–6. Fr Lobo on condemned ancestors: AFH, VIII (1915), 584. Modern anxiety: on his conversion, Gerard Manley Hopkins asked 'Is my Anglican family damned?'

40   'Polygamy no sin' in early America: Friar Toribio de Motolinía, *Memoriales*, (Madrid, 1970), 146.

41   Navarrete on pagans' salvation and fate of Confucius: NC 173, 176, 194, 218–9, 381, 449–450; NR fol. 15.

42   Fu-an, north-west of Funing, founded by Juan Bautista Morales: 'it is the centre of our China mission' (Dehergne, 'Chrétientés', 32).

43   NT 341. Biermann, *Anfänge*, 77. AOPM, 'Ritos: tratados del siglo 17' (Friar Jacinto Gali). On 'face': Latourette, *Chinese*, 583–4.

44   NE fol. 47v.

45   *Documenta*, 119; González, *Varo*, 12–13.

46   Zürcher, 427, 429; T'ien Ju-k'ang, 100; on conversion through missionary tracts: Price, 382.

Chapter 5

1   Cortés Osorio, *Reparos*, 63–5.

2   Semedo, *Hist.*, 93. For Schall: Hummel, II: 890. Verbiest's defence of Schall's calendar work: *Corr.*, 41–103 (ARSI, JapSin 143, No. 8, fols. 161–79).

3   Schall, *Rel. Hist.*, 193–4 (Pih, 56). Magalhães's 'Tractatus' (1649) in ARSI, JapSin 142, No 14, fol. 2 *et seq*.

4   Schall, *Rel. Hist.*, 6–7, 101, 268–9; Pih, 101–9, 167, 184, 231; Needham, *Science*, III: 191; Rowbotham, 69–70.

5   Wakeman in Spence-Wills, 50. Spence, *Search*, 21–25. On Jesuit cannon-masters: Verbiest, 309–19; Wakeman, 77; Gernet, *Chine*, 88; Pih, 315. Needham, *Science*, V (3), 240–41; V (7), 55 quotes a sarcastic Isaac Vossius on ecclesiastical gunners; see also 394–5.

6   Ajuda 49/V/15, fol. 14r; ARSI, JapSin 142, No. 25; NC 63; Zürcher, 421–22; Pih, 76; Hummel, I: 37, 491.

7   NC 427; Hummel, I: 255–9; Wakeman, II: 929n; Dunne, 329; Fu, 12; Needham, *Science* III: 444. Pih, 330.

8   ARSI, JapSin 142, No 29. Fu, 447; Pfister, I: 172; Dunne, 329.

9   ARSI, JapSin 162, fols. 44, 55; NC 66.

10   ARSI, JapSin 142, Nos. 14, 20, 22, 32; JapSin 162, fol. 55v. Vaeth, 256; Pih, 81, 309.

11   ARSI, JapSin 142, No. 11, fols. 44–5; JapSin 142, No. 14, fol. 11.

12   ARSI, JapSin 142, Nos. 11 and 12.

13   ARSI, JapSin 142, No. 32; Pih, 83, 314, 329; Fu, 16.

14   ARSI, JapSin 162, fol. 42–44; Pih, 83–5, 326, 330. Summary of the accusations, based on ARSI documents, in Pih, 353–57.

15   ARSI, JapSin 162, fol. 44, 58. Pih, 277–8; and for round-up see Pih, 319–48.

16   ARSI, JapSin 162, fol. 55, 59.

17   Vaeth, 251; NC 60, 134, 330, 432–3. Buglio's fears over the calendar-almanac

work: ARSI, JapSin 162, fols. 58, 59, but Riccio had already (1651) written to Propaganda (ARSI, Phils. II, fols. 259–80) mentioning 'another matter, though this isn't the place for it' (fol. 279). Philippine Jesuits' anxieties: ARSI, JapSin 142, No. 40.

18 ARSI, JapSin 162, fols. 55, 59, 63. Pih, 71–2, 96–7, 359–66.

19 ARSI, JapSin 142, Nos. 4, 20, 21, 29, 40, 45. Pih, 70, 95, 108, 264–5, 336.

20 Pih, 73, 80, 338; Fu, 13.

21 ARSI, JapSin 142, No 29; Vaeth, 260. Fu, 434.

22 Fu, 13. For Schall's last confession: *Etudes*, 88 (1901), 64–67, and *Zeitschrift für Katholische Theologie* XXV (1901), 332; ARSI, JapSin 142, fols. 231–2; Ajuda, Jes. na Asia 49-V-15, ff. 22-24; RAH, Leg. Jes 22, fols. 1–20.

23 Pih, 231. Verbiest, 351–2.

24 *Studies in the Spirituality of Jesuits*, V (1973), 40; and on the dangers of neglecting mental prayer: Ledóchowski, 403–4, 414.

25 Ch'ien Chung-shu, 138; Ranger, 119; Hinsch, 130–1.

26 Price, 287. The 'Silence extraordinaire': Thomas, 105, 112n.

27 On Yang Kuang-hsien, whose anti-Christian arguments survived into the 19th century: Gernet; Young; Cohen, *China*. Shun-chih's death: Schall, *Hist. Rel.*, 415.

28 Hummel, II: 890–91; Spence, *Emperor*, 72; Rowbotham, 84–85.

29 Pandzic, 182.

30 On prison conditions: Spence, *Woman Wang*, 134. On homosexuality in China: Hinsch; van Gulik; Wakeman; Meijer; and for its prevalence in Fukien: Idema, 460.

31 On the churches: Gouveia (1653) in ARSI, JapSin 162, fol. 2; Devine, *Four Churches*. On Peking in 1656: Baddeley, II: 147–50.

32 Fu, 38.

33 NC 234.

34 Pray, 67.

35 NC 63; Verbiest, 333. Yet in Peking Verbiest led him to think he favoured the friars' policy (NC 428).

36 NT 24, 348–53.

Chapter 6

1 For fuller details of the Canton detention: NH 229–45, 413–24. Pandzic, 193. 'More than fifty works': Varo, 'Breve respuesta a Brancato', AOPM, vol. 58: fol. 133v.

2 Magalhães's account of events in Peking is at RAH, Jesuitas leg. 22, fols. 204–209.

3 NC 260. The Dominicans still working were Varo, Verge, Riccio, García, Valle, and Lo.

4 NC 64, 246, 259, 260; NR 54–6.

5 NH 246–9.

6 NC 10, 396, 411, 621. Bontinck 108.

7 NH 216, 244. NC 351–2.

8 Varo, 5 Dec 1667 (AOPM, Unclass. mss). La Motte: NC 207, 284, 285.

9 NC 190–252.

10 NC 191, 193. Seventy years later the formula was still a concern: González, *Misiones* II, 77.

11 NC 221–6.

12 NC 39–40, 229–30. Against tampering with mass-rite and ritual: Wills, *Choirs*, 65; and on how the Church would never permit vernacular mass, see Jung, 'Transformation Symbolism in the Mass', *Works* (London, 1977), XI: 208–16.

13 NC 193.

14 NC 199.

15 NC 65, 68, 252, 367.

16 Detailed discussion of this episode in NH 413–424. ARSI, JapSin 109, fols. 126–7; *ibid.*, 162, fols. 297–8. Sarpetri's letter to Manila, 30 Sept 1670 (AOPM, unclassified mss) and Navarrete's *Certificatoria hecha en Roma,* in *Documenta,* original in BNP mss. esp. 155. Le Gobien, 272.

17 NC 330. For contradictory sworn evidence: Pih, 22–27; SinFran II: 281–2.

18 NC 323–38; Bernard-Maitre, 'Dossier', 57–8; *Classica Japonica* (Facsimile Series), I (1975), 192; Le Gobien, 275–322.

19 Cortés Osorio, *Reparos,* 90–1. NC 228, 279, 292, 329, 617, 650. SinFran II: 374. Costello, *Scholastic Curriculum,* 98. On Spanish gravity and silence as ploys to hide shaky Latin, and so escape Italian ridicule: Gil Fernández, *Panorama social,* 67 and *passim.* On the Spanish Jesuits' Latin: Sohier-Ceyssens, *Bulletin,* 48. On the Jesuits' twice-daily recreation periods: Ribadeneyra, *Tratado,* ch. 38.

20 NC 605, 617, 621.

21 Verbiest, 316.

22 ARSI, JapSin 162, fols. 207, 220. Sarpetri report: AOPM, vol. 87 fol. 29. Navarrete, confessor of Lubelli and Augery: NC 404; and of Rougemont: NE fol. 52r.

23   AHN, Inquisición 4440.13.

24   For melancholy as temperament, as illness, and in moral theology, see Klibansky, *Saturn and Melancholy*; also Tanqueray, *Spiritual Life*, appendix.

25   Gama, *Diary*, 114–15. ARSI, JapSin 162, fol. 210.

26   ARSI, JapSin 162, fols. 235, 239–40, 249–50, 278, 363.

27   ARSI, JapSin 162, fol. 298.

28   Yang's end was noted by the Jesuits: 'a few months later God struck him down with a fatal ulcer' (Couplet, 103).

29   Needham, *Science*, III: 173, 258–9.

30   *Ibid.*, 193.

31   ARSI, JapSin 162, fol. 269 (in Verbiest 130–53). Pih, 131, 220.

32   Pinot, 24.

33   NC 205; Bosmans, 'Verbiest', 233; Hummel, II: 891; Pfister, 342.

34   Biermann, *Anfänge*, 170n. Bernard-Maitre, 'Dossier', 47.

35   *Ibid.*, 58; Caballero on Longobardi, MEP, vol. 474, fols. 46, 75.

36   On Longobardi: Ferrari, in Intorcetta's *Testimonium*, 226; NT Tr. 5; Gernet on authenticity of text: *Chine*, 19, 49. Background: Rosso, 96–103.

37   NC 201, 331, 340, 344–5. Jesuit fears of Jansenism in the missions: Maggs's Catalogue 455 (1924), 66–67, 73.

38   BL, Add. Mss. 16,933, fol. 227. NC 344, 353, bis. Biermann, *Anfänge*, 118–128.

39   NC 366, 397; SinFran, II: 331, 606.

40   NE fols. 44–5. Sarpetri, letter of 1670 (AOPM, unclass. mss. and vol 87, fol. 44r). Friar del Valle dreamt Caballero's ghost came to him, saying 'Strike hard against those tablets!' ('Vida de fray Raimundo del Valle', AOPM, unclass. mss.).

41   NC 235, 357–8.

42   NC 250, 316, 358, 359, 361, 391.

43   NC 407 and cf. NT 445. NC 367.

44   NC 372, 373.

45   NC 19, 196, 368. NT, 160, 197.

46   NC 416 (in Rome, 15 Sept 1673).

47   Gama, *Diary*, II: 755.

48   'Convine con él en un acuerdo hasta tener resolución de nuestros padres': Biermann, *Anfänge*, 123.

49   'Gouveia insisted': NE fol. 44. González, *Misiones* I: 446.

50   Gouveia to the general (March, 1670): ARSI, JapSin 162, fols. 297–8.

51   NC 605; NT 352.

52   NC 360; NT 358.

53   NC 605.

54   ARSI, JapSin 162, fols. 164–5. CASA, 1074, fol. 290. On Sarpetri's evidence: his letter (30 Sept. 1670) in AOPM, unclassified mss. NC 61, 605–6.

55   AHN Inquisición 4440. 13; Dehergne, *Répertoire*, 129.

56   NT 358.

57   NC 370, 605; NT 352. Varo on the embassy: CASA 1074, fol. 299; and Wills, *Embassies*, 82–126.

58   Brancati in MEP, vol. 280, fol. 290.

59   ARSI, JapSin 162, fols. 297–8, 302. AHN Inquisición 4440.13.

60   Varo: CASA 1074, fol. 299. On adopting a Chinese name: Fu, *T'oung Pao*, XLIII (1955), 94.

61   Rougemont, *Hist. Tart.*, 304. Gama, *Diary*, II: 752.

62   NT 358; NC 604–10.

63   NR 47.

64   NT 351, 358; NC 624.

Chapter 7

1   NT 359. NC 473–4, 609. Duncanson, 166.

2   Boxer, *A propósito*, 17 and appendix.

3   NT 371.

4   Vieira, III: 179. For Needham's use of Navarrete on nautical science: *Science*, IV (3) *via* 876.

5   Letter of Juan Camacho OP, Manila, July 1670: MEP, vol. 121, fol. 256. NT 371, 422.

6   NT 377–9. Survey in Boxer, *India*.

7   NT 169, 380, 384–7.

8   IOL, Original Correspondence, 5 Mas. 41. EF (ns), II: 203. Clément, *Lettres de Colbert* III (ii), 418, 524, 753, 777. Makara on Japan: NC 35.

9   Conversions of Protestants in India: EF (ns), II: 166, 179.

10   NH 327.

11   Varo reported a sighting of Navarrete in Goa: CASA, 1074, fol. 291. 'Caron told me [about Japan] in Surat on 18 January 1671': NC 35.

12   NT 390–94. On the Madagascar mission see Metzler, I (ii), 515–46.

13   BNP, Mss. esp. 381: fol. 387. NT 399. NC 318. Pallu, *Lettres*, I: 35, 392; II: 36, 38, 48, 207. Pastor, XXX: 193–7; XXXI: 150–60; XXXIV: 76, 81.

14   Pallu, *Lettres*, I: 129. He also wrote about Navarrete to Wm. Leslie, Cardinal Barberini's Scottish chaplain: a copy in the Blairs College Archives, Scotland, differs slightly from the printed version.

15   Lo baptized 3 000 during the persecution, and managed to visit the internees in Canton (NC 30, 246); half a century later his work was remembered (González, *Misiones*, II: 23). By 1681 Pallu had a seminary with 18 boys and the Jesuits resolved to outdo him before any of his 'neomysti' reached ordination: Maldonado, AHEB, XXXVI (1910), 86; cf. ARSI, JapSin 163, fol. 5.

16   NE 44r; NC 109–37, 312, 327. Gernet, *Chine*, 48; Dehergne, *Répertoire*, 328. Bernard-Maitre, 'Dossier', 45–6, 60–61.

17   References to their conversations are scattered throughout NC 193–452. Pallu praises Navarrete: MEP, vol. 107, fols. 209–10; vol. 856, fol. 499 *et seq.* and BNP, Mss. esp. 381. Pallu, *Lettres*, I: 135, 206, II: 206–7, 350–52.

18   Navarrete to Lo: CASA 1074, fol. 298. NR 46r. Pallu, II: 37. MEP, 107, fols. 209–10.

19   NT 401–2.

20   IOL Orig. Corr. (1673), vol. 33, item 3681, fol. 15; NT 404; Gosse, *St Helena*.

21   NC 128; NH 434.

22   AROP, IV, 145, fol. 107; IV, 157, fol. 151. NT 391, 407–8; NC 602.

23   NT 408–9. Valencia as bandit-country: Newsletter (1676), BL, Harl. Mss. 4520, fol. 112v. Casey, *Valencia*.

24   NT 409. Pastor, XXXI: 433–5, 444–5, 470, 507. Forte, *Cardinal-Protectors*.

25   APF, Informationum lib. 118, fols. 34–51, 88–101; NT 465; NC 61–8, 96, 105, 333, 637; NE 45–6; NR 46; Bontinck, 130; Moreton, 149; Bernard-Maitre, 'Dossier', 60.

26   BL Add. Mss. 16933, fol. 257. NT 75–6, 245, 361, 501, 511, 513; NC 84, 414, 416. Pastor, XXXI: 410.

27   NT 466, 495, 505. Pinot, 79.

28   NC 102.

29   NT 493–505. Pastor XXXI: 478–9; *Corpo diplomatico Portuguez*, XV: 17, 83, 321; MEP, vol. V: fol. 293–4.

30   APF Acta, vol. 43: fol. 166. MEP vol. V: fol. 279. Vieira, II: 629.

31   APF Acta vol. 43, fol. 394–96; *Corpo diplomatico Portuguez*, XV: 294; NC 476. Frequent quotations from the Chinese Ritual submitted to Rome in NC 377–414.

32   Burnet, *Travels*, I: 245. Bayle, *Reflections*, 506. Pastor, XII: 75; Ledóchowski, 823; Daineville, 113. Mir, I: 326.

33   SinFran III: 44, 50; NC 51, 477; Fernández, *Historia*, 7; Santa Cruz, *Historia*, 424; Purchas, I: 56; Dawson, *Mongol Mission*, 228.

34   NT 438; NC 108, 658; Burnet, *Three Letters*, 130; Purchas, V: 586; Hennepin, ed. Thwaites, II: 584. For Japan: friar Juan Pobre in Indiana Library, Lilly Mss. BM 617, prologue. On the dangers of misleading volunteers: Acosta, *De procuranda*, ch. 1.

35   Dainville, 134. Maggs's Catalogue 455 (1924), i; Cepari, *Life of St Aloysius*, 39; Moorhouse, *Missionaries*, 190. Ledóchowski, 340, 683. For Von Moltke: Keegan, *Face of Battle*, 20.

36   NC 282; Pastrana ms., Sig. 11, fol. 29r; SinFran III: 319.

37   NT 432–3; NC 628, 653.

38   AROP, IV, 145, fols. 161, 302, 316. NT 410; NC 57, 645.

39   Masson, *Queen Christina*, 252–71.

40   APF, Acta (1673), fols. 115–6. NT 390, 394. Launay, *Documents*, 289–90. Ambrosini, 260.

41   BNM, Ms. 8512, fol. 221.

42   AROP, IV, 145, fols. 28, 132, 223, 248, 258, 263, 363. NT 95; NC 106.

43   Burnet, *Travels*, I: 244–45.

44   APF, Acta vols. 43, fols. 394–6; 44, fol. 3. Pastor, XXXI: 460.

45   AROP, IV 142, fols. 22, 296, 363.

46   NT 288. Guy, *Image*, 54. Bernard-Maitre, 'Dossier', 60–66. *Catholic Encyclopedia*, XIV: 96.

47   NR 8; NT 410.

Chapter 8

For background I have followed H. Kamen's *Spain in the Later Seventeenth Century 1665–1700* (London, 1980) which gives fuller details and references; also relevant for religious and social history is *Itinera M. de Arezzo per Hispaniam*, ed. D'Alatri (Rome, 1973).

1   NT 57; Boxer, *South China*, 248.

2   AROP, IV, 145, fols. 368, 409, 413, 456. VAT, Cons. Proc. 81: 231. NT 59, 408; NC 282, 601.

3   AHN, Clero 7634, fols. 124, 158, 164, 172. On Rocaberti: Mortier, VII: 103, 144, 151, 259. Riccio's ms: González, *Misionero diplomático*, 85.

4   AROP, IV 147: fols. 34, 47, 72. NC 273, 457. San Antonio, *Chronicas*, 2; Baltasar de Santa Cruz's prologue to San Agustín's *Conquistas* (1686). In 1688 the Dominican General ordered each province to appoint an historian (AOPM, Libro de consejos de provincia, 1621, fol. 21). León Pinelo's *Epitome* (1629), dedication and prol.

5   NT 91, 111, 226. For royal generosity to the friars' missions and a wish for chairs of Chinese language and institutions: Newberry Library, Phil. Ms. 1440, fols. 2-5; SinFran V: 363; VI: 14, 236, 237, 1354; Metzler, I (i), 388. Don John's interest in missions: Maggs's Catalogue. 442 (1923), 129. Vieira, II: 664.

6   Dolores Franco's *España como preocupación* (Madrid, 1960) is an anthology of texts. Contents of NC in NH cv-cvi, and Streit, V: 862-3. The lengthy Latin quotations in NC show it was aimed at a different audience from that of NT.

7   Núñez de Castro, 209. Varela Hervías, *Gazeta*. Vernet, 'Copernicus in Spain', 274. Ambassador Sandwich even found Spanish inventions judged to be worth taking to England, and he translated a technical treatise: A. A. Barba, *The Art of Mettals* (London, 1670) (Harris, *Life of Montague*, II: 153, 231-2).

8   Juanini's *Nueva physica* (1685) cites Robert Boyle and Copernicus, 2, 14, 51, 57. On the *novatores*: López, Forner, 41-54; and Maravall, *Cuadernos*, 28. Sta Teresa, *Libro de las fundaciones*, ch. 12.

9   Varela Hervias, xxviii-xxxv; Schulte, *Spanish Press*; Guinard, *La Presse espagnole*.

10   Lynch, II: 125-30.

11   For Rocroi, Lynch, II: 120.

12   Paul Rycaut's prologue to his *Critick* (London, 1681). He was owed £23 000; in 1654 Cromwell tried vainly to help him (Thurloe, *State Papers*, III: 75).

13   Stanhope, *Letters*, 138. Tizón, *La España borbónica*, 8.

14   NT prelims, 91; NR 67. For the emperors in NT: Philips, *Oriental History*.

15   Maverick, 12. Gregory Blue (personal communication) compares NH 146 with Le Comte, *Memoirs* (London, 1698), 242.

16   NT 107; BNM Ms. 18212, fol. 33; Codoin LXVII: 109; G. Maura Gamazo, *Supersticiones*, 204. Nicolini's Diary, *Rev. Hisp.*, vol. 67, 305.

17   NT 51, 97-8, 106, 108, 111-16, 124-7, 136, 143, 185-7, 231, 384-5, 428, 434-5; NC 640; NR 67.

18   NT 96, 105-6, 109, 124, 137, 158, 419.

19   NC 617. Royal confessors: Astrain, VII: ch. 6. Mir, II: 247, 648. Getino, 68-9. Lea, *Inquisition*, IV: 562-3. Vieira, III: 238. English confessors: Basset, *English Jesuits*, 266. See also Zürcher, 421.

20   Nidhard as Inquisitor: *Historia de la Inquisición en España y América* (Madrid, BAC, 1984), 1079–89. Lea, *Inquisition*, IV: 310–313, 498.

21   NT 63, 164. BNM Ms. 6590, fols. 66ff. Lafuente, *Historia*, XXVII: 30; Juderías, *España en tiempo de Carlos II*, 232–38; Michaud, *Louis XIV et Innocent XI*, I, 9; Sandwich in Harris, *Life of Montague*, II: 64.

22   Nidhard's 21-volumes of mss. memoirs: BNM 8344–64; Pastor, XXXI: 475, 516.

23   Nidhard as 'ambassadeur capon': Bayle's *Dict.*, 'Nidhard'. Sánchez Alonso, *Fuentes de la historia*, II, 368, 369, 413. Relevant letters: *Epistolario español* (BAE), 116–36. Vieira, II: 369, 384.

24   NT 115–6.

25   BNM, Ms. 18211, fol. 4. Codoin LXVII: 73, 99, 123. NT's dedication describes Don John as 'devoted to my order'. Spanish Jesuits in this period: Dominguez Ortiz, *La sociedad*, II: 69–83.

26   NC 595, 614; NR 41.

27   BNM, Ms. 18211; BL, Add. Mss. 10262, fols. 250–262; Codoin LXVII: 74; Díaz, 799; Schons, *Notes*, 35.

28   Codoin LXVII: 73, 84, 97.

29   BNM, Ms. 18211, fols. 7–9; Vieira, III, 290.

30   Pepys' *Diary*, July 1–2 1663; Vieira, III: 424; Juanini, *Carta a Francisco Redi*, 17–8.

31   BNM, 18211, fols. 9–10; AROP, IV 145, fol. 456; IV 147, fols. 72, 128, 222, and *ibid.*, letters of 13 July and 5 Oct 1675.

32   NT 184: 'Writing this in Canton'. NT 289: 'writing in Madagascar'. NC 139: diary-like entries: NT 169, 289–90. AROP IV, 147: fols. 222, 296

33   NT preliminaries, no pagination. On getting a book through the press: Cruickshank, 'Spanish book-production', 1–19; J. Simón Díaz, *El libro español antiguo*; Lea, *Inquisition*, III: 480–550.

34   NT 'Advertencias', no pag. NT 11, 18, 62, 140, 347. NC 97, 417, 612. NR fol. 44.

35   NT 394, 397; NC 139, 380.

36   AROP, IV, 145: fol. 456; IV, 147: fol. 296. NT 420; NR 44.

37   Meléndez, *Tesoros*, III: preface.

38   BR, XXXVII: 18; XXXVIII: 10; Fu, *T'oung Pao*, XLIII (1955), 78n. Twitchett, BSOAS, XXVII (1964). Boxer, personal communication. Leslie, *Essays*, 157. Needham, *Times Literary Supplement*, 19 July 1963, and for his use of Navarrete, especially in technology and civil engineering matters: *Science*, IV (3), 47, 148, 158, 311, 347, 423, 518–9, 537, 673.

39   NC 72, 284; NR 24, 48, 58.

40   NT 407; NC 284; NR 44, 65. Hamilton, *New Account*, I: 5; Raleigh in Hakluyt's *Voyages*, XII, 101. Navarrete's criticism of Colín on anthropological and geographical points: Retana, *Aparato*, I: 35.

41   NR 58. López Piñero, *Ciencia moderna en España*, passim.

42   Verbiest, *Corr.*, 117, 249–50.

43   'Lucky days': NC 92.

44   NT 14, 65; NC 180.

45   NT 38, 45, 388, 394; NC 71; NR 70.

46   AROP, IV 147, fols. 222, 269. NR 42–3. 'Prestigious bookshops': Ribas, no pag.

47   AHN, Inq., 4440. 13, fol. 2. Juanini, *Discurso físico y político*, 17v.

48   BNM, 18211, fol. 225. 'Jesuit's nib': Manucci, *Storia do Mogor*, III: 282.

Chapter 9

1   NC 591, 595, 597, 601.

2   Cortés, *Reparos*, 16, 20, 25, 27, 29, 37, 39, 47, 48, 49, 64, 71, 119. Cortés's combative character: Etreros (ed.), *Cortés Osorio*, 17–78, esp. 24.

3   Cortés, *Reparos*, 11, 15–16, 22, 37, 44, 46.

4   NC 640. Navarrete follows Las Casas: NT 'Advertencias', 115; NC 620.

5   Cortés, *Reparos*, Dedication, 11, 40.

6   NT 293, 296, 425; NC 107, 613, 617, 619–23, 636–38; NR 51, 73.

7   NC 613, 622.

8   NT 'Advertencias'. Cummins, 'Las Casas'.

9   NC (54, 62, 65, 66, 102, 330, 420, 426, 444, 607) refers to a third volume including an anthology of reports by friars expelled from China. Cordier, II: 33, 34. The Conde de la Viñaza (*Escritos*, 72) claimed the ms. was in the Minerva (Rome); and Retana believed he had once seen it without realizing what it was (*Catálogo*, 10). One modern Dominican historian knew its whereabouts but was unable to reveal it, presumably for ecumenical reasons or because of a promise. See also González, *Misiones*, V: 91.

10   AHN, Inq., 4440. 13, fol. 34 ff.

11   NT 398. AROP, IV 147, fols. 406, 500, and letter of 14 Nov 1676.

12   Steele, *Account of the RC Religion*, 77.

13   AHN, Inq., 4440.13, ff. 47, 54, 59. AROP, IV 147, 23 Jan 1677.

Improbably, jeering nicknames were forbidden by the Inquisition. Oliva's rebuke (10 July, 1676) in Bernard-Maitre, 'Dossier', 60.

14 AHN, Inq. 4440, 13, passim.

15 Pallu's arrest: APF, Acta 45 (1675): fol. 306; 47 (1677): fol. 180. Metzler, I (i): 388; AROP, IV 147, fol. 269; ARSI, JapSin 162, fols. 378–83, 389; AGI, Fils 305 (Navarrete's defence of Pallu). González, *Misiones*, I: 580–85, 687; Maggs's Catalogues, 442 (1923), III: 109, and 455 (1924), 79; BR, XXXIX: 215; XLII: 14, 136–40, 211–13; *Relations des missions*, 278–371. NC 103, 608, 625. Pallu, *Lettres*, I: 134, II: 44, 50.

16 AGI, Fils. 305 (letter of 11 July 1676). AROP, IV 147, fol. 269.

17 MEP, 6: fols. 402, 427; vol. 202: fol. 105. Pallu, *Lettres*, II: 96, 296, 358, 362.

18 NE, fol. 44.

19 CASA, 1074, fols. 290, 298–9. NC 101–2, 420. 468. SinFran III: 385, 398. Navarrete offers copies of material to interested readers (but this is still done: Dunne, 'Foreword').

20 NC 101, 419, 476; SinFran III: 75, 89, 100, 116, 139, 223–4; VII (i) 68. MEP, vol. 426, fol. 196.

21 Baltasar Navarrete in Arriaga, *Historia*, II: 482. NC 163, 363, 476, 657.

22 NC 106, 370, 418, 424. Pasquinades in Manila (1680): BR, XXXVIII: 8.

23 NC 359, 591, 621, 640.

24 NC 5, 39, 56, 63, 94, 189–91, 299, 403, 477, 649. AHN, Inq. 4440. 13, fols. 34 ff.

25 He hints that he is holding material back: NT 340, 352; NC 186, 330, 410; 476; NR 14, 68.

Chapter 10

1 Informers in Madrid: Codoin 67: 107.

2 The papers in the case are at AHN, Inquisición 4440, 13, which I follow throughout this chapter.

3 Vieira, III: 354. Suppression rumours: Sohier-Ceyssens, *Bulletin*, 63–4.

4 BNP Mss. esp. 155; Quétif-Echard, *Scriptores OP*, II: 723b. On Spanish Indexes 1551–1878, see Sierra Corella, *La censura*, 217–303; Defourneaux, *Inquisición y censura*, 33; Pardo Tomás, *Ciencia y censura*. Bernard-Maitre, 'Dossier', 60–61.

5 BNP, Mss. esp. 155; and see reference 9 to chapter IX above.

6 Montesquieu, *OC* (1950–55), II: 153, 171; see also Neveu, 5 (1977), 44–45.

7 Santillana, 155, 194, 233, 290.

8   Noronha, *A India portuguesa*, II, 260, 278. Not a uniquely Jesuit characteristic: Alexander VI would 'rather offend a great monarch than the least brother of the mendicant orders' (Erasmus, *Colloquies*, ed. Bailey, II (1878), 249, 298). Saint-Simon, II: 199.

9   Pascal, *Provincial Letters* No. VII. Some mendicants were nervous: 'anyone taking on the Jesuits needs Paciencia, Prudencia, Pesos, y Pasos', and must 'never be hopeful' (Augustinian procurator's report, Lilly Library, Indiana, Ms. 21533 (3), fols. 147–8). On Benedictine fear of the Jesuits: Mabillon, *Corr.*, II: 236.

10 ARSI, JapSin 163, fol. 9; AHN, Inq., 4440.13; MEP, v. 426: fol. 196, 239; APF, Lib. informationum 120 pro miss. sin. , II: fols. 22–31. BNM ms. 18,533 (6), fol. 1; Maggs's catalogue, 455 (1924), 28; Bernard-Maitre, 'Dossier', 28, 29. *Classica Japonica: sect. 8*, 29. For an allegation that Lubelli himself was no sinologue: CASA 1074, fol. 298. Jesuit approval of Navarrete as a judge of Chinese: Pfister, I: 160.

11 Verbiest, *Corr.*, 266–72, 280–342.

12 Bernard-Maitre, 'Dossier', 61; Brou, *Légende*, II: 55. Navarrete remembered (and hated): Lilly Library, Phillipps collection: OSA Ms letters II: 174–5 (I owe this ref. to Professor C. R. Boxer).

13 On lack of scruple in publishing: NC 7, quoting the Jesuit Lessius.

14 Brancati: MEP, 476: fol. 296. Locke, *Corr.*, VII: 299, 733.

15 Mesina: MEP, 426: fol. 196; Tolomei: BL Add. Mss. 26, 816, fol. 203b; Fénelon, *OC.*, VII (Paris, 1848), 559. Cordier, II: cols. 870–925.

16 AOPM, 87: fol. 1; 301: fols. 110–142. Unclass. mss: letter of Magino Ventallol, 3 Jan 1692.

17 AGN, Inquisición 531, fol. 265; APF, Informationum Lib. 134 pro miss. sinen., III: 89; MEP, 423, fol. 208; Murillo Velarde's attacks (*Geographia*, 14, 24) on Navarrete: Retana, *Aparato*, I; 150 and for bibliography of more recent quarrels over the rites: Pastor, XXIX: 249n.

18 NT 188; NC 265, 424.

19 Sebes, *Diary of Thomas Pereira*, 38; Fu, 114.

20 Jesuit views of Tournon: Pastor, XXXIII: 429–90; Rouleau in AHSJ, XXXI (1962), 264–323. Cf Pinot, 115. Rosso, 472. Impartial view in Latourette, III: 352–4. Arxo's letters to Aveiro (4, 11 and 22 Sept, 1709), property of C. R. Boxer.

21 *Trans. Asiatic Society of Japan*, IX (ii), (1881), 167. Pastor, XXXIII, 451.

22 Noel in Maggs's Catalogue, 455 (1923), 52. Verbiest, 163, 255, 442. Spence, *Emperor*, 72; Fu, 105.

23 Bernard-Maitre, *Dictionnaire*, XII: 736. Not all Jesuits agreed with the appeal to K'ang-hsi: Bernard-Maitre, *Concilium*, VII (3) (1967), 42–3.

24   Pastor, XXXIII: 412.

25   Spence, *Emperor*, 75.

26   One of the friars denounced was later martyred: Fernández Arias, 162–65. Porquet in González de San Pedro, 182.

27   Arxo letters property of C. R. Boxer; González de San Pedro, 278.

28   Banchieri letter in AOPM vol. 8: 'Tratados sobre ritos chinos'; Pastor, XXXIII: 455; Pinot, 121; SinFran V: 631, 643.

29   Benedict XIV, ed. Heeckeren, I: 386. Streit, VII: 158, 172, 175, 196. Pinot, 121. *Synopsis historiae*, col. 282. ISJ VI (May, 1974), 138.

30   Pinot, 129–31; Latourette, 354; Pastor, XXXIII: 460; Boxer, *Portuguese Seaborne Empire*, 240; Spence, *Emperor*, 81. Jesuit lobbying: Maggs's Catalogue, 455 (1924), 56.

31   Pinot, 99, 130, 180–81; Fernández Arias, 196–201. Guy, *Image*, 51.

32   Saint-Simon, II: 112; Pinot, 129–38; Pastor, XXXII: 219; González de S. Pedro, 19; Ceyssens, 'Unigenitus'; Charles, *Dossiers*, 338; Knox, *Enthusiasm*, 197. Hillenaar, 239–40; Brou, *Légende*, II: 90. For an example of Jesuit ability to argue their corner, see Verbiest, 196–207, questioning an order from his general.

33   Text of *Ex quo singulari* in Benedict XIV, *Opera*, XV: 216–30. Biermann, 150; Pastor, XXXV: 433–48; Boxer, *Fidalgos*, 168; González, *Misiones*, I, 297–319.

34   Pinot, 132.

35   Cummins, 'Suppression', 846.

36   Fernández Arias, 442, 455; P. Fernández, *Dominicos*, 228; González, *Misiones*, I: 93–4.

37   Rickaby, 79.

38   *Acta Apost. Sedis*, XXXII (1940), 24–26; Metzler, III (ii), 786. Bouscaren, *Canon Law Digest*, II, 367–8. Joy, 787–90; P. Gutiérrez, *Missionalia Hispanica*, III: 514. Brou, 'Le point final', *Etudes*, 275–77.

39   Rickaby, 77.

40   Benedict XIV, *Lettere*, ed. Morelli, II, passim. Bernard-Maitre 'La Correspondance Becker-Brucker', 424.

41   *Reponse*, 296; Pastor, XXXIV: 77; Pinot, 92, 120.

42   Arnauld, *Lettres*, VI: 12, 43, 50.

43   Ibid., 55, 540–47.

44   NT 92. NR fol. 46v. *Herder Correspondence* (Dec 1966), 376.

45   Bernard-Maitre, 'Dossier', 59–61; Maverick, 14; Rosso, 130; Pastor, XXXIII: 408; Jarry, XIX: 174; Brou, *Légende*, II: 56; DTC, II: 2372.

46   Guy, *Image*, 65–6; the best guide to the chronology problem is Pinot (Needham, *Science*, III: 173).

47   NT 4, 250; NC 224, 646; Cortés *Reparos*, 75; Pascal, *Pensées*, No. 397; Needham, *Grand Titration*, 252, 285; some Chinese, approaching modern hypotheses, put the age of the world at 97 million years (Needham, *Science*, III: 120); Pinot, 191, 227; Chadwick, *From Bossuet to Newman*, 77.

48   For religious-philosophical background: Kinsman, *Darker Vision*; Walker, *The Ancient Theology*; Seznec, *The Survival of the Pagan Gods*; Lynch, *Christ and Apollo*; Smalley, *Study of the Bible*. (Typology is found in hymns such as 'Lauda Sion' and 'Adoro te devote'.) Augustine's rules for figurative interpretation: *De doc. christiana*, III: 16. Figurism and modern science: R. Hooykaas, *Rheticus's Treatise*. French Jansenist Figurism: Kreiser, 246; Pastor, XXXIV: 450.

49   Manila commission of enquiry (1649) into Morales's theories: AOPM vol. 6; Martini, *Decas prima* (1658), 131, 366; Bouvet: Beckmann, 129, 132; Guy, *Image*, 76–8, 83; Pinot, 251–2, 347–67; America in the Bible: Luis de León, *Obras completas*, 440. Cf. Juan Pérez de Moya: *The Secret Philosophy*.

50   On the *I Ching*, see Needham, *Science*, II: 304ff, 672. For problems in interpreting the classics: Van Zoeren, *Poetry and Personality*.

51   Pfister, I: 550.

52   Damboriena, 143–149.

53   NT 185, 262; Gernet, *Chine*, 169.

54   Pinot, 251–2; Guy, *Image*, 331. On Ricci's 'perhaps', and the compromising of his probabilist stance by 'the fantastic ideas of Bouvet and others', see Bernard-Maitre, 'La Correspondance Becker-Brucker', 422, 424; idem, *Hist.*, II (1957): 331–32; and 'Dossier', 38. In agreement with him are Frs Gutiérrez, *Missionalia Hisp.*, III, 540, and Brou, *Revue d'histoire des Missions*, XI (1934), 188, and Dehergne, *Répertoire*, 328–9. On the other hand, see Fr D'Elia's sharp personal criticism of Bernard-Maitre in *Gregorianum*, XLIII (1962), 206, after which the latter seems to have been 'silenced' and to have written less on the rites: see Dehergne, *Bull.* LXIII, 467–81; and in AHSJ, XLIV (1975), 421–3.

55   Technical definition of 'the philosophical sin': Denzinger, 479; cf. Pastor, XXXII: 557; Lea, *Confession*, II: 256; and as the subject of French street-songs: Mabillon, *Corr.*, II: 219. Bouhours, *Sentiment*.

56   Couplet, *Confucius Sinarum Philosophus*, lx, lxxvii, lxxxii, lxxxix, 87, 105. For the Goa version: Boxer, 'Tentative Checklist', *Arquivos*, 567–99. Verbiest, *Corr.*, 549. Maggs's Catalogue, 455 (1924), vii–viii; Guy, *Image*, 99; Pinot, 88–9, 151; Needham, *Science*, II: 162, V (3), 223; Walker, 200; background in Maldonado, *Analectes*, 81; for its intellectual significance see two essays by

Lundbaek and Mungello, in *China Mission Studies*, III (1981) 2–22, and also Lundbaek in *Journal of History of Ideas*, XLIV (1983): 19–30.

57   NC 166. Damboriena, 144. Needham, *Science*, II: 163. Pinot, 158, 298. Bontinck, 220.

58   Le Comte, *Memoirs* (1737), 320. Lovejoy, *Essays*, 105. Pinot, 90–105. Glimpses of the turbulent background in Mabillon's *Corr.*, III: 109.

59   Bernard-Maitre, 'Dossier', 54; idem, *Concilium*, 42, and *Hist.*, II (1957) 171; Walker, 196–9; Guy, *Image*, 94; Damboriena, 144–5; Capéran, *Le problème du Salut des Infidèles*, 362–7; Delumeau, *Le Catholicisme*, 150; J. Davy, 'La Condamnation en Sorbonne des "Nouveaux Mémoires" ' in RSR, XXXVII (1950), 366–97; Bayle, *Dict.*, *s.v.* 'Milton'; Atkinson, *Relations*, 89–93.

60   NC, 49; Etiemble, 54 ff.

61   Needham, *Science*, II: 497, following Pinot.

62   NT, 98, 123, 342; Tindal, *Christianity*, 371–2.

63   Bernard Hung-Kay Luk, 'Aleni's *Chih-fang wai chi*', BSOAS, XL (1977), 58–84, and J. L. Mish in MS, XXIII (1964), 1–87; Zürcher, 426.

64   von Wolff, *Oratio*; Lovejoy, 108; Hazard, *European Thought*, 40.

65   'China as paradise of the present world': Astley, *Voyages*, vi; Vossius, *Observationes variae*, 85; Atkinson, *Extraordinary Voyage*, passim; Needham, *Science*, II: 361; Colton, 'Garden Art as Political Propaganda', *Eighteenth Century Studies*, 1–20; Sullivan, *Eastern and Western Art*, 108–15.

66   Goldstein, *Philadelphia and the China Trade*, 16–17, 94. South America: Mariluz Urquijo, 'La China', *Revista de Historia de América*, 98 (1984), 7–31.

67   Charles, *Les dossiers*, I: 86; Duyvendak, 'The Last Dutch Embassy', 1–137.

68   Hennepin, ed. Thwaites, II: 363; Arber, *Term Catalogues*, viii.

69   *Correspondence of John Locke*, ed. De Beer, VI, 463, 569, 603, 615, 731;. Locke saw the page-proofs of Churchills' *Voyages* ('in which is Naveretti') on 26 Feb 1703 (VII, 753). Harrison–Laslett, *Library of John Locke*, 28, 134.

70   Valera, *Obras completas*, III: 153.

Epilogue

1   Nunez de Castro, *Solo Madrid es corte*, 168, but cf. AGI, 5. Dgo. 3 where the salary is 6000 ducats; Eubel, *Hierarchia catholica*, V (1667–1730), 186; Utrera, I: 83, 88; Vazquez de Espinosa, 762; Vallellano, 79; Domínguez Ortiz, *Sociedad*, 268.

2   Depopulation: Navarrete to king: AGI, S. Domingo 93; NR 72. Decreasing

church finances: VAT, Proc. consist. 81.225, para 9, 'ab aliquibus annis'. Rodríguez Demorizi, 94, 110, 125. Gage to Cromwell: Thurloe, III: 60.

3   Rodríguez Demorizi, 128, 246–7.

4   Carvajal (1692) in Hiersmann Katalog, 427 (July, 1913), 9; Situado: BL Add. Mss. 13. 992, fol. 93; Palm, I: 31.

5   Relic: VAT, Process. consist. 81.226/6, 239. NR 71. The university: BL, Add. Mss 17,627, fol. 10. Palm, I: 104.

6   Carrillo, *El obispado de Yucatán*, II, 523–590.

7   BNM, Ms. 3034, fol. 340.

8   AROP, IV, 147, 33, 72, 279, 296, 406; AGI, S. Domingo 93. NT 402, 406, 422, 425; NC 251, 273.

9   AGI, S. Domingo 3. AROP, IV, 145, fol. 276. Palafox, *Obras*, VII (1762), 14.

10 NR 43; AGI, Contratación 5441; AGI, S. Domingo 93; Pallu Mss. in MEP, vol. 103, 272; *Recopilación de leyes*, Lib. I, tít. VII, ley ii.

11 AGI, S. Domingo 84, 93, 94, 98, 874.

12 AGI, S. Domingo 98.

13 AGI, S. Domingo 93, 98.

14 AGI, S. Domingo 84, 93, 98.

15 AGI, S. Domingo 93, 98.

16 AGI, S. Domingo 93, 98.

17 AGI, S. Domingo 65, 84, 93, 98. Vallellano, 104, 115. Escalante's end: Ignacio Rubio Mañé (personal communication).

18 NR 10, 38. AGI, S. Domingo 3, 93, 94, 98; AGI, Contratación 5441; Barcelona Univ., Mss, 968/13, fol. 14v; Jesuit annua (1699): BL, Add. Mss. 17,627, fols. 9–10.

19 NR 35. AGI, S. Domingo 94.

20 NR 70.

21 AGI, S. Domingo 94. For Navarrete as pastor-administrator: Nouel, *Historia eclesiástica*, I: 280.

22 NR 11. AGI, S. Domingo 65, 93, 874. BL, Add. Mss. 17, 627, fol. 5. Vallellano, 83. Konetzke, *Col. de documentos*, II, 697. Lugo, *Historia*, I: 328.

23 NR 2, 4, 70. AGI, S. Domingo 93. Henríquez Ureña, *Panorama histórico*, 44. English translation of the *Relación* in NH 399–410. Colonial law-code: Schäfer, *Consejo*, I: 306–22.

24 AGI, S. Domingo 65, 93, 94, 874. NT 428. Cf. *Recopilación de leyes*, Lib. I, Tit. VII, Ley iv.

25   AGI, S. Domingo 93.

26   AGI, S. Domingo 65, 72, 79, 874, 875. NT 154. NC 423. Konetzke, II: 758. Lugo, *Historia*, I: 368.

27   AROP, IV, 154, fol. 76. AGI, S. Domingo 93, 98. Barcelona Univ. Mss 968/13.

28   APF, SRN Congressi: America, Antilles vol. I: fol. 256–8. Vallellano, 80, 97, 140, and passim. AHSJ, LIX (1990), 95–104. Breathett, 'Jesuits in colonial Haiti', *Historian*, XXIV, 153–71.

29   Jesuit anua (1699): BL, Add. Mss. 17,627, fol. 2.

30   ARSI, Fondo Gesuitico 841, doc. 9 (Vallellano, 310; and Nouel, 274); there is a slightly different copy in BNP, Mss. esp. 409.

31   Jesuit anua: ARSI, NR 13. 1, NG. et Quit. (1655–93). AGI, S. Domingo 93, 94. BL, Add. Mss. 17,627, fols. 11–12. The Jesuit college was opened in 1701.

32   Vallellano, 86, 110, 117.

33   BNP, Mss., esp. 409, fols. 397–404.

34   NT 318. NR 11. The letters are in Fr Le Tellier's *Défense des nouveaux chrétiens*, II (1687). Cf the *Apologie des Dominicains*, defending him. Navarrete mentions (NR 24) two affirmations of his attitude over the rites (as does a report of 1693 in AOPM, vol. 275, fol. 91), but only the 'Ratificación' (May 1680) is known to me. 'Hang a Jesuit': Rodríguez Marín, *21,000 refranes*, 227.

35   Cahour, *Des Jésuites*, II: 109. A. Jaramillo, *Memorial* (1691), in AOPM, vol. 117, fol. 79.

36   NR 1, 5, 20.

37   NT 56; NR 11, 62, 70. On the 'Wonders of the coconut tree': NH 97.

38   AGI, S. Domingo 93, 94, 875. Utrera, *Dilucidaciones* I: 317. Lugo, I: 296.

39   NT 65. Lugo, I: 243, 256. Palm, I: 113.

40   AGI, S. Domingo 93. NT 237. Utrera, *Dilucidaciones*, I: 184.

41   AGI, S. Domingo 72, 93, 94, 875. Simancas, Ms. Estado 4136 (antiguo).

42   Embajada de España cerca de la Santa Sede, Madrid, Leg. 116. Simancas, Tesoro, leg. 25, fol. 228. AGI, S. Domingo 93, 94, 316.

43   Utrera, *Dilucidaciones*, I: 115.

44   BL, Add. Ms. 117627 fol. 12. NS 9–10.

45   HSA, Ms. 427/4. Utrera, *Dilucidaciones*, I: 41; Lugo, I: 319.

46   NT 442. AGI, S. Domingo 93, 94, 875. Howell, *Instructions for Foreigne Travell*, 63. Aubrey, *Brief Lives*: 'Raleigh'.

47   AGI, S. Domingo 65, 94.

48   AGI, S. Domingo 93.

49   VAT, Proc. Consist., 81.226/4, fol. 228. AGI, S. Domingo 93, 94. NR 16.

50   AGI, S. Domingo 875.

51   AGI, S. Domingo 65.

52   AGI, S. Domingo 65. Vieira, III, 424.

53   NT, 394. Utrera, *Inmaculada*, 112. For an official appreciation of his 'zeal, moderation, love of peace', etc., see the letter of Andrés de Robles, President and Governor of Santo Domingo to the king, April 1685 (AGI, S. Domingo 65).

Bibliography

1. Navarrete's principal works

NT *Tratados / historicos, / politicos, ethicos, / y religiosos de la monarchia / de China. / descripcion breve / de aquel imperio, y exemplos raros / de emperadores, y magistrados del. / Con narracion difusa de varos sucessos, / y cosas singulares de otros reynos, / y diferentes navegaciones. / Añadense los decretos pontificios, / y proposiciones calificados en Roma para la mission / Chinica; y una Bula de N. M. S. P. Clemente X. en favor de los / Missionarios. Por el P. Maestro Fr[ay] Domingo Fernandez de Navarrete / Cathedratico de Prima del Colegio, y Universidad de S. Thomas de Manila, / Missionario Apostolico de la gran China, Prelado de los de su Mission; / y Procurador General en la Corte de Madrid de la Provincia del Santo / Rosario de Filipinas, Orden de Predicadores. Dedica su obra al Serenissimo Señor don Juan de Austria. / año 1676, con privilegio / en Madrid: En la imprenta real. Por Juan García Infançon. / A costa de Florian Anisson, Mercader de Libros* [Madrid, 1676].

NC *Controversias antiguas, y modernas de la mission de la gran China. Repartidas en nueve tratados con lo que toca al culto y beneracion que el chino da a su Protho maestro Confucio y a sus progenitores difuntos con respuesta a diversos tratados de los P[adr]es. de la Compañia de Jesus. Obra mui util y necessaria para todos los Missionarios por el M. fr[ay] Domingo Fern Navarrete Cathedratico de prima del collegio y universidad de S. Thomas de Manila, Missionario Apostolico de la gran China, Vicario Provincial y veses Prelado de los de su mission y Procurador General de la Provincia del Santo Rosario de Philippinas orden de Predicadores. A nro. santissimo P. Innocencio XI que oi rige la Igliesa y sus sacras congregaciones del Santo Officio, de Propaganda Fide y tribunal santo de la general Inquisicion de los reinos de España. tomo 2* [Partially printed Madrid, 1679, but not published].

NE The manuscript of the unprinted conclusion of the *Controversias*; it is bound in the back of the copy of the printed *Controversias* in the Biblioteca nacional, Madrid, Sección de Raros 2012.

NH *The Travels and Controversies of Friar Domingo Navarrete, 1618–1686.* Edited from manuscript and printed sources by J. S. Cummins. 2 vols., Cambridge University Press for the Hakluyt Society, 1962.

NR 'Ratificacion de verdades y retractacion de engaños, dirigida al entendimiento del Lector, no a la voluntad.' (Biblioteca nacional Madrid, Ms. 7522).

NS 'Synod of Santo Domingo' [5 November, 1683], (Ms. in Archivo general de Indias, Santo Domingo 93). [There is a very rare printing, Madrid: Fernández, s. a.] The synod was 'evidence of Navarrete's zealous reform of the island's clergy' (Utrera, *Dilucidaciones*, I:115).

NT See above: *Tratados historicos*.

For some commentary on the above works, and for details of other writings by Navarrete not mentioned here, see NH, lxxxiv–cxiv, and González, *Misiones*, V: 76–117.

2. Manuscript sources

AGI Archivo general de Indias, Seville
Contratación 5441, 5539
Contaduría general 373 B
Indiferente general 2873
Filipinas 5, 81, 86, 305, 330A, 1051
Santo Domingo 3, 65, 72, 79, 84, 93, 94, 98, 305, 316, 874, 875

AGN Archivo general de la nación, Mexico City
Inquisición 446, 485, 531, 585, 1548
Reales Cédulas LII

AHN Archivo histórico nacional, Madrid
Clero regular, legs. 1118, 1123
Clero, 7634
Inquisición 4440.13

Ajuda Biblioteca da Ajuda, Lisbon
Cod. 49–V–12. 49–V–15. (Jesuitas na Asia: 61 vols. of 18th-century transcripts of documents in the Jesuits' Macao archive)

AOPM Archivum Ordinis Praedicatorum, Manila
Vols. 6, 8, 28, 58, 73, 87, 117, 223, 275, 353
Libro de consejos de provincia
Documentos sin clas. (unclassified mss.)
'Ritos chinos' (Tratados breves, 1702)
Ms. 'Hist. de la Provincia' by fray Juan de los Angeles.
Ms. 'Hechos' by fray Vittorio Riccio

APF Archivum Cong. de Propaganda Fide, Rome
Acta vols. 15, 43, 44, 45 (1675), 47 (1677).
Scrit. rif. cong. generali (1622–1668), vols 108, 142, 145, 193
Scrit. rif. cong. generali, America, Antilles, vol. 1

Informationum lib. 118, 120, 134

AROP Archivum Romanum Ordinis Praedicatorum, Rome
Vol. X, 2569
Reg. IV, 142, 145, 146, 147, 154, 157

ARSI Archivum Romanum Societatis Jesu, Rome
Fondo Gesuitico 841
JapSin 109–10 (Dunin-Szpot's 'Collectanea'),
JapSin 112, 142–3, 161, 162–64 ('Sina Epistolae', 1652–1690)
An. litt. Novi Regni (1655–1693), NR. 13. 1
Phils II

Barcelona – University Mss. Dept.
Mss. 968 / 33

Barcelona – Jesuit Archives, San Cugat
Pastells Ms. LVI

BL British Library, Dept of Mss., London
Additional. Mss. 10262, 13992, 16933, 17627, 26816, 26818
Harleian Ms. 4520
Egerton Ms. 406

Blairs Seminary, Aberdeen, Scotland
Documents from the Lesley Papers (courtesy of Rev. Fr Anderson)

BNM Biblioteca nacional, Madrid
Mss. 3034, 5758, 6590, 7522, 8344–64, 8512, 18211, 18533(6)
Raros 2012

BNP Bibliothèque Nationale, Paris
Mss. esp. 155, 381, 409

CASA Biblioteca Casanatense, Rome.
Vols. 1070, 1074

EESS Embajada de España cerca de la Santa Sede [Spanish embassy to the Holy
See], Madrid
Leg. 116

HSA Hispanic Society of America, New York
Mss. HC. 411/636
HC. 427/4

IOL India Office Library, London.
5 Mas. 41 (1673)
Orig. Corresp. (1673), vol. 33

Lilly Lilly Library, Bloomington, Indiana, USA
Phillipps Mss. 8469, 21533(3),
Ms. BM 617

MEP Archives du Séminaire des Missions Étrangères, Paris
Vols. 5, 6, 103, 107, 121, 202, 280, 423, 426, 474, 476, 856, 858, 972

Newbury   Newberry Library, Chicago
   Phillipps Ms. 1440

Pastrana   Franciscan archives, Pastrana, Spain:
   Sig. 11–2

RAH   Real Academia de la Historia, Madrid
   Mss. 9/2664, 9/2667–8
   Jesuitas Legajo 22

Simancas, Archivo General
   Estado 4136 (antiguo)
   Tesoro Legajo 25 (1677–1682)

TCD   Trinity College, Dublin
   Ms. K3. 20

VAT   Vatican archives, Rome
   Processus consistorialis 81,225, 81,226/4, 81,226/6
   81, 233/5
   Acta Cameralia 23

3.   Printed sources: Short-title bibliography (with some annotations)

Acosta, J. de   *De procuranda indorum salute* [1577], 2 vols. (Madrid, 1984–87).

Acta Cap.   *Acta Capitulorum provincialium: provinciae Sacratissimi Rosarii Philippinarum ab anno 1588*, 3 vols. (Manila, 1874–76).

Acta Cong.   *Acta Congressus Missionum SI* [Ad usum nostrorum tantum] (Rome, 1925).

Acta Apostolicae   *Acta Apostolicae Sedis*, VII (Rome, 1940).

Aduarte, Diego   *Historia de . . . la Orden de Predicadores en Filipinas, Japón, y China* (Manila, 1640).

AFH   *Archivum Franciscanum Historicum*, I (Quaracchi, 1909).

AFP   *Archivum Fratrum Praedicatorum*, I (Rome, 1931).

AHEB   *Analectes pour servir à l'histoire ecclésiastique de la Belgique*, I (Louvain, 1863).

AHSJ   *Archivum Historicum Societatis Jesu*, I (Rome, 1932).

AIA   *Archivo Ibero-americano*, I (Madrid, 1914).

Ajuda   See Manuscript sources above.

Alatri, M. d', (ed.)   *Itinera Min. Gen. Bernardino ab Arezzo per Hispaniam* (Rome, 1973).

Alembert, J. d'   *Sur la destruction des Jésuites en France* (Paris, 1765).

Alonso, D.   *Ensayos sobre poesía española* (Buenos Aires, 1946).

Ambrosini, M. L.   *The Secret Archives of the Vatican* (London, 1970).

Anscombe, G. E. M. *The Collected Papers, II: Metaphysics and the Philosophy of Mind* (Oxford, 1981).

AOPM See Mss. sources above.

APF See Mss. sources above.

Apologie *Apologie des Dominicains . . . de la Chine, ou Réponse au Livre du P. Le Tellier Jésuite* [by Alexandre Noël OP.] (Cologne, 1699).

Aquinas *Summa contra gentiles*, 3 vols. (Rome, 1961–67) [with appendices relating the text to the modern missionary situation].

Arber, E. *Term Catalogues, 1668–1702*, III (London, 1906).

Arlington, L. C. *In Search of Old Peking* (Peiping, 1935).

Arnauld, A. *Lettres*, 9 vols. (Nancy, 1727–43).

Arriaga, G., ed. Hoyos *Historia de San Gregorio de Valladolid*, 3 vols. (Madrid, 1928–40).

Arteaga, C. de la Cruz *Una mitra sobre dos mundos* (Seville, 1985).

Astley, T. *A New Collection of Voyages*, vol. III (London, 1745).

Astrain, A. *Historia de la Compañía de Jesús . . . en España*, 7 vols. (Madrid, 1900–25).

Atkinson, G. *Les nouveaux horizons de la Renaissance française* (Paris, 1935).

Atkinson, G. *Les relations de voyages du XVIIe siècle et l'évolution des idées* (Paris, 1924).

Atkinson, G. *The Extraordinary Voyage in French Literature before 1700* (New York, 1920).

Aubrey, J. *Brief Lives* [1693], ed. Oliver Lawson Dick, (London, 1949). [Like Navarrete, Aubrey displays a passion for first-hand information and an interest in everyday details; once convicted of credulity, he now appears more in the role of amateur anthropologist.]

Baddeley, J. F. *Russian, Mongolia, China*, 2 vols. (London, 1919). [Deals (II, 130–66) with the Russian envoy F. I. Baikov who was in Peking throughout 1656; there are some passing references to Schall and other Jesuits in the capital (II, 144–58), and a description of the city (II, 147–50).]

BAE *Biblioteca de autores españoles*, I (Madrid, 1846).

Barrett, D. B. *World Christian Encyclopedia: A Comparative Survey* (Oxford, 1982).

Barthes, R. *Sade, Fourier, Loyola* (London, 1976).

Basset, B. *The English Jesuits from Campion to Martindale* (London, 1967).

Bataillon, M. *Annuaire du Collège de France*, 51 (Paris, 1951).

Bayle, C. 'Impedimenta de misioneros', *Missionalia Hispanica*, IV (1947), 403–9.

Bayle, P. *Dictionnaire historique et critique*, 5th edition, 4 vols. Amsterdam, 1740. [Bayle's *Summa Sceptica*].

Bayle, P. *Reflections on the Comet* (London, 1708).

Beckmann, J. 'The Church's Dialogue with Chinese Religion', in P. Beyerhaus, *The Church Crossing Frontiers* (Uppsala, 1969), 124–138.

Beltrán de Heredia, V. *Las corrientes de espiritualidad entre los dominicos de Castilla: la primera mitad del s.16* (Salamanca, 1941).

Beltrán de Heredia, V. *Domingo Bañez y las controversias sobre la gracia. Textos y documentos* (Madrid, 1968).

Beltrán de Heredia, V. 'Examen crítico de la historiografía dominicana en . . . España', *Archivum Fratrum Praedicatorum* 35 (1965), 195–248.

Benavente, A. de 'Itinerario', *Missionalia Hispanica*, 2 (1945), 291–364.

Benedict XIV *Opera*, 17 vols. (Prati, 1839–47).

Benedict XIV *Correspondance*, ed. E. de Heeckeren. 2 vols. (Paris, 1912).

Benedict XIV *Le Lettere di Benedetto XIV al card. de Tencin*, ed. E. Morelli, 3 vols. (Rome, 1955–84).

Bennett, R. F. *The Early Dominicans* (Cambridge Studies in Medieval Life and Thought) (Cambridge, 1938).

Bernard-Maitre, H. 'La Correspondance Becker–Brucker sur la question des rites chinois (1885–1907)', *Recherches de science religieuse*, 54 (1966), 417–24.

Bernard-Maitre, H. 'Un dossier bibliographique de la fin du XVIIe siècle sur la question des termes chinois', *Recherches de science religieuse*, 36 (Paris, 1949), 25–79.

Bernard-Maitre, H. *Aux Portes de la Chine* (Tientsin, 1933).

Bernard-Maitre, H. in *Histoire universelle des missions catholiques*. ed. S. Delacroix, 4 vols. (Paris, 1956–59).

Bernard-Maitre, H. 'The Chinese and Malabar rites: an historical perspective', *Concilium*, VII (3), (London, 1967), 38–45.

Bernard-Maitre, H. 'Chinois (Rites)', *Dictionnaire d'histoire et de géographie ecclésiastiques*, XII (Paris, 1953), 731–41.

Biermann, B. *Die Anfänge der neueren Dominikanermission in China* (Münster in Westfalen, 1927).

Biermann, B. 'Chinesische Sprachstudien in Manila. Das erste chinesische Buch in europaischer Ubersetzung', *Neue Zeitschrift fur Missionswissenschaft*, VII (1951), 18–23.

BL See Mss. sources above

Blackwell, R. J. *Galileo, Bellarmine, and the Bible* (London, 1991). [Chapter 6: 'The Jesuit Dilemma: Truth or Obedience?', is relevant to the China mission.]

Blair and Robertson   E. H. Blair and J. A. Robertson, ed., *The Philippine Islands 1493–1898*, 55 vols. (Cleveland, 1903–1909).

BNP   See Mss. sources above.

Boin, M.   'When the twain met: an analysis of "A mirror to encourage self-improvement",' *Itinerario* VIII, No. 1 (1984), 58–77.

Bonet, A.   *La Filosofía de la libertad en las controversias teológicas del s.16 y 17* (Barcelona, 1932).

Bontinck, F.   *La lutte autour de la liturgie chinoise aux XVIIe et XVIIIe siècles* (Paris, 1962).

Borges, P.   *Análisis del conquistador espiritual* (Seville, 1961).

Bosmans, H.   'Correspondance de J-B Maldonado', *Analectes pour servir à l'histoire ecclésiastique de la Belgique*, 36 (1910), 39–86, 187–238.

Bosmans, H.   'Verbiest, Directeur de l'Observatoire de Pekin', *Revue des Questions Scientifiques*, 3rd series, 71 (Louvain, 1912), 195–273, 375–494.

Bottazzi, E.   'Francesco Brancati e la questione dei riti cinesi', *Humanitas*, 39 (Brescia, 1984), 47–62.

Bouscaren, T. L.   *Canon Law Digest*, II (Milwaukee, 1949).

Bouhours, D.   *Sentiment des Jésuites touchant le peché philosophique* (Paris, 1690).

Boxer, C. R.   *The Christian Century in Japan (1549–1650)* (London, 1951).

Boxer, C. R.   *South China in the Sixteenth Century* (London, 1953).

Boxer, C. R.   *Fidalgos in the Far East 1550–1770* (The Hague, 1948).

Boxer, C. R.   *The Portuguese Seaborne Empire, 1415–1825* (London, 1969).

Boxer, C. R.   *Portuguese India in the Mid-Seventeenth Century* (New Delhi, 1980).

Boxer, C. R.   *Race Relations in the Portuguese Colonial Empire, 1415–1825* (Oxford, 1963).

Boxer, C. R.   *Salvador de Sa and the Struggle for Brazil and Angola, 1602–1686* (Westport, 1975).

Boxer, C. R.   *Francisco Vieira de Figueiredo: a Portuguese Merchant-Adventurer in South East Asia, 1624–67* (The Hague, 1967).

Boxer, C. R.   *The Church Militant and Iberian Expansion 1440–1770* (London, 1978).

Boxer, C. R.   *A propósito dum livrinho xilográfico dos Jesuítas de Pequim: Ensaio histórico.* (Macao, 1947).

Boxer, C. R.   'A tentative check-list of Indo-Portuguese imprints', *Arquivos do Centro Cultural Português*, IX (Paris, 1975).

Boxer, C. R.   'The Dominican Mission in Japan (1602–1622) and Lope de Vega', *Archivum Fratrum Praedicatorum*, 33 (Rome, 1963), 5–88 (with Cummins, J. S.).

BR See Blair, E. H., & Robertson, J. A., ed.

Brading, D. A. *The First America* (Cambridge, 1991).

Breathett, G. 'Jesuits in colonial Haiti', *Historian*, XXIV (Allentown, PA, 1962), 153–71.

Brodrick, J. *Robert Bellarmine 1542–1621*, 2 vols. (London, 1950).

Brooke, C. N. L. 'St. Dominic and his first biographer', *Transactions of the Royal Historical Society*, 5th ser., 17 (1967), 23–40.

Brou, A. *Les Jésuites de la legende*, 2 vols. (Paris, 1907).

Brou, A. 'De certains conflits entre missionnaires au 17e siècle' *Revue d'Histoire des Missions* XI (Paris, 1934). 187–202. [This is a Jesuit review of Pinot's study which is deplored as an 'oversimplified survey'.]

Brou, A. 'Le point final à la question des rites chinois', *Etudes*, CCXLII (Paris, 1940). 275ff.

Bruckberger, R-L. *La Nef*, 55 (Paris, 1974), 146–54.

Brzezinski, Z. 'How to control a deviation', *Encounter*, 21 (No 3), (September, 1963), 77–89.

BSOAS *Bulletin of the School of Oriental and African Studies*, I (London, 1940).

Bulletin de l'Institut *Bulletin de l'Institut historique Belge de Rome*, I (Rome, 1928).

Burnet, G. *Travels* (London, 1689).

Burnet, G. *Three Letters* (London, 1687).

Cahour, A. M. *Des Jésuites. Par un Jésuite* (Paris, 1844).

Camden Society 'Documents relating to dissension among the RC clergy, 1597–1602: Quarrels with the Jesuits', T. G. Law (ed.) *Camden Society Publications*, vol. LVI (London, 1896), 1–62.

Cammann, S. *China's Dragon Robes* (New York, 1952).

Canal, M. 'El P. Luis Aliaga y las controversias teológicas de su tiempo', AFP, I (1931), 107–57.

Candidus, L. [pseud.] *Tuba magna mirum clangens sonum de necesitate reformandi Societatem Jesu* (Argentinae, 1713).

Cano, M. *De locis theologicis*. The best edition: the *Opera*, ed. T. M. Tucci, 3 vols., (Rome, 1900).

Capéran, L. *Le problème du Salut des Infidèles*, 2 vols. (Toulouse, 1935). [Re-written and updated in a 1961 edition.]

Carreño, A. M. *Cedulario de los siglos 16 y 17: Palafox y el conflicto con la Compañía de Jesús* (Mexico, 1947).

Carrillo, C.   *El obispado de Yucatán*, 2 vols. (Merida, 1895).

Carro, V. D.   La teología y los teólogos-juristas españoles, 2 vols. (Madrid, 1944).

Cartas selectas   *Cartas selectas de los generales* [SJ] (Oña, 1917).

CASA   See Mss. sources above.

Casey, J. G.   *The Kingdom of Valencia in the 17th Century* (Cambridge, 1979).

Castleton, Wm.   'Domingo de Salazar: Life and work' (unpublished PhD, University of London, 1974).

Castro, A. A. de   *Osario venerable*, ed. Merino (Madrid, 1954).

Cath. Dict. Theol.   *A Catholic Dictionary of Theology*, vols. I–III (Abandonment-Paradise), (London, 1962–71). No more published.

Catholic Encyclopaedia   *The Catholic Encyclopaedia*, 15 vols. (New York, 1907–12).

Cayre, F.   *Manual of Patrology and History of Theology*, 2 vols. (Paris, 1940).

Cepari, V.   *Life of St Aloysius Gonzaga* (London, 1885).

Ceyssens, L.   'Autour de la bulle *Unigenitus*', *Revue d'histoire ecclésiastique*, LXXX (1985), 369–414, 732–759.

Ceyssens, L.   'Autour de Caramuel', *Bulletin de l'Institut historique Belge de Rome*, XXXIII (1961), 329–410. Reprinted in *Jansenistica minora*, VII, fasc. 59.

Ceyssens, L.   *Jansenistica Minora*, 12 vols. (Malines–Amsterdam, 1951–1975).

Ceyssens, L.   See also Sohier-Ceyssens.

Chadwick, O.   *From Bossuet to Newman* (Cambridge, 1957).

Chan, Wing-tsit   *Religious Trends in Modern China* (New York, 1953).

Chappoulie, H.   *Rome et les missions d'Indochine au xviiie siècle*, 2 vols. (Paris, 1943–48).

Charles, Pierre   *Les Dossiers de l'action missionnaire* (Louvain, 1938).

Ch'ien Chung-shu   'China in English literature: 18th century', *Quarterly Bulletin of Chinese Bibliography*, 2 (1941), 7–48, 113–152.

Churchill, A. and J.   *A Collection of Voyages and Travels: Some now first printed from original manuscripts*, 6 vols. (London, 1704).

Clancy, T. H.   *An Introduction to Jesuit Life* (St. Louis, 1976).

Clancy, T. H.   *The Conversational Word of God* (St. Louis, 1978).

Classica Japonica   *Classica Japonica (Facsimile series)* I (Tenri, 1975).

Classica Japonica   *Classica Japonica: Far Eastern Catholic Missions: Section 8: Christian Materials* II (1663–1771) (Tenri, 1978).

Clément, P. *Lettres de Colbert* (Paris, 1865).

CMS *China Mission Studies (1550–1800)*, I (1979).

Cobo, Juan OP. *Beng Sim Po Cam o Espejo rico del claro corazón {1592}*, ed. Carlos Sanz (Madrid, 1959). [See Piet van der Loon's masterly study of this, the first Chinese book to be translated into Spanish.]

Codoin *Colección de documentos inéditos para la historia de España*, 113 vols. (Madrid, 1842–95).

Coemans, A. *Commentarium in regulas SJ omnibus nostris comunes* (Rome, 1938).

Cohen, Paul *China and Christianity 1860–70* (Cambridge, Mass., 1963).

Cohen, T. V. 'Why the Jesuits Joined, 1540–1600', *Canadian Historical Papers*, (Dec. 1974), 237–58.

Colín, F. *Labor evangélica* [1660], ed. Pastells, 3 vols. (Barcelona, 1900–1902).

Collectanea SCPF *Collectanea de Propaganda Fide*, I *(1622–1886)*, (Rome, 1907).

Colton, J. 'Garden Art as Political Propaganda', *Eighteenth Century Studies*, X (1976–77), 1–20.

Contaduría See Mss. sources above at AGI.

Cordier, H. *Bibliotheca Sinica*, 5 vols. (Paris, 1904–24).

Corpo Diplomático Port. *Corpo Diplomático Portugues, Actos*, XIV: *(1661–1677)*, ed. J. C. Freitas Moniz (Lisbon, 1910); XV: *(1677–78)*, ed. A. Ferrão (Lisbon, 1936).

Cortés Osorio, J. *Reparos historiales* (Pamplona-Madrid, 1676).

Cortés Osorio, J. *Memorial apologético* (Madrid, 1677).

Cortés Osorio, J. see also Etreros.

Costa, H. de la *The Jesuits in the Philippines, 1581–1768* (Harvard, 1961).

Costello, W. T. *The Scholastic Curriculum at Seventeenth-Century Cambridge* (Harvard, 1958).

Coulton, G. G. 'The failure of the friars', *Ten Medieval Studies* (Boston, 1959).

Couplet, Ph. *Confucius sinarum philosophus* (Paris, 1687).

Cranmer-Byng, J. L. (ed.) *An Embassy to China: Being the Journal Kept by Lord Macartney, 1793–94* (London, 1962).

Crehan, J. H. 'Foreknowledge', *A Catholic Dictionary of Theology*, II: 301–4.

Cruickshank, D. W. 'Spanish book-production in the Golden Age', *The Library*, XXXI, 5th series (1976).

Cummins J. S. 'Las Casas Goes East', *The Hakluyt Society Report* (London, 1985), *Annual Lecture 1985*, 10–22 [Reprinted in *Culture and Belief in Europe, 1450–1600* (Open University Texts: Milton Keynes, 1990), 30–35.]

Cummins, J. S.   *Jesuit and Friar in the Spanish Expansion to the East* (London, 1986).

Cummins, J. S.   'Two missionary methods in China: Mendicants and Jesuits', in Cummins, *Jesuit and Friar*, fasc. V.

Cummins, J. S.   'Palafox and China', in Cummins, *Jesuit and Friar*, fasc. III.

Cummins, J. S.   'The suppression of the Jesuits', *History Today*, XXIII (December, 1973), 839–848.

Curtius, E. R.   *European Literature and the Latin Middle Ages* (London, 1953).

Dainville, F. de   *La Géographie des Humanistes* (Paris, 1940).

Damboriena, P.   *La Salvación en las religiones no cristianas* (Madrid, 1973).

Dawson, C.   *The Mongol Mission: Franciscan Missions in China in the Thirteenth Century* (London, 1955).

Defourneaux, M.   *Inquisición y censura de libros en España* (Madrid, 1973).

Dehergne, J.   *Répertoire des Jésuites de China, 1552–1800* (Rome, 1973).

Dehergne, J.   'Les Chrétientés de Chine de la période Ming', 1581–1650', *Monumenta Serica*, 16 (1957), 1–136.

Dehergne, J.   'Henri Bernard-Maitre: Select bibliography of writings on East Asia', *Bulletin de l'Ecole française d'Extrême-Orient*, 63 (Paris, 1976), 467–81.

Dehergne, J. & Leslie, D.   *Juifs de Chine* (Rome, 1980)

D'Elia, P. M.   *Fonti Ricciane*, 3 vols. (Rome, 1942–49).

D'Elia, P. M.   'Les Rites chinois', *Gregorianum*, 43 (1962), 206.

D'Elia, P. M.   *Galileo in China* (Rome, 1947).

Delumeau, J.   *Le Catholicisme entre Luther et Voltaire* (Paris, 1973).

Denzinger, H.   *Enchiridion Symbolorum* (Rome, 1976).

Devine, W.   *The Four Churches of Peking* (London, 1930).

DHGE   see *Dictionnaire d'histoire et de géographie*.

Díaz, C.   *Conquistas de las islas Filipinas, Parte segunda*. (Valladolid, 1890). [The first part is by Gaspar de San Agustín (Madrid, 1698).]

Diccionario   *Diccionario de historia eclesiástica de España*, 5 vols. (Madrid, 1972–87).

Dictionnaire   *Dictionnaire d'histoire et de géographie ecclésiastiques*, ed. A. Baudrillart, I (Paris, 1912).

Documenta   *Documenta controversiam missionariorum . . . spectantia . . . ac apologiam Dominicanorum . . . confirmantia* (Cologne, 1699).

Documentação   *Documentação para a história das missões do Padroado português do Oriente: India* ed. A. Silva Rego, 12 vols. (Lisbon, 1949–58); V (*India 1551–1554*), (Lisbon, 1951).

Domínguez Ortiz, A. *La Sociedad española en el siglo 17*. II: *El estamento eclesiástico*, 2 vols. (Madrid, 1970).

Domínguez Ortiz, A. *The Golden Age of Spain* tr. J. G. Casey (London, 1971).

DTC *Dictionnaire de théologie catholique*, ed. A. Vacant *et al.*, 15 vols. (Paris, 1903–1950).

Du Halde, J. B. *Description de la Chine*, 4 vols. (Paris, 1735).

Duncanson, D. Review in *The Journal of the Royal Asiatic Society* (No. 1, 1986), 166.

Dunne, G. H. *Generation of Giants* (London, 1962). [Reviewed *Zeitschrift für Missionswissenschaft*, 51 (1967), 381–83, and the London *Times Literary Supplement*, 29 March 1963.]

Duviols, P. *La lutte contre les religions autochtones dans le Pérou colonial* (Paris–Lima, 1971).

Duyvendak, J. J. L. 'The last Dutch Embassy to the Chinese Court, 1794–5', *T'oung Pao*, XXXIV (Leiden, 1938). 1–137.

Duyvendak, J. J. L. *T'oung Pao*, XXXIX (1949–50), 193–4: a review of Boxer's *Fidalgos in the Far East*.

Dyer Ball, J. *Things Chinese; Or, Notes Connected with China*, 5th ed. (Hong Kong, 1925).

Ebrey, P. B. (tr.) *Chu Hsi's 'Family Rituals'* (Princeton, 1991).

Edwards, T. 'A Monastic Hegira', *History Today*, XXIV (1974), 275–9.

EF *The English Factories in India* (New Series), (*1670–84*), ed. Sir Charles Fawcett (Oxford, 1936–55).

Eliade, M. *Encyclopedia of Religion*, 15 vols. (New York, 1987).

Elison, G. *Deus Destroyed* (Cambridge, Mass., 1973).

Enciclopedia *Enciclopedia cattolica*, 12 vols. (Vatican City, 1948–53).

Epistolae selectae *Epistolae selectae Praepositorum Generalium ad superiores Societatis* (Rome, 1911).

Ernst, C. *Multiple Echo: Explorations in Theology* (London, 1979).

Espinosa Polit, M. M. *Perfect Obedience* (Westminster, MA, 1947).

Etiemble *Les Jésuites en Chine (1552–1773)* (Paris, 1966).

Etreros, M. (ed.) *Cortés Osorio: Invectiva política contra don Juan de Austria* (Madrid, 1984).

Eubel, C. *Hierarchia catholica*, 8 vols. I (Munster, 1913).

Farmer, E. L. *Technology Transfer and Cultural Subversion: Tensions in the early Jesuit Mission to China*, James Ford Bell Lecture No. 21 (Minneapolis, 1983).

Farrington, A.   *The English Factories in Japan: 1613–23*, 2 vols. (London, 1991).

Fénelon, F. de   *Oeuvres complètes*, 10 vols. (Paris, 1848–52).

Fernández, Alonso   *Historia eclesiástica de nuestros tiempos* [Part II deals with East Asia], (Toledo, 1611).

Fernández. P.   *Dominicos donde nace el sol* (Barcelona, 1958).

Fernández Arias, F.   *El Beato Sanz y compañeros* (Madrid, 1893).

Flew, A.   *Dictionary of Philosophy* (London, 1979).

Fliche–Martin   A. Fliche and V. Martin, eds., *Histoire de l'Eglise*, I (Paris, 1935).

Focher, J.   *Itinerarium catholicum proficiscentium ad infideles convertendos* [1574], ed. Eguiluz (Madrid, 1960). [Franciscan; the first-ever investigation of mission theory.]

Ford, R.   *A Handbook for Travellers in Spain*, [1845], 3 vols. (London, 1966). [The classic study of Spanish psychology.]

Forte, S.   *The Cardinal-protectors of the Dominican Order* (Rome, 1961).

Franco, D.   *España como preocupación* (Madrid, 1960).

Franke, W.   *Studia Sino-Altaica: Festschrift für Erich Haenisch* (Weisbaden, 1961).

Fu, Lo-shu   *A Documentary Chronicle of Sino–Western Relations (1644–1820)*, 2 vols. (Tucson, 1966).

Fu, Lo-shu   'Two Portuguese Embassies to China', *T'oung Pao*, XLIII (Leiden, 1954), 75–94.

Furtado, F.   *Informatio antiquissima de praxi missionariorum sinensium SJ. circa ritus Sinenses data in China 1636–40.* (Lyon–Paris, 1700).

Gage, T.   *Travels in the New World*, ed. Thompson, (Norman, OK, 1958).

Galbraith, G. R.   *The Constitutions of the Dominican Order, 1216–1360* (Manchester, 1925).

Gallego, A.   'Por qué el Oriente no se convierte', *Missionalia Hispanica*, 4 (1947), 209–247.

Gama, L. da   *Diary*, ed. J. F. Marques Pereira as 'Uma resurreição historica (Paginas inéditas . . . 1665–71)', *Ta-Ssi-Yang-Kuo*, 1 (Macao, 1899), 31–41, 113–19, 181–8, 305–10; II (1901), 693–702, 747–63.

Garrigou-Lagrange, R. M.   *Grace* (London, 1952).

Gaubil, Antoine   *Correspondance de Pékin, 1722–1759*, ed. R. Simon (Genève, 1970).

Gazeta   *Gazeta nueva.* (Madrid, 1661–1690).

Gernet, Jacques   *Chine et christianisme: Action et réaction* (Paris, 1982). English translation: *China and the Christian Impact: A Conflict of Cultures* (Cambridge, 1985).

Getino, A. *Dominicos españoles confesores de Reyes* (Madrid, 1917).

Gibbon, Ed. *A Vindication of some passages in the 'Decline and Fall'* (Dublin, 1779).

Gil Fernández, L. *Panorama social del humanismo español (1500–1800)*, (Madrid, 1981).

Godwin, J. *Athanasius Kircher. Renaissance Man* (London, 1979).

Goldstein, J. *Philadelphia and the China Trade, 1682–1846* (Pennsylvania State University Press, 1978).

González, J. Ma. *Historia de las misiones dominicanas en China (1632–1954)*, 5 vols. (Madrid, 1955–1965).

González, J. Ma. *Biografía del primer obispo chino: Gregorio López, OP.* (Pamplona–Manila, 1946).

González, J. Ma. *Semblanzas misioneras: P. Francisco Varo* (Madrid, 1955).

González, J. Ma. *Un misionero diplomático: Victorio Riccio* (Madrid, 1955).

González, J. Ma. 'Filología misional dominicana de Oriente', *España misionera*, 12 (Madrid, 1955), 143–79.

González de S. Pedro, F. *Relation de la nouvelle persecution de la China* (s. 1., 1714).

Goodrich, L. C. *Dictionary of Ming Biography 1368–1644*, 2 vols. (New York, 1976).

Gosse, P. *St Helena* (London, 1938).

Gray, J. H. *China*, 2 vols. (London, 1878).

Guia *Manuscritos da Ajuda (Guia)*, 2 vols. (Lisbon, 1973).

Guibert, J. de *The Jesuits: Their Spiritual Doctrine and Practice* (St. Louis, 1972).

Guinard, P. J. *La Presse espagnole* (Paris, 1973).

van Gulik, R. H. *Sexual Life in Ancient China* (Leiden, 1961).

Gutiérrez, P. 'Dos métodos del apostolado en las misiones modernas de China', *Missionalia Hispanica*, 3 (1946), 511–73.

Guy, Basil 'AMDG', in G. S. Rousseau and Roy Porter, *Exoticism in the Enlightenment* (Manchester, 1990).

Guy, Basil *The French Image of China before and after Voltaire* (Geneva, 1963).

Hakluyt, R. *Voyages and Discoveries*, 12 vols. (Glasgow, 1903–05).

Hamilton, A. *A New Account of the East Indies*, 2 vols. (London, 1931).

Hamilton, B. *The Medieval Inquisition* (London, 1981).

Hamilton, C. D. *Western Civilization: Recent Interpretations*, I (New York, 1973).

Harnack, *History of Dogma*, 7 vols. (London, 1894–99).

Harris, F. R.   *The Life of Edward Montague, Earl of Sandwich*, 2 vols. (London, 1912).

Harris, G. L.   'The Mission of Matteo Ricci: A Case Study', *Monumenta Serica*, 23 (Los Angeles, 1968), 1–168.

Harrison, J. & Laslett, P.   *The Library of John Locke* (Oxford, 1965).

Hastings, J.   *Encyclopaedia of Religion and Ethics*, 13 vols. (Edinburgh, 1908–27).

Hazard, P.   *European Thought in the Eighteenth Century* (London, 1954).

Hennepin, L.   *A New Discovery of a Vast Country in America* [1698], ed. R. G. Thwaites, 2 vols. (Chicago, 1903).

Henríquez Ureña, P.   *Panorama histórico de la literature dominicana* (Rio de Janeiro, 1945).

Heras, E.   *La dinastía Manchú en China* (Barcelona, 1918).

Herder Correspondence   *Herder Correspondence*, I (Dublin, 1963).

Herrero, M. (ed.)   *China y Oriente por Fr Domingo de Navarrete* (Madrid, 1946).

Hillenaar, H.   *Fénelon et les Jésuites* (The Hague, 1967). ['It is rare to find so realistic a view of the Society of Jesus from a Jesuit pen' (L. Ceyssens, OFM, *Revue d'histoire ecclésiastique*, LXIII (1968), 565–69).]

Hinsch, Bret   *Passions of the Cut Sleeve: The Male Homosexual Tradition in China* (Berkeley, 1990).

Historia . . . Inquisition.   *Historia de la Inquisición en España y América* (Madrid, BAC., 1984).

Hoàng-Manh-Hiên, J.   *Thyrse Gonzáles et le probabilisme*, (Cholon, Vietnam, ed. Chan-ly, 1959).

Hobson-Jobson   *Hobson Jobson: A Glossary of Anglo-Indian Words and Phrases*, ed. Wm Crooke (London, 1969).

Hooykaas, R.   *Rheticus's Treatise on Scripture and the Motion of the Earth* (Amsterdam, 1984).

Hopkins, G. M.   *The Hopkins-Dixon Correspondence*, ed. Abbott (Oxford, 1935).

Hostie, R.   *Vie et mort des ordres religieux. Approches psycho-sociologiques* (Paris, 1972). [Attempts a comparative examination of different religious orders and argues that most have a built-in life-cycle.]

Howell, J.   *Instructions for Foreigne Travell* (London, 1642).

Hsü, Aloysius   *Dominican presence in the Constitutions of the Society of Jesus*, (an unpublished thesis: Rome, 1971).

Huang, Ray   *1587. A Year of No Significance: The Ming Dynasty in Decline* (London, 1981).

Huerga, A.   'Escolástica', in *Diccionario de historia eclesiástica de España*, II (Madrid, 1972), 810–849.

Hummel, A. W.   *Eminent Chinese of the Ch'ing Period, 1644–1912*, 2 vols. (Washington, 1944).

Ibáñez, B.   *Cartas, Informes y Relaciones*, ed. S. Alcobendas, (Madrid, 1933).

Idema, W. L.   'Cannon, Clocks and Clever Monkeys: Europeana, Europeans and Europe in some early Ch'ing Novels', in Vermeer, 459–488.

Imago   *Imago primi saeculi* (Antwerp, 1640).

Intorcetta, P.   *Testimonium de cultu sinensi datum anno 1668* (Paris, 1700).

ISJ   *Información SJ*, I (1969) [Spanish edition of a private international newsletter for Jesuits].

Israel, J.   *Race, Class, and Politics in Colonial Mexico, 1610–70* (Oxford, 1975).

Iyer, R.   *The Glass Curtain between Asia and Europe* (Oxford, 1965).

Jarry, E.   In A. Fliche and V. Martin, eds., *Histoire de l'Eglise*, I (Paris, 1935).

JHI   *Journal of the History of Ideas*, I (Lancaster, PA, 1939).

Jonsen, A. & Toulmin, S.   *The Abuse of Casuistry. A History of Moral Reasoning* (London, 1988). [An impartial academic study of probabilism, casuistry, Pascal, etc.].

Journ. Oriental Studies   *Journal of Oriental Studies*, I (Hong Kong, 1953).

JRAS   *Journal of the Royal Asiatic Society*, I (London, 1835).

Joy, P.   'Nova instrucão sôbre os ritos Chineses', *Boletim eclesiástico de Macau*, no. 435, año 36 (Macao, 1940), 785–99.

Juanini, J. B.   *Nueva idea physica* (Madrid, 1685).

Juanini, J. B.   *Discurso físico y político* (Madrid, 1679–89, French trans. Toulouse, 1685).

Juanini, J. B.   *Carta a Francisco Redi* (Madrid, 1689).

Juderías, J.   *España en tiempo de Carlos II* (Madrid, 1912).

Kamen, H.   *Spain in the Later Seventeenth Century* (London, 1980).

Keegan, J.   *The Face of Battle* (Harmondsworth, 1978).

Kelly, Celsus   *La Austrialia del Espíritu Santo*, 2 vols. (Cambridge, for the Hakluyt Society, 1966).

Kendrick, T.   *St James in Spain* (London, 1960).

Kinsman, R. S. (ed.)   *The Darker Vision of the Renaissance: Beyond the Fields of Reason* (London, 1974).

Kirk, K. E.   *Conscience and its Problems. An Introduction to Casuistry* (London, 1933). [Kirk was Bishop of Oxford. His work in this field was dismissed by the English

Jesuits as 'amateur moral theology' (*Month*, 136 (1920), 563–4); but Jonsen-Toulmin (*op. cit.*, viii) find him a 'a genius of casuistry in the Anglican tradition'.]

Klibansky, R.   *Saturn and Melancholy* (London, 1964).

Knowles, Dom David   'Portrait of St Dominic', *Blackfriars*, 39 (1958), 147–55.

Knowles, Dom David   *From Pachomius to Ignatius* (Oxford, 1966).

Knowles, Dom David   *The Religious Orders in England*, 3 vols. (Cambridge, 1948–59).

Knowles, Dom David   *The Historian and Character, and Other Essays* (Cambridge, 1963).

Knowles, W. E.   'Science in Rome, 1675–1700', *British Journal for the History of Science*, 8 (1975). ['Jesuits and the New Science', 149–51.]

Knox, Ronald (Mons.)   *Enthusiasm* (Oxford, 1950).

Knox, Robert (Capt.)   *An Historical Relation of Ceylon* [1681] (London, 1911).

Koch, L.   *Jesuiten-Lexikon*, 2 vols. (Paderborn, 1934, reprinted 1962).

Konetzke, R.   *Colección de documentos para la historia de la formación social de Hispanoamérica, 1493–1810*, 2 vols. (Madrid, 1958).

Kowalsky, N.   *Inventory of the History Section of Propaganda Fide* (Rome, 1983).

Kreiser, B. R.   *Miracles, Convulsions, and Ecclesiastical Politics in early 18th-Century Paris* (Princeton, 1978).

Kristeller, P. O.   'The Contribution of the Religious Orders to Renaissance Thought and Learning', *American Benedictine Review*, 21 (1970), 1–55.

Lach, D.   *Asia in the Making of Europe*, I (Chicago, 1965), in progress.

Lafuente, M.   *Historia general de España*, 30 vols. (Madrid, 1887–90).

Lancashire, D.   'Anti-Christian polemics in 17th-Century China', *Church History*, XXXVIII (1969), 218–41.

Lapide, Cornelius à   *Commentaria in Apocalypsim* (Lyon, 1627). [Navarrete (NT, 255) cites Lapide's references to Asia.]

Latourette, K. S.   *A History of the Expansion of Christianity*, vol. 3 (London, 1939).

Latourette, K. S.   *The Chinese: History and Culture* (London, 1964).

Lattimore, O.   *The Month*, XI, 2nd New Ser. (1978), 170.

Launay, A.   *Documents historiques* (Paris, 1905).

Laurentin, R.   *Chine et Christianisme. Après les occasions manquées* (Paris, 1977).

Lea, H. C.   *A History of Auricular Confession and Indulgences*, 2 vols. (London, 1896). [Vol. 1 was criticised by Fr. H. Thurston SJ, in *How History is Miswritten* (London, 1938).]

Lea, H. C.   *The History of the Inquisition in Spain*, 4 vols. (New York, 1906–1907).

Le Bachelet, X-M. *Auctarium Bellarminianum* (Paris, 1913).

Lebégue, R. 'Les ballets des Jésuites', *Revue des cours et conférences*, XXXVII (1936–37).

LEC *Lettres édifiantes et curieuses*, 4 vols. (Paris, 1838–1843). [First edition in 34 vols. (Paris, 1702–73); there is also a 26-volumed edition (Paris, 1780–83) where China is represented in vols. 16–26 and vol. 24 has a useful table (Guy, *Image*, 456).]

Le Comte, L. *Memoirs and Remarks* (London, 1737).

Ledóchowski, W. *Selected Writings* [Ad usum nostrorum privatum tantum] (Chicago, 1945).

Le Gobien, C. *Histoire de l'Edit de l'Empereur de la China* (Paris, 1698).

Lemoine, R. *Le Monde des religieux* (Paris, 1976) [Covers the period 1563–1789; studies the Jesuits at 121–160; the Dominicans at 73–86.].

León Luis de *Obras completas*, 2 vols. (Madrid, 1957).

León Pinelo, A. de *Epitome* (Madrid, 1629).

Leslie, D. D. *Essays on the Sources for Chinese History* (Canberra, 1973).

Le Tellier, M. *Défense des nouveaux chrétiens et des missionnaires de la Chine.* 2 vols. (Paris 1687–90).

Le Tellier, M. *Defensa de los nuevos Cristianos*, translation of the above by Gabriel de Parraga (Mexico, 1690). [Dedicated to 'The Affronted Christ'.]

Lettre *Lettre de Messieurs des Missions etrangeres au Pape, sur les idolatries et les superstitions chinoises* [Paris, 1700].

Lewis, N. *The Missionaries* (London, 1988). [For a Catholic counterpart of this distressing survey, see Victor Daniel Bonilla, *Servants of God, or Masters of Men?* (Harmondsworth, 1972).]

Locke, J. *Correspondence*, ed. E. S. de Beer, 8 vols. (Oxford, 1976–1989).

Longobardi, N. *De Confucio ejusque doctrina tractatus* [published Paris, 1701 as *Traité sur quelques points de la religion des Chinois*, trans. from Navarrete (NT, *Tratado quinto*)].

van der Loon, P. 'The Manila Incunabula and early Hokkien Studies', *Asia Major*, 12(i)–13(i-ii) (London, 1966–67), 1–42, 95–186.

López, F. *Forner* (Bordeaux, 1976).

López Piñero, J. *Introducción de la ciencia moderna en España* (Barcelona, 1969).

Lovejoy, A. O. *Essays in the History of Ideas* (New York, 1960).

Lugo, A. *Historia de Santo Domingo*, I (Ciudad Trujillo, 1952).

Luk, Bernard Hung-kay 'Aleni's *Chih-fang wai-chi*', *BSOAS*, XL (1977), 58–84.

Lundbaek, K. 'The Image of neo-Confuciansim in *Confucius Sinarum Philosophus*', *Journal of the History of Ideas*, XLIV (1983), 19–30.

Lynch, J. *Spain under the Habsburgs*, 2 vols. (Oxford, 1969).

Lynch, W. F. *Christ and Apollo* (New York, 1960). [Relevant to the tradition of Figurism.]

Maas, O. *Cartas de China*, 2 vols. (Seville, 1917).

Mabillon, J. *Correspondance inédite*, ed. M. Valery, 3 vols. (Paris, 1846).

Macaulay, Lord *History of England*, 10 vols. (Leipzig, 1849).

McHugh-Callan J. A. McHugh, OP., and C. J. Callan, OP., *Moral Theology: A Complete Course based on Aquinas*, 2 vols. (New York, 1929–30).

Magalhães, G. de *New History of China* (London, 1688).

Maggs's Catalogues 442: *Bibliotheca Asiatica. Pt. III* (London, 1923).

Maggs's Catalogues 455: *Bibliotheca Asiatica. Pt. II* (London, 1924).

Maggs's Catalogues 515: *Bibliotheca Asiatica. Pt. III* (London, 1929).

Maldonado, J-B. 'Correspondance de J-B. Maldonado', *Analectes pour servir a l'histoire ecclésiastique de la Belgique*, 36 (1910), 39–86, 187–238.

Manucci, N. *Storia do Mogor or Mogul India (1653–1718)*, ed. W. Irvine, 4 vols. (London, 1907–08).

Maravall, J A. 'Novadores y pre-ilustrados', *Cuadernos hispanoamericanos*, 340 (Madrid, 1978).

Mariluz Urquijo, J. M. 'La China, utopia rioplatense del siglo 18', *Revista de Historia de América*, 98 (1984).

Maritain, J. *Peasant of the Garonne* (London, 1968).

Martini, M. *Sinicae historiae decas prima* (Munster, 1658).

Masetti, P. T. *Lettere edificanti scritte dai Frati Predicatori martirizzati nel Giappone* (Rome, 1868).

Masson, G. *Queen Christina* (London, 1968).

Maura Gamazo, G. *Supersticiones y hechizos de Carlos II* (Madrid, 1943).

Maverick, L. A. *China: A model for Europe* (San Antonio, 1946).

Meersman, A. 'Chapter Lists . . . India, 1569–1790', *Studia*, 6 (Lisbon, 1960), 123–349.

Meijer, M. J. 'Homosexual Offences in Ch'ing Law', *T'oung Pao*, 71 (1985), 109–33.

Meléndez, J. *Tesoros verdaderos de las Indias* (Rome, 1682).

Melo, C. M. de *Recruitment and Formation of the Native Clergy in India* (Lisbon, 1954).

MEP Archive of Missions Étrangères de Paris, see Mss. sources above.

Métraux, A. 'The Revolution of the Ax', *Diogenes*, 25 (1959), 28–40.

Metzler, J. *S. C. de Propaganda Fide: Memoria rerum*, 3 vols. in five parts (Rome, 1971–76).

Meyer, A. O. *England and the Catholic Church under Elizabeth* (London, 1916).

Meyere, P. Liévin de *Historiae controversiarum de divinae gratiae auxiliis*, 2 vols. (Venice, 1742).

MH *Missionalia Hispanica*. I (Madrid, 1944).

Michaud, E. *Louis XIV et Innocent XI* (Paris, 1882).

Mims, S. L. *Colbert's West India Policy* (New Haven, Conn. 1912).

Mir, M. *Historia interna documentada de la Compañía de Jesús*, 2 vols. (Madrid, 1913). [Fr Mir (1841–1912) left the Jesuits in 1891; for an official view of his story see the *Memorias* of Jesuit General Martín, II (Rome, 1988), chapter 49.]

Mish, J. L. 'Creating an image of Europe for China: Aleni's *Hsi-fang ta-wen*', *Monumenta Serica*, XXIII (1964), 1–87.

Molina, L. de *Concordia*, ed. J. Rabenech (Madrid 1953).

Molina, L. de *On Divine Foreknowledge* (Pt 1V of the '*Concordia*'), tr. and ed. Alfred J. Freddoso (Cornell University Press, 1988).

Mon. Historica *Monumenta Historica S. J.*, XXVII (*Epistolae Nadal*, IV), (Madrid, 1905), 214–15).

Montesquieu, M. de *Oeuvres Complètes*, 3 vols. (Paris, 1950–55).

Moorhouse, G. *The Missionaries* (London, 1973).

Moorhouse, G. *Against All Reason* (London, 1969).

Morale pratique A. Arnauld, *La Morale pratique des Jésuites*, vol. VII (Cologne, 1716). ['This unjust, unchristian, prejudiced book is calculated to stir up hatred of a religious order [SJ] approved by the Church', Benno Bierman, OP., *Die Anfänge*, preface.]

Morelli, E. (ed.) *Le Lettere di Benedict XIV*, 3 vols (Rome, 1955–84).

Moreton, H. A. V. 'Some Aspects of Jansenism' (M. Litt. dissertation, University of Durham, 1962).

Mortier, D.-A. *Histoire des Maitres Généraux de l'Ordre des Frères Prêcheurs*, 8 vols. (Paris, 1903–1920) ('bristling with facts and as objective in its conclusions as can fairly be expected from a distinguished and devoted Dominican' [G. G. Coulton, *Five Centuries of Religion*, IV, 447]).

von Mosheim, J. L. *Authentic Memoirs of the Christian Church in China* (London, 1750).

MS *Monumenta Serica*, 1 (Peking, 1935).

Mungello, D. E.   *Curious Land: Jesuit Accommodation and the Origins of Sinology*, (Stuttgart, 1985).

Mungello, D. E.   'The Jesuits' use of Chang chü-Cheng's commentary in their translation of the Confucian Four Books (1687)', *China Mission Studies (1580–1800) Bulletin*, III (1981), 12–22.

Murillo Velarde, P.   *Historia de la [SJ] Provincia de Philipinas* (Manila, 1749). [The second part of a series; the first part is Colin's work listed above.]

Murillo Velarde, P.   *Geographia historica de las islas Philipinas y del Africa*, 10 vols (Madrid, 1752). [Vol. 8, dealing with the Philippines, criticizes Navarrete's 'filthy lies and falsehoods' (14, 24).]

Muro Orejón, A.   *Cedulario americano*, 2 vols. (Seville, 1956–69), Vol. 1 (*Cédulas de Carlos II: 1679–1700*).

Mustapha, M.   'José de Acosta on "de auxiliis" ', *Annales de la Faculté des lettres et sciences humaines de Nice*, 23 (1982), 209–16.

NC   See Navarrete, Principal Works.

NCE   *New Catholic Encyclopedia*, 16 vols. I (New York, 1966–74).

NE   See Navarrete, Principal Works.

Needham, J.   *Science and Civilisation in China*, I (Cambridge, 1954), in progress.

Needham, J.   *Within the Four Seas: The Dialogue of East and West* (London, 1979).

Needham, J.   *The Grand Titration: Science and Society in East and West* (London, 1969).

Needham, J.   'Roles of Europe and China in the evolution of oecumenical science', *Journal of Asian History*, I (Weisbaden, 1967), 1–32.

Neveu, B.   'Saint-Simon, les Jésuites et la Chine: Correspondence inédite avec le Père Foucquet', *Cahiers Saint-Simon*, Nos. 5–7 (Paris, 1977–79).

New Cambridge History   *New Cambridge Modern History*, V, ed. F.L. Carsten, (Cambridge, 1961).

New Catholic Encyclopaedia   See NCE.

NH   See Navarrete, Principal Works.

Nicolini, M.   'Diario', *Revue Hispanique*, 67 (Bordeaux, 1926). [Nicolini visited Madrid (1686) during his tour of duty as papal nuncio to Portugal.]

Noroña, A. de   *A India portuguesa*, 2 vols. (Goa, 1923).

Norton, L.   See Saint-Simon, *Mémoires*.

Nouel, C.   *Historia eclesiástica de la arquidiócesis de Santo Domingo*, 3 vols. (Rome–Santo Domingo, 1913–15).

NR   see Navarrete, Principal Works.

NS   see Navarrete, Principal Works.

NT   see Navarrete, Principal Works.

Núñez de Castro, A. *Sólo Madrid es Corte* (Madrid, 1669).

Ocio y Viana, H. M. *Compendio de la reseña biográfica de los religiosos de la provincia del S. Rosario de Filipinas* (Manila, 1895).

Ohm, T. *Asia Looks at Western Christianity* (London, 1959).

Palafox, J. de *Obras*, 13 vols. (Madrid, 1762).

Pallu, François *Lettres 1658–1684*, ed. A. Launay, 2 vols. (Angoulême, 1905).

Palm, E. W. *Los Monumentos arquitectónicos de La Española*, 2 vols. (Ciudad Trujillo, 1955).

Pandzic, Bazilije 'Quinque nondum editae P. Antonii Caballero OFM de Sinarum Missionibus litterae', *Archivum Franciscanum Historicum*, 61 (Firenze, 1968), 176–200.

Pardo Tomás, J. *Ciencia y censura. La Inquisición española y los libros científicos* (Madrid, 1991).

Parker, J. 'Windows into China: The Jesuits and their Books, 1580–1730' (5th Annual Bromson Lecture, 1977, Boston Public Library, 1978).

Pascal, B. [PL] *The Provincial Letters* (Paris, 1656), ed. Stewart (Manchester, 1920).

Pascal, B. *The Pensées*, ed. J. M. Cohen (Harmondsworth, 1961).

Passman, B. *The Experience of Priesthood* (London, 1968).

Pastells, P. *Catálogo de documentos relativos a las islas filipinas*, 9 vols. (Barcelona, 1925–34).

Pastine, D. *Juan Caramuel Lobkowitz: Probabilismo ed Enciclopedia* (Florence, 1975) [For this picaresque Cistercian, the 'Leader of the Lax', see Ceyssens, above.]

Pastor, L. *A History of the Popes*, 40 vols. (London, 1891–1953). [On the attitude to Spain of Pastor and his collaborators: P. Leturia SJ., *Razón y Fe*, 85 (1928), 136–55; and L. Ceyssens OFM., *Jansenistica Minora*, XII, fasc. 103. Pastor is also rebuked by G. G. Coulton for 'frequent mis-statements and silences which it is charitable to palliate as mere blunders' (*Medieval Studies*, X (London, 1931), 10).]

Pastrana See Mss. sources.

Pérez, L. *Cartas y relaciones del Japón*, 3 (Madrid, 1923). [Reprinted from *AIA* vols. 13–19.]

Pérez de Moya, J. *Philosofía Secreta [The Secret Philosophy wherein under the veil of fabulous histories may be found much useful doctrine]* (Madrid, 1585).

Petrocchi, M. *Il problema del lassismo nel secolo xvii* (Rome, 1953).

Pfister, L. *Notices biographiques et bibliographiques sur les Jésuites . . . de China*, 2 vols. (Shanghai, 1932–34). ['gingerly written', Needham, *Science*, V (3), 221.]

Philips, C. H. *A Handbook of Oriental History* (London, 1963).

Piedad, F. de la *Teatro Jesuitico* (Coimbra, 1654).

Pih, Irene   *Le P. Gabriel de Magalhães* (Paris, 1979).

Pinot, V.   *La Chine à le Formation de l'Esprit philosophique en France* (Paris, 1932).

Plattner, F. A.   *Jesuits Go East* (Dublin, 1950).

Playfair, G. M. H.   *The Cities and Towns of China: A Geographical Dictionary* (Shanghai, 1910).

Pollak, M.   *Mandarins, Jews, and Missionaries* (Philadelphia, 1980).

Poulain, A.   *The Graces of Interior Prayer* (London 1928; reprinted 1950).

Pray, G.   *Historia controversiarum de ritibus sinicis* (Budapest, 1789).

Price, M. T.   *Christian Missions and Oriental Civilizations: A Study in Culture Contact. The Reaction of Non-Christian Peoples to Protestant Missions: Individual and Collective Behaviour* (Privately printed, Shanghai, 1924). [Described as 'a natural history of missionary propaganda.']

Pritz, J. G.   *In missionem Tournonii a Clem. XI in Regnum Sinense ad componendas lites de cultu Confutii Jesuitas inter atque Dominicanos agitatas, ablegati, Io. Geo. Pritius* (Gripswaldiae, 1709).

Pritz, J. G.   *Relatio de statu Religionis Christianae in regno sinensi ob cultum Confucii perturbato* (Hamburg, 1709).

Puebla   *Evangelization Present and Future in Latin America: Conclusions of 3rd General Conference of Bishops* (London, 1984).

Purchas, S.   *Pilgrimes*, 5 vols. (London, 1625).

Quarterly Review   'The doctrines of the Jesuits', *Quarterly Review*, 138 (Edinburgh, 1877), 57–106. ['A blot upon English fairness and disreputable to the *Quarterly Review*', *The Month* (May, 1875), 88.]

Quéti-Échard   J. Quétif and J. Échard, *Scriptores Ordinis Praedicatorum*, 5 vols. (Paris, 1719–23; reprinted New York, 1959).

RAH   See Mss. sources.

Ramière, H.   *Compendium Instituti Societatis Jesu Praepositorum generalium responsis illustratum* (Toulouse, 1896).

Ranger, T. O.   'From Humanism to the Science of Man: colonialism in Africa and the understanding of alien societies', *Transactions of the Royal Historical Society*, XXVI (1976), 115–41.

Recopilación   *Recopilación de Leyes de los Reynos de las Indias* [1680], 3 vols. (Madrid, 1943).

Redondi, P.   *Galileo Heretic* (Harmondsworth, 1988).

Relation   *Relation Des Missions Et Des Voyages Des Evesques Vicaires Apostoliques, 1672–75* (Paris, 1680).

Réponse   *Réponse De Mrs. Des Missions Etrangères à la Protestation Et aux Reflexions Des Jesuites* (s. l., 1711).

Retana, W. E.   *Aparato bibliográfico de la historia general de Filipinas*, 3 vols. (Madrid, 1906; reprinted 1964).

Retana, W. E.   *Catálogo abreviado de la biblioteca filipina* (Madrid, 1898).

RHA   See Mss. sources.

RHE   *Revue d'histoire ecclésiastique*, I (Louvain, 1900).

RHM   *Revue d'histoire des missions*, I (Paris, 1924).

Ribadeneira, M. de   *Historia del archipiélago filipino y reinos de la Gran China . . . y Japón* (Barcelona, 1601).

Ribadeneyra, P. de   *Epistolae* [1590], 2 vols. (Madrid, 1923).

Ribadeneyra, P. de   *Tratado en el qual se da razón de la Compañía de Jesús* (Madrid, 1605).

Ribas, Juan de, OP   'Antilogia o Defensa de la Historia de China de Fray Domingo Navarrete', (Madrid, 1714): (Hispanic Soc. of America, MS. HC/411/636; formerly the property of the Oratorians of Murcia).

Riccio, Vittorio   'Hechos' (1676). Ms. in three books and thirty chapters, in AOPM: see Mss. sources.

Richards, J.   *Sex, Dissidence and Damnation in the Middle Ages* (London, 1991).

Rickaby, J.   'Clement XI and the Chinese Rites', *The Month*, 73 (1891), 70–79. [Fr Rickaby's account is accepted as 'impartial' by the editor of the *The Month*, 162 (1933), 420.]

Ripa, M.   *Memoirs of Fr Ripa during 13 Years' Residence in Peking* (London, 1844).

Robles, A. de   *Diario (1665–1703)*, 3 vols. (Mexico City, 1946).

Rodríguez Demorizi, E.   *Relaciones históricas de Santo Domingo*, III (Ciudad Trujillo, 1957).

Rodríguez-Marín, F.   *21,000 refranes españoles* (Madrid, 1926).

Rosso, A. S.   *Apostolic Legations to China: 18th Century* (South Pasadena, 1948).

Rougemont, F.   *Historia Tartaro-Sinica nova . . . ab anno 1660* (Louvain, 1673).

Rouleau, F.   'Tournon at the Court of Peking (1705)', *Archivum historicum Societatis Jesu*, XXXI (Rome, 1962), 264–323.

Rowbotham, A.   *Mandarin and Missionary* (Los Angeles, 1942). [Now largely superseded, and limited to French sources, but this is a lively and impartial introduction to the subject.]

RQS   *Revue des questions scientifiques*, 1 (Louvain–Paris, 1877).

RSR   *Recherches de science religieuse*, I, (Paris, 1910).

Ruthven, K. K.   *Myth* (London, 1976).

Rycaut, Paul (tr.)   *The Critick* (London, 1681).

Saint-Simon, Duke of *Memoirs*, tr. E. L. Norton, 3 vols. (London, 1974).

San Antonio, J. F. de *Chrónicas* [of the Franciscans in the Philippines, 1738], (Manila, 1977).

San Agustín, G. de *Conquistas de las islas Philipinas: Parte primera* (Madrid, 1698).

San Cugat Mss. in the Jesuit archives in San Cugat, Barcelona.

Sánchez Alonso, B. *Fuentes de la historia española e hispano-americana*, 3 vols. (Madrid, 1952).

Santa Cruz, B. de *Historia de la provincia del Santo Rosario de Filipinas, Japón, China* (Saragossa, 1693).

Santillana, G. de *The Crime of Galileo* (London, 1961).

Schäfer, E. *El Consejo real y supremo de las Indias*, 2 vols. (Seville, 1935–47).

Schall, Adam *Historica relatio*, ed. H. Bernard-Maitre and P. Bornet (Tientsin, 1942).

Schneemann, G. *Controversiarum de divinae gratiae liberique arbitrii concordia initia et progressus* (Friburg, 1881).

Schons, D. *Book Censorship in New Spain* (Austin, Texas, 1949).

Schons, D. *Notes from Spanish Archives*, I (Ann Arbor, 1946).

Schulte, H. F. *The Spanish Press, 1470–1966. Print, Power and Politics* (Urbana, 1968).

Schurhammer, G. *Francis Xavier*, tr. M. J. Costeloe, 4 vols. (Rome, 1973–82).

SCPF Congregation of Propaganda Fide, Rome. See Mss. sources above at APF.

Sebes, J. *Diary of Thomas Pereira SJ* (Rome, 1961).

Secret, F. 'Quand la Kabbale expliquait le "Yi King" ou un aspect oublié du Figuratisme du P. Joachim Bouvet', *Revue de l'histoire des religions*, 195 (Jan. 1979), 35–53.

Semedo, A. de *The History of the . . . Monarchy of China* (London, 1655).

Serry, J. H. *Historia Congregationum de auxiliis divinae gratiae* (Venice, 1742).

Seznec, J. *The Survival of the Pagan Gods* (London, 1940).

Shryock, J. K. *Origins of the State Cult of Confucius* (New York, 1932).

Sierra Corélla, A. *La censura de libros en España* (Madrid, 1947).

Silva Rego, A. da *Documentação para a história das missões do Padroado português do Oriente: India*, ed. A. Silva Rego, 12 vols. (Lisbon, 1949–58); V (*India, 1551–54*), (Lisbon, 1951).

Simón Díaz, J. *El libro español antiguo* (Kassel, 1983).

SinFran *Sinica Franciscana*, 8 vols. (Quaracchi-Firenze, 1929–1975). [Seventeenth-

and eighteenth-century letters from China which include incidental data on social and economic life, travel routes, etc.]

Sipe, A. W. R.   *A Secret World: Sexuality and the Search for Celibacy* (New York, 1990). [The author, a former Benedictine monk, and currently a professor in John Hopkins Medical School, also discussed the subject in the London *Tablet* (9 and 16 May, 1992), 576, 605.]

Sivin, N.   in *Isis* LVI (1965), 201–5.

Smalley, B.   'Novelty', in *Studies in Medieval Thought and Learning* (London, 1981).

Smalley, B.   *The Study of the Bible in the Middle Ages* (London, 1951).

Sohier-Ceyssens   A. Sohier and L.Ceyssens, 'La activités antijansénistes à Madrid (1679–84)', *Bulletin de la Commission royale d'histoire*, 118 (1953), 1–114 [Repr. *Jansenistica minora*, II, fasc. 18.]

Southern, R.   *Western Society and the Church in the Middle Ages* (Harmondsworth, 1970).

Spence, J. D.   *Emperor of China: Self portrait of K'ang-hsi* (New York, 1974).

Spence, J. D.   *The Death of Woman Wang: Rural Life in China: 17th Century* (Harmondsworth, 1980).

Spence, J. D.   *The Search for Modern China* (London, 1990).

Spence, J. D & Wills, J. E.   *From Ming to Ch'ing* (New Haven, 1979).

Standaert, N.   'Jesuit presence in China (1580–1773): a statistical approach', *Sino-Western Cultural Relations Journal*, XIII (1991).

Stanhope, A.   *Letters* (London, 1846).

Steele, R.   *An Account of the Roman Catholic Religion* (London, 1716).

Stewart, H. F. (ed.)   *Pascal's Provincial Letters* (Manchester, 1920).

Streit, R.   *Bibliotheca Missionum*, 5 (Freiburg, 1964).

Studies in Spirituality   *Studies in the Spirituality of Jesuits*, I (1965).

Sullivan, M.   *The Meeting of Eastern and Western Art* (London, 1989).

S-WCRJ   *Sino–Western Cultural Relations Journal* XIII (Cedar Rapids, 1991). [Formerly the *China Mission Studies (1550–1800) Bulletin*.]

Synopsis   *Synopsis historiae Societatis Jesu* (Louvain, 1950).

Tanquerary, A.   *The Spiritual Life* (Tournai, 1930).

Tapia, P. de   *Catenae moralis doctrinae*, 2 vols. (Seville, 1654–57).

TCD   See Mss. sources.

Tellechea Idígoras, J. I.   'Martín Ignacio de Loyola', *Salmanticensis* XXXVI (Salamanca, 1989), 341–62.

Terrien, J.   *Historical inquiry into the tradition that 'To die in the Society of Jesus is a* *certain pledge of Salvation'* (Woodstock, 1874; reprinted (1974) as *Prophecies and revelations about the Jesuits*).

Thomas, A. (SJ)   *Carta circular* [1691] (Madrid, 1692).

Thomas, A. (pseud.)   *Histoire de la mission de Pékin*, 2 vols. (Paris, 1923–25) [Privately printed, hostile to the Jesuits, and described by Pastor as 'swarming with inaccuracies and arbitrary assertions' (XXXV, 457).]

Thurloe, J.   *A Collection of the State Papers of John Thurloe, Secretary of State to Oliver Cromwell*, 7 vols. (London, 1742).

Thwaites, R. G.   *Jesuit Relations and Allied Documents*, 66 vols. (Cleveland, 1896–1901).

T'ien ju-k'ang   'The decadence of Buddhist temples in Fu-chien in late Ming and early Ch'ing' in Vermeer, 83–100.

Tindal, M.   *Christianity as Old as Creation* (London, 1730).

Tizón, H.   *La Espana borbónica* (Madrid, 1978).

TP   T'oung Pao, I (Leiden 1890).

Tugwell, S.   *The Early Dominicans: Selected Writings* (New York, 1982).

Utrera, C. de   *Dilucidaciones históricas*, 2 vols. (Santo Domingo, 1927–29).

Utrera, C. de   *La Inmaculada Concepción. Documentos para la historia de la arquidiócesis de Santo Domingo* (Ciudad Trujillo, 1946).

Vaeth, A.   *Johann Adam Schall von Bell S. J.* (Cologne, 1933).

Valera, J.   *Obras completas*, 3 vols. (Madrid, 1947).

Vallellano, A.   *La Compañía de Jesús en Santo Domingo* (Ciudad Trujillo, 1959).

Valles, C. G.   *Living Together in a Jesuit Community* (St Louis, 1984). [Described as a 'how to do it' book.]

Van Zoeren, S.   *Poetry and Personality: Reading, Exegesis, and Hermeneutics in Traditional China* (Stanford, 1991)

Varela Hervías, E.   *Gazeta nueva, 1661–1663* (Madrid, 1960).

Varo, F.   'Facilis et perspicua methodus ad linguam mandarinam addiscendam' (Ms. of 1684; see González, J. M. *Historia*, I: 686). [The first Chinese grammar printed in China by a Westerner.]

Vázquez de Espinosa, A.   *Compendium and Description of the West Indies*, ed. C. U. Clark (Washington, 1942).

Verbiest, F. de   *Correspondance*, ed. Josson and Willaert (Brussels, 1938).

Verbrugge, M. R.   'Molinism: "Fact with Fancy"; Heresy with Truth', *Victorian Poetry*, XXI (1983), 229–40.

Vermeer, E. B.   *The Development and Decline of Fukien Province in the 17th and 18th Centuries* (Leiden, 1990).

Vernet, J. 'Copernicus in Spain', *Colloquia Copernicana*, 1 (Warsaw, 1972).

Verricelli *Quaestiones morales seu Tractatus de apostolicis missionibus* (Venice, 1656).

Vieira, António de *Cartas*, ed. J. Lúcio de Azevedo, 5 vols. (Coimbra, 1926).

Viñaza, Count de la *Escritos de los Portugueses y Castellanos referentes a las lenguas de China y el Japón* (Lisbon, 1892).

Visschers, P. *Onuitgegeven brieven van eenige Paters der Societeit van Jesus, missionarissen in China van de XVIIde en XVIIIe eeuw* (Arnhem, 1857).

Vossius, I. *Observationes variae* (London, 1693).

Vranich, S. 'Carta de un ciudadano de Sevilla: La guerra mariana de Sevilla en el siglo 17', *Archivo hispalense*, 44 (Seville, 1966), 241–74.

Wakeman, F. *The Great Enterprise. The Manchu Reconstruction of Imperial China*, 2 vols. (London, 1985).

Walker, D P. *The Ancient Theology* (London, 1972).

Walz, A. M. *Compendium Historiae Ordinis Praedicatorum* (Rome, 1930).

Wedgwood, C. V. *The Thirty Years' War* (Harmondsworth, 1957).

Wicks, J. 'Doctrine and Theology', in O'Malley, ed., *Catholicism in Early Modern History* (St Louis, 1988).

Wilhelm, R. *I Ching* (London, 1980).

Wills, Garry *Bare Ruined Choirs* (New York, 1972).

Wills, J. E. *Embassies and Illusions: Dutch and Portuguese Envoys to K'ang-hsi, 1666–1687* (Harvard, 1984).

Wolff, C. von *Oratio de Sinarum philosophia practica* (Halle, 1721).

Young, John D. 'An early Confucian attack on Christianity: Yang Kuang-hsien and his Pu-te-i', in *Journal of the Chinese University of Hong Kong*, 3 (1975), 159–186.

Zagzebski, L. T. *Dilemma of Freedom and Foreknowledge* (Oxford, 1991).

Zaide, A. G. F. *Philippine Political and Cultural History*, 2 vols. (Manila, 1957).

Zeuli, C. *Matteo Ricci: Lettere del Manoscritto Maceratese* (Macerata, 1985).

Zürcher, E. 'The Jesuit Mission in Fujian in late Ming times: levels of response', in Vermeer, 417–457.

Index

Abbreviations: N refers to Navarrete throughout
CRC to the Chinese Rites Controversy
SJ to the Jesuits
OP to the Dominicans
OFM to the Franciscans

332